MEDIEVAL
QUEENSHIP

Also by John Carmi Parsons

THE COURT AND HOUSEHOLD OF ELEANOR OF CASTILE IN 1290

HUNTINGDON BOROUGH COURT ROLLS (*with J. Ambrose Raftis, CSB*)

MEDIEVAL QUEENSHIP

EDITED BY JOHN CARMI PARSONS

St. Martin's Press
New York

First published in the United States of America in 1993

Printed in the United States of America

ISBN 0-312-05217-0

Library of Congress Cataloging-in-Publication Data

Medieval queenship / edited by John Carmi Parsons.
    p. cm.
    Includes bibliographical references and index.
    Contents: Family, sex, and power : the rhythms of medieval
queenship / John Carmi Parsons — Roles and functions of queens in
Árpádian and Angevin Hungary (1000-1386 A.D.) / János M. Bak —
Queenship in medieval Denmark / Inge Skovgaard-Peterson (with Nanna
Damsholt) — Women at the court of Charlemagne: a case of monstrous
regiment? / Janet L. Nelson — Mothers, daughters, and power : some
Plantagenet evidence, 1150-1500 / John Carmi Parsons — Queens
dowager and queens regent in tenth-century Léon and Navarre / Roger
Collins — Capetian women and the regency / André Poulet — The
king's mother and royal prerogative in early-sixteenth-century
France / Elizabeth McCartney — The portrayal of royal women in
England, mid-tenth to mid-twelfth centuries / Pauline Stafford —
Reigning queens in medieval Europe : when, where, and why / Armin
Wolf — Female succession and the language of power in the writings
of twelfth-century churchmen / Lois L. Huneycutt.
    ISBN 0-312-05217-0
    1. Monarchy — Europe — History. 2. Queens — Europe — History.
I. Parsons, John Carmi, 1947- .
JC375.M43 1993
321'.6'0940902 — dc20   93-10879
                                            CIP

Interior design by Digital Type & Design

T·A·B·L·E O·F C·O·N·T·E·N·T·S

L·I·S·T O·F I·L·L·U·S·T·R·A·T·I·O·N·S

A·B·B·R·E·V·I·A·T·I·O·N·S

b.	born
bef.	before
ch.	chapter
cm.	centimeter
col.	column
ct.	count
d.	died
dau.	daughter
emp.	emperor
esp.	especially
ff.	and following pages
fol.	folio
hss	heiress
m.	married
MS	manuscript
nos.	numbers
n.p.	no place of publication (or publisher) given
pl.	plate
r.	reigned
rpt.	reprint
s.a.	*sub anno* ("see under the year")
s.n.	no volume number given
s.v.	*sub voce* ("see under the word")

R·E·F·E·R·E·N·C·E A·B·B·R·E·V·I·A·T·I·O·N·S

AASS	[Bollandists] *Acta Sanctorumï*
BIHR	*Bulletin of the Institute of Historical Research*
EHR	*English Historical Review*
JMH	*Journal of Medieval History*
MGH	Monumenta Germaniae Historica
SS = Scriptores	
SSRG = Scriptores, Rerum Germanicarum	
SSRM = Scriptores, Rerum Merovingicarum	
London, P.R.O.	Public Record Office
S.C. 1/	Ancient Correspondence
C 47/	Chancery Miscellany
Just 1/	Justices Itinerant
CPR	*Calendar of Patent Rolls*
CClR	*Calendar of Close Rollsï*
CLR	*Calendar of Liberate Rolls*
Migne, *PL*	*Patrologia Cursus Completus, Series Latina*
Paris, AN	Archives nationales
Paris, BN	Bibliothéque nationale
RS	Rolls series
SCH	*Studies in Church History*
TRHS	*Transactions of the Royal Historical Society*

CHAPTER 1

INTRODUCTION

Family, Sex, and Power: The Rhythms of Medieval Queenship

JOHN CARMI PARSONS

While this anthology reflects current interest in the queens of medieval Europe as an outgrowth of feminist historical studies since the 1960s, it also highlights the curious fact that only recently has much notice been taken of queenship itself. It is almost deplorably easy to account for this state of affairs. A renewed interest in women's history first produced accounts of prominent women—nobles, abbesses, saints—including that handful of medieval queens who have always excited popular interest: Eleanor of Aquitaine, Blanche of Castile, Margaret of Anjou, Isabella of Castile. These works are, however, limited by the tendencies to depict queens as moral pendants to husbands or sons, and to dwell on their lives but not their offices (N. Davis 1976; Stuard 1987b: 62-63, 72). More recently, queens and queenship have fallen into some disrepute as feminist historical scholarship has shifted its focus to socioeconomic studies that concentrate on the less fortunate sisters of the well-known; a current distaste for administrative and institutional history has, moreover, impeded investigation of queenship's resources, its links to the king's office and, most important, queens' relationships with kingdoms and communities.

Recent publications suggest an awakening of interest in the institutions and workings of queenship: for the early medieval period the work of Pauline Stafford (1978a, 1978b, 1981a, 1981b, 1983); for Ottonian Germany, Karl Leyser (1979); for France, Marion Facinger (1968), Elizabeth A. R. Brown (1976), and André Poulet (1989); for England, F. D. Blackley and G. Hermansen (1971), John Carmi Parsons (1977, 1988, 1991, forthcoming), Margaret Howell (1987), Marjorie Chibnall (1991), and Lois Huneycutt (1989a, 1989b, 1989c, 1990, forthcoming). Queenship in art and ritual has been discussed by Ernest Kantorowicz (1957, 1965), Claire Sherman (1976), Robert Deshman (1976, 1988), Janet Nelson (1986b), Marion Clayton (1990), and Rosamund McKitterick (1990), though liturgical studies continue to favor kings (e.g., Le Goff 1990; but compare Enright 1988; J. Parsons 1991). The divorce of "history" from "political history" and of "power" from "political power," moreover, has opened fresh approaches to discussions of gender and power in the Middle Ages (Erler and Kowaleski 1988; Fradenburg 1991a). Queens were the closest of all women to the center of magisterial authority, and their prominence left them exposed to scrutiny—just the circumstances in which (as Stafford's essay in this volume shows) it was likely they would become lightning rods for thoughts on gender and power.

The present volume shares in this evolving tradition. The contributors, all historians, offer no biographical sketches of individual queens, but have instead sought to dissect the ways in which queens pursued and exploited means to power, and how their actions were interpreted by others. The essays are not source-specific (compare Rosenthal 1990); rather, they bring to bear on their discussions as many materials as possible and examine queenship from a broad geographical and chronological perspective. Lois Huneycutt's essay, however, reminds us that (as Eileen Power stated), this wealth of sources and breadth of subject is liable to present us with divergent pictures of medieval women. To an extent these essays reflect that conundrum—compare, for example, the status of medieval women as reflected in André Poulet's chapter, drawn from patristic writings and scriptural exegesis, and the contrasting picture that emerges from Pauline Stafford's examination of chronicles and saints' lives, many of them the work of monks, and Lois Huneycutt's investigation of medieval writings on queens who ruled in their own right. It is partly to avoid a deluge of such pronounced contrasts at the very beginning of this book that I have chosen to lead off the collection with the accounts by János Bak and Inge Skovgaard-Petersen (with Nanna Damsholt) of the little-known queens of medieval Denmark and Hungary: the paucity of relevant sources for those kingdoms permits (or compels?) the authors to identify some basic themes of queenship that can help to unify an otherwise disparate collection.

Of these motifs, the one fundamental to all the essays in this collection is the familial context in which queens operated. In the early Middle Ages, when rulership and power were thought of in terms of personal inheritance, when the king's "family" and household were the government and ill-defined succession customs allowed many members of royal kindreds to hope for the throne, the king's wife could be a pivotal figure, her actions (in Stafford's words) "magnified by the status of royal dynasties and extended by the fraught politics of royal succession." A preference for inheritance in the male line that evolved from the eleventh century is held to have relegated women to the margins of the feudal family; in the same period, as royal succession customs crystallized and as government became increasingly bureaucratized, the relationship between royal families and kingdoms was transformed, and it is often said that these changes banished queens to marginal roles in royal houses now defined by descent in the male line. Huneycutt's examination of representations of reigning queens by chroniclers and other writers, however, leads her to question whether the position of women in the feudal aristocratic family was indeed as peripheral as has been argued. Marriage, motherhood, and kinship (agnatic or cognatic) were indispensable to the family whether or not the lineage defined itself in agnatic terms; women thus retained claims to power and influence within the feudal family. That a more nuanced view should also be taken of women's position in royal houses is suggested by the widely varied aspects of "family" in queens' experiences as examined in these essays.

Royal marriage, for example, is often discussed as merely supportive of kings' diplomatic alignments—a frame of reference that can obscure queens' origins in royal or noble lineages and the crucial role such connections could play in their careers. (Aspects of royal women's relations with their birth families are discussed here in Janet Nelson's essay on Charlemagne's daughters and in mine on royal daughters' importance as international brides, both of which indicate that "marginalized" women retained an important presence in kingly sensibilities.) Not surprisingly, "family" had a multifaceted role in the complicated process of queen-making; as Skovgaard-Petersen notes, the issues were weighty enough that chroniclers expressed opinions on the choice of queens. There was, first, the question of the queen's descent. Her *desirability* came from her male kin's sphere of influence, but high lineage established her *suitability* for matrimony and maternity—as chroniclers said, good trees do not bear bad fruit (Riley 1865: 49-50), and the magnates who objected to a royal union (usually on fairly obvious political grounds) often justified their actions by claiming the bride was of ignoble birth (Paris 1872-84: iii, 206; Paris 1866-69: ii, 336; A. Lewis 1981: 54-55). Kings also had to negotiate Church doctrines on marriage and consanguinity. Canonical strictures were a handy resource in that "proof" of kinship within the prohibited degrees allowed for disposal of unwanted or barren consorts (Duby 1984), but to avoid marrying within those degrees kings often sought wives from remote realms (e.g., A. Lewis 1981: 20-21). The ramifications here reveal affinities between politics and the choice of queens, who brought with them both the promise of alliance and the threat of division (Stafford 1985: 35; Fradenburg 1991a: 4-5). The king who chose a wife within his own realm exalted her kin and upset the balance among his nobles, while the queen might use her family for political leverage; an alien queen, though the linchpin of a valuable alliance and a token of the social gulf between king and subjects, could divert his wealth to her kin and countrymen. Bak describes the fatal resentments aroused by some foreign-born queens, and notes a solution adopted in the early modern period—sending royal brides to their new homes as mere children, to immerse them in new cultures and weaken ties to their homelands, a practice compared to banishment by the eleventh-century monk Goscelin, who likened himself in exile to a young princess married in a foreign court whose language she did not know (cited by Stafford, note 17). As my chapter implies that access to power was easier for queens who commanded strong cross-cultural perspectives, prospective in-laws might have demanded the handing over of very young brides precisely to deprive future queens of such avenues to influence. Whatever their origins, queens as daughters and wives had to negotiate divided loyalties, an essential aspect of queens' understanding of themselves and others' understanding of them (Wood 1991: 127; Freccero 1991: 134).

If "family" invested the choice of a queen with potential for division, so did her behavior as a wife—especially in the bedchamber. Royal marriage helped to construct social order, but at the same time had to be made subtly "different," and its sexual and other anomalies were closely scrutinized. The king's marriage, for example, could model loving submission and peaceful community, but by marrying as they often did (by papal dispensation) within prohibited degrees, kings committed permissible incest, common in royal annals but denied to others (Lincoln 1989: 162-63; Fradenburg 1991b). Scrutiny was not inspired merely by prurient curiosity: obsessive attention focused on the birth of heirs, guarantee of the integrity and continuity of the realm (Nelson 1986b: 304), and the apprehensions aroused by barren queens can be judged from similar patterns evident in two eleventh-century cases, from England and the Holy Roman Empire. Early in their marriage, Edward the Confessor's wife Edith was advertised as his bedfellow (*gebedda*, in Robertson 1956: no. 105), and her failure to produce an heir undoubtedly contributed to her repudiation in

1051. Edward soon took her back, but there were still no children (Barlow 1970), and in Stafford's words, Edith as a widow "staked her survival on the construction of Edward's sanctity," explaining her childlessness by claiming a chaste marriage. Closer to contemporaries' real opinion of Edith may have been the rumors of adultery she felt compelled to deny on her deathbed in 1075, as told by William of Malmesbury, who wrote sixty years later but before Edward's 1161 canonization made Edith's allegations of chastity the authorized version of their marriage. In much the same way, contemporaries of the Emperor Henry II noted his barren marriage and found it remarkable that he forbore to dismiss his childless wife; it is only in later *vitae* promoting and celebrating their sanctity that he is said to have persuaded Kunigunde to share a prenuptial vow of chastity. Given the rumors of the childless Edith's adultery, some interest attaches to the legend that Kunigunde too was accused of adultery, though the story surfaces in a *vita* written a century and more after her death in 1033, and in the hagiographer's hands the charge (attributed to satanic apparitions) serves chiefly as the springboard for a miraculous demonstration of her purity (Rodolf Glaber 1989: 94-96; AASS, March i: 265-80; Waitz 1841: 816-20; Klauser 1957). (As regards queens' relations with their birth families, it should be noted here that both Edith and Kunigunde were really saved from repudiation by the political influence of father or brothers as well as the Church's evolving position on the indissolubility of marriage [Stafford 1983: 76].) Regardless of whether allegations or attributions of chastity were based in fact any more than were the charges of adultery, society undoubtedly found childless royal marriages troubling, and with good reason: the deaths of Edward the Confessor and Emperor Henry without direct heirs ended their respective dynasties and led to succession crises. In both these cases posthumous claims of chastity were perhaps made attractive by the desire to believe that it was not the king who failed the people whose vitality he embodied (Klaniczay 1985: 64-65), but his wife. The suspicions that beset barren queens might also be discerned in the fact that charges against them could go well beyond adultery: the royal wives accused of witchcraft, whether or not to justify repudiation, were often childless (Myers 1940; R. A. Griffiths 1969; Duby 1984: 204-05).

  If the royal bedchamber was the site of proper reproductive behavior, it could also be the crucible of conflict and upheaval. The adulterous queens noted by Poulet, Skovgaard-Petersen, and Bak sparked civil wars and succession crises. Stafford discusses twelfth-century concern for queens' seductive power over their husbands, and as he, Bak, and Nelson show (see also Levin 1986), the preoccupation with queenly sexuality in part underlies chroniclers' invention after the fact of adultery and other royal misbehavior to blame queens for past conflicts. Such factors help, too, to explain the collapse of Elizabeth Woodville's position after Edward IV's death in 1483. Queens rarely had to exert their sexuality to attract a mate, but as a comely widow Elizabeth did just that to win Edward's interest; grounding her queenship in her carnality—combined with her lack of exalted forebears and the horde of impecunious relatives to whom she diverted Edward's patronage—left Elizabeth isolated and easily defeated (Wood 1991: 126-28).

It was in the passage from daughter's descent and wife's sexuality to maternal care that a queen's family contexts were most subtly and profoundly altered. As wives, queens were interlopers and potential adulteresses who inspired distrust and suspicion, but their maternal instinct to protect their children and their children's inheritance deserved sympathy and respect—as Charles Wood has stated, medieval views on women acknowledged a "capacity to transcend the natural inferiority of the female gender whenever their actions were perceived as flowing from their role as mothers." Thus the legitimacy of Edward II's children by Isabella of France was cause for disquiet only so long as Edward was her husband; once he was disposed of, and Edward III safely crowned, the focus shifted to Isabella's proper solicitude for her son (Wood 1988b, and 1991: 121-24, 128; Menache 1984). Poulet and Elizabeth McCartney show that a maternal authority's exemplary lack of self-interest paved the way for French queens to act as regents—an uncrowned mother might be preferred as regent to a crowned wife—and that queens' maternal behavior won them a voice in royal affairs even during their husbands' lives is shown in my essay on the training of royal daughters as diplomatic brides.

The delicate nexus of lineage, nationality, and sexuality that royal women had to negotiate is concisely illustrated by Roger Collins' discussion of the career of Elvira, a tenth-century regent of the kingdom of León. Here there were no stable customs of succession: if a king left a young son, any adult male of the family could claim the throne, and as a young heir's mother might play an important (and complicating) role in such crises, Leonese royal widows were expected to remove themselves from the political arena by taking the veil. In Elvira's case, a lack of adult males brought to the throne her young nephew Ramiro III, and as her diplomatic connections through her mother were acceptable to the more influential segment of the Leonese nobility, she was preferred as regent over Ramiro's foreign-born mother. Elvira was, moreover, from childhood a professed virgin whose vows eliminated the hazards of sexual misconduct or a husband who might take the throne. Virginity or chastity in fact extended the power of many women from the exalted lineages whose members already had claims to extraordinary spiritual graces (Vauchez 1977; Klaniczay 1980); Stafford notes that the English throne was said to have been offered to a royal nun on one occasion, and remarks parallels with contemporary women regents in Ottonian Germany who were also widows or nuns, as with Mathilda of Quedlinburg who, like Elvira, ruled for a nephew.

The regencies incidentally mentioned here—family crises that associated royal women with change and anomaly—are an appropriate way to emphasize how family roles both limited and empowered queens, as shown in Stafford's discussion of Aelfgifu-Emma's manipulation of matrimonial and maternal loyalties during the crises that followed the deaths of both her husbands. These regencies also recommend that an eye be kept open for shifting inflections of locality and custom. Poulet and McCartney link the success of French queens' claims to the regency to an aggressively enunciated patrimonial relationship between royal office and agnatic lineage that inspired belief in a dynastic blood-right to that throne (see also A. Lewis 1981): women's exclusion from the succession guaranteed the disinterested exercise of power by mothers already naturally devoted to their children's welfare. In England, royal succession remained volatile and women theoretically could occupy the throne; here royal women were influential in succession crises, but no English queen ever became regent for a minor son. León, like England, had no stable succession customs, but avoided regencies by rejecting young children as heirs to the throne in favor of adult kinsmen. The Leonese throne would ultimately be inherited by a woman, but its royal widows were excluded from legitimate political activity, and a king's daughter was accepted as regent only when religious vows divorced her from worldly concerns—though her terrestrial family connections still helped recommend her for political responsibility. Amidst such diversity, the terms "daughter," "wife," and "mother" themselves develop nuances that argue against a static, generalizing view of women within medieval ruling families.

If royal wives could find and develop means to power through families, the reigning queens of medieval Europe discussed by Huneycutt, Skovgaard-Petersen, Bak, and Armin Wolf are the ultimate irony of political authority considered as patrimony, and the final proof of royal women's integration into the family—as Wolf shows, the exaltation of agnatic descent itself held out the possibility that women might inherit.

Huneycutt's examination of chroniclers' representations of reigning queens suggests the conundrum could be surmounted by representing such a woman, daughter of a reigning father, as a locum-tenens for her son. (Chronic speculation that Victoria and Elizabeth II of England might abdicate in favor of their sons implies that such tendencies survive.) At this point, however, the implications of "family" assumed negative aspects for a reigning queen. The expectation that a woman who inherited supreme authority would marry and produce a son to replace her implied submission to a husband as prescribed by Christian teaching—and the submission of her people to one who in most cases was not native to the kingdom; Bak and Wolf note the sometimes tragic results. Or reigning queens could be fictively masculinized; Stafford, Wolf, Huneycutt, Bak, Nelson, and Skovgaard-Petersen remark queens who used male titularies or were referred to by such circumlocutions, and it is instructive to note the links between such masculine topoi and virginity—real in the case of nuns-regent or fictive and subtly Marianized for queens-consort (King 1991: 192-93; J. Parsons 1991). But the virginal or Marian imagery appropriate to a consort, at once exalted and submissive, chaste yet fertile, posed insoluble dilemmas for a queen-regnant—as Nelson remarks, Mary does not reign—until Elizabeth I put herself outside the genealogical continuum by asserting her virginity: as Elizabeth entered her forties and the likelihood of her marriage and motherhood diminished, English poets invested the Protestant queen with recognizable Marian attributes (Wilson 1980: 22; Wells 1983: 14-21).

That the most positive images of medieval queens grew from their maternal role is reflected in queenship's ritual context. This volume attends more precisely to queenly power in the family arena than to the Christian imagery often summoned to define them, and perhaps for this reason the essays refer only obliquely to queens' ritual roles. The topic needs investigation: as the king's wife was neither warrior nor lawgiver, ritual had an especially crucial role in the construction of queenship, beginning with the fundamental queen-making act of coronation; and here too, underlying patterns of familial status cannot be ignored. That queens swore no coronation oath, as Poulet stresses, left their power helpfully undefined, but allowed them no effective claims to deference save as royal wives and mothers. But with blessings, prayers, and exhortations based on marriage rites, coronation in effect consecrated queens as lawful royal consorts and mothers of legitimate royal heirs—indeed, the hallowing of the queen's maternal role is made explicit in those elements of medieval coronations properly described as "fertility charms" (Kantorowicz 1965;

Stafford 1983: 7-12, 15). Nelson's reference to the first recorded coronation of a Frankish queen, that of Pippin the Short's wife Bertha in 754, reminds us that the event signaled that it was not only Pippin who was raised to the throne but his lineage as well (Stafford 1983: 131), and, as Bak notes, Hungarian queens began to be crowned only as hereditary succession assured their role as dynastic mothers. Coronation for Scandinavian queens may also have been linked to efforts to assure hereditary succession (Hoffmann 1990), and in England, Lancastrian queens' childbearing became the focus of rituals that may have been of some significance for the strengthening of a weak hereditary principle (J. Parsons 1991, and forthcoming).

Ritual constructions of queenship could also help secrete the areas of conflict noted above. Even as the queen was ceremoniously exalted, rituals prescribed a submissive role that secluded her from authority. The boudoir influence or improper behavior threatened by her sexuality were allayed by ritual imagery that inscribed chaste demeanor and fictive virginity while it celebrated her fertility; ritual emphasis on virginal imagery could suggest liminal masculine identities less threatening than the feminine to a social hierarchy reckoned according to male roles (J. Parsons 1991). These liminal spaces recall as well the many boundaries queens traversed—geographical and cultural as they were changed from daughters into wives and mothers, or those between margin and center (Fradenburg 1991a: 9-10)—and again insinuate the family sphere, for whether such boundaries should include those between the "public" arena and the "domestic," "familial," or "private" domain to which medieval women are said to have been marginalized, is a question to which the present anthology turns implicit attention.

The validity of the public-private distinction in the history of medieval women has been questioned, especially for medieval and early modern queens (Erler and Kowaleski 1988: 4-5; Fradenburg 1991: 9; Freccero 1991: 132), and while queens are not the only case studies available, their prominence offers strong arguments for a reconsidered terminology. That the French legal writers McCartney discusses deduced a queen's right to act as regent of the kingdom from feudal widows' right to act as guardians of children and fiefs is a reminder that the feudal Middle Ages were characterized by "public power in private hands," as "the estate became the state" (and incidentally offers further proof of women's integration into the family). Other areas of medieval queens' familial activities also challenge the distinction: as Huneycutt and I discuss elsewhere, a queen's intercession with her husband was an important element in the public personae of both king and queen that could betoken an intimate and suspect influence; that queens received petitioners in their bedchambers — sites of that intensely scrutinized procreative activity — in effect publicized intimacy as a base of their power (Huneycutt, forthcoming; J. Parsons 1991: 67-8, and forthcoming). Queens were "marginalized" to a "private" sphere in the narrow sense that patrimonialization of authority or bureaucratization of administration lessened their direct role in government, but they retained power, however "unofficial" or informal, and it was by paths inarguably linked to family roles that they preserved a share in rulership on a not-insignificant basis. The regency was only the most official of these; Nelson shows how daughters could wield informal power as they helped a father to control rivalries among his sons, and Nelson's sources imply that the activities of these "crowned doves" resonated in observers' awareness. The wealth of extant evidence from Charlemagne's court highlights a lack of it for much of the medieval period, but McCartney's study of the imagery applied to Louise of Savoy demonstrates that Louise's right to the regency was braced by perceptions of the pedagogical relationship between mother and son as she fulfilled the "private" maternal obligation of educating the future Francis I for his duties as king. (My essay makes a very similar point about queens who trained their daughters as diplomatic brides.) That these essays reveal women as fully functioning members of royal families argues against describing their position and roles as "private" or "domestic," and in favor of a flexible and inclusory "interstitial" (as suggested by Fradenburg 1991a: 5).

If one point is to be distilled from the array of issues raised by the single, familial aspect of medieval queenship discussed in these introductory pages, it is that the variety of queenly experience contained in that one area argues that all aspects of medieval queenship need much further investigation, especially on the specific territorial scale suggested by Bak and Skovgaard-Petersen, and that more comparative anthologies are needed. One approach marked out by the present collection is to seek a redefined chronology of medieval queenship in relation to shifting patterns of "family," to changes in the relationship between the king's family and the kingdom, and to consequent growth, restraint, or redirection of queens' power and influence. Attention to such changes, to variety in local custom and experience and its impact on queenship, may help explain why the Middle Ages only slowly developed its vocabulary of gender and power.

This volume originated in a conference session on medieval queenship at the Twenty-Fifth International Congress on Medieval Studies at Western

Michigan University in May 1989, a session organized by the present editor on behalf of *Majestas*, an international scholarly organization founded in 1985 to promote the study of medieval rulership. Three of the essays published here were read on that occasion and two others during a *Majestas* session on royal mothers at the Twenty-Seventh International Congress in 1991. The remaining essays were contributed by the authors, to whom I owe my thanks for their generosity, cooperation, and patience. I must also thank Mr. Simon Winder of St. Martin's Press, whose suggestion inspired the collection, and his assistant, Ms. Laura Heymann, for their invaluable advice and support.

Centre for Reformation and Renaissance Studies
Victoria University, Toronto
November 1992

CHAPTER 2

Roles and Functions of Queens in Árpádian and Angevin Hungary (1000-1386 A.D.)

JÁNOS M. BAK

robably much less has been written on Hungarian queens than on those from other European kingdoms in the Middle Ages. While the neglect of queens was common to all medieval historians until recently, in Hungary no renewed interest in women's history has as yet begun to rectify the imbalance.[1] Queens are no exception, moreover, to the reticence about women shown by medieval Hungarian sources; some royal consorts are in fact unknown to us by name, their existence surmised from references to a known wife as the king's second or third spouse. This is not really surprising, as Erik Fügedi, the authority on medieval Hungarian family history, was able to establish the origins and family connections of only eight wives of the greatest magnates between 1000 and 1250 (Fügedi 1986b: 32-33). Consequently, this discussion will be exploratory, summarizing the little that is known of Hungarian medieval queens and suggesting a few promising areas for future inquiry.

The first aspect worth noting is the queens' origins. The list given at this article's conclusion of the known consorts from the Árpád dynasty contains the essential information. Though it tells us little of the queens themselves, it does elucidate the dynastic and international orientation of the ruling house. The social and political gulf between the king and even the most ancient and powerful aristocratic families was apparently so vast that until the fifteenth century nearly all Hungarian kings married foreign princesses. About half the known queens between 1000 and 1300 came from countries west of Hungary; half the rest were from neighboring countries such as Poland, Kievan Rus' or Serbia, and the remainder were of Byzantine aristocratic background (Kerbl 1979). There were very few exceptions. A niece of the founding monarch St. Stephen (r. 997-1038) married a Hungarian magnate, Samuel Aba, who reigned briefly as king of Hungary (1041-44) in opposition to St. Stephen's Venetian nephew Peter Orseolo (of whom more below). Two centuries later, King Béla IV (r. 1235-70) married his son Stephen II (r. 1270-72) to a daughter of the chieftain of the Cumans, a warlike nomadic people who had sought refuge in Hungary from the Mongols; Béla hoped the marriage would reinforce the alliance with the Cumans, giving him, in the face of imminent Mongol invasion, a force more reliable than the feudal levy. That most queens came from abroad was important for their role in the country's cultural life; I shall return to this point.

Even though we know relatively little about any of the early medieval Hungarian queens, a few of their "functions" can be outlined. First, they may have served as real or ideological scapegoats for abuses resented by the nobility; second, they were agents of foreign influence and immigration; third, they were owners of extensive estates, in connection with which they headed reginal households with their own officers and with distinct roles in the royal *curia*, including its little-known ceremonial functions. They were also, of course, the kings' wives, and as such were expected to provide heirs to the throne, but this aspect of their functions apparently did not develop political significance until the end of the thirteenth century, when the male branch of the founding dynasty became extinct and the question of inheritance in the female line became an issue. In the earlier Middle Ages (at least until around 1100) male primogeniture was not the accepted norm in the Árpád house; hence the lack of a legitimate son was not of critical importance. The first king, St. Stephen, predeceased by his only son in 1031, was succeeded by a sister's son, then a nephew, and later two distant cousins. A century later, King Coloman (r. 1095-1116) expelled his second queen, an alleged adulteress, from court and country in 1113, and her son Boris was barred from the succession (though he caused much trouble in later decades [Makk 1989]). But the sources suggest no further implications of these matters.

There were three significant cases in which queens served as scapegoats; in one of these, accusations surfaced when the woman was long dead and hurt only her memory, but in the other cases the accused lost their lives. The first (posthumous) victim was Queen Gisela, first Christian queen of Hungary, wife of St. Stephen and a sister of Emperor Henry II. After the death of his only son, Stephen selected as his heir the Venetian Peter Orseolo, the son of one of his sisters. At the same time, an uncle or cousin of the king named Vazul (Vasilij or Basilios), accused of conspiring to kill Stephen, was imprisoned, blinded, and later killed.

Ultimately neither Peter Orseolo nor Stephen's other close relative, Samuel Aba, was able to consolidate power in Hungary, and the expatriate sons of the dead Vazul were recalled from Bohemia and Poland to rule the kingdom; they were the ancestors of the later Árpáds. The earliest redaction of the Hungarian chronicles, written during their reigns in the mid-eleventh century, had to accommodate both growing veneration for the founding King Stephen (canonized in 1083 under one of Vazul's grandsons), and the fact that that same "holy king" had ordered the gruesome murder of the reigning king's grandfather. Building on Hungarian resentment against foreigners like Peter and his supporter the German emperor, it was easy to blame Stephen's "German" queen Gisela for the tragedy and to depict the aging, ailing, and heartbroken Stephen as the victim of court intrigue—even making him counsel Vazul's sons to flee the country to evade the queen's wrath (Szentpétery 1937: i, 318-20). Of course there is not a shred of evidence to support this legend. Judging from Stephen's earlier actions in assuring the development of his realm as a Latin Christian, western-oriented kingdom, in opposition to some of his relatives who clung to paganism or leaned towards the Eastern Church, there is no reason to assume that he did not order the elimination of Vazul, who could have had strong claims to the throne under the prevailing custom of *senioratus* and who, as his name suggests, could have been closer to Byzantium than to the West. That a "vicious wife" caused King Stephen's bad reputation had purely topical implications that should be noted only in passing.

The fabricated story of Gisela already contains one element that two centuries later cost a queen her life: anti-foreign rhetoric. In 1213 Queen Gertrudis of Andechs-Meran, wife of Andrew II (r. 1204-1235), was assassinated by a group of aristocratic rebels; what exactly triggered this palace revolt is not known, but it is clear that Andrew favored his wife's relatives who had acquired important posts in the Hungarian church and the royal government. The rebels belonged to a group of magnates who feared a loss of influence at court, and blamed the "Meranians" for all the measures taken by Andrew in strengthening royal power. It is significant that Andrew did not succeed in punishing all the powerful conspirators, many of whom retained or regained their high posts. It was only thirty years later that his son Béla IV managed to punish the last of his mother's murderers (Féjer 1829-44: vi part 1, 41, 129, 203; Osgyányi 1985). Legendary elements were already being added to this story in the later Middle Ages, including Gertrudis' role in her lascivious brother's alleged seduction of the wife of the count palatine, Ban Bánk. These events were immortalized in Grillparzer's drama *Ein treuer Diener seines Herrn,* and by a national opera that still plays to full houses in Budapest.

More than 170 years later, the dowager Queen Elizabeth Kotromanic of Bosnia, widow of Louis I of the house of Anjou, and her daughter Maria, the only reigning queen of medieval Hungary, were imprisoned by a group of rebellious barons (Bernath and von Schroeder 1974-81; iii, 51-54, 95). Elizabeth was strangled by one of them, though Maria finally regained her freedom and was able to join her husband, Sigismund of Luxembourg, for a few years before her death in a riding accident (Halecki 1991: 219-20). In this case the two queens were accused of misgovernment, especially Elizabeth who, according to many contemporaries, was indeed a forceful but ruthless politician. The details of this rebellion are still unclear; it was connected with the competing bids for influence at court from the Garai clique, confidants of the Angevin royal family on the one hand, and on the other some Croatian lords allied with the Neapolitan branch of the dynasty (Bard 1978: 11-15). Whatever the case, it is noteworthy that throughout the history of Hungary only four crowned members of the royal house were assassinated and three of them were queens (unless we add Empress Elizabeth, Franz Josef's popular wife, murdered by an anarchist in 1898). The one murdered king was Charles of Durazzo, crowned on the last day of 1385 and killed a month later by men of the dowager Queen Elizabeth Kotromanic—who paid for it with her life.

Probably the most important aspect of the early medieval queens' careers was that foreign knights and courtiers came with them to Hungary even before the mass migration of Germans and Rhinelanders into the Carpathian basin. It is likely, though not certain, that the first Western knights known in Hungary, who girded King Stephen *more teutonico* on the eve of his major battle against his pagan uncle Koppány, and that Vecelin who killed Koppány next day, were members of Queen Gisela's Bavarian escort. Hermann, the ancestor of the clan Hermány, was also reputed to be Gisela's retainer, though conjectures based on his family's estates would put his arrival in Hungary a few generations later (Szentpétery 1937: i, 189, 190). The powerful noble family of Gutkeled were descendants of two knights from the retinue of Queen Judith, daughter of Emperor Henry III. The ancestors of the Ratold (Rátót) clan came from Apulia with Queen Busilla. The French knights from whom the Kukenus-Renold family traced their origin, and a certain count Smaragdus Aynard, accompanied Margaret Capet, sister of Philip Augustus of France and wife of Béla III. The Aragonese *comes* Simon and his brother Martin came to Hungary with Constance, first the wife of King Imre/Henry and later of Emperor Frederick II; they were the founders of the Martinsberg comital family (Fügedi 1974: 495-98). In a few cases we can also follow the fate of ladies who accompanied their mistresses to the Hungarian court. Lady Thota, from Aragon, became the wife of Voivode Benedict, a Hungarian magnate, and remained at the court even after Queen Constanza's departure (Szentpétery and Borsa 1923-87: i, nos. 198, 362 [at 60, 120]). The French lady Ahalyz seems to have been one of Queen Yolande's entourage, and when Ahalyz married a local nobleman the queen granted her a sizeable property as a kind of dowry (Szentpétery and Borsa 1923-87: i, no. 357 [at 119]; Fejér 1829-44: iii part 1, 285).

Cultural and ecclesiastical historians have pointed out that French influence, in the form of Parisian studies and the spread of Cistercian foundations, was greatly enhanced under Queen Margaret Capet. Perhaps the popularity of romance, reflected in many "Trojan" names among the aristocracy, was also due to her influence and her entourage (Gabriel 1944: 24-26; Kardos 1941: 92-93). Sources are too scanty to establish similar cultural links in the cases of many other foreign-born queens. Their arrival and acculturation in Hungary, however, does raise the puzzling question of linguistic pluralism. With few exceptions these queens arrived as grown women (albeit sometimes young ones) in Hungary, where the spoken language, Magyar, was not only unknown to them but was linguistically totally alien to their Latin, Germanic, or Slavic mother tongues (Bak, forthcoming). It would be most interesting to know how, and over what period of time, they and their retinues learned the local language — or how much of the queens' native tongues the Hungarian kings knew when their brides arrived. How were communications managed between husband and wife? Did chaplains and confessors act as go-betweens, using Latin as a major vehicle of acculturation? Only in the later Middle Ages were future queens sent to Buda as children, to learn the language and customs of their new country.

As a systematic study of reginal properties is still wanting, only fragmentary information is available on the estates and cities under the queens' jurisdiction. The most ancient piece of reginal real estate seems to have been in western Hungary: the palace at Veszprém and properties attached to it. As early as the tenth century St. Stephen's mother Sarolt lived there, and Stephen's widow was exiled to Veszprém by King Peter. The connection between queen and city—and its bishopric—was always a very close one; the bishops of Veszprém had the right to crown the queens of Hungary (and seem to have done so throughout the Middle Ages), and several of them served in the queens' households, as will be seen later. Obuda ("Old Buda") and the island close to it (now called St. Margaret's Island) were reginal estates and frequently served as queens' residences. Other lands and towns designated as *reginales* appear in some charters recording donations, but as authentic documents of this nature are rare before the thirteenth century the evidence is too scanty to make it certain whether distinct estates in the royal domain were regularly designated as the queen's property. According to a charter of 1284, for example, the village of Veröcze *ultra Dravam* was "commonly known as the queen's property" (Szentpétery and Borsa 1923-87: ii, nos. 3310-11); on the other hand, in 1279 Queen Elisabeth was in possession of the northern district of Szepes/Zips only to be made administrator of the southern vassal Banate of Macva a year later (Féjer 1829-44: vi part 3, 35-37).

The character of these possessions can be understood from the custom of marriage gifts. In a custom similar to the Germanic *Morgangabe*, a Hungarian noblewoman received a wedding gift (*dos*) from her husband or his clan upon marriage; this remained under her control, was retained by her if she became a widow, and seems sometimes to have been inherited in the female line. Such women did not bring landed property to the marriage, for their own clan satisfied their claims to family property with the so-called filial quarter, rendered mostly in cash (Bonis, Bak, and Sweeney 1988: 98-99). Queens who came from distant lands likewise added no lands to their husbands' property, but just like any noble wife they were given at marriage property from the kings' possessions. The royal domain remained impressive until the mid-thirteenth century, comprising roughly one-third of the kingdom; hence there was plenty of land, including royal cities, that could be assigned the queen. In the earlier Middle Ages, however, few references give us some idea of the extent of reginal properties, or claims. The dowager Queen Constance was promised 12,000 silver marks if she left the country after King Imre's death in 1204; but she later complained to the pope that her brother-in-law was reluctant to hand over the money to her. When Andrew II married Yolande of Courtenay, her *dos* was secured on the income of a banate and four western counties. Later, when he left for the Crusade, he assigned Yolande as security against her claim to an 8000-mark dower, the income from salt sales on the river Maros, the taxes from the Ishmaelites of Pest, and the revenues from a major county (Fejér 1829-44: iii part 1, 263; see also Szentpétery and Borsa 1923-87: nos. 321-22).

As far as the queens' administrative functions are concerned, fragmentary references prove their existence and importance, though we cannot establish their extent. There are indications Queen Margaret Capet initiated a reginal household parallel to the more formalized royal *curia* of her husband Béla III. The first reference to a *comes curiae reginae* dates from *ca.* 1205; a queen's chancellor is mentioned in a charter of 1224, and a treasurer occurs in 1261-62 (Fejér 1829-44: xiv part 3, 405, and v part 3, 210), though as the records are in no sense continuous these offices could have existed earlier. In 1269 Bishop Paul of Veszprém, Queen Maria Laskaris' chancellor since 1263, obtained assurance that this office would always be connected with his church. This claim was disregarded for some time, however, and although Bishop Peter of Veszprém had his rights again confirmed in 1277, only fourteenth-century successors of his were reginal chancellors (Fejér 1829-44: v part 2, 337). In the last decades of the thirteenth century the queens also had vice-chancellors, suggesting that the title of chancellor, like that of the king's chancellor, had become a prestigious dignity, while the actual writing office was headed by a lesser cleric. It is significant, however, that the queens' household officers are best known to us when they are mentioned as performing duties entrusted to them by the king, be it the supervision of property transactions or diplomatic missions abroad. They were part of a gradually growing group referred to as attached to the king's *aula* or *curia* (compare Engel 1990: 46-47); they acted as the government of the realm and were "reginal" only insofar as their regular tasks involved administration of the queens' estates.

From a few references in royal charters to the queens' approval or intercession in various matters (mostly regarding property donations), one may assume that some early medieval queens participated actively in royal councils and routine governmental matters. Evidence for such activities before 1300, however, is too slim to confirm or challenge this conclusion. There is no evidence for the assumption that Turkic and steppe-nomadic traditions, in which powerful women were influential figures at the heads of tribes and tribal alliances, survived in Hungary into the Christian Middle Ages (Szentpétery 1930: 117). Thietmar of Merseburg indeed reports that Prince Géza's wife Sarolta, the "White Lady" (St. Stephen's mother), was just such a commanding person, and chides her for violent actions against Géza's enemies (Thietmar of Merseberg 1955: viii part 5, 498; Szekfü 1974); but there is no indication of continuity from Sarolta to the medieval queens. A few queens in the twelfth and thirteenth centuries did wield considerable power, though this was the result of specific circumstances and not by custom or tradition. To mention only the most conspicuous example, King Béla II was blinded as a child; his

Serbian wife Helena/Jelena and her brother, Ban Belus, often had to act in Béla's name and thus acquired a degree of authority that no wife or brother-in-law of a fully capable king would have enjoyed. Several dowager queens acted as virtual regents for their sons, but only Elizabeth, widow of Stephen V, was formally entrusted with that office, and it is significant that after her son came of age the donations made by her and her co-regents had to be submitted to the king for his confirmation (see, e.g., Szentpétery and Borsa 1923-87: ii, no. 2999 [at 246]). Tomasina Morosini, mother of Andrew III (r. 1290-1301), was influential in the first years of her son's reign, but probably because of her Venetian background and forceful personality, not through any specific tradition. The two queens of Hungary who were probably most powerful reigned in the fourteenth century and were hence beyond the limits set for this inquiry; they were wives of kings of the Angevin-Sicilian dynasty, moreover, and thus surely unconnected to any Eurasian traditions. Elizabeth Piast, last wife of Charles I (r. 1301-42), was especially influential during the reign of her son Louis I (r. 1342-82); she travelled widely in order to support the claim of her younger son Andrew to the throne of Sicily, and later served as Louis' rather unpopular regent in Poland (1370-80) (Ferdinandy 1972; Halecki 1991: 50-52, 59-60). She came quite close to becoming another "scapegoat" when a disgruntled nobleman, Felician Záh, attacked her and her family, reputedly in revenge for the seduction of his daughter in the queen's court (Marczali 1911). Actually, this episode may have been telescoped into the story of Queen Gertrudis in late medieval historical-literary tradition. The tragic fate of Elizabeth's daughter-in-law, Elizabeth Kotromanic, murdered by rebels, is discussed above.

Evidence for the symbolic role of queens as consorts of their royal husbands is even slimmer than that for other functions. Pictorial sources are lacking for this period. That Queen Gisela is not shown with her husband on what is the only authentic image of him, the coronation mantle, is regrettable but not really surprising. This garment was originally a pluviale embroidered by Gisela and her ladies for the royal basilica in Fehérvár; though the queen could have appeared on it as a donor, it may not have been considered proper for her to include herself in a royal iconography (Kovács 1985). There are no reginal seals surviving before 1382 (Szentpétery 1930: 119), nor are *ordines* or reliably detailed descriptions of Hungarian coronations known before 1312. Hence, we have no information on the regalia attributed to Hungarian queens, though there is good reason to assume that medieval queens were crowned together with their husbands, with the same crown which since the early thirteenth century was known as the "Holy Crown of St. Stephen": two thirteenth-century queens refer in charters to their *dies appositionis coronae*. Of course, both kings and queens owned other crowns as well; these feature, for example, in the treasure that Princess Anna, daughter of Béla IV, took with her when she fled to her son-in-law, King Ottokar, sometime in the 1270s (Deér 1966: 256-58). Actually, the lower part of the "Holy Crown of Hungary," the so-called Greek crown, was originally a woman's diadem, possibly a Byzantine gift to Queen Synadene in 1075; its size fits only a head with elaborate hairdo and veil, and even Deér, who considered other possibilities, admitted that it fits nicely into the series of Byzantine empresses' crowns (1966: 76-77). In the twelfth or thirteenth century this diadem, perhaps slightly reworked, received its well-known cruciform arches and became the venerated royal insigne of the kings of Hungary.

The earliest surviving Hungarian coronation order, from the fourteenth century, is essentially an adaptation of the order found in the Pontifical of Guillaume Durand (composed 1292-95), the Roman Pontifical of the later Middle Ages (Andrieu 1938-41: iii, 318-20). This order prescribes the coronation of the queen but tells nothing about the actual ceremony (Bak 1973: 168-70). Our first close look at a reginal coronation dates from a period later than our survey: Queen Maria's investiture in 1382, which was anomalous as she was medieval Hungary's only reigning queen, elected and acclaimed. King Louis I left only two daughters to inherit his Polish and Hungarian thrones; a few years earlier, he had required the magnates of both realms to swear to accept these girls as their rulers. According to Maria's inaugural charter, she was "by hereditary right accepted by the prelates, nobles and notables" of the kingdom, and was crowned *rex Hungariae*. The legal construct was crafty: in a country where women did not usually inherit and were often not even recorded by name, it was somewhat problematic to hand the scepter to a woman, or to be precise, two women, because the queen-mother was formally made regent for her young daughter. The conundrum was therefore hidden behind the title *rex*. Foreign observers, such as the Venetian Lorenzo da Monacis, apparently accepted this usage, and he for one called Maria *rex foemineus!* The constitutional questions were not faced squarely, however, because the few charters Maria issued bear the style *dei gratia regina Hungariae* (Bak 1973: 24-26, 93). At her crowning, moreover, a quarrel broke out between the archbishop of Esztergom and the bishop of Veszprém, the latter claiming the ancient privilege of crowning Maria as queen, the former as primate of Hungary naturally asserting his right to crown the reigning monarch. Maria was finally crowned by the archbishop, who also became her archchancellor, but she issued a charter guaranteeing the privilege of Veszprém to crown the queens-consort (Fejér 1829-44: xi, 29).

With this episode we have already left the time limit set to this inquiry. Hungarian queens in the later Middle Ages deserve special study—not that any essential legal or constitutional changes can be identified in the fourteenth or fifteenth centuries, but because rather more is known about reginal properties and administrative functions in that period. For example, the political and economic role played by Queen Barbara of Cilly (second wife of King-Emperor Sigismund) was due to her family's wealth, and the cultural influence of Queen Beatrice (second wife of Matthias Corvinus) was nurtured by her Neapolitan, humanist entourage. Perhaps Maria of Habsburg, wife of the hapless Louis II and later governor of the Netherlands (Bernath and von Schroeder 1974-81: iii, 96), was the only one of those late medieval-early modern queens who conducted independent politics and tried to introduce serious changes in the royal court. Too late, however, for Hungary, which lost its king and its independence at the disastrous battle of Mohács in 1526.

Central European University
Budapest

Kings and Queens of Hungary, 1000-1301[2]

St. Stephen I, r. 1000-1038	Gisela of Bavaria (∂. 1065)
Peter (Orseolo), r. 1038-44, 1044-46	1. Tuta of Formbach (∂. 1046?) 2. Judith of Steinfurt (∂. 1058)
Samuel Aba, r. 1041-44	a kinswoman of St. Stephen?
Andrew I, r. 1046-60	1. "a pagan woman" 2. Anastasia of Kiev (∂. 1096)
Béla I, r. 1060-63	Richeza of Poland (∂. 1059?)
Salomon, r. 1063-74	Judith, dau. of Emp. Henry III (∂. 1093/95)
Géza I, r. 1074-77	1. Sophia of Looz (∂. 1065) 2. N. Synadene (∂. 1077?)[3]
St. Ladislas I, r. 1077-95	1. unknown 2. Adelaide of Zähringen (∂. 1079)
Coloman, r. 1095-1116	1. Busilla (Felicia) of Sicily (∂. ca. 1102) 2. Eufemia Vladimirovna of Kiev (div. 1113, ∂. 1139)
Stephen II, r. 1116-31	1. Christiana (?) of Capua 2. Adelaide of Riedensburg
Béla II the Blind, r. 1131-41	Helena/Jelena of Serbia (∂. ca. 1146)
Géza II, r. 1141-62	Euphrosina Mstislavna of Kiev (∂. bef. 1186)
Ladislas II, r. 1162	Judith (?) of Poland

Stephen III, r. 1161-63

1. A dau. of Jaroslav of Galicia
2. Agnes of Babenberg (∂. 1182)

Stephen IV, r. 1163-65

Maria Komnene[4]

Béla III, r. 1172-96

1. Maria Komnene (div. 1168)[5]
2. Agnes/Anne of Châtillon
   (∂. 1184)[6]
3. Theodora Komnene
4. Margaret Capet (∂. 1197)

Imre/Henry, f. 1196-1204

Constance of Aragon (∂.   1222)

Andrew II, r. 1205-35

1. Gertrudis of Meran (d. 1213)
2. Yolande of Courtenay (∂. 1233)[7]
3. Beatrice of Este (∂. 1245)

Béla IV, r. 1235-70

Maria Laskaris (∂. 1270)

Stephen V, r. 1270-72

Elizabeth, dau. of Zayhan,
Khan of the Cumans (∂. 1290?)

Ladislas IV, r. 1272-90

Elizabeth of Anjou-Naples
(∂. 1290)

Andrew III, r. 1290-1301

1. Fennena of Cujawia
   (∂. ca. 1295)
2. Agnes of Habsburg (∂. 1364)

CHAPTER 3

Queenship in Medieval Denmark

INGE SKOVGAARD-PETERSEN
(*in collaboration with* NANNA DAMSHOLT)

THE SOURCE MATERIAL

aterial for studying the queens of medieval Denmark is very scarce. Among the best sources relevant in this connection are diplomas, coins, annals, chronicles, and saints' lives. Diplomas provide evidence of Danish queens acting as donors or receivers of land, or as witnesses to royal acts. Only one coin, from the 1120s, mentions the name of a queen *expressis verbis*: King Niels (r. 1104-34) and his wife Margaret "Fredkulla," daughter of King Hakon of Norway. We also have some small bracteates (Fig. 3.1) from *ca.* 1160 on which both a king and queen are represented, but the lack of inscriptions makes their identity uncertain (Jørgensen and Skovgaard 1910). Chronicles and annals, Danish as well as foreign, give a more qualitative representation of the queens although the chroniclers' bias must be taken into consideration.

Figure 1. Danish bracteates from the middle of the 12th century (P. Hauberg, Danske Udmyntninger fra Tidsrummet 1146-1241. Det kongelige danske Videnskabernes Selskabs Skrifter, 1906).

THE PATRIARCHAL SYSTEM

The status of women in society was determined by their relation to men, and whether they were virgins, wives, or widows. According to the law, every woman was considered to be underage and in the custody of a man, though widows had a certain independence. A woman could temporarily take the place of a man and function as the head of a household or institution. A married woman could be in charge during the absence of her husband, or because of his weak health. A widow could manage a farm or household until a male heir came of age. Women could thus substitute for men if it was in the interest of house, lineage, or kingdom. Within the patriarchal framework, therefore, women had positions of high esteem as leaders of that part of the household belonging to women: the mistress of the house carried the keys to the storerooms, a symbol of her power.

Here we are concentrating on the study of powerful married women, namely queens, and must leave out the interesting subject of kings' concubines. Some of these latter women may have had a position that gave them respect and security, as indicated by some passages in the Icelandic sagas. Sven Estridsen (r. 1047-74) had a number of sons by different women, but we know nothing of the fate of these women apart from their not being married to the king.

THE ORIGINS AND CHOICE OF DANISH QUEENS AND THE ROYAL MARRIAGE

Medieval Danish queens came from a wide variety of backgrounds. If we begin with the tenth century when the evidence becomes sufficient for our purposes, a list of the queens reveals certain instructive patterns. During the Viking Age, Slavonic princesses were preferred; then, in the eleventh and at the beginning of the twelfth centuries, most of the queens were chosen from the Scandinavian countries, apart from the wives of Waldemar II. Danish kings also married princesses from Russia and from countries as far away as Portugal and Bohemia; in the later Middle Ages, German-born queens abound. Only one queen was of Danish origin, namely Bodil, the wife of King Erik "the Evergood" (r. 1096-1102), though the women attached to the Danish kings as "friller," or concubines, were probably Danish, as for instance the mothers of the sons of Sven Estridsson (r. 1047-74). But queens were usually selected from foreign royal families, and no doubt these matrimonial choices are a mirror of foreign politics.

An interesting study is the account of queens in Saxo Grammaticus' *Gesta Danorum*, written in Latin around 1200 and regarded as the culmination of Danish medieval historiography. A few examples from this rich source show the author's attitude toward queens, probably colored by his attitude toward women in general. In the fifth book of his work, Saxo maintains that kings ought to marry princesses from neighboring countries, not from faraway lands: Frode III (in later texts called "the Peaceful") is asked to propose to a daughter of the Hunnish king, but the marriage turns out badly: she betrays him with one of his men, and when the affair is disclosed Frode hands her over to another of his followers. Frode then marries a Norwegian princess and the marriage seems to succeed. A queen born in a neighboring country had certain advantages: she would speak a Nordic language and belong to the same culture as the king. The political reasons were less idealistic, and an example of these having the upper hand will be shown, together with the other side of the coin: a foreign princess was isolated from her kindred and they could not intervene in Danish affairs to help her.

Saxo's narrative is a moral lesson based on clerical views. The point is that in the Middle Ages many marriages, not only royal ones, were alliances between kindreds with elaborate rules for inheritance. Saxo was fully aware of the real conditions, so he put Christian ideas, which in his view stemmed from natural law, into the legendary past to create a Utopia to imitate a future age in which people could understand what the best relationship between men and women should be. In the first, legendary, half of his work, Saxo thus insists upon the wife's consent to marriage even if she is of royal descent. This is a canonical doctrine which Saxo adopted and used in that part of his work in which he was not bound by his sources. When he crosses the border into recorded history, he admits that royal alliances were negotiated by the relatives of the two parties. There is no evidence that future queens were involved in the planning of their marriages; some of them were small children when they were betrothed to young princes. Only three times does Saxo tell of queens or princesses who acted against the wish of their male wardens, were seduced, or left their husbands of their own will. Almost every time that sort of thing happens in Saxo's work, disastrous consequences follow.

For instance, during the twelfth century rebellions or wars point back to matrimonial unhappiness: the rebels are born outside wedlock, or to mothers tainted by seduction or rape. The first example is the tale of King Niels' wife, who was seduced by the Swedish king Sverker. When their son Johannes became an adult he raped two distinguished Danish ladies, one a virgin and the other married to the duke of Halland, and compelled them to have intercourse with him night after night. After he was forced to give them up, he had the temerity to appear at a public assembly, where he was killed by the outraged Swedish people. The Danish king then waged war upon the Swedes and many were killed. The other instance is told with tongue in cheek. The unfortunate prince Henrik had a lively wife who one day ran away with a young man, both of them dressed as servants. Henrik had to fetch her home; in Saxo's opinion he deserved no better because he had participated in the murder of his cousin, St. Canute. But the lady, called Ingerid, gave birth to a son, Buris Henriksson (his paternity was not disputed), who afterwards rebelled against King Waldemar the Great and died in captivity.

Ingerid appears in a famous chronicle of Norwegian kings and queens, the so-called *Heimskringla* written by the Icelander Snorri Sturlason about 1230. Of Ingerid, Snorri wrote that when her first husband, Henrik, was killed in a battle in Skania, she married the Norwegian king and had by him three sons who made civil war in Norway. When that king died, she took a third husband, and had a son by a lover; this last son, Orm, called "king's brother," also made war on Denmark. Ingerid indeed seems to have been *la femme fatale du Nord!* A third instance of seduction, told by Saxo in a more serious manner, occurred in the early 1170s. A royal prince, and two other princes whose mother was the duchess of Halland mentioned above, hatched a plot against King Waldemar; the plan was discovered and they fled, but were later imprisoned. Thus all three rebellions noted by Saxo had some connection with willing or unwilling transgressions of matrimonial vows.

Saxo is not the only chronicler who tells about princesses who rebelled against the destiny intended for them. The Swedish author of *Erikskrönikan*, from *ca.* 1320, tells of the daughters of the Danish king Erik "Ploughpenny" (r. 1241-50). As their father was murdered by one of his brothers, their fate depended upon the succeeding kings, their uncles. The two elder princesses were married to the kings of Sweden and Norway, but the two younger were less lucky. Agnes went into a new convent in Roskilde dedicated to her patron, St. Agneta, and Jutta followed her some years later; both swore that they took the conventual vows voluntarily but eventually they abandoned the cloister. Jutta sought refuge with her sister in Sweden; the *Erikskrönikan* says she arrived "like an angel from Heaven"—but then her brother-in-law, the king, made love to her. As a result, he lost his kingdom, and Jutta returned to Denmark. The sisters' property had been given to their convent, and a dispute over the rights arose between the convent and the crown. The Danish king prevailed, but in 1284 he was compelled to give the land back to Agnes and Jutta, who then lived there. Both the conventual vows and the fight over the estates are well documented in charters.

It must be remembered that Saxo invented much of the legendary part of his work (Books I-VIII)—if not the whole, then at least the dating, background, and connections among these stories. To create this sort of thing he had to use other sources than historical ones, for instance, events from his own time. Of course it can only be guesswork, but it is tempting to look for parallels at the Danish court at the end of the twelfth century. King Waldemar I, the Great, took a Russian princess as his consort (see list at the end of this chapter). Saxo disliked her, and she was perhaps the model for the Hunnish princess Frode III married, though her faults were not the same: she was rather poor but was nevertheless very ambitious for the marriages of her children. One of them was betrothed to a son of the emperor Frederick Barbarossa; a huge sum of money was to be given as her dowry, but the marriage never came off. It must be added that Saxo's opinion of Queen Sofia was not the only one. In another chronicle from the same period, Sven Aggesen praises her beauty and in Sven's *Brevis historia* she appears as a lady worthy of the songs of the troubadours.

Both Aggesen and Saxo finish their narratives in the mid-1180s and so avoid writing about the scandals at Waldemar's court in the 1190s, but a famous royal wedding in 1193 must have loomed large in their thinking during the decades around 1200, the marriage of Ingeborg, daughter of King Waldemar and Queen Sofia, who married the French king Philip Augustus. For unknown reasons the bridegroom wanted to divorce her the morning after their wedding, but the young queen refused to yield to his wishes. For about twenty years Philip tried to divorce her, but the papacy and the Danish king fought stubbornly for Ingeborg's rights. From her isolated and prison-like residence Ingeborg sent letters that give a touching description of her situation and of the way she handled it, and of the importance that Ingeborg attached to her status as queen: she claimed the right to be with her husband and to be dressed and served according to her rank. At last, Ingeborg was accepted as queen of France and remained there, even after King Philip's death. Obviously it is impossible to tell

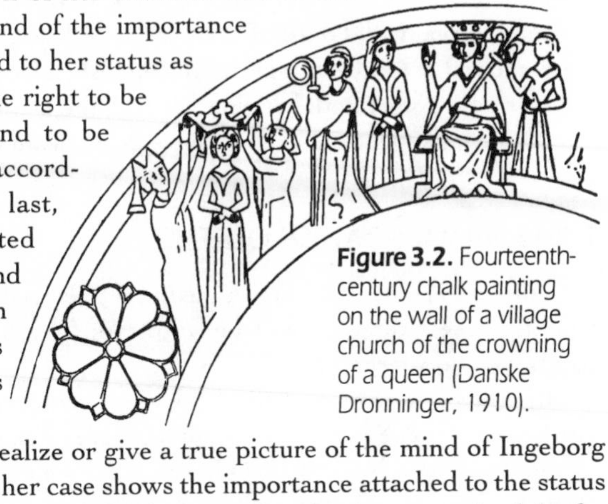

Figure 3.2. Fourteenth-century chalk painting on the wall of a village church of the crowning of a queen (Danske Dronninger, 1910).

whether the letters idealize or give a true picture of the mind of Ingeborg and her advisers. But her case shows the importance attached to the status of a crowned[1] and acknowledged queen. A princess was raised in the expectation of being treated truly and honorably as the first lady of the realm, mother of a future king, and the mistress of royal estates.

THE DUTIES OF MEDIEVAL QUEENS

Like every wife in a medieval household, the queen held the keys—that is to say, she managed the household—but as that sort of thing belongs to the private sphere, it does not appear in the source material. Only in elaborate chronicles like Saxo's can we get an idea of what that meant, and we must always keep in mind that Saxo invented much information, especially in the legendary part of his work. One of his most famous incidents is the story of Amleth's mother weaving wall-hangings to be hung up at his funeral. Whether queens really did that kind of thing we cannot know, but it seems plausible; of Queen Gunhild, whom Sweyn Estridsson divorced, it is told that she afterwards lived as a nun and wove church-cloths. (Altar-cloths could also be bought, however; when Canute IV was canonized his widow Adela, who had then married the king of Sicily, sent a beautiful Byzantine antemensale of which a fragment is still preserved.) A very humble type of housework was the repairing of courtiers' clothes. Saxo says that King Frode needed a wife to do the mending, but this seems to be an antiquarian's dream.

From diplomas from the early twelfth century we know that several prominent functions were performed by specially entrusted men, and the same must have been true of household duties. Cooking and baking were performed by both men and women, while washing was a female duty; but of course servants did most of these jobs. In the tenth-century Norwegian grave-mound at Oseberg, where a distinguished lady, presumably a queen, was buried together with her elderly maid, the magnificent burial deposits included a milk-sieve which must have been meant for the old servant.

THREE FAMOUS DANISH QUEENS

In order to show that Danish medieval queens could rule on their own behalf, three examples will be adduced: Thyra Danebod, Margaret Sambiria, and Margaret I.

Thyra lived in the first half of the tenth century; her Anglian origin is known only from Saxo, whose statements are often self-contradictory. She is commemorated by several runic stones, of which the most famous is the smaller of two stones at the village of Jelling in Jutland (Fig. 3.3), whose inscription reads: "King Gorm erected this monument in honor of his wife

Thyra Danebod." In the last two hundred years there has been much discussion of this epitaph. The meaning of the appellation "Danebod" is uncertain; it may mean the fine or the penalty of the Danes, or it may derive from the verb "bøde," to repair. The latter interpretation has been preferred, but this begs the question as to what sort of mending was done.

Fig. 3.3. The small runic stone at Jelling. The last words of the inscription, "Sina Tanmarkaar But," are carved on the side of the stone (Danske Dronninger, 1910).

By the twelfth century "Danebod" was connected with "Danevirke," the dyke from Schleswig to the North Sea, the old frontier between Denmark and Germany. The dyke was first erected in A.D. 737, and archaeologists have shown that later extensions and rebuilding took place through the end of the twelfth century. No doubt some such emendations took place in the tenth century. Both Sven Aggeson and Saxo tell exciting stories of Thyra's achievement as an architect of Danevirke, though it seems the stories were invented to explain the word "Danebod." Aggesen's charming tale of Thyra's organization of the Danish people to build the dyke, for example, has been compared to Virgil's story of Queen Dido's building of Carthage. There is no necessity, however, to connect "Danevirke" with "Danebod." The surname could denote other quite different things, such as "the pride" or "the flower" of the Danes. Another problem is that "Danebod" could apply to King Gorm; there are other instances of such connections between the first and last words of a runic inscription, and if that is the case, Gorm is boasting of his own achievement regardless of the meaning of the surname. Still, the most natural explanation is that Thyra was called "Danebod," and much guesswork has been done not only as to how Thyra won the name but also as to what Gorm did on that occasion. In the royal genealogies he is called "the Dull" and several explanations have been offered about why he let his wife do the work; was he dull, "Løge," as one text says? Or was he too old—in royal genealogies he is invariably called "den Gamle"? Or was he dead when the challenge came? The latter assertion arose when people had forgotten the runic inscriptions and needed to explain why it was Thyra who contrived the building of Danevirke.

One story was already told in the twelfth century and seems to derive from Icelandic historians, though it is first met in Saxo's *History of the Danes*. There is no need to think that Saxo did not know runes, but if he read or was told a good story by the Icelanders he did not compare it to the Jelling inscription. So he wrote that when Gorm and Thyra were to be married, she demanded the whole of Denmark for her morning gift. Birgit Strand (Sawyer) has noticed that in old Scandinavian laws the morning gift became the maternal inheritance of the children; that way one of Thyra's sons could be guaranteed the succession to the throne even though Denmark was an elective monarchy.

Nanna Damsholt supports this interpretation by stressing Saxo's ambiguous representation of Queen Thyra. She and Gorm had two sons. The younger was Harald, who succeeded to the throne because the elder, Canute, was killed beforehand in a battle in Ireland. King Gorm had once said that he would put to death anyone who delivered the message that Canute was dead; when Canute was killed, nobody dared tell the king until Thyra conceived the idea of putting a funeral cloak on him. When he saw this Gorm exclaimed, "So my son Canute has died." Thyra answered, "You have said it yourself," and Gorm fell dead. It has been assumed that Saxo told the story in this way to explain how Thyra secured the inheritance for her younger son. It may be so, but in outline the same story is told in later Icelandic texts whose authors do not seem to have known Saxo. There is no reason why an independent story about Canute should not have been transmitted, but the death of Gorm before Thyra is another matter: it contradicts the contemporary evidence of the runic stone at Jelling, so it must be rejected.

Much more is known of queens from the thirteenth century. Admittedly the chronicles and annals are rather poor, but several other pieces of evidence can be unearthed in the way of diplomas and seals. Still, we do not know why the youngest son of Waldemar II, Christopher, in 1249 took a bride from Pomerania. It may be that he wanted to offset his elder brother Abel, who had married a wife from Holstein and so gained considerable influence over Schleswig and Holstein, the southernmost provinces of

Denmark. In fact, this was the beginning of Schleswig's independence (Holstein was always German, though a fief of the Danish crown).

The eldest of the royal brothers, King Erik "Ploughpenny," was murdered in the Schlei firth in 1250. Rumor accused Abel of provoking the murder, but he succeeded to the Danish throne, to be killed two years later in a battle in Frisia. His sons were passed over and imprisoned, so that the third brother, Christopher, took the throne. During the long struggle with the princes of Schleswig-Holstein, Abel's descendants tried to regain the Danish crown but were invariably repulsed by Christopher. One of his tactics was to kindle hatred against Abel by publicizing the latter's responsibility for King Erik's murder. That was done by a detailed narrative in a letter to the pope describing the struggle between the two brothers, and how Erik was beheaded and his body thrown into the Schlei. Fishermen netted the corpse and the head, and brought them to a Dominican priory where they were buried; in 1258 Erik's body was transferred to the royal sepulchral church in Ringsted.

Some people had recognized the body as King Erik's, and before Abel could be crowned king he had to swear that he had no part in the hideous crime. Still, many believed him guilty of the murder, most important among them King Christopher and Queen Margaret; she was the author of the letter to the pope, which is known only through its quotation in the pope's preliminary response. We do not know why it was the queen who requested Erik's canonization while King Christopher was still alive. A commission was appointed but refused the canonization; nevertheless Erik was venerated as a popular saint and several guilds of merchants took him as their patron.

As mentioned above, Erik had only four daughters, of whom two married the kings of Sweden and Norway while the two youngest went at Queen Margaret's instigation into a convent at Roskilde; when they later abandoned the convent there was a great struggle for their property. A more significant quarrel was the fight between Kings Erik and Christopher and the Danish archbishop, Jakob Erlandsen. An account of this conflict in the "Acta processus litium inter regem Danorum et archiepiscopum Lundensen" shows that Queen Margaret had a significant part in the quarrel, which was concluded in a way that was rather favorable for the crown. Margaret participated in politics both while her husband was alive and after his death in 1259; he was poisoned, it was whispered, by means of sacramental wine. At that time Margaret became the guardian of her young son Erik, called "Glipping," and shouldered the royal tasks very seriously indeed. She fought the princes of Holstein and was captured with young Erik in 1261; they were released only in 1264.

Fig. 3.4. Queen Margaret Sambiria and her
son King Erik in a law manuscript in Tallinn,
Estonia (Danske Dronninger, 1910).

Margaret's best weapon was her chancellery. Many of her diplomas,
and sixteen seals, have been preserved. Niels Skyum-Nielson has studied
the original diplomas from the later thirteenth century and has shown the
distinction between the queen's and the king's chancelleries. The king had
to procure his income by travelling around the kingdom, while the dowager queen could stay in her castle in Nykøbing and keep the same scribes
to a much greater extent than was possible for the king. The result was
that her charters were much more firmly implemented. Several times she
seems also to have taken the initiative; the king's letters would follow
afterwards, more or less explicitly agreeing with Margaret's. She reaped
the fruits of her efforts by having conferred on her the government of
Estonia and Virland; on some of her seals she is called "Domina Estoniae."
She died in 1282, only four years before her son was murdered at
Finderup in Jutland, one of the most debated events in Danish history.

King Waldemar Atterdag shrewdly arranged that his younger daughter
Margaret (born in 1353) should marry Haakon, the young king of Norway,
though the Norwegian nobility wanted Elizabeth of Holstein as their
queen. When Elizabeth arrived in Danish waters she was taken into custody until the marriage between Haakon and Margaret was solemnized at

Copenhagen in 1363. Two years afterwards, Margaret was taken to Norway to be brought up under the supervision of a daughter of St. Birgitta of Vadstena. This connection with the Order of St. Birgitta had a lasting influence on Margaret; she often went to Vadstena, founded Birgittinian convents, and saw to it that her daughter-in-law, Philippa of Lancaster, later sought the same support from the order. Philippa was buried at Vadstena in 1430. In 1371 Margaret gave birth to a son, Olaf. As Norway was a hereditary realm, the young prince was guaranteed the succession to the throne when King Haakon died in 1380. Denmark, on the other hand, was an electoral monarchy, so that when Waldemar died in 1375 leaving no sons, the choice lay between the sons of his two daughters. The elder daughter, Ingibjorg, was dead, and her son Albert of Mecklenburg had already become king of Sweden; when the Danish counsellors succeeded in choosing Olaf as their new king, they were supported by the Hanseatic League, who did not want to see the same king reigning over both Denmark and Sweden.

Olaf's power, or in fact his mother's, was at first restricted. He had to sign a coronation charter which stressed the enforcement of the law and ensured the privileges of the clergy and nobility. No doubt a certain distrust of the kingship lingered from the reign of Waldemar IV, who was criticized for successfully laying doubtful claims on lands. Margaret took over this course of action, thereby enriching the royal family.

During the next fifteen years Margaret revealed her diplomatic abilities. She had good advisers indeed, for instance her father's "drost" (seneschal) Henning Podebusk, and the bishop of Roskilde, Niels Jacobsen Ulfeldt, but in the long run her most important counsellor was the canon and later bishop Peter Jensen Lodehat. Still, there is no doubt that the queen herself was the soul of Danish politics. The first issue was an arrangement with the Hanseatic League. At a peace negotiation in Stralsund in 1370, the league had won the supervision of the royal castles in Scania for fifteen years. When the time came to restore the castles the Hansa refused to do so; and in 1380 when King Haakon died, Margaret declined to renew the Hanseatic privileges connected with trade in Norway. Thus the Danish crown lost some income from the league, but on the other hand the necessity of cooperation became evident, not only in the case of Norway but also for the important herring trade in Øresund. Margaret succeeded in having the castles returned. A contemporary chronicler, Dietmar of Lübeck, praised her skill not only as regards the Scanian castles but also her politics concerning Schleswig-Holstein; when in 1386 she and her son King Olaf drove through Jutland, official homage was paid to him and the fiefs of Schleswig and Holstein were restored to the Danish crown. It was stressed that these prominent vassals should in the future adhere to King Olaf. Later on, however, Margaret infringed part of this agreement, and it has been said by a modern Danish historian that "neither King Waldemar nor his daughter were remembered by the Hanseatics for fidelity to their promises."

Now the time had arrived for a decisive battle between Margaret and her nephew Albert of Mecklenburg, the king of Sweden. The opportunity arose when the richest Swedish nobleman died and left his estates to the king of Norway, Margaret's son Olaf. They at once claimed the inheritance although they would have to fight for it. Just as they were preparing for war with Albert, Olaf died in August 1387. In this dangerous situation Margaret had to act quickly. She assembled a meeting of noblemen who, on behalf of all the people of Denmark, pronounced that Margaret had been appointed "fuldmætig frue og husbonde og ganska rigens af Danmarks formynder," as it was phrased in the language of the fourteenth century; the title means something like "principal mistress and house-holder and guardian of all the realm of Denmark." At the same time it was decided that all parties involved should choose a new king. The next year, Margaret received the same title in Norway, with the addition that as queen of Norway and Sweden she was inheritor of Denmark.

Fig. 3.5. A marble bust, presumably of Queen Margaret I (Museum für Kunst und Kulturgeschichte der Hansestadt Lübeck).

These magnificent titles were new and were meaningful only insofar as she could gain control over the three countries. First and foremost, the war with Albert of Mecklenburg provoked a final decision. Supported by Swedish nobles, Margaret went to battle with her nephew near Falköping in 1389 and won the day; Albert was captured. In name he was still king of Sweden and soon the Swedes' hostility towards foreign rulers was transferred from the Germans to the Danes. In order to ensure a more certain sovereignty over the three Nordic countries, Margaret chose her nearest male relation, her sister's grandson Erik of Pomerania, as the elected king of the three realms. In 1397 a grand coronation ceremony was held in the town of Kalmar, and a magnificent document of the coronation was signed and sealed by sixty-seven noblemen from all three countries. At the same time a letter describing the coronation was written in a more modest form; only seventeen men signed it and only ten signatories, most of them Swedish and only one Norwegian, impressed their seals onto it. The explanation may be its content: In this letter of the "Kalmar Union" each country stresses its independence of the others in many ways, for instance, that the castellans should be indigenous. As Margaret had much trouble with Swedish noblemen it must have been her intent to keep this document in a preliminary form. She did not wish to commit herself beforehand, and when the chance arose, she appointed Danish or Germans castellans of royal castles in Sweden and Norway as well as in Denmark. The government was centralized around her and her adopted successor Erik.

In a letter she wrote to Erik when he was going to Norway for the first time in 1406, the same carefulness appears. She tells him what he should be aware of in particular places, which people he can trust, and that while he should always appear as a kind and liberal regent, he must not take any decisions by himself "because we know more of the issues involved than you yourself"! As can be seen, Margaret was as shrewd as her father, though a velvet glove covered her iron hand. Despite her asperity there is every reason to believe in her piety. Shortly before she died in 1412 she made a will; apart from many legacies to individuals and monasteries (especially the Birgittinians) she appointed monks to visit all Scandinavian and many other places of pilgrimage, in order to intercede for her soul.

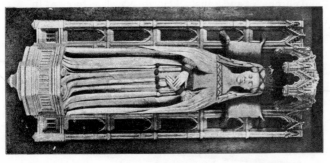

CONCLUSIONS

It has been said that Scandinavian women had a better position than other European medieval women. The idea is founded on what is told in the Icelandic sagas. Now these can be divided into several categories: although they were written down in the thirteenth century, some of them deal with the time before Iceland was inhabited and so take place in Scandinavia, the British Isles, or some part of continental Europe. Another group tells of Icelandic families who lived in the tenth and eleventh centuries, a time when the change from the Northern religion to Christianity took place. A third group deals with contemporary history. The most famous group of sagas is that of the so-called family sagas: *Njal's saga, Egil's saga Skallagrimsson, Laxdaela saga,* and so on. Here we meet renowned female heroes who played great roles. These "strong women" have been considered the archetypes of Nordic womanhood, much more independent than their sisters in other countries. Recently this conception has been much disputed: some scholars have stuck to the idea of the strong woman while others see it as an "Idealtypus" that never existed in real life. Whichever interpretation is preferred, it seems to be a fact that there were a number of influential Danish queens in the Middle Ages, but they were very different from each other.

One explanation of the differences can be found in the source material, as we noticed. Of Thyra we hardly know anything—when or where she was born, or when she died. The most substantial evidence is her nickname, whose very meaning is uncertain. On that account, various stories of her career have arisen. We are much better informed about Margaret Sambiria, thanks to the many diplomas she issued (it does not matter whether she was able to read or write herself, because she could act regardless of her literacy). Although the chronicles of her time were poorer than those of Saxo or Aggesen, they are a better help for the dating of events.

When we arrive at Margaret I, we can rely on many sources: diplomas, private letters, and chronicles and annals, Danish as well as foreign. In fact, we know so much that the contours of her personality can be drawn. Clearly she had an exceptional career and it is possible to see that her achievements had two certain consequences for the following queens of Denmark.

A reigning woman was accepted. We have seen that Margaret Sambiria had already taken part in the government, both when her husband was alive and after his death, when she was guardian for her young son. Nevertheless, the man who was the cause of her role was never forgotten, for obviously he was the real ruler. But Margaret I ruled in her own right and had a special title. Among her particular accomplishments was the fact that she named not only her heir but also his consort; and she took care of Philippa's upbringing so that the younger woman did her adoptive mother-in-law credit. When Margaret died, Erik of Pomerania decided that Philippa should be in charge when he himself was prevented from reigning, and she was the regent during his absence from 1423 to 1425. At that time she negotiated with the Hanseatic League, and the Hanseatics were rather shocked to meet a woman of such strength. Among other things she and they together decided that the Danish coinage should be stabilized. Philippa also took care of the relationship with the Union, especially with Sweden. A good part of the lands allotted to her as queen were in the middle of Sweden, where she also enjoyed the companionship of the nuns at Vadstena. In fact, Philippa followed the style of Margaret's government more than did her husband.

The next queen after Philippa, Dorothea of Brandenburg, was independent in another way. Erik was expelled from Scandinavia in 1439 and his nearest male relative, Christopher of Bavaria, became king of the three realms. He married Dorothea in 1445 when she was fourteen, but he died three years later. Dorothea tried to have a hand in the arrangements for her next marriage, but she had to accept the man whom the Danish counsellors appointed, a distant relative of the old dynasty, Christian of Oldenburg, who founded the line that ruled Denmark until 1863. He was charming and extravagant, rather a handful for his young wife. Whatever she had been beforehand, she now had to be a good manager, and compared to other queens of Denmark she was quite a different sort of person. Time and again she had to go to the so-called Kielerumschlag, a yearly money-market in the town of Kiel, to pay her husband's debts or to arrange new mortgages. At the same time, she took good care of her own money and estates, bore several children, and saw to their upbringing. When King Christian went to Rome in 1474 he showed the utmost extravagance, whereas the next year Dorothea drove there quietly, if not anonymously, with a small train of attendants, and secured results Christian had not obtained. Among other things she had the patience and the needed family connections to induce the papal curia to issue the bull for the establishment of the University of Copenhagen, which came into being in 1479.

To conclude, Denmark existed under the same patriarchal conditions as prevailed elsewhere, and in many ways the history of its queens was the same as in other European countries. Everywhere during the Middle Ages there were queens who wanted to live up to the maxim from the Gospels "pious as doves, wise as serpents," and some of them fulfilled this ideal.

Historisk Institut
Københavns Universitet

Danish Queens in the Middle Ages

Thyra, from Anglia (?), married Gorm the Old (r. *ca.* 918-958).

Tove, daughter of the Abodrite Slavonic prince Mistiwoi, married Harald Bluetooth (r. *ca.* 958-986).

Gunhild, daughter of Duke Mieszko of Poland, married Sweyn Forkbeard (r. *ca.* 986-1014).

Emma, daughter of Richard, duke of Normandy, and Ælfgifu, daughter of Ealdorman Ælfhelm of Deira, married Canute the Great (r. 1018-35). (Emma's first husband was the Anglo-Saxon king Æthelred II.)

Gunhild of Sweden married Sweyn Estrithson (r. 1047-74), but they were divorced because of their consanguinity.

Margaret (?) married Harald Hen (r. 1074-80).

Adela, daughter of Robert, count of Flanders, married Canute IV (St. Canute) (r. 1080-86).

Ingegerd of Norway, daughter of King Harald Harderade, and Tora, daughter of Thorberg and Elizabeth of Russia, married Olaf "the Hungry" (r. 1086-96).

Bodil, daughter of the Danish nobleman Trugot, married Erik "the Evergood" (r. 1096-1102).

Margaret Fredkulla, daughter of King Inge of Sweden, and after her death Ulfhild, daughter of the Norwegian Hakon Finsen, married Niels (r. 1104-34).

Malmhild, daughter of Mstislav of Kiev and Christina of Sweden, married Erik Emune (r. 1134-37).

Liutgard, daughter of Ludolf, margrave of Salzweden and count of Stade, married Erik Lam (r. 1137-46).

From 1147 until 1157 there was civil war between the rival claimants Sweyn, Canute, and Waldemar. Their consorts were:

Adela, daughter of Conrad margrave of Meissen, married Sweyn Grathe.

A daughter of the king of Sweden married Canute Magnusson.

Sophia, daughter of Prince Volodar of Novgorod and his Swedish wife, Richza, married Waldemar I the Great (r. 1157-82).

Gertrude, daughter of Duke Henry the Lion of Saxony and his first wife, Clementia of Zähringen, married Canute VI (r. 1182-1202).

Dagmar of Bohemia and then Berengaria of Portugal married Waldemar II "the Victorious" (r. 1202-1241).

Jutta, daughter of Duke Albert of Saxony, married Erik "Ploughpenny" (r. 1241-50).

Matilda, daughter of Count Adolph of Holstein, married Abel (r. 1250-52).

Margaret Sambiria, daughter of Duke Sambor of Pomerelia, married Christopher I (r. 1252-59).

Agnes, daughter of Margrave John of Brandenburg, married Erik Glipping (r. 1259-86).

Ingeborg, daughter of King Magnus Ladulas of Sweden, married Erik Menved (r. 1286-1319).

Euphemia, daughter of Duke Bogislav of Pomerania, married Christopher II (r. 1319-32).

Helvig, daughter of Duke Erik of Sunderjutia, married Waldemar IV Atterdag (r. 1340-75).

Margaret I (regent 1387-1412), daughter of Waldemar IV, married King Hakon of Norway.

Philippa, daughter of Henry IV of England, married Erik of Pomerania (r. 1412-39).

Dorothea, daughter of Margrave John of Brandenburg, married first Christopher of Bavaria (r. 1439-48) and then Christian I (r. 1448-81).

Christine, daughter of the Elector Ernst of Saxony, married Hans (r. 1481-1513).

Literature

All the queens discussed above are mentioned in Jørgensen and Skovgaard 1910; both kings and queens can be found in *Dansk biografisk leksikon*, vols. i-xvi (1979-84). Other useful multivolume works are Christensen, Ellehøj, Clausen, and Mørch 1977-90, a work with elaborate references, and Olsen 1988-90.

Recent single-volume works and articles are Damsholt 1984, 1985, 1987; Horby 1977; Skovgaard-Petersen 1988; Skyum-Nielsen 1981; Strand 1980. Of the proceedings of St. Gertrud's symposium two volumes are published in English: Carle, Damsholt, Glent, and Trein 1980, and Glente, Winther-Jensen, and Reitzel 1989.

CHAPTER 4

Women at the Court of Charlemagne: A Case of Monstrous Regiment?

JANET L. NELSON

I begin with an image: the rape of Proserpina, as depicted on a late second-century Roman marble sarcophagus (fig. 4.1), now in the Cathedral Treasury at Aachen, and at Aachen, apparently, since the time of Charlemagne (Schramm and Mütherich 1981: no. 18 [at 120]; Schmitz-Cliever-Lepie 1986: 8). Pluto, god of the underworld, abducts Proserpina with the help of Minerva, goddess of wisdom. On the viewer's right, Mercury, messenger of the gods, leads a *quadriga,* a four-horse chariot—symbol of triumphal rulership. Behind, on the viewer's left, preceded by female attendants with baskets symbolizing plenty, comes Proserpina's mother, Ceres, goddess of fruitfulness, in a chariot drawn by serpents.[1] A brief gloss can be added. The Proserpina myth was borrowed by the Romans from the Greeks and was popular throughout Antiquity. Ceres (Demeter) was one of the twenty "select deities" who had care of the universe; her rites at Eleusis were one of the best-known cults of the ancient world, and there were Roman equivalents. Ceres was identified as the Great Mother, "procuring the emission of the seed of women," which (according to ancient medical theory) joined with the male seed to produce the foetus. Proserpina was the special goddess of fertile seeds.

Fig. 4.1. A late Roman marble sarcophagus depicting the rape of Proserpina (Cathedral Treasury, Aachen).

The fact that all of the above "gloss" comes from St. Augustine's *The City of God*,[2] a work familiar to Charlemagne's entourage—he liked having it read out during dinner (Einhard 1911: ch. 24 [at 29])—assumes some importance if we accept the medieval tradition that the sarcophagus was reused for Charlemagne himself (Schramm and Mütherich 1981: 120 [note 1]; Dierkens 1991: 166-67).[3] Since he was buried on the day of his death, 28 January 814, the sarcophagus must have been at Aachen, probably already chosen and prepared for the funeral.[4] Why it was chosen, and what it may have signified to the chooser(s) and to other ninth-century viewers, are not simple questions to answer. The Classical tradition thrived at Charlemagne's court; but it was also contested (Nees 1991: ch. 4). For while Roman texts, objects, and visual styles were reused and imitated, and invested with new Christian meaning,[5] no comfortable synthesis was possible for those who grasped Augustine's *City of God*. Anyone viewing the sarcophagus through that lens would recognize the Proserpina myth, but might *not* therefore endow it with an uplifting Christian significance. Augustine uncompromisingly rejected Varro's attempt to "mitigate the offensiveness of pagan rites" by suggesting that in some way they referred to a "natural order," and his whole lengthy discussion in Books VI and VII of *The City of God* aims to show that pagan deities were "unclean demons."[6] Thus while whoever chose the Proserpina sarcophagus may have had no "programmatic" purpose, but may simply have wanted to convey a "Roman effect" of imperial prestige, other contemporaries, including those who buried Charlemagne, might have responded differently to this object. It's possible that gender further affected their response—that, disturbed by the frequency of more or less violent abduction in their own world, and encouraged by Augustine, they turned a hostile gaze on the Rape of Proserpina (compare J. Rose 1986).[7]

A second image gives an indirect entrée to Charlemagne's entourage and suggests the allocation of gender roles within it. St. Jerome and his students (fig. 4.2) were depicted by the artist of the Vivian Bible, illuminated at St.-Martin of Tours, for presentation to Charlemagne's grandson Charles the Bald, perhaps in 845. The image comes from the frontispiece to the prefaces supplied by St. Jerome for his Vulgate translation; its caption says: "Jerome gives to Eustochium and Paula divine laws of salvation."[8] It has been suggested that this frontispiece had special meaning at Tours, where during Charlemagne's reign Alcuin (abbot 796-804) had produced a new edition of Jerome's Vulgate text and begun the production of large single-volume Bibles. Mütherich and Gaehde describe the miniature as follows: "St. Jerome instructs Paula and Eustochium and other ladies . . . in the Holy Scriptures which are transcribed by the clerics to the right"; but there is also—invisible to Mütherich and Gaehde—a woman writer on the left (Mütherich and Gaehde 1977: 75, 77; Kessler 1977: 95).

Fig. 4.2. The frontispiece to Jerome's Prefaces, Vivian Bible (Tours, c.844), showing St. Jerome and his students (Paris B.N. MS. lat. 1, fol. 3v).

While any depiction of a woman writing is extremely rare in the Carolingian period, Rosamund McKitterick has not only drawn attention to the possible significance of Jerome's writings to Paula and Eustochium as authorizations for early medieval "female students," and hence to a quite specific contemporary relevance for the image, but has also assembled a good deal of evidence that the copying of manuscripts was a widespread activity in early medieval convents (McKitterick 1990: 82, 84, 85-6; McKitterick 1991: 68-76; McKitterick 1992 [forthcoming]; Gaehde 1971: 361-65).[9] In the Carolingian period it was practiced, notably at Chelles near Paris where Charlemagne's sister Gisele was abbess in the late eighth and early ninth centuries. Some women in the Carolingian period were authors too; there were a number of female letter-writers, especially at royally patronized convents like Chelles (Nelson 1991: 150-51, 157-60; McKitterick 1991: 95-97, 104-11). Women were thus not debarred by gender from being active partners in the networks of friendship and power maintained through the exchange of letters and of manuscripts. High status, and specifically membership of a wider royal family, allowed some women to participate in these aspects of the Carolingian Renaissance even in its early stages during the reign of Charlemagne

(Nelson 1990: 74-75, though for a more positive view see McKitterick 1991: 106, 118).

A third type of representation of women, and one more widely available to Charlemagne's contemporaries, is illustrated by a red silk fragment depicting the hunt of the Amazons (fig. 4.3), made in Byzantium in the late eighth or early ninth century; measuring 34.5 x 39 cm, the fragment came from the convent of Faremoutiers (Seine-et-Marne) and is one of half a dozen extant examples of Byzantine silk with a similar pattern from churches in various parts of the Carolingian world.[10] It was used to wrap the relics of a saint, perhaps of St. Fara, the seventh-century founder of Faremoutier, presumably on the occasion of a *translatio* during the period in the ninth century (*ca.* 840-852) when Charlemagne's daughter Ruothild was abbess of Faremoutiers (T. Schieffer 1966: no. 49 [at 142]; Werner 1968: 445). If Ruothild chose this piece of silk, she and her contemporaries would surely have recognized the subject of its design, because a basic textbook for Carolingian readers was Orosius' *Seven Books of Histories against the Pagans*, in which there appears a little excursus on Amazons (Orosius 1889: i, 15; Goetz 1980: 148-65; Werner 1980: 7-17). Orosius praises their skill in archery, which he links with their one-breasted state: they burned off the breasts of female children to give them a freer hand with the bow. Orosius describes the Amazon princess who was specially good in war because of her virginity, and the warrior-queens who at one point conquered the whole of Europe before being subdued by Hercules. Did Carolingian readers and viewers, Ruothild and her sisters perhaps, regard the Amazons in any sense as role models?

Fig. 4.3. A fragment of red silk depicting the hunt of the Amazons, Byzantine, late 8th century/early 9th century (Museum of Meaux)

A fourth image, depicting the Empress Irene, appears on a Byzantine gold solidus (fig. 4.4) issued by the empress in the late 790s. An Athenian noblewoman, bride, then widow, of the Emperor Leo IV, Irene on her husband's death in 780 became regent for her nine-year-old son Constantine VI. She had Leo's five half-brothers tonsured and ruled with eunuch-advisers until 790, when her son, long since of age, banished her from court and took over the government. In 797, after seven years of fairly disastrous rule, Constantine was arrested by his mother's supporters and blinded. Irene then ruled alone until 802, using the title *basileus*, or "emperor," (not *basilissa*, "empress") in documents, and issuing coins like the one illustrated here, where she is depicted on both obverse and reverse wearing the imperial *loros* and holding the cross-scepter and orb (Wroth 1908: no. 10, plate xlvi; Grierson 1966-73: iii part 1, 347-51 and plate xv).[11] Irene had an eye for ritual effect and could reinvent tradition: during Easter Week 799, when she had just dealt successfully with a plot against her (and blinded the plotters), she scattered imperial largesse from a golden chariot drawn by four white horses (Theophanes 1982: 156).[12] Her constitutional position was exceptional, but it was accepted—if only because of the exceptional circumstance that Irene, for the triumphant iconophiles, represented the guarantee of orthodoxy (Herrin 1987: 408-31; Runciman 1978: 101, 113; Theophanes 1982: 154-55).[13]

Fig. 4.4. A Byzantine gold solidus of Empress Irene, 797/802 (American Numismatic Museum, New York)

During her regency, Irene had resumed more or less continuous contacts with the West. Envoys were sent to the court of Charlemagne, whose conquest of Italy had brought him into Mediterranean politics, to negotiate a match between Charlemagne's daughter and Irene's son. There were indirect contacts, too, via the papacy: in 787, Irene summoned papal representatives to the Seventh Oecumenical Council which, with her encouragement, renounced iconoclasm. No Frankish representatives were invited; in 786-7, Irene had become worried about Charlemagne's advance into southern Italy. She had a useful card to play, sending back to Italy with military support an exiled

Lombard prince harbored (since 774) at the Byzantine court. Friendly relations faded between the Franks and the Byzantines, and the proposed marriage alliance was dropped (Classen 1965: 558-63; Noble 1984: 165-6, 176-81). (It was a *Greek* saying, according to Einhard [1911: ch. 16 (at 20)], that if a Frank was your friend, he was certainly not your neighbor). In 792, in the *Libri Carolini* written at Charlemagne's behest, Theodulf of Orléans protested fiercely against Irene's role in the Seventh Oecumenical Council, where she played Helena to her son's Constantine as imperial co-defenders of orthodoxy (Freeman 1957: 663-705; A. Freeman 1965: 203-89; A. Freeman 1971: 597-612; Dahlhaus-Berg 1975). Theodulf countered with a negative model: the presumptuous Irene was like the wicked Queen Athaliah in the Old Testament, "who `destroyed nearly all the seed royal' because with unfitting desire she had an appetite for command over men" (". . . dum viris praesse incompetenti desiderio appetiit" [Theodulf 1881: 129]). Pope Hadrian had accepted Irene's role at the council, invoking the New Testament examples of Mary and Martha: "Christ himself used the services of women" (Hampe 1899: 39-40).[14] Theodulf riposted: "Frailty of sex and changeableness of heart do not allow a woman to put herself in supreme authority over men in matters of doctrine or command (*praelatio*). She must submit to a man's authority. . . . It is one thing to sit at the feet of the Lord, quite another to organise synods, teach men in councils, hand down perverse decrees. . . ." (Theodulf 1881: 127, 129).[15] Brusque as this démarche was, it never reached Irene; the pope, aghast at the threatened breach, smoothed the indignation of the Frankish court. The *Libri Carolini* got no further than the papal library (Dahlhaus-Berg 1975: 215-16).

Immediately after her coup in 797, Irene sought to revive the Frankish connection: under the year 798, the Royal Frankish Annals record that an embassy came from Irene to Aachen to inform Charlemagne that Constantine VI had been blinded, hence by implication removed from power. "But this embassy was only about a peace" (Kurze 1895: 104). Though there may have been an ironic note here, with the emphasis on "this," the Frankish annalist offered no comment. Irene doubtless expected an outcry, and worse. It was probably now that to secure the Franks' recognition, she made a major concession, transferring authority over formerly Byzantine territory in Italy: hence a Frankish annal noted the coming to Charlemagne of eastern envoys *ut traderent ei imperium* (Löwe 1949: 12-21).[16]

But *imperium* has a wider sense too—one with which westerners were all too ready to invest the word in this case. How, they demanded, could

Irene exercise *imperium* at all? The answer was a foregone conclusion, and in explaining why Charlemagne became emperor on Christmas Day 800 it had a larger part than most historians have acknowledged. The Lorsch Annals are perfectly explicit (Pertz 1826: 38).

> Because the title of emperor was at this time lacking among the Greeks and they had among them the rulership of a woman [femineum imperium], it seemed to the pope, the holy fathers and the rest of the Christian people that they ought to give Charles himself the title of emperor.

It was as simple as that: *femineum imperium* was a contradiction in terms — a monstrous regiment. The argument didn't even need to be spelled out. A vacancy therefore existed, and Charlemagne was the man to fill it.

A Carolingian ivory plaque depicting the Virgin Mary (Fig. 4.5) takes us directly to the Court of Charlemagne, where this curious object was very probably made *ca.* 800.[17] It has recently been argued that the plaque's model was among Irene's gifts to Charlemagne, and that the *virgo militans* represented "a superannuated Byzantine conception of the Mother of God as an invincible military commander," an image that Irene saw as an apt analogue for her own position. In western eyes, however, this was "a fundamentally repugnant conception of Mary as an independent and aggressive female power." Charlemagne's own cult of the Virgin was an enthusiastic imitation of Constantinople's traditional practice: the dedication to her of the church at Aachen was intended to secure for Charlemagne's empire the special protection the Virgin had long offered to Byzantium (Cameron 1978: 79-108). But in this function, the Virgin was to operate strictly in a maternal role. By contrast, an image of the "militant Virgin," though it perhaps caught Charlemagne's "passing fancy" (S. Lewis 1980: 93), was bound to raise hackles at his court, and almost immediately to become redundant. Hence the uniqueness in the West of the *virgo militans* plaque.

This argument, to my mind not wholly convincing,[18] nevertheless does draw attention to a crucial point: that in the years around 800, in both eastern and western Christendom, any representation of female power was bound to be a sensitive and controversial area. The question is whether the Virgin's power as represented in the ivory really is "independent and aggressive." Though she carries a cross-scepter signifying power, she herself wears no crown: by implication, the power is her son's, and she offers all Christians a model of enlistment in Christ's service (compare Sears 1990: 616). She also carries crossed spindles, signifying an essentially domestic and female function, often associated symbolically with the Virgin at the Annunciation (S. Lewis 1980: 73). The image is not explicitly military or political. The Virgin was not claiming "independent" power.

Fig. 4.5. A Carolingian ivory of the Virgin Mary, School of Reichenau (The Metropolitan Museum of Art, New York, Gift of J. Pierpont Morgan, 1917 [17.190.49])

She might work as an adjutant, a mediator and patron, or counsellor; above all as the nurturer of a future king (here, if anywhere, was Irene's Achilles' heel). But Mary was never a ruler in her own right. And when writers of the Carolingian period celebrated Mary as queen, *regina*, they meant to specify precisely the role of consort, never that of queen-regnant. Significantly, while benedictions for kings spoke of *regimen*, those for queens (extant from the late ninth century onward) did not (e.g., the "Erdmann" *ordo* [Schramm 1968, 2: 218-19, 221]).

What then were the uses, and what were the limits, of queenly power when it was exercised by women in real life? At what point could it be perceived as regiment (*regimen, imperium*) and therefore unnatural, wholly unacceptable? I want now to look at the regime of Charlemagne with these questions in mind. First I will make some observations about the queens in his life, and about the roles these queens played in early Carolingian courts. Then I will look at the latter years of Charlemagne, especially the years after 800 when there was no queen as such. In what follows, the images discussed above should also be kept in mind: available representations of women's activity and of women's power, mythic where Proserpina and the Amazons were concerned but real enough in the cases of Irene and (in a very different sense) of female scribes, yet always ambiguous, need to be set against, and may have affected, the ways in which women at the court of Charlemagne viewed their own actions, and were viewed in turn by male contemporaries.

The Carolingians, as everyone knows, were upstarts. One day, Pippin was just a noble like others—the next, he was an anointed king. In many ways his rule was quite traditional. But one problem was new: the urgent need to canalize and concentrate power within a family that had suddenly become royal. Pippin had to cut down the rights of Carolingian co-heirs. Already two bastard half-brothers, Jerome and Remi, had been offered to the Church, whose resources then endowed them (Duchesne and Vogel 1886-1957: ii, 451; Kurze 1891: 7; Pertz 1892: 286; Adrevald of Fleury 1879: col. 918). Pippin's brother Carloman had announced a monastic vocation in 746 and left for Monte Cassino; even if he withdrew voluntarily to strengthen Pippin's hand, he clearly hoped that his sons would have something of his inheritance, but they were excluded from the patrimony of Charles Martel (Affeldt 1980). Pippin's ancestors, the mayors of the palace, like other Frankish aristocrats partitioned their lands among close kin, but this old practice was now abandoned. Pippin's half-brother Bernard remained in secular life and had two sons by successive wives; the lands they inherited seem to have come to them from their mothers, not their father's kin (Weinrich 1963: 11-12; Hlawitschka 1985: 1-61). The royal family was a nuclear family, and a small family. That meant highlighting the royal couple as a couple. Pippin's short-term need for allies may have driven him briefly (apparently in 751-52) to consider repudiating his wife Bertrada and marrying again (Gundlach 1892: no. 45 [at 561-62]; Enright 1985: 92-3). But the pope dissuaded him, and in July 754 consecrated Bertrada alongside Pippin and their two sons (Gundlach 1892: no. 11 [at 505]). Husband and wife needed and deserved each other: it was to Bertrada that Pippin handed over his brother Carloman, who had returned to Francia in April 754 to plead his sons' cause. Bertrada could be relied on to secure her *own* sons' future; Carloman was still in her custody when he died, and his sons were tonsured (Kurze 1895: 12-13). Thereafter Pippin was a model husband. He had no bastard offspring. In addition to the two sons, one daughter survived, Gisele, born in 757; there was talk of diplomatic marriage for her with more than one foreign potentate, but in the end she became abbess of Chelles (Werner 1968: 431). Pippin also needed to cut down the claims of in-laws. He arranged the marriages of his two sons to Frankish noblewomen (Konecny 1976: 65-66), but contemporary sources say little about these brides and nothing about their male kin (any more than they do about Bertrada's), though the family of Charlemagne's wife, Himiltrude, may well have thought their prospects fairly rosy when she bore a son, especially when he was named Pippin after his grandfather. Himiltrude's marriage does seem to have been a legal one, although this was to be denied by an admirer of one of Charlemagne's later queens (Gundlach 1892: no. 45 [at 561]; see also Paul the Deacon 1829: 265).

At Pippin's death in 768 Charlemagne and his brother Carloman divided the kingdom between them. Their mother, Bertrada, "mother of kings" (*mater regum*), now assumed a new importance, and sided with her older son against her younger son (Wallace-Hadrill 1960: 121; Kurze 1895: 31).[19] She encouraged Charlemagne to repudiate his Frankish wife and marry a Lombard princess, to seal an alliance with the Lombard king Desiderius; in 771, Bertrada went to Rome herself to conciliate the pope (who, as ever, feared Lombard aggression), and, returning via the Lombard court, escorted the bride back to Francia: a notable exercise in personal diplomacy (Lappenberg 1859: 496; Hauck 1968: 93-94). But this marriage was short-lived; within scarcely more than a year Charlemagne rejected the Lombard princess and soon married for a third time (Classen 1965: 545-47). This was the one occasion, according to Einhard (1911: ch. 18 [at 23]), that there was ever a cross word between the dowager and her son. The apparent ease with which Charlemagne twice divorced and twice remarried within three years is striking, especially given Pippin's very different behavior. Rather than explain the contrast by reference to Charlemagne's temporarily diminished respect for canon law (Wemple 1981: 78), I attribute his marital shifts to the extreme fragility of his political position during these early years of his reign—as long as his brother lived.[20] Charlemagne's decision in 771 was no whim: he feared his brother's intrigues in Rome, and his marriage to a noble Alaman, Hildegarde (Thegan 1829: 590-91), was calculated to consolidate support in Alemannia, through which lay the route to Italy. Divorcing Desiderius' daughter was a very dangerous move, not only because it would arouse Lombard wrath, but also because the queen, *ex officio*, had an especially close relationship with the young warriors in the royal household whom she "nurtured," literally and metaphorically (Nelson 1978: 36, 40, 47; Stafford 1983: 104-06; Enright 1988: 170-203). Hence a royal divorce could put key loyalties at risk, and the abrupt change of career of two young nobles at Charlemagne's court in 771 hints at their refusal to transfer their personal service to another queen: Both found an escape route from political dilemma in the monastic life.[21]

Charlemagne was able to weather the storm mainly because his brother died in December 771 (a courtier frankly recommended gratitude to God for this [Cathwulf 1892: no. 7]),[22] and former supporters of that brother now hastened to accept Charlemagne's lordship. Thus his new bride, Hildegard, was able to secure her position at court. If Bertrada remained there too "in great honor" until her death in 783 (as implied by Einhard 1911: ch. 18 [at 23]), there is no evidence for her activity after 771. That there is not much evidence for Hildegard's either may have something to do with Bertrada's continued presence in the household (she just outlived her daughter-in-law),[23] but perhaps still more to do with Hildegard's numerous pregnancies: in twelve years of marriage she produced four sons (including twins) and five daughters, and died along with her last daughter shortly after the delivery. "Alas," mourned the author of her epitaph, "alas, O mother of kings, the glory and the pain!" (Paul the Deacon 1829: 266 [line 40]). The glory was posthumous. Hildegard had no time to capitalize on her offspring, and it is significant that her brother appears as a great magnate in Bavaria only some years after her death (Borgolte 1987: 122-26). One of the few things known of Hildegard is her friendship with the Anglo-Saxon St. Leoba, follower and blood relative (on the maternal side) of St. Boniface. According to Leoba's hagiographer, she was a favorite counsellor of the queen, and made her final visit to the court in response to Hildegard's pleas "because of their deep friendship" (Rudolf of Fulda 1887: 130). It is possible the queen knew Leoba was dying and wished to keep her at court until her death in order to control her relics (in the event, Leoba's remains were taken to Fulda).

From the mid-780s, more evidence survives to allow life in Charlemagne's entourage to be reconstructed. This is not entirely fortuitous: on the one hand, as Charlemagne's patronage attracted more scholars, more was written to and from persons at court, and on the other, as Charlemagne's family increased and grew up, as new tensions arose and factions formed, a queen came into her own. This was Charlemagne's fourth wife, Fastrada. Einhard is quite explicit about her influence: it was considerable, and it was bad. Her cruelty caused conspiracies and revolts—the only two Einhard mentions—in 785 and 792 (Einhard 1911: 26). In the latter case, the rebels' figurehead was Charlemagne's eldest son, Fastrada's stepson Pippin (handsome enough, says Einhard, but a hunchback [Einhard 1911: 26]), whose mother had been spurned by Charlemagne so long before. By 792 Charlemagne had installed Hildegard's three surviving sons as subkings in Italy, Aquitaine, and Neustria, and the hunchback clearly feared that he would be excluded from any share in the realm. In fact, exclusion was precisely the outcome of his unsuccessful revolt: that was what it meant to be tonsured. Einhard may not have exaggerated Fastrada's role.[24] Several snippets of evidence suggest that she was very influential indeed. Lacking sons of her own (she had two daughters), Fastrada involved herself in maneuverings around her stepsons: the thirteen-year-old Louis (the future Louis the Pious) spent with Fastrada at Regensburg the entire winter preceding Pippin's revolt (791-92)—one is tempted to add, under her surveillance (Astronomer 1829: 610). Charlemagne's sole surviving letter is addressed to Fastrada: he reports (and assumes she will appreciate) the victories of his son the subking of Italy against the Avars, and instructs her to organize fasts and litanies to ensure continuing military success for the Franks (Dümmler 1895: no. 20 [at 528-29]).[25] An interesting case, probably of 793, shows Fastrada at the royal residence of Frankfurt. A killing was committed in her presence and the killer's property was then confiscated as punishment. Presumably it was Charlemagne who actually carried out the sentence, but in his enforced absence it was Fastrada who apparently declared the judgment. The image of the queen holding court in a judicial as well as a sociological sense is an arresting one (Zeumer 1886: 323). The ninth-century treatise *The Government of the Palace* epitomized the queen's function as "to release the king from all domestic or palace cares, leaving him free to turn his mind to the state of the realm" (Hincmar 1980: 74). The implied distinction is misleading: Palace cares were political affairs and intimately affected the state of the realm.

If Fastrada was unusual in operating virtually as vicereine, the queen's normal "domestic" role as played by Charlemagne's fifth and last wife, Liutgard, was also a political and public one. Suppose you wanted to know (as Alcuin did in 797) in what palace the king would spend that winter? You wrote to the queen (Alcuin 1895: letter 50 [at 93-94]). When her husband won fabulous treasures from the destruction of the Avar realm, Liutgard helped distribute them to deserving churchmen (Alcuin 1895: letters 96, 102, 190 [at 140, 149, 317]). In 798, the childless queen and her stepdaughters went to pray on the Feast of the Assumption at Nivelles, the convent founded by the Carolingian St. Gertrude (Alcuin 1895: letter 150 [at 246]). A liturgical women's network linking earth and heaven represented the entirely acceptable face of feminine power.

But it was not regiment. To see what some came to regard as such, and therefore as unacceptable, we must look at other women around the court of Charlemagne. Not all were there continuously. Charlemagne's cousin Gundrada, for instance, was a virgin who spent much time at the palace where she was *familiarior regi* (Paschasius Radbertus 1879: col. 1526). Still closer to him was his sister Gisele, abbess of Chelles. To her Charlemagne confided his imperial relic collection, believed to be an essential source of supernatural aid (Laporte 1988: 115-50). He placed in Gisele's care one of his daughters, Rotrude, and also the daughter of his defeated enemy Tassilo of Bavaria. The Psalter brought from the Bavarian house of Mondsee to Chelles lets us imagine the young Bavarian princess joining

Abbess Gisele in the commemoration of deceased Carolingians (Stoclet 1986: 250-70; McKitterick 1989: 253-55).[26] Gisele and Rotrude expected swift compliance when they asked for a Bible commentary from the Anglo-Saxon scholar Alcuin, abbot of St.-Martin of Tours (Alcuin's letters reveal, suddenly, so much about the court in the 790s). When he apologized for delay, they reminded him that St. Jerome had quickly sent works requested by Paula and Eustochium all the way from Bethlehem to Rome, "and the Mediterranean is a lot wider than the Loire"! (Alcuin 1895: letter 196 [at 323-25]). Alcuin may have had tongue in cheek when he hailed Gisele as *femina verbipotens* (Alcuin 1881: poem 12, line 6 [at 237]). But she was a woman who knew how to use the written as well as the spoken word, if, as I suspect, she was responsible for the writing at Chelles, *ca.* 806, of the *Annales Mettenses Priores*, and thus for the imperial ideology contained therein (Nelson 1991: 157-59).

There were other women, more permanently with Charlemagne. After Liutgard's death in 800, he did not remarry but had a series of concubines. Einhard names four: Madelgard, Gervinda, Regina ("Queenie"?), and Adallinda (Einhard 1911: ch. 18 [at 23]).[27] We can only guess at what informal influence they may have wielded. Regina and Adallinda produced sons whose names—Drogo, Hugh, Theuderic—had been borne by kinsmen of Charlemagne's grandfather, clearly chosen to signify lack of throneworthiness (Hlawitschka 1965: 72-73).[28] There were also Charlemagne's daughters, and here the evidence, as we'll see, is sufficient to tantalize. Einhard again lists them: Rotrude, Bertha, and Gisele (Hildegard's surviving daughters), Theoderada and Hiltrude (Fastrada's daughters), and three by concubines: Hruodhaid, Ruothild, and Adaltrude. That wasn't all: when Charlemagne's son Pippin of Italy died before his father in 810, his daughters too were brought up to Aachen to join their grandfather—Adelheid, Atula, Gundrada, Berthaida, and Theoderada, whose mother's name Einhard forgot (Einhard 1911: chs. 18-19 [at 22-24]).

A veritable "regiment of women," you might say, using the term regiment in its modern sense. What about regiment in the sense intended by John Knox, meaning government (Knox 1558)? After all, it was Knox's sixteenth-century blast against the regiment of women that was responsible for the popularity of the expression down to the present day; and Knox too who associated (again, the link is hardly broken yet) women's regiment with monstrosity. What did those women do at the court of Charlemagne? Back in 792, when a young cleric wanted to unmask the revolt of Charlemagne's hunchback son, he arrived one night at the palace. He had to pass through seven doors to reach the king's bedroom: it was guarded by women "who were constantly with Charlemagne to serve the queen and the daughters" (Notker 1962: 72). And several of the daughters remained there, even after 800 when there was no queen; stayed indeed throughout the reign. None of them married. Einhard explains: ". . . because they were very beautiful and because they were very much beloved by their father, amazing as it is to relate, he refused to give any of them in marriage, either to one of his own men or a foreigner, but kept them with him in his household right up to his death, saying that he could not be without their company." There was a drawback: Einhard refers delicately to the fact that some of the unmarried daughters were also unwed mothers, but Charlemagne himself "pretended there was nothing wrong at all" (Einhard 1911: ch. 19 [at 25]).

Charlemagne loved his sons too, of course, and according to Einhard, was so conscientious a father to all his children that (presumably when they were at court) he never took a meal or went on a journey without them (Einhard 1911: 24-25). But, in the memorable phrase of Heinrich Fichtenau, "the sons were too valuable to serve as toys, and to be used as mere objects of fatherly love" (Fichtenau 1963: 42-43). So the boys went off to do valuable things like wage war, and the girls stayed behind in their father's "company." The word Einhard uses here, *contubernium*, deserves a closer look; it is a little unexpected, for classical and Carolingian authors generally used it to refer to comradeship between men, often in military contexts. If Charlemagne found the *contubernium* of his daughters indispensable, was that just because they served *in domo sua* as toys? Those "crowned doves who flitted through the windows and through the private apartments" (Alcuin 1895: letter 244 [at 392]), alluding to *Isaiah* 60:8) — did they do more than play?

Naturally the "official" histories, the Royal Frankish Annals, for instance, or the capitularies, say nothing about them. We have to look to other, "private" witnesses. Eleven of Alcuin's letters are addressed to Charlemagne's sister and/or daughters, and six more mention them.[29] But it is court poetry above all — by Alcuin, Theodulf, Angilbert, Dungal the Irishman — that lets us through those seven doors and into the heart of the court. There we find a number of women playing political roles. In a well-known poem, Theodulf describes the daughters in a splendid procession: they participate in feasts, banquets, and the hunt, central rituals of the court (Theodulf 1881: no. 25, lines 79-108 [at 483-39] = Godman 1985: 150-63; Angilbert 1881: 300-03 [lines 43-53] = Godman 1985: 114-17). In another poem, less well known, Theodulf depicts the king ("David") in his citadel (*in arce*) with a number of young women, while the flute of the Muses whispers songs. Here is "Delia," one of the daughters (perhaps Bertha, the oldest remaining in secular life): "she makes the Muses of Flaccus blush." Here Theodulf has a laugh at Alcuin's expense, for "Flaccus" was Alcuin's nickname: "the old man with his boys has to leave the town in the evenings and come back next day, but the girls stay with their father all the time" (Theodulf 1881: 490-93 [lines 27-44]). The humor of this little battle of the sexes would be the sharper if we follow John Boswell's suggestion that Alcuin was gay (Boswell 1980: 188-91). But there is more here than teasing. With Charlemagne's daughters, the great men of the court—Alcuin, Theodulf, Angilbert—needed to establish *amicitia* and *familiaritas*, that is, political friendship. There could be sexual "familiarity" too: Angilbert was Bertha's lover and fathered her sons Nithard and Hartnid. The daughters' permanent position at the palace gave them a tremendous advantage. In the 790s, Alcuin hints that they may have taken sides in the jostling for power between Charlemagne's sons (Alcuin 1881: no. 14 [at 238], and Angilbert 1881: 360-63, both imply that "Delia" favored Pippin of Italy; Classen 1971-72: iii, 112-13, 123). Through the poets' artificial language, almost the language of courtliness (Bezzola 1944-63, vol. 1), can be glimpsed the real power of these *puellae*. We know almost by chance, from Pope Leo III's biographer, that more than one of Charlemagne's daughters were with their father in Rome at Christmas 800 (Duchesne and Vogel 1886-1957: ii, ch. 24 [at 8]), and it looks as if his sister Gisele was there too (Alcuin 1881: no. 216 [at 359-60]). These women were, even when Charlemagne journeyed, with him at the political center of the realm.

Unfortunately, the distribution of the sources is uneven, and the last years of Charlemagne's reign are virtually empty of both poetry and letters (Alcuin died in 804). But could we not expect that precisely in those last years when there was no queen and the *turba puellarum* functioned, so to speak, like a collective queen; when the court was fixed more or less permanently at Aachen as *the* palace, that the influence of Charlemagne's daughters would have become still greater than before? That is in fact just what the biographer of Charlemagne's successor, Louis the Pious, implies when he describes the difficult beginnings of Louis' reign. On 28 January 814, it was "the children of Charlemagne at the palace" who assumed the task of organizing the dead emperor's funeral. Louis himself was in northern Aquitaine, waiting for news of his father's demise. Only then, when the news had come, could he install himself at Aachen and "chase out that whole female mob, which was very large" (*coetus—qui permaximus erat—*

femineus). These women presented a real problem for Louis. Their expulsion, and that of their male associates, was the precondition for the establishment of a new regime.[30] This is clear from the violence Louis used to deal with the crowned doves of yesteryear, and also from the violent propaganda his partisans now used. The reconstitution of the court became a moral clean-up, a reformation. The women of Charlemagne's court were depicted as whores; only one, his cousin Gundrada, had been able to remain a virgin "and so pass unscathed through the lustful heats of the palace and the sexual appetites of young men and the seductions of pleasure and all the blandishments of fleshly desire" (Paschasius Radbertus 1879: ch. 33 [at col. 1526]). If Irene's *imperium femineum* in Byzantium had been monstrous regiment, that *coetus femineus* at the court of Charlemagne was a monstrosity of some kind as well. Let's briefly return to the word *contubernium* used by Einhard to specify Charlemagne's relationship with his daughters. It had another sense too, apart from comradeship, namely, illicit sexual relations (Niermeyer 1976, *s.v.* "contubernium"). Was Einhard hinting that Charlemagne had practiced incest? Would that explain the peculiarly sharp criticism of Charlemagne's sexual behavior in several texts, couched in the "safe" form of visions of the next world, written within only a few years of Charlemagne's death (Godman 1985: 214-15; Traill 1974: 144-49)? The afterglow of Charlemagne's last years had the lurid tinge of a possibly unnatural, hence monstrous, sexual appetite.

Every court has its women. Indeed, women can be said to be especially at home in the *höfische Gesellschaft* (Elias 1983: 243-44). But the role of women at the court of Charlemagne was surely extraordinary. It was not just that they generated lust: that was the oldest accusation in the book, and it was the pretext that enabled Louis the Pious and his supporters to pose as moral reformers with puritan values, bent on cleaning up the unreformed style of Charlemagne's ancien régime. Louis' pose is unconvincing. After all, it was only a few years later that his own court was being denounced as a sink of vice (Ward 1990b: 15-26). Such charges were a code for political opposition. Still, the unmarried daughters in Charlemagne's household were sufficiently unusual for Einhard to feel obliged to explain them—even to explain them away. Perhaps Charlemagne did love them a lot. But I will end by offering another explanation for their presence at court in Charlemagne's last years. There was the factor of chance: Charlemagne was exceptionally prolific and exceptionally long-lived, which meant that he ended up as the paterfamilias of a three-generation household. For the same reason, he coexisted in the latter half of his reign with adult sons, at least one of whom (according to his biographer) "felt the desire for power grow in him" (Astronomer 1829: ch. 20 [at 617]). This suggests to me that the daughters' presence was not coincidental, but that considerations of policy were also involved. It was the presence of the women, especially some of the daughters, that allowed Charlemagne to contain the rivalries, otherwise intolerable, that in a reign so prolonged inevitably developed between an aging father and grown sons (Schieffer 1990a: 148-64). Charlemagne did not let his daughters marry because he had to prevent excessive dispersal of Carolingian blood, but also because he needed their political help within the household and the court. There they flitted in and out of the windows of the royal apartments, operating as multiple channels of patronage and information—channels that Charlemagne himself could control because they were informal and because his daughters were entirely dependent upon his favor. They had been trained in obedience to their father: Carolingian childrearing instilled a religion of paternity (Riché 1975: 27). The father decided that his daughters should remain unmarried, though with his permission they might have lovers. In turn, the daughters kept the keys of the inner doors: the keys of power. They constituted a cadre functionally similar to Byzantine court eunuchs, offering no rivalry as potential heirs to formal power, nor producing offspring with claims to a share in rulership or patrimony. Eunuchs had been especially crucial agents of Irene's regime; Charlemagne chose his daughters for an equivalent role.[31]

He chose well. And the absence of rebellion in the second half of his reign therein finds at least a part of its explanation. The *contubernium* of his daughters gave him an entourage of advisers, a kitchen cabinet whose loyalty, unlike that of their brothers, was guaranteed and who, if they proved unhelpful, could be readily dismissed. Did these women wield the power behind the throne as Charlemagne suffered increasingly, in his latter years, from bouts of ill health? It was power, and it could be construed as monstrous—but it was not regiment. For these women exercised no formal authority, could issue no capitularies, could not summon or lead armies, could not even request charters (at any rate, no such activity is recorded). Their power thus remained ancillary, dependent on their father and on his survival. Once he was gone, that dependence became all too evident, and the daughters' departure followed swiftly. But perhaps before they left the palace, they performed one last political act, one last service for their father—and left one last bit of evidence for their activity. When Charlemagne died on 28 January 814, it was "the children of the defunct emperor at the palace" who arranged for his funeral. Did they perhaps also choose his sarcophagus? They must at the very least have supervised the laying in it of their father's body. Did they intend that the dramatic scene of Proserpina's rape should function as a metaphor which, in Christian terms, would express their confidence in their father's life after death? Did that scene convey, at the same time, a message of their own—equating their brother with the man in the four-horse chariot, themselves with Proserpina, forcibly carried off? For those erstwhile crowned doves, Ceres and her female attendants moving in behind Proserpina may have seemed a reminder, if not of women's regiment, then at least of women's often potential and always conditional, yet irreducible, power.

King's College, London

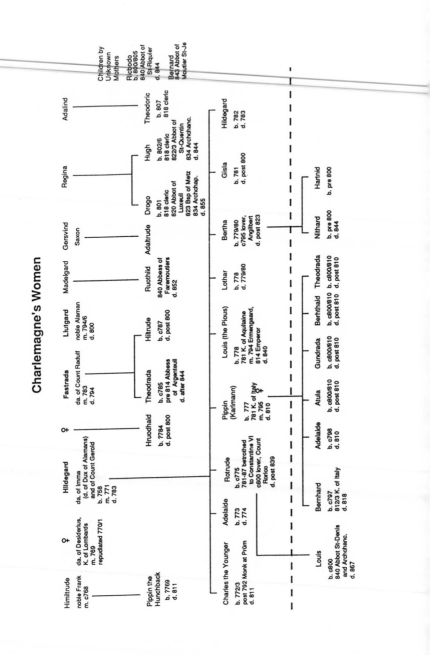

Charlemagne's Women

CHAPTER 5

Mothers, Daughters, Marriage, Power: Some Plantagenet Evidence, 1150-1500

JOHN CARMI PARSONS

In the spring of 1282, envoys of Edward I of England were sent to Aragon to conclude negotiations, begun in 1273, to marry Edward's eldest daughter to the Aragonese heir. The English agents were unexpectedly faced with the queen of Aragon's demand that her future daughter-in-law be sent there at once, but the instructions Edward dispatched on 19 June show that Queen Constance would not have her way: Edward directed his envoys to tell her that his wife and his mother opposed sending the girl to Aragon, "propter teneritatem suam." Thirteen that same week, she was old enough for marriage according to canon law, but the queens wanted to wait eighteen months from the next Michaelmas, and preferably two years (Francisque-Michel and Bémont 1885-1906: ii, no. 597; J. Parsons 1984: 260).[1] The two queens were not out to stop the marriage—which was soon concluded by proxy (Prestwich 1988: 321, 325-26)—but this was not an isolated incident: two centuries later, for example, Margaret Beaufort asked her son Henry VII (born when she was thirteen) not to marry his daughter Margaret to the Scottish king until the girl was older (Jones and Underwood 1992: 40).

At a time when society lacked an abstract notion of the state, and power was conceived of in patrimonial terms, marriage was an important instrument of royal alliance (Ganshof 1970: 45)—as Henry III of England put it when seeking a wife for his son Edward in 1254, "friendship between princes can be obtained in no more fitting manner than by the link of conjugal troth" (Rymer 1816-69: i, 209). The role of marriage in alliance formation, as women were exchanged to serve a patriarchal sociopolitical system, throws into relief the English queens' 1282 intervention and raises questions about noblewomen's claims to a role in matrimonial diplomacy. Certainly their cooperation was solicited—and advertised. In 1254 Henry III consulted the widowed queen of Castile when seeking her daughter

Eleanor's marriage to his son Edward (Francisque-Michel and Bémont 1885-1906: i, no. 3845); Edward in 1279 prominently associated Eleanor with the preliminaries for a younger daughter's marriage to the duke of Brabant's son, and one of her ranking officials helped conclude another daughter's marriage to the count of Holland's son in 1284 (Sturler 1936: 157; Rymer 1816-49: i part 2, 643; Byerly and Byerly 1977: no. 280). Eleanor's approval of her daughters' marriages was also implied in her supervision of wedding festivities and the allocation of gifts (J. Parsons 1977: 59, 102, 103, 109-10, 124, 126-27, 134-35), and special links among royal women at such times are indicated by the records for two of the unions just mentioned. When young Eleanor consented to her proxy marriage to Alphonso of Aragon in 1282 she had no seal of her own, so the queen-mother's was used (not the king's); the charter whereby Margaret accepted her dower in Brabant in 1290 states that as her seal was not yet widely known, her mother (not her father) would seal it for her (Rymer 1816-69: i part 2, 209, and i part 3, 74).

It was not only through ceremony or formality that royal mothers shared in international matrimony. Their awareness of the role marriage played in diplomatic alignment was sophisticated—in 1282 the king of Aragon was at odds with both France and the papacy, and his wife would have had good reason to want young Eleanor safely in hand as proof of a solid alliance with England (Prestwich 1988: 315, 320-21); clearly, too, Constance's role in the process was important enough that Edward felt he must respond to her demand. Queens even formed marriage projects on their own and attempted to manipulate them. Edward I's aunt, Queen Margaret of France, promoted a marriage between his daughter Joan and a son of Rudolf of Habsburg, but after the treaties were sealed Margaret asked Edward to postpone the marriage until Rudolf made peace with her cousin the count of Savoy; she also suggested a marriage between her granddaughter and Edward's son (Bréquigny and Champollion-Figéac 1839-47: i, nos. 163, 170; Prestwich 1988: 317).

It is a commonplace of current scholarship that a sense of identity for medieval people was largely shaped by an awareness of belonging to a group or groups with identifiable patterns of behavior—guild, religious order, family (Bynum 1982). Recent work suggests that the activities and models medieval noblewomen shared in common allowed them to see themselves as just such a group. Lois Huneycutt (1990) so expounds queens' role as intercessors, urged upon them by prelates who cited the Biblical model of Esther; I deal in the same vein with queens' religious observances and their relations with the Church, functions incumbent upon them that were shaped by popular expectations (Parsons 1992). That royal women's participation in matrimonial diplomacy was another such area of experience is suggested by Natalie Davis' study of ways in which the patriarchal family in early modern France "could stimulate people within its borders toward self-discovery," as "common experience [fed] the sense of one's own distinctive history": Davis theorizes that women's sense of being bartered as brides was the origin of a "thread of female autonomy" as they occasionally reversed the formula and gave themselves away (Davis 1986: 59, 61, 63). Carla Freccero, considering one royal mother's role in her daughter's contested marriage in sixteenth-century France, adopts Davis' formulations to discuss women's leverage within a sociopolitical system that did not serve women's interests as a group but enlisted individual women's cooperation, and examines how women's sense of self allowed them "to resist or claim control" over their matrimonial destiny (Freccero 1991: 133).

That medieval noblewomen indeed felt a bond based on their matrimonial experiences is argued by the material cited above, and that so much of the limited evidence for community of feeling among medieval noblewomen (Westphal-Wihl 1989: 162-63) involves marriage implies that their endeavors in this area might reward investigation along lines indicated by the work described above. This chapter, then, will explore the possibility that despite their membership in patriarchal families that traded them in marriage, noblewomen's unique participation in matrimonial politics did afford them opportunities to claim power and to achieve some degree of self-realization. The ramifications will be examined from the perspectives of women's position within English kings' families (especially mother-daughter relationships), the effects on royal women's role in preparing matrimonial alliances, and the contributions the process might make to such women's self-awareness.

These questions are best broached by first considering the stated reason for the English queens' 1282 protest. The youthful aristocratic bride, packed off to a distant land perhaps unfriendly to her homeland, condemned to endless childbearing if not an early grave, is an affecting image cherished by popular historians, but its validity and implications for the history of noble family relationships have been given only sporadic scholarly scrutiny (Walker 1976: 160-61, and 1982: 125).[2] A recent study of Eleanor of Aquitaine's family stresses the isolation of noble children from their parents, portraying royal daughters as marginalized members of agnatic lineages, sent "from their childhood homes to their husband's courts without ever spending much time in their parents' company"

(Turner 1988: 321-25 [compare Brown 1976: 9-34]; Turner 1990: 17-52). David Herlihy (1975) thought that while a girl might marry and consummate her marriage at the canonically approved age of twelve, conjugal relations and the risks of childbirth might be delayed for humane reasons until she was older, but despite his belief that medieval parents did value their children, Herlihy posited elsewhere (1985: 82, 185) that girls in agnatic lineages were indeed marginalized and devalued once they ceased to be "the nodules through which pass[ed] the surest kinship ties."

The provocative and contradictory theses of these articles touch upon some of the most debated aspects of medieval family relationships and fairly beg for further attention. Elise Boulding's *The Underside of History* (1976: 429-39) suggested a fresh approach by essaying a wider survey of English royal women than Turner uses, though in the context of her lengthy study Boulding could not develop her material broadly enough to answer ancillary questions. To this end, I have assembled a compilation of the matrimonial and maternal careers of women from three well-documented English noble houses between 1150 and 1500: the Plantagenets, the Mortimers of March, and the Holands of Kent. Supported by my own research and by authorities whose work I have verified whenever possible, the compilation includes all known offspring who lived to adulthood and married.[3] I focus on females' ages at first marriage and at the birth of a first child; only daughters' first marriages are considered, but all sons' marriages are included provided their wives' ages at marriage and first childbirth could be ascertained. The compilation thus defined contains the names of ninety-eight individuals who contracted 105 marriages, eighteen of them omitted from consideration because a woman's age at marriage or first childbirth could not be reckoned; thus the number of marriages is reduced to eighty-seven. On the basis of the 1282 incident with which I began, the age of fifteen is taken as the watershed year for marriage and conjugal relations.[4]

The conclusions germane to this discussion are quickly stated. Politics occasionally required that a girl married at twelve or younger, but forty-nine of the eighty-seven documented marriages were solemnized when the bride was fifteen or older. Of the thirty-eight brides who were under fifteen at marriage, fifteen were childless and the age at which they undertook conjugal life cannot be suggested. Of the twenty-three who married before the age of fifteen and did bear children, however, sixteen had their first child three years or more after marriage, when past fifteen. In only seven cases did women bear children before the age of fifteen (five of these kings' wives or daughters); two of the seven, married at fourteen, bore their first children in the months of their fifteenth birthdays. Thus in only five of eighty-seven documentable cases was marriage followed by childbirth when the mother was appreciably younger than fifteen (and one of the five remains conjectural).[5]

With regard to those youthful brides who did not bear a child for some years after marriage, there is the undocumentable possibility that some were not yet nubile at marriage (Post 1971: 83-87; Amundsen and Diers 1973: 363-69). But for others there is evidence that conjugal relations were delayed.[6] Henry II's daughter Eleanor, born in 1162, was sent to Castile in 1170 and may have wed Alphonso VIII then; the union was probably consummated in 1177 and she had her first child *ca.* 1180 (Lane 1910: i, 83-84; Gonzalez 1960: i, 190-91, 916-917). Henry III's daughter Margaret, eleven, wed Alexander III of Scotland in 1251 and it is attested that the guardians of that realm kept the couple apart for some four years after that; reportedly anxious to consummate her marriage at fifteen, Margaret bore her first child at twenty (Paris 1872-84: v, 501, 504, 505). Edward I's brother Edmund wed Aveline de Forz in 1269 when she was ten; the marriage was consummated in February 1273 as she turned fourteen, and she is reported to have borne two children before her death in November 1274 (Cokayne 1910-40: vii, 378-87; Rutherford 1932: 127-28; *CClR 1272-1279, 7*). Mary de Bohun married the future Henry IV in July 1381, when she was just twelve; to guarantee Henry her inheritance the marriage was consummated at once, with the result that Mary bore and lost a son in April 1382. The couple then lived apart for some years; their second child was born probably in September 1387 (Macfarlane 1972: 13, 16-17; Kirby 1970: 11-12).

Other cases suggest that such delays were not uncommon. King John married Isabella of Angoulême in 1200, when she was twelve; their first child arrived seven years later (Newman 1971: ii, 335-36). Eleanor of Provence was not yet thirteen when she married Henry III in January 1236, and bore her first child in June 1239.[7] Edward I heeded his wife and mother and kept his daughters unmarried until they were past fourteen; in the single case in which one of them did marry that young, the husband left England just after the wedding, but Edward kept his daughter with him until she was past fifteen (Prestwich 1988: 127-28). The nature of Edward II's relationship with Piers Gaveston admits of little doubt, but Edward is now known to have fathered at least one bastard son, which suggests that Gaveston was not the only reason Isabella of France slept alone for some time after she married, at twelve (Doherty 1975: 246-48; Brown 1988: 573-95; Hamilton 1988; Phillipps 1990:

1180-81). Edward may simply have postponed marital relations until Isabella could safely tolerate pregnancy and childbirth.[8]

These considerations suggest that marriage for a bride fifteen or older was more common among the Plantagenets and their kin than at twelve (compare Russell 1948: 156-59; Post 1974: 110-14; Walker 1982: 125). This is not, of course, to insist that adolescent international brides were unknown in the Middle Ages; a wider survey of such marriages on an international scale might, however, bear out the Plantagenet indications that even when noble girls were married so young, conjugal relations could well be postponed except in urgent cases governed by diplomacy or inheritance. For present purposes, though, the numerical incidence of adolescent international marriage is less important than are the implications of the two queens' intervention in 1282 to delay the marriage of a thirteen-year-old. Mothers or grandmothers, aware of the dangers facing the young women who were thus handed about, were concerned for their survival, and it may be assumed that fathers, brothers, and husbands had at least some practical regard for the physical well-being of their daughters, sisters, and wives: an early death in childbirth could jeopardize a valuable alliance. Such reflections, however, cover only one aspect of queens' power to intervene in these matters, and they solicit wider reconsideration of the relationships between noble parents and daughters.

We need no reminders that kings who fathered many sons were both blessed and cursed. Male offspring represented secure succession but had legitimate demands on the patrimony, and their loyalty could never be guaranteed: as Jane Beitscher suggests, emergence of the agnatic lineage family may have fostered the kind of rivalry between fathers and sons Turner sees in Henry II's family (Beitscher 1976: 181-91; Turner 1988). That queens' relationships with sons were likely to be dominated by politics, as demonstrated by Pauline Stafford and Janet Nelson, echoes Turner's thesis that Eleanor of Aquitaine concerned herself with her sons only when they were old enough to serve her political ends (Stafford 1978, 1981: 24-27, 1983: 143-68; Nelson 1978: 35, 38, 43-44, 48-52; Turner 1988). Daughters, in contrast, had no immediate claims on the patrimony, and they offered a father certain advantages—extending his influence abroad, improving relations with foreign princes, bearing children to increase the pool of supporters upon whom he could draw; if they took the veil, he and his house would benefit from their prayers, perhaps from their reputations for sanctity.[9] While kings might hope for sons, then, the birth of a daughter was not necessarily calamitous,[10] and we may expect that kings' relations with their daughters would be more tranquil than with sons. Janet Nelson's essay in this volume shows this was the case with Charlemagne, and Michael Prestwich and Elizabeth Brown find the same for Edward I of England and Philip IV of France (Prestwich 1988: 127-29; Brown 1987: 300-01, 303-07). Though jealousies would appear likely, relations among thirteenth-century Plantagenet daughters and their brothers seem to have been close, and a son in disgrace might seek a sister's support in placating an angry father, as Edward of Caernarvon did in 1305 (Stevenson 1839: 81; Johnstone 1931: 70, 75, 115).

Relationships between royal daughters and their mothers, however, remain poorly elucidated, and this brings me back to the 1282 incident with which I began. That the two Queens Eleanor were married at virtually the same age as the girl they were protecting implies that they were acting on the basis of their own experience (compare Jones and Underwood 1992: 40).[11] Eleanor of Castile's anxiety resonates, moreover, with Nicholas Trevet's well-informed account of her objections to the dedication of her fourth daughter, Mary, in the convent at Amesbury when the girl was only six (Trevet 1845: 310; Rutherford 1932: 346), and her opposition to having her daughters' futures settled for them when they were so young argues against the idea that royal mothers had little interest in daughters. True, we have scant evidence for Plantagenet personal lives in Eleanor of Aquitaine's day; but as Lois Huneycutt points out it may be merely this lack of material that obscures the earlier Eleanor's relations with her children (Huneycutt 1990; see also Brown 1976).

It hardly stands to reason that royal or noble parents would ignore the daughters who were to serve as matrimonial ambassadors. For one thing, the idea that royal daughters were raised in isolation from their families implies that for them, the imperatives of that group were greatly attenuated; if they were meant to represent a father's interests as informants or go-betweens, it is more likely that parents would cultivate relationships with them and train them for their future roles, a pattern suggested by behavior in cultures in which daughters' marriages are arranged to serve family interests. These daughters are prepared from childhood for their roles as peace-weavers; since their early marriages are seen as deplorable events that consign them to the authority of tyrannical mothers-in-law or to hostile environments where they lack the support of relatives, they are indulged with every luxury while under their parents' roof. Even among peoples who allow women no claim to paternal property and do not expect close companionship between fathers and daughters, mutual affection underlies their reciprocal obligations, and fathers watch out for their daughters' married happiness (Rosaldo 1974: 32-33; Kuper 1950: 96-97; Lewis 1962: 24-25, 39-40; Lerner 1986: ch. 3).

Whether there was a profound shift in parental attitudes between Eleanor of Aquitaine's day, when we have little evidence for private royal lives, and the next century when evidence does begin to survive, is a question impossible to settle within the scope of this discussion (see, however, Attreed 1983: 43-58). When relevant sources do survive from the thirteenth century, however, it at once appears that while English kings' children lived apart from their itinerating parents while too young for constant travel, adults were keenly attentive to the welfare and training of their young. Henry III and Eleanor of Provence have been called exemplary parents; Matthew Paris has a vivid account of her behavior when her son Edward fell ill at Beaulieu Abbey where she insisted on staying for three weeks while he recovered (Paris 1872-84: iv, 639).[12] In 1253 Henry asked King Alexander of Scotland to allow Queen Margaret to visit her pregnant mother, and both parents intervened repeatedly after learning in 1255 that Margaret was badly treated by the Scots guardians. When Margaret found herself pregnant while visiting England in 1260 she insisted on staying with her mother to bear a Scottish heir on English soil (Shirley 1862-66: ii, 497; Luard 1890: ii, 463; Paris 1872-84: v, 272, 340, 501, 504). Edward I's abounding self-confidence has been ascribed to the close familial relationships of his early years, and as an adult he loved to speak of his own children (Prestwich 1988: 122-23; Riley 1865: 48). In 1289-90 his three oldest daughters lived at court most of the time, and the earl of Gloucester incurred the king's wrath when he took the second daughter from court too soon after their April 1290 wedding. Edward endlessly indulged his fourth daughter, Mary, veiled at Amesbury in 1291, often visited her there and brought her to court, and kept her supplied with firewood, food, jewels, and wine; not surprisingly, Mary was deeply attached to her father whom she once begged, for the ease of her heart, to send her news of himself "by every messenger." King Edward's favorite child was probably his youngest daughter, Elizabeth, whom he kept with him much of the time in his later years, while his relationship with his son was deteriorating (Green 1859-69: ii, 275-317, 318-62, 363-401, 404-42, and iii, 1-59; Prestwich 1988: 128-29).[13]

Philip IV of France kept himself well-informed of his daughter Isabella's welfare in England, as Henry II welcomed his daughter Matilda and her family after her husband lost his duchies to Frederick Barbarossa (Brown 1988: 582-84; Warren 1977: 603). Such cases of parental concern echo that of Henry III and his wife and are paralleled by examples of married daughters who supported relations among husbands, fathers, or brothers. Despite the early age at which she left her family to live in

Castile, Henry II's daughter Eleanor afterwards assured critical contacts between her husband and King John; Margaret, duchess of Brabant, Edward I's daughter, handled business with her nephew Edward III, and her namesake, Edward IV's sister the duchess of Burgundy, gave her brother important diplomatic support (Rymer 1816-69: i part 1, 94, 96, 100; *CCIR 1333-1337*, 96; Weightman 1989). Of course, royal women sensibly exploited such means to sustain influence with husbands or sons; but it is tempting to think that the unruffled relations these women could enjoy with fathers and brothers were a good part of what made them such ideal choices as go-betweens, and that husbands and sons knowingly capitalized on such relationships (as when Edward II sent his wife in 1325 to treat with her brother, the French king [Menache 1984: 110-11]).

Even before marriage, moreover, royal women could find in kingship's evolving ritual setting many opportunities to serve their families. Edward I's daughters, for example, often went on pilgrimage to shrines associated with Plantagenet kingship, dispensing alms to attract prayers for the king and adding their own at their destinations.[14] Following their mothers' example, royal daughters interceded for petitioners, implying that the supplicants had reason to think the king would listen to his daughters' requests; by doing so, he confirmed the young women's status as mediators with him, and thus tacitly encouraged others to seek their friendship and patronage.[15] The birth of a daughter to the king served the glorifying functions of royal pageantry by providing the occasion for a courtly display just as sumptuous as that laid on for the birth of a son, and even the burials of kings' infant daughters could further the development of royal mausolea, which were becoming significant elements in the construction of popular perceptions of kingship (above, note 10; below, p. 86).

There is little here to suggest that these girls were ignored while they lived at home. Their activities before marriage linked them closely to the interests of their family; it is far from certain that they forgot ties to homeland and family that were bases of influence to them in their new homes, and still less that their parents wrote them off after marriage. The idea that kinship ties through women weakened as the agnatic lineage family evolved implies the unanswerable conundrum that kings arranged marriages meant to be advantageous to themselves and their heirs, only to devalue the living tokens of such alliances. That the English throne was heritable in the female line, moreover, meant that daughters and their offspring were potential heirs; the news that they had borne children was welcome (e.g., Paris 1872-84: iii, 518) — admittedly, a messenger who reported a new grandson or nephew was likely to be more richly

rewarded than one who announced a granddaughter or niece—and fifteenth-century uncertainty over the succession generated much interest in
royal descents through women.[16] Grandchildren often visited the courts of
grandfathers and uncles; some settled in England, and even became
Plantagenet matrimonial pawns (Prestwich 1988: 129, 132).[17] The point is
that while the male line may carry greater prestige as the preferred avenue
for inheritance, female descents are not necessarily reduced to insignifi-
cance in the wider net of kinship—after all, dispensations for marriage
were needed whether a couple were related through male or female lines
(Goody 1983: 222-39; Herlihy 1985: 83; Ariès and Duby 1988: 111-15;
Turner 1990: 29-30).

With this in mind, Pierre Bourdieu's study of the Kabyle people allows
us to approach the heart of relationships between royal mothers and
daughters. A Kabyle man's marriage to a paternal relative is socially desirable and he will prefer to identify his wife as his father's brother's daughter;
but as Kabyle mothers seek to provide themselves with domestic allies by
marrying their sons to women of their lineage, the son's wife may really
have been chosen because she is also, say, the mother's uncle's granddaughter (Bourdieu 1977: 40-42, 45-46, 66). The ritual and diplomatic
activities of royal daughters benefited the male relatives in whose interests
international marriages were arranged; but if anyone understood the
ongoing inner workings of such marriages, queens did, and it was this
knowledge that allowed them to assert their influence in concluding their
daughters' marriages. There can hardly be a better example than Eleanor
of Castile, who must be counted among the champion matrimonial manip-
ulators of all time. During her thirty-five years in England, Eleanor
involved herself in some twenty marriages involving cousins, godchildren,
and courtiers, purchasing marriages of noble youths for her kinswomen or
offering a favored knight's daughter a marriage "to advance her"; the
queen's executors rewarded a knight who married "at the queen's will." In
all but four of these cases, the partner with whom Eleanor had her long-
established initial contact was the wife. Especially noteworthy is the skill
with which she deployed the marriages of her women and their daughters
with men of the king's household to shape a wider presence for herself
within the court's male enclave; the only household knights to whom
Eleanor granted land were those married to her women, and it was the
offspring of these couples who were raised with her children to assure the
next generation of loyal service (Botfield 1841: 104; Beardwood 1969:
106-08; J. Parsons 1977: 32-55, 103, 155-56; J. Parsons 1982: 335-40; J.
Parsons 1989: 141-44).[18]

It is an obvious inference that Eleanor, herself partner in a marriage arranged to stabilize ties between kingdoms, saw women's roles in marriage and family as the likely means to foster the dependability and loyalty that were clearly her aims—an echo of the notion that women were the originators and first masters of matrimonial diplomacy (Lerner 1986: 48; compare Hanawalt 1988: 202-04, and Ward 1990a: 216). This raises interesting questions about the way Eleanor saw herself as participant in a marriage exchange and as a manipulator of marriages, and these self-perceptions must be taken into account in considering her attitudes towards her daughters' marriages (compare Wood 1991: 127). Any queen must have anticipated that her daughters would marry outside the realm, and it is not impossible that Eleanor's elaborate female networks functioned as surrogate families that would support her after her daughters departed. This may relate as well to ideas that emotional relationships in medieval domestic groups were more diffused than in the modern nuclear family: cousins, goddaughters, and attendants were potential emotional centers if daughters left (Mitterauer and Sieder 1982: 61-63). There are evident similarities in Eleanor's attitudes toward relatives and affines, and toward her daughters. Her relationships with her curial brides were longstanding, and their presence at court near her helped prepare them for the roles she meant them to fill; if this were true for her cousins, goddaughters, and attendants, we may well ask how much more so it would have held true for the daughters whose interests Eleanor unquestionably had very much at heart (on household and family as parallel agents of social reproduction, see Mertes 1988: 169-70).

The role taken by such a mother in educating her daughters and preparing them for their adult careers is thus a pertinent consideration. To encourage their consent to an illustrious marriage she could stress prestige or wealth, representing the marriage as an opportunity for the exercise of power through patronage and other informal channels—all implied in the response of Richard II's seven-year-old fiancée as she received his envoys at her mother's knee: "If it please God and the king my father that I should be queen of England I shall welcome it, for I have been assured I shall be a great lady" (Froissart 1867-77: xv, 185-86). (Of course, if a marriage was thus made attractive, it must have been clear to the bride—or been made clear—that she was dependent upon a senior male relative to place her there.) A queen's role in preparing her daughters for marriage, however, involved practical considerations of much greater urgency. An untrained daughter might prove incapable of managing her affairs after marriage, fail to establish an influential presence in her new home, and never develop the capacity to uphold her family's interests. The cultural differences such brides confronted on arrival in their new homes, for example, could present baffling obstacles to progress in settling into new lives. The linguistic barriers noted by János Bak in this volume are an obvious case in point, but there are other examples: Alphonso X of Castile, for example, scorned the notion of royal thaumaturgy and one can only guess at his sister Eleanor's reaction to the sight of her father-in-law and husband touching for "the King's Evil" (Barlow 1980: 3-27; Ruiz 1985: 128; Prestwich 1988: 113). The sophistication international brides derived from their unique multicultural perspectives thus emerges as an important base of influence and power to them (Lerner 1986: 48). The training essential to the integration and manipulation of such contrasts was crucial to a royal wife's success, and it is unthinkable that a queen seeking to maximize her own power would deny these tools to the daughters she knew would share the same destiny.

That royal daughters imitated their mothers by interceding with the king indicates that the unofficial arena they shared with her did help shape their skills in dealing with others in a responsive and informal way, integrating them vertically into the family and preparing them to solicit the centers of power (Chodorow 1974: 43-66; J. Parsons, forthcoming). That a queen's part in her daughters' training could be more immediate and far-reaching is often deduced from international brides' roles in the creation and dissemination of literary works, but the implications go beyond what has been called mere bibliophilia as noble feminine pastime (Bell 1988: 149-87; Galbraith 1935: 215). Literary inclinations nourished in her childhood at an aggressively literary court may have helped Eleanor of Castile assimilate the cultural differences she found in England: Castilian kings never evolved a heroic ancestral figure, nor fostered the cult of a dynastic saint like Edward the Confessor, but Eleanor obtained a vernacular life of the latter probably on arrival in England in 1255, and after succeeding her mother as countess of Ponthieu in 1279 she commissioned a romance on a supposed Ponthevin ancestor to promote a political agenda for her inheritance (Ruiz 1985: 126; J. Parsons 1977: 13-14; J. Parsons 1988: 376, 395). In England, Eleanor had a major role in her children's training; she was responsible for many appointments to their households, settled her favored Dominican friars among them, and in 1290 added a scribe from her personal scriptorium (Parsons 1977: 10 [note 29], 13-14, 95-96; Parsons 1991: 37-39).[19] Interest thus attaches to the persuasive evidence that Eleanor's oldest daughter—she of the 1282 incident—was literate, and to indications of literary interests among the queen's younger daughters (Byerly and Byerly 1977: no. 403; Dean 1976: 339-49).[20]

By training her daughters on the basis of her international experience, moreover, a queen could prepare them as disseminators or gatherers of symbolic capital.[21] Henry II's daughters, for example, carried to Germany, Spain, and Sicily the Arthurian legends he promoted as the heroic evocation of a kingship these women represented abroad (Labande 1986: 319-37; Benton 1961: 551-91; McCash 1979: 698-711; Legge 1986: 113-18). His Castilian granddaughters then exported royal burial traditions derived from the pantheon at the Cistercian abbey of las Huelgas; only after Alfonso II of Portugal wed Urraca of Castile did his lineage adopt Cistercian Alcobaça as their mausoleum, and her sister Blanche founded the Cistercian abbey at Royaumont where Capetians other than reigning kings were buried. Eleanor of Castile subsequently carried those traditions to England, where they influenced Westminster Abbey's evolution into a royal pantheon, beginning in the 1260s with the burials of her children (including two infant daughters), and her own in 1290 (Korrodi 1929: 35-38; Chaves de Almeida 1944; J. Parsons 1984: 258-59; Brown 1985; Hallam 1991: 14-15).

Queens knew their daughters had serious roles to play, and keeping them at home until they were old enough for married life was only partly a question of preserving them from the physical perils of early childbirth; it allowed them to be prepared to meet uncommon challenges and pursue family interests effectively. No one was better equipped to supervise such training than their mother, who thereby added to her daughters' value as diplomatic brides and made herself a natural point of contact between her husband and their married daughters.[22] Queens thus obligated husbands toward themselves, ultimately increasing their influence in matrimonial diplomacy and foreign relations. And however "domestic" or "private" an activity the education of children may appear, the implications of the queen's role as instructor—and her capacity to object (if temporarily) to a diplomatic marriage—point up the inadequacy of positing modern boundaries between public and private when considering the power of medieval noblewomen. Daughters and their marriages in effect emerge as a practical means by which queens crossed limits between the unofficial sphere to which popular expectations and royal ritual directed them (J. Parsons 1991) and the magisterial sphere in which their husbands functioned. The sons who could succeed to supreme authority were always likely to remain the apples of a royal mother's eye, but daughters too were a resource no wise queen would overlook.

That queens effectively claimed power through their active participation in matrimonial diplomacy leads to consideration of the remaining point raised at the beginning of this discussion: the possibility that medieval noblewomen derived a sense of self from these endeavors. On a primary level, the careful protection of Plantagenet brides, the watchful care given royal offspring, and the evidently favorable relationships within this family (in some reigns at least) recall links suggested between the increase during the Middle Ages in nurturing care given children, and the growing perception of the worth of the individual (Benton 1977: 156-57; Benton 1982: 289-90, 293-94).[23] But the experiences of diplomatic marriage were played out on other, deeper levels. The record evidence from the royal court upon which this discussion has centered naturally privileges the royal parents or parent-figures, and rarely witnesses the parent-daughter conflicts over marriage evident in other sources (e.g., Haskell 1973; Davis 1986; Freccero 1991). Such friction was by no means unknown in exalted circles. At least two curial women declined Queen Eleanor's offers of husbands: she reacted graciously when one of them preferred the cloister, but when a wardrobe buyer's daughter refused to marry a son of King Edward's physician, Eleanor seized £200 deposited in the woman's name with Italian bankers; still single, the victim recovered it only after Eleanor died ten years later.[24] Queens and noblewomen were known to compel women subjects to marry, or were represented as doing so (Lambert of Ardres 1879: 625; John of Marmoutier 1913: 135-36); their daughters were not exempt from coercion, and two of Queen Eleanor's own daughters—collectively called a headstrong lot (Prestwich 1988: 128-29, 567)—left indications of their reactions to the process. Margaret (1275-ca. 1333) wed the duke of Brabant's son in 1290 and they lived in England until his father died in 1295. The marriage was unhappy, and Margaret's behavior in the weeks before she finally left for Brabant (as late as 1297) suggests that the sums her father spent on a new trousseau were a necessary inducement to her departure (Green 1859-69: ii, 363-401; Prestwich 1988: 128-29). Joan "of Acre" (1272-1307) was far more explicit: at eighteen she married the forty-seven-year-old earl of Gloucester, who died in 1295, and in 1297 Joan secretly married one of his squires. Soon revealed by an inopportune pregnancy, the marriage provoked a convulsion of regal wrath stilled only when Joan, it is said, retorted that "it is neither shameful nor disgraceful for a great earl to marry a poor and simple woman; nor is it blameworthy or too strange that a countess should thus promote a likely youth" (Cokayne 1910-40: v, 702-12, and ix, 140-43; Green 1859-69: ii, 318-62; Riley 1865: 27).[25]

These words were reported by a St. Albans chronicler who wrote some ten years after the fact, and they ring true in the sense that any number of women deployed in prestigious first marriages took less exalted second husbands. To cite only English examples, Adelicia, widow of Henry I, wed William de Albini; Henry V's widow married Owen Tudor, and their great-granddaughter Mary Tudor married Charles Brandon within a scandalously short time after the death of her first husband, Louis XII of France. Edward IV's daughter Cecily, a young widow at the death of her first husband Lord Welles, took as her second one Thomas Kyme (Green 1859-69: iii, 434). André Poulet's essay in this volume shows that French kings feared a widowed queen's second marriage might lead to non-royal meddling in government, but clearly were powerless to prevent such unions except by providing that a remarried queen lost her powers as regent. Such marriages suggest the workings of canonical doctrines of personal consent to marriage, often held (however guardedly) to have afforded medieval women some freedom of choice in contracting marriage (Sheehan 1971; Helmholz 1974); they may represent a personal choice noblewomen felt free to make after they agreed to an illustrious first marriage. Whether or not Joan "of Acre" really uttered the words attributed to her, the chronicler convincingly conveyed a virtually contemporary sense that such women understood the consequences of their marriages and their capacity to dispose themselves in marriage. Perhaps it was no coincidence that Joan as a child lived with her maternal grandmother, the dowager queen of Castile, who had taken as her second husband the *seigneur* of Falvy; nor that Joan marked her 1297 reconciliation with King Edward by having masses celebrated for the soul of her mother, that matrimonial dynamo Eleanor of Castile (Green 1859-69, 2: 347-48; J. Parsons 1977: 39 [note 146], and 1988: 388).

Marriage and matrimonial endeavors were a common ground that closely touched upon the self-perceptions of medieval noblewomen. That these women so utilized the incidents of international marriage to vindicate for themselves an active role in that arena, and thereby won a not-insignificant modicum of power, resonates (if in rather circular fashion) with Davis' notion that the lack of power is a major obstacle to self-realization (Davis 1986: 53). To consider briefly a related line of reasoning, a man's place in the medieval world was defined by his membership in a single patrilinear family, a woman's place by multiple family allegiances — a point fundamental to medieval women's understanding of themselves (Freccero 1991: 134; Wood 1991: 127). Women's passages from one family to another, from one stage of family life to another — daughter, wife,

mother, widow—distinguished their lives from men's. Royal women experienced these passages in exaggerated form as they crossed cultural,
geographical, and linguistic boundaries as well as familial—transitions
that, with attendant choices and decisions, might well give them a strong
sense of self (compare Bynum 1987: 286-87, 293). That these women
objected on the basis of their own experience to premature marriages for
their daughters and granddaughters implies a self-awareness perhaps bol-
stered by the uniqueness of each bride's experience as she traversed
boundaries and cultures—a Bohemian queen in England, a Hungarian
queen in Aragon, a Portuguese in Denmark—and this uniqueness could
inform royal roles with individual responses that herald a personal identity
(Marsh 1985: 20-21). Self-awareness would surely have been sharpened
by a queen's articulation of her experience as she imparted it to her daughters, offering herself as a model for them—an oral autobiography implying
some degree of introspection (Morris 1973: 79-85; Benton 1982: 264-60;
Bynum 1982: 95-102; Davis 1986: 57-58). If emphasis on personal consent to marriage indeed heightened the sense of self, a queen's persuasion
of her daughters' consent could intensify that sense in them by emphasizing their consent as something of value to their parents, highlighting as
well their choice to conform to their families' desires and to the behavior
of royal women as a group (Bynum 1982: 107).

If the evidence argued here implies a "specifically maternal authority"
(Freccero 1991), it shows too how a queen's power was intimately linked
to her position within the families to whom she owed allegiance. That this
power was both diplomatic and personal (personal to the extent that a
cosmopolitan outlook gave her the advantage), further confounds distinctions between public and private with regard to medieval noblewomen's
activities. The material implies yet further ramifications that may reward
attention. I suggest above, for example, that literary elements in queens'
international formation were critical to the assimilation and manipulation
of the cultural differences they met in their careers; does the prominence
of the inner space in the vernacular literary works these women so often
sponsored, reflect to a degree the extent of their self-perceptions (Morris
1973; Hanning 1977)? The lives of medieval noblewomen require much
further consideration before such areas can be fully fathomed.

Centre for Reformation and Renaissance Studies
Victoria University, Toronto

CHAPTER 6

Queens-Dowager and Queens-Regent in Tenth-Century León and Navarre

ROGER COLLINS

In the spring of the year 975 a large Christian army, composed of contingents drawn from the kingdom of Navarre, the county of Castile, and the lesser lordships of Peñafiel and Alava, besieged the recently refortified Arab stronghold of Gormaz. The siege, which had begun by early April, dragged on for over two months. A relieving army sent by the caliph al-Hakam II (r. 961-76) was unable to cross the Duero to assist the besieged garrison, and it must have looked as if the fortress, the most powerful Muslim stronghold in the central March, would fall. At this point the fourteen-year-old king of León, Ramiro III (r. 966-85), put himself at the head of the Christian forces to ensure that the imminent triumph was secured under his leadership rather than that of the overly independent frontier counts who had instigated the campaign. The young king's decision to take this personal role was inspired by his aunt Elvira, who had exercised the regency of the kingdom since the death of her brother King Sancho the Fat in 966. She accompanied her nephew to Gormaz (García Gomez 1967: sections 218-20, 223, 229-30, 233-36, 239-42; Pérez de Urbel 1969-70: ii, 339-45).

Sieges, however, are notoriously unstable forms of warfare, and as had happened on several other occasions in the previous history of early medieval Spain, that of Gormaz in 975 turned suddenly into a humiliating débacle for the besiegers.[1] The protracted nature of the operation may have caused a loss of concentration or, despite the presence of Elvira and Ramiro III, inherent divisions within the ranks of the Christians may have resulted in a less-than-integrated structure of command. Whatever the cause, the Muslim garrison was able to make a sortie that caused the disintegration of the besieging forces. Although the relieving army waiting south of the Duero was not then able to make any useful inroads into Christian territory, the collapse of the siege of Gormaz put an end to such large-scale cooperative ventures between the kingdoms of León and Navarre and the frontier counties for over a quarter of a century, and may have contributed directly to the end of Elvira's ascendancy in León.

Although the claim that she was killed in the rout of the Christian forces at Gormaz, accepted by some historians, is based on a mistranslation of a passage in the principal Arab account of these events (Pérez de Urbel 1979: 45), it is true that Elvira disappears from the documents emanating from the Leonese royal court after the spring of 975. While, as will be suggested, she may have lived on into the 980s, her political influence came to an end in that year. It is possible, though not provable, that her espousal of Ramiro III's personal intervention in the Gormaz campaign played a part in this. That this episode marks the end of an interesting royal career, of central importance in the history of the Leonese kingdom in the period *ca.* 966 to 975, is significant in its own right. But the roles played by Elvira Ramírez in those years are also illuminating in the understanding of the nature of the queen's office in early medieval Spain and of the different traditions underlying it, which could serve to make the queenship subtly different from its counterparts in other Western societies in these centuries.

Elvira was the only daughter of the Leonese King Ramiro II (r. 931-51) by his second wife, Urraca Sánchez, daughter of the Navarrese King Sancho Garcés I (r. 905-25). Born no earlier than *ca.* 934-35,[2] Elvira by September of 946 had become "deovota," a consecrated virgin dedicated to divine service. It is likely that her dedication coincided with her father's foundation in the city of León of the monastery of San Salvador de Palaz de Rey, of which Elvira became titular abbess. The first of the *Infantados*, monasteries created deliberately for daughters of royal or comital families, San Salvador was located in the vicinity of the now-vanished royal palace and may have been created as the royal pantheon; it became the burial place of Ramiro II and then of his sons, Elvira's half-brother Ordoño III (r. 951-56) and her full brother Sancho I the Fat (r. 956-58, and 959-66).[3]

With the accession of her brother Sancho in 956, Elvira's role became increasingly important. In the last years of her father and under Ordoño III she occasionally appeared at court, as testified by her signature on a number of royal charters of this period. In the reign of Sancho her attendance was more frequent, and not confined to periods in which the court was resident in León (Rodríguez 1972: documents 61, 70; Rodrígues 1982: documents 19, 27). The lack of any substantial narrative history produced in the Leonese kingdom in the tenth century makes it extremely difficult, if not impossible, to delineate the factional politics of the period, but the almost total absence of Elvira's name from the documents of her half-brother's reign would suggest that her influence was slight at this time, and that most of her time was passed in San Salvador.[4]

Thus the succession of her full brother Sancho I in 956 may have altered her standing, but his first reign was brief. Faced in 958 with the successful revolt of Ordoño IV the Bad (r. 958-59), whose supporters included the count of Castile and other leading figures in the kingdom, Sancho was forced to flee from León to his mother's kinsmen in Navarre. The coup proved short-lived, in that Sancho, on the advice of his uncle the Navarrese King García Sánchez I (r. 932-70), obtained military assistance from the caliph of Córdoba. By early March of 959 Sancho (slimmed down by the caliph's doctors) was restored to power in León, and after a fruitless attempt to hold out in the Asturias, Ordoño the Bad fled into exile in the south (Rodríguez 1987: 137-85).

In the remaining years of her brother's reign, Elvira appears as a signatory of all the extant royal documents, indicating an almost continuous attendance at court. In most cases her signature follows that of Sancho's wife Teresa Ansúrez (Tarasia regina), whom he married shortly after his restoration.[5] That Elvira's role was not merely formal is suggested by the account of Sancho's reign in the two versions of the Chronicle of Sampiro. Sancho and Elvira are jointly attributed the responsibility for sending envoys to Córdoba to try, successfully, to obtain the body of the supposed martyr Pelagius, who died as a hostage in Arab hands in 924 or 926 (Pérez de Urbel 1952: 337-38). The story of this "St. Pelagius" is unusual, in that he is reported to have volunteered to replace Bishop Ermogius of Tuy, a relative of his who had been captured by the Arabs and was being held captive in Córdoba; the young Pelagius was put to death for refusing the amorous advances of the caliph 'Abd ar-Rahman III (r. 912-61). A *Vita Pelagii* was written in Córdoba by the priest Raguel, possibly around the time of the translation of the relics under Sancho I, and the cult rapidly, if briefly, spread beyond the Pyrenees. A second, metrical *vita* was composed by Hrothswitha of Gandersheim later in the century.[6]

A new monastic house was founded in León by Sancho and Elvira to receive the relics. A lack of surviving documents obscures the early history of this foundation, which was to develop in the eleventh century into the great collegiate church and royal pantheon of San Isidoro. The sack of León by the Arabs in 988 was probably the major cause of this lack. It seems probable, however, that Sancho and Elvira transformed a preexisting male monastic house into a double monastery by the addition of a new community of nuns, and the previous dedication to St. John the Baptist was extended to include the new St. Pelagius. The community was initially ruled by abbesses, of whom Elvira Ramírez was the first; one of its earliest members, herself later to become abbess, was Teresa Ansúrez, widow of Sancho the Fat (Viñayo 1982: 123-35).

Sancho did not live to see the arrival of Pelagius' relics from Córdoba; he died in December 966, poisoned by a member of the Galician aristocracy. The agreement on the part of Caliph Al-Hakam II (r. 961-76) to send northward the body of Pelagius was among other things a sign of the good relations existing in the 960s between the Arab ruler and the Christian king of León, who was effectively his client. Freed of any threat from the south, Sancho sought to impose his authority more effectively on the western parts of his kingdom, in particular on the frontier district around the lower Duero that would form the nucleus of the later kingdom of Portugal. Unable to resist the king militarily, one of the leading nobles of this region, probably Count Gonzalo Muñoz, gave him a poisoned apple. Sancho died three days later, leaving the kingdom to his five-year-old son Ramiro III (Pérez de Urbel 1952: 339; Rodríguez 1987: 94-104).

Apart from one significant case in Navarre, this was the first royal minority, not only in the history of the Leonese kingdom which is conventionally seen as beginning in 910, but at any time since the deposition of the child king Tulga in 642. In the seventh-century Visigothic kingdom the accession of a minor had invariably triggered a political crisis, culminating in the murder or enforced removal of the young monarch (Collins 1983: 112-16). Under the Asturian kingdom the problem of how to combine with dynastic succession a kingship still seen primarily in terms of war leadership was effectively solved by the adoption of a very fluid approach to inheritance within the royal kindred. Thus, when Fruela the Cruel was murdered in 768, his infant son Alfonso was temporarily passed over in favor of a cousin of the late king (Aurelius, r. 768-74), and then of his aunt's husband (Silo, r. 774-83).

Whether such an expedient was contemplated in 966 is unknown, but in fact the ranks of the Leonese royal family had by this date become very thin. The only other male of the line was Vermudo, later known as the Gouty, a probably illegitimate son of Ordoño III, who was being brought up in Galicia.[7] The political alignments within the Leonese kingdom would have made the selection of Vermudo, albeit possibly ten years older than Ramiro III, highly unlikely. Since its inception the Asturian monarchy, like its Leonese successor, had depended on a delicate balance between the varied interests of its components. On the one hand, a number of families had built up powerful landed interests on the expanding frontiers in the West, in Galicia and later north of Portugal; on the other a similar process in the south-east had seen the emergence of a strongly entrenched regional aristocracy in Castile, dependent on a largely Basque resettlement of the region (Baliñas 1988; Pérez de Urbel 1969-70). In the Asturias and then León, which itself grew from a frontier march, yet other lay and ecclesiastical landholdings were built up from war and resettlement. Crudely put, an alliance with any two of the three major component aristocracies was sufficient to maintain effective royal authority in the kingdom, though in practice this also normally involved playing off local rivalries within the regions. A complicating factor was the existence of the Basque kingdom of Pamplona or Navarre to the east, which could on occasion draw into its orbit Castile and other peripheral areas of the Leonese realm, such as Alava.

Similarly, the matrimonial policies of the Leonese kings were expected to play a part in tilting the factional balances within the monarchy. Thus, the first wife of Ramiro II, Adosinda Gutiérrez, was a member of a major Galician family, and her son Ordoño III enjoyed considerable support in that region, as in due course would his son Vermudo II the Gouty (Fernandes 1972: 91-93). On the other hand, Ramiro II's second wife, Urraca Sánchez, was a member of the Navarrese royal house, and this led to considerable Navarrese support for her son Sancho I and her daughter, the regent Elvira Ramírez.

In general, it may be thought that the balance of forces tended to favor the eastern, Navarrese and Castilian, connections of the Leonese monarchy at the expense of the Galician-Portuguese ones. Thus it is notable that both Ramiro II (r. 931-41) and Vermudo II (r. 984-999) came to the throne married to Galicians, only to repudiate them in the opening years of their reigns in order to marry easterners.[8] Possibly the same was true of Ordoño III (r. 951-56), though his hypothetical first marriage is debated. Although the lack of narrative sources makes it impossible to take account of the role of personalities in these domestic rifts, such a pattern would suggest that kings such as Ramiro II and Vermudo II, who obtained the throne through Galician support, found it expedient to expand and alter their power bases through new marriages into the Navarrese and Castilian aristocracy.

Following the death of Ordoño III in 956 it is possible to see from the witness lists of royal charters that an identifiable body of aristocrats emerges at the royal court, largely of Leonese and Navarrese origin, who thereafter feature together consistently until around the year 980.[9] Such a group was inherently likely to prefer the claims of Sancho's son to those of the Galician Vermudo, despite the problems implied by Ramiro's youth and the need for nearly a decade of regency.

The question of the person of the regent may initially have been unclear. As previously mentioned, there were no precedents more recent than the mid-seventh century, nor could much have been found bearing on the matter in the seventh-century collections of civil and ecclesiastical law that provided the norms around which Leonese political life was structured. What might be deduced from such texts was that queens played a very limited role in the Visigothic kingdom. The names of few of them have been recorded. Apart from the attendance of Reccared's queen Baddo at the Third Council of Toledo in 589, they did not take part in the most important political assemblies of the kingdom. They were not mentioned at all in the *Forum Iudicum,* the compilation of secular law, and only feature in the canonical collections in respect of various enactments concerning their protection after the deaths of their royal husbands (Orlandis 1957/58). One of these conciliar legacies of the late Visigothic period that seems to have been enforced ever since did, however, have a direct influence on decisions made by the Leonese court following Sancho the Fat's death in December 966.

In the reigns of the Visigothic kings Ervig (r. 680-87) and Egica (r. 687-702) a series of conciliar enactments forbade the remarriage of a royal widow, requiring her to enter religious life immediately upon her husband's death (Vives 1963: 421-22, 479-80). This sharply distinguished practice in Spain from that of other kingdoms in western Europe in the early Middle Ages (Stafford 1983: 143-90). The Visigothic conciliar regulations have been seen, perhaps wrongly, as a piece of cynical manipulation of the Church by a king who wished to free himself of his obligations to his wife's family (Thompson 1969: 242-43). Whatever the actual circumstances of the making of these canons, they were regarded as mandatory and a part of normal royal practice in the succeeding Asturian and Leonese kingdoms. All too little is known of the queens of the eighth and ninth centuries, but those who are recorded as outliving their husbands always entered convents. This was the case, for example, with Adosinda, the widow of King Silo (r. 774-83), and with Gotona Muñoz, the widow of King Sancho Ordoñez of Galicia (r. 925-29); the latter outlived her husband by about twenty years, living as abbess of the Galician monastery of Castelo (Saéz 1949). The same procedure was almost certainly applied in the cases of wives repudiated by the Leonese kings: Adosinda Gutiérrez, the first wife of Ramiro II, entered the monastic life in Galicia, and Velasquita, the first wife of Vermudo II the Gouty, appears as a nun in the convent of San Pelayo in Oviedo after the dissolution of their marriage.[10]

It is thus not surprising to find Teresa Ansúrez, widow of Sancho the Fat, described as "ancilla Christi" ("handmaid of Christ") or "conversa" in the earliest documents of her son's reign. Willingly or otherwise, she was forced by canonical rules to enter religious life. What is unprecedented, however, is that Teresa was not made the abbess of some suitable monastic house, but entered as a nun into the monastery of San Pelayo under the authority of its abbess—her sister-in-law Elvira Ramírez (Viñayo 1982: 125-28). Her signature to royal acts, moreover, always followed that of Elvira, and from April 970 until December 975 she appears in no documents emanating from the royal court (Mínguez Fernández 1976: document 256; Saéz and Saéz 1990: ii, document 442).

It is clear, both from the extant charters of the years 966 to 975 and from the references in the surviving fragment of the narrative history of this period written by Ibn Hayyan, that control of the kingdom during this time was in the hands of the young king's aunt, the abbess Elvira Ramírez. Although her style was not uniform (suggesting that no formal act underlay it), three relevant charters of the Leonese monastery of Sahagún ascribe to her the title "regina," or queen, as well as that of "ancilla Christi" (Mínguez Fernández 1976: documents 261-62, 276). The latter, or "deovota/deodicata," combined on occasion with the epithet "filia regis" remains her normal style in other Leonese and Galician charters. One Leonese text shows her presiding over a judicial assembly in the royal court, something otherwise normally the king's role (Saéz and Saéz 1990; ii, documents 403, 405, 410, 411; Collins 1985: 489-512). In the eyes of the Arab historians, the contemporary account of one of whom is preserved in the slightly later work of Ibn Hayyan, it was Elvira who made the various political submissions to and truces with Córdoba in the early 970s, and she is explicitly recorded as guardian of the young Ramiro III (García Gómez 1967: sections 32, 157, 239).

The lack of Leonese narrative histories, other than the brief account in the two later recensions of the chronicle of Sampiro, makes it impossible to do more than speculate as to why Elvira Ramírez was able to impose herself in place of Ramiro's mother as the young king's guardian, or as to what policies she espoused during her tenure of power, which lasted for nearly a decade. It is clear enough that she had the backing of the court nobility of her late brother's reign; they continue to appear with commendable regularity as signatories to the documents of the regency. As previously mentioned, many of these were from the kingdom of Navarre. Also, the policy of maintaining good relations with Córdoba, pursued by Sancho the Fat, who owed his 959 restoration to the caliph, was clearly preserved until 975.

An equally important factor in the external relations of the Leonese kingdom at this time was the preservation of accord with the kingdom of

Navarre. Not only were Sancho and Elvira closely related to the Navarrese royal house; their uncle King García Sánchez (r. 932-70) had played a vital role in the events of 958-59 and was able to exercise considerable pressure on the county of Castile, probably the most turbulent frontier march of the kingdom of León. In the 970s, however, the relationship between Navarre and Castile may well have been becoming too close. The new king of Navarre, Sancho Garcés II (r. 970-94) was married to the sister of the recently succeeded count of Castile, García Fernández (r. 970-75), and the county came increasingly under the domination of its powerful eastern neighbor. The support given by Sancho Garcés II of Navarre to the Castilian-directed attack on Gormaz may, then, have been decisive in leading Elvira Ramírez into placing her ward Ramiro III at the head of an expedition that would otherwise have passed out of Leonese control. It is unknown whether the ensuing debacle was crucial in undermining her influence, or in causing her voluntarily to relinquish power in the interests of returning to monastic seclusion. What is clear is that she disappears from the documentary records of the royal court, and by December 975 her role had been taken over by Ramiro III's mother, Teresa Ansúrez.

Appealingly dramatic as was the interpretation based on the misreading of Ibn Hayyan's text, that would make Elvira a victim of the fighting at Gormaz; not only is that reading based upon an error, but evidence exists to suggest that she was still alive in the early 980s. In a document dated 18 January 982, Ramiro III is recorded as giving "his aunt" Elvira an estate in the Campos Góticos, a donation witnessed by some of the survivors of the court nobility who had supported Elvira during her years as regent. Apart from the explicit reference to her as "tia nostra," no mention is made of any office or status, lay or ecclesiastical, that she might then have enjoyed (Mínguez Fernández 1976: document 313).

Although the limited survival of evidence makes it unwise to draw too many conclusions on the basis of only a relatively small number of charters, it is perhaps notable that this gift by the king to his aunt was made in the period in which he had broken free of his mother's influence. Until the winter of 978-79 Ramiro III issued charters in the names of both himself and Teresa Ansúrez, using such phraseology as "Ranimirus, nutu divino rex, una cum consessum domina et ienetrix mea domna Tarasia, regina et Christi ancilla . . . ." (Saéz and Saéz 1990: ii, document 461). Teresa, however, soon disappears once more from royal charters and was clearly definitively supplanted by the time Ramiro married Sancha Díaz in 980 (Mínguez Fernández 1976: document 309). Not least significant in this respect was that the king's wife was a member of the family of the counts of Saldaña, rivals and enemies of the Ansúrez counts of Monzón, Queen Teresa's relatives (Rodríguez 1982: 203-11; Pérez de Urbal 1969-70: ii, 121-36, 151-60). The latter seems to have retired once more into monastic life and was possibly the last survivor of the complex events of the 970s; she outlived her son by a decade and appears as abbess of San Pelayo in 966 (Fernández Conde 1978: 19-22). The date at which she succeeded her sister-in-law Elvira Ramírez in that office is unknown.

While some aspects of the activities of queens in the Leonese kingdom were still directly conditioned by the normative rules of the Visigothic period, it would be unwise to assume that other traditions did not have a part to play. It is possible, for example, that the very active role of Elvira Ramírez was made possible by precedents from the land of her mother, the Navarrese kingdom. Also, as will be seen, there were a number of tenth-century Spanish queens, all of Navarrese origin, who were in no sense constrained by the canonical legislation forbidding their remarriage and requiring them as widows to embrace the religious life.

While the evidence for political life in the kingdom of Pamplona or Navarre in the tenth century is even more limited in quantity and more problematic in character than that pertaining to the Leonese monarchy, it is not difficult to uncover the presence in it of another powerful female regent. This was Queen Toda Asnárez, wife of the first king of the second Pamplonan dynasty, Sancho Garcés I (r. 905-25) (Collins 1986a: 163-71). Their marriage took place before 912, but their only son, García Sánchez, was still a minor at his father's death (Martín Duque 1983: document 5). The royal title was then taken by the late king's brother Jimeno Garcés (r. 925-33), but with its reversion apparently secured for the young García.[11] In 933 the boy began his long reign (933-70) under his mother's tutelage.

As in the case of Elvira Ramírez in León, it is the Arab sources that validate the tentative deductions that can be drawn from the formal styles used in royal charters. From 933 until the late 950s many of the charters of the kingdom of Pamplona and of the county of Aragón, which was attached to it, refer to García Sánchez and his mother, Queen Toda, as reigning together (Ubieto Arteta 1962: document 18; Ubieto Arteta 1976: document 65). It is the lucky survival of another section of the great *al-Muqtabis* of the eleventh-century author Ibn Hayyan, this covering the years 912-42, that puts some flesh on these very bare bones. It is clear from this that it was Toda whom the Arabs saw as ruling the kingdom of Pamplona in the 930s, and as responsible for making diplomatic, political, and military decisions (Viguera and Corriente 1981: sections 225-27, 271-75, 285).

It is not until 940 that Ibn Hayyan's narrative presents García Sánchez as lord of Pamplona in his own right without reference to his mother (Viguera and Corriente 1981: sections 308, 316-17, 323, 326). The loss of the sixth book of this work is thus particularly regrettable, in that the Navarrese documentary evidence suggests continuing periods of influence for Toda, and a series of shifting relationships between herself and her son in the course of the next two decades. Thus, while Toda does not feature in royal documents of the early 940s, the formal language of the charters reveals her again ruling jointly with her son by 947 (Ubieto Arteta 1981: documents 8, 16; Ubieto Arteta 1962: document 18).

By 943, García had married, probably for the second time, and in a number of documents his new wife Teresa appears with him, jointly making donations or confirming charters (Ubieto Arteta 1976: documents 30, 41, 45). The style "I, García Sánchez, king by the grace of God together with my wife Queen Teresa . . ." is used both in the preamble and in the confirmatory section of these documents; the same formula, with the names changed, is employed in documents of García and his mother: "I, García Sánchez, king by the grace of God, together with my mother Queen Toda . . . ." What is peculiarly perplexing is that Teresa and Toda never feature together in the same document. Thus, from *ca.* 943 to 947 García appears with his wife, and from 947 to *ca.* 955 he is found exclusively with his mother. By 956-57, however, Teresa reappears while Toda vanishes in 957, only for the process to reverse itself by 959 when García is found issuing documents with his mother; no further mention is made of his wife (Ubieto Arteta 1976: documents 65, 68, 69, 72-78; Ubieto Arteta 1981: document 20; Lacarra 1965: document 1). The lack of Navarrese or Aragonese royal documents dating to the 960s makes it impossible to follow these strange maneuverings into the next decade.

Inevitably, part of the explanation may lie in the nature of the evidence itself. All of these texts are preserved in later cartulary copies, and there is the real possibility that scribal errors have crept into the dating clauses of some of them. Furthermore, the relatively late development of a charter tradition in the kingdom of Pamplona and the county of Aragón means that there was an unusually large amount of subsequent fabrication of texts to provide documentary titles for properties earlier obtained through exclusively oral transactions (Goñi Gaztambide 1963; Collins 1986b: 85-104; Goñi Gaztambide 1979: i, 441-54). It must be admitted, however, that no one has yet been able to cast doubt on the validity of any of the documents upon which the above analysis of the alternations of the Navarrese queens has to be based. Formally, and in terms of the composition of their

witness lists, there is nothing in them that would impugn their genuine-
ness (García Larragueta 1983: 7-22).

To complicate the issue further, one of the documents in the cartulary of
the monastery of Albelda implies that in 958 at least Toda was ruling a
subordinate kingdom centered on "De[g]io" and "Lizarrara" (Ubieto
Arteta 1981: document 24). The first of these places has not been identified,
but the second may be Lizárraga in the district of Aoíz or the identically
named place in the upper valley of the Rio Araquil, respectively south-east
and north-west of Pamplona.[12] The practice of creating small subking-
doms for members of the royal family, normally younger sons, was frequently followed by the Navarrese royal house in the tenth and eleventh
centuries, and it is reasonable to suspect that Toda may have been exercising such authority for some or all of the times that she is not found with
her son ruling from Pamplona (Ubieto Arteta 1950: 3-24). It must be
admitted that no evidence whatever survives by which it is possible to
work out the nature and extent, geographical and otherwise, of the
authority exercised by most of these Navarrese subkings and subqueens.[13]

That such dowager queens as Toda continued to enjoy special authority
in the kingdom, and probably also superior status to their sons' wives or
other royal ladies of younger generations, is also indicated by another
charter from a slightly later period. This comes from the reign of Sancho
III the Great (r. 1004-35), who succeeded as a minor under the tutelage of
his mother Jimena, widow of García Sánchez II the Tremulous (r. 994-
1004). In a document of 1 March 1005, Sancho III and his mother remit-
ted the annual tax payable by the monastery of Fontfrida, but, strikingly,
in the charter's dating clause Sancho is said to be "regnante . . . cum avia
sua Urraca regina." This was the king's grandmother Urraca Fernández,
widow of Sancho Garcés II (Ubieto Arteta 1962: document 25). It would
seem that while she lived, she remained the senior female member of the
royal family, and that the child-king was deemed to rule with her.

Another example that would seem to establish that special local juris-
dictions could be created for royal mothers as well as for younger brothers
in the tenth-century Navarrese kingdom, comes from the reign of Sancho
Garcés II. He was the son of García I's first wife, Andregoto Galíndez;
their marriage, which must have taken place no earlier than 938, was dissolved by 943, and she retired into her father's county of Aragón. The
usual lack of documentation makes it difficult to delineate her career during the next few decades, but it is clear that she was still living in 971. Her
son Sancho Garcés inherited the county of Aragón through her, and ruled
it at least from 948 (Ubieto Arteta 1962: document 18; Durán Gudiol

1988: 204-11). After his accession to the kingdom of Navarre in 970, however, a document in the cartulary, or Becerro, of Leire records Sancho "ruling in Pamplona" and his mother "donna Endergoto" as ruling in Lumberri (Lumbier). In the document Andregoto, who is here given the title of queen, intervened to solve a dispute over an estate between two local landowners and the church of St. Mary and St. Saturninus in Lisabe (Ubieto Arteta 1972b: 113-28). Thus it would appear that just as Sancho II invested his half-brother Ramiro with a subkingdom centered on Viguera, so he gave his mother one on the frontier between Pamplona and Aragón.

For all the unsolved, indeed insoluble, problems concerning the political careers of Toda, Jimena, Urraca, Andregoto, and others, what is clear is that queens enjoyed a pronounced public role in the kingdom of Pamplona. Formally, in the royal charters king and queen are represented as ruling jointly, and making and confirming grants and giving judgments together. Some of the Leonese documents also present the king and queen as acting together in the making of donations to religious foundations, but this mirrors the normal practice of non-royal donors. The preservation of a wife's property rights in Visigothic law meant that both spouses had to be seen to consent to the alienation of their matrimonial possessions (King 1972: 222-50). The same applied in Navarre, but the documents indicate that ideas of shared royal authority in that kingdom went far beyond that. For example, confirmations of gifts made by earlier monarchs or others would be made jointly by the reigning king and queen and not, as was the case in León, by the king alone, with his wife possibly appearing as a witness (Ubieto Arteta 1981: document 29).

It is also notable that widowed or divorced royal wives were not required to retire into monastic life; though she never remarried, Andregoto Galíndez never entered a convent. The best example here, however, is Queen Urraca Fernández, whose career spans the boundaries of both the Leonese and Navarrese kingdoms. She was the daughter of Count Fernán González of Castile and of Sancha Sánchez, daughter of the Navarrese rulers Sancho Garcés I and Toda. Her father's growing power in the frontier county made her diplomatically a valuable spouse. Her first marriage was to the Leonese king Ordoño III (r. 951-56), who was the grandson (though via another wife) of her mother's first husband.[14] After his death, she returned to her father in defiance of Leonese tradition, but within two years reappeared as queen of León, this time married to her first cousin Ordoño IV the Bad (r. 958-59):

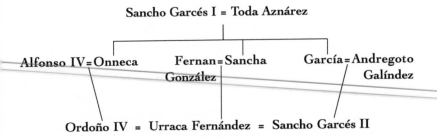

Sancho Garcés I = Toda Aznárez

Alfonso IV = Onneca   Fernan = Sancha   García = Andregoto
                          González   Galíndez

Ordoño IV = Urraca Fernández = Sancho Garcés II

Urraca did not follow Ordoño into exile in the south after his expulsion from the kingdom, and upon his death soon afterward she married yet another first cousin, the future Navarrese King Sancho Garcés II (r. 970-74). As has been seen, she outlived him and their son García the Tremulous, to rule jointly with her young grandson Sancho III for a few years. Uniquely among early medieval Spanish queens, she is depicted in a contemporary manuscript illumination.[15] The roots of the differences in tradition between León and Navarre are harder to delineate than their effects. The Leonese monarchy, like its Asturian predecessor, was a self-conscious heir to the seventh-century Visigothic kingdom, and could articulate its ambitions and justify its territorial expansion by reference to the peninsula-wide dominion of that realm. The kingdom of Pamplona or Navarre, on the other hand, was a creation of the first quarter of the ninth century and was much less ideologically committed to an idealized Gothic past (Collins 1986a: 99-163). Though not explicitly Basque in its self-presentation, the majority of its population would have been Basque-speaking, and inevitably the influence of Basque social norms prevailed. These will have included a much greater role for women in the transmission of property and within individual households. Earlier matriarchal traditions in Basque society can still be detected in this period; charters from some Pyrenean valleys show that matronyms were used rather than patronyms, and examples survive of the inheritance of family property through the female line (Collins 1986a: 99-101, 159-61, 206; Ortiz-Osés and Mayr 1980). In this context, it is interesting to note that Andregoto Galíndez appears to have been able to pass on her father's county of Aragón to her son Sancho, though she had seven half-brothers, some of whom themselves had sons (Lacarra 1945: 244-45; Ramos Loscertales 1961: 39-44).

In general, in the absence of even moderately detailed narrative accounts of the history of this period in the two northern Spanish kingdoms, it is unwise to push conclusions too far or to be too confident about the real significance of events obscurely hinted at in charter collections, whose own formal problems are not always securely settled. It is at least clear, however, that two rival traditions existed in the Christian states of tenth-century Spain: one that was essentially more passive and restrictive of the formal roles of the queen, and one that was far more dynamic, and which invested her with much greater potential for taking an active role in the political life of the realm. Obviously, the role of individual personality, almost concealed from us by the problems of evidence so frequently noted here, will have played a vital part in determining how great or how little influence any particular queen was able to exercise in practice on the public stage. All that the evidence can really allow us to do is to highlight differences within the formal framework within which such queens were able to put their own personalities to work.

The Royal School, Bath

CHAPTER 7

Capetian Women and the Regency: The Genesis of a Vocation

ANDRÉ POULET

To be born male or female has never been a neutral biological factor. Every society conceives its own distribution of roles unrelated to the natural distinctive capacities of the sexes. The absence of natural determinism explains the multiplicity of conditions of the female in history: theoretical or practical equality, or hierarchial difference from the male group. The conception of the woman has its source in an essentially temporal ideology that determines the specific and substantive functions assigned to males in society. Medieval woman did not escape from the connotations of these innate male rights responsible for the division of space and function; and beyond the prestigious office that established her as a living role model, a queen was the archetypical woman of her time. Despite the superficial splendor in which she lived, a queen was not exempt from the ideology that defined the female. In absolute terms, the marriage that raised her to royal rank gave her a juridical and social status identical to those of her anonymous sisters, and closed her in a domestic setting in contrast to that of the male, which centered on the exercise of power in the public and private spheres. Repressed by theology, law, and attitude, the feminine sex was the object of constant marriage speculation, organized around the requirements of male authority—or in the queen's case, those of the royal lineage and the material signs of its power. The social differentiation of the sexes and the dialectic of their relationship, however, intervened in the social game of which they were creator, product, and driving force. Beneath a rigid ideology that demeaned women and confined them to the domestic sphere, society—static only in appearance—discreetly shed the status of object conferred upon them. Thus the queen, following the example of less-favored sisters both common and noble, was able to rise above her theoretical position and escape subjection by a subtle method which was really the defense and preservation of male supremacy: the regency, essential to the survival of the dynasty, opened to her a specific and indispensable institutional role.

I. "THE SECOND SEX"

Rare were the voices raised against the injustice of men and against women's state of ignorance from which men benefited, the most distinct and persuasive that of Christine de Pizan in the early fifteenth century. Her feminist crusade was directed against a multilayered misogyny, rooted like a truism, which appeared socially impregnable (Pizan 1986: 37; Pinet 1927; Dulac and Dufournet 1988). The narrow vision of a "second sex" that Christine combatted was conceived and defended by moral philosophers and poets, the intellectuals who were the source of her erudition.

A completely negative image of the fair sex had been developed by the Church and adopted by the nobility, the former with an almost purely bookish knowledge of women, the latter a narrow segment of the population, largely cut off from the mass of women. The misogynist line of thought was that of the élite who shared the monopoly of knowledge and power: on the one hand the scholar, celibate conceiver and defender of marriage, with his command of the written word; on the other the knight, for whom woman came second to his principal possession, land. The seemingly universal and everlasting dogma of damnable woman originated in Scripture and the Church Fathers: women, by their essence inferior, lustful, and demonic, required constant strict subjection. The prototype of this contemptible being, held up to public obloquy, was Eve, second born after man, her descendants and sisters heirs to the opprobrium of learned minds. Condemned first for lust and later for volubility, the weaker sex could and should inspire scorn and fear (Power 1976; Dalarun 1991: 31-54).

To counterbalance Eve, restless, curious, and lascivious, who worships the body and its finery, the Church and aristocracy introduced the Marian cult and the ideal of courtly love. Devotion to Mary developed in the twelfth century, the age of cathedrals that extolled the Virgin, but did little to put right the insults directed at women. Putting this extraordinary femininity on a pedestal and praising it extravagantly, as churchmen did in accordance with evangelical tradition, had no effect on the belief that to protect himself, every man must suspect the cunning and corrupting female. The Virginal ideal came close to divinity, and thus the superficial contradiction between the adoration of Mary and the harsh judgement of Eve—who was more real—was dealt with without notable difficulty. Eleventh-century esteem of Mary Magdalene, repentant sinner and accessible model of redemption, argued more for the cause of women without, however, leading to their rehabilitation (Dalarun 1991: 45-49).

The counterpart in fiction of the Virgin's cult—the exaltation of the Lady and the spiritualization of loving fervor—heralded the emergence of a civilized society and the rebirth of literature in the vernacular. Courtly love, based on the freedom of those who sought and conceded it, could only be imagined outside marriage, ignoring the way of the Church. Ennobled yet real, civilizing yet morbidly refined, this ecstatic, narcissistic love refused to attain too quickly its logical carnal end, lest it cut short the exquisite emotional turmoil it generated. Love was "feudalized": like a vassal, the lover would wait subserviently upon the Lady. This led to feats of arms that exalted the gallant knight and enhanced masculine prestige. But while courtly love at its height of perfection lessened the inferiority of women, it was practiced only in the narrow and chivalrous milieu of the aristocracy. And even if this elite welcomed courtly love, the fleeting, extraordinary outburst of the ideal became a clumsy academic attitude: courtly gallantry opened the way for bourgeois literature to reenunciate misogynous criticism. Though distorted and practiced only by the ruling minority, the new code of love did not liberate the lady, though it saved her from brutal masculine assaults such as rape and abduction (Duby 1991b: ii, 261-76; Marou 1971: 151-63, 173-81).

The cults of the Virgin and the Magdalene, and courtly love, modified only superficially the status of women. Inferior to man by their nature and in their Biblical past, they could achieve salvation only with difficulty. Marriage, a consensus between Church and society long distanced from the sacred, was offered as an institution of salvation, the least sinful of states and a refuge for those repulsed by clerical celibacy or virginity (Duby 1981). Marriage took on a new definition in the twelfth century, as the Gregorian reform battled the difficult circumstances from which it had arisen. Its development concomitant with that of courtesy, marriage became an element of social cohesion, monogamous, binding, and lifelong; in keeping with prevailing misogyny, however, it was a universe of subjection for women. What choices other than married life, guarantee of virtue based on controlled sexuality and marital chastity, might exist for women concerned for their salvation, and for men convinced of their supremacy? The chaste behavior that virtuous women were invited to adopt by scholars' teachings against the lust of the flesh—of varying strictness depending on virginity or marital status—was not accepted unanimously throughout the Middle Ages. In fifteenth-century Christendom, depopulated by recurrent plague, was born a way of thinking not properly described as libertine, but populationist, stigmatizing chastity and even rehabilitating the *prostibulum* and the *meretrix* as an apprenticeship to a married life where pleasure, source of procreation, was imperative to the regeneration of humanity. This "naturalist" approach, tolerant of lust, did not, however, improve the inferiority of women nor their weaknesses, vulgarized by the traditionalists' morality, which was rarely and only belatedly contested (Rossiaud 1988: 96ff; Thomasset 1991: 55ff; Bologne 1988: 296ff).

Marriage remained almost the only way for women to obtain salvation, but the subservience to which it relegated them was perpetuated by the imitation of exemplary women, either legendary or Biblical, or real examples chosen from the top of the social hierarchy. Aristocratic ladies occupied a privileged position as participants in pastoral and pedagogical views. Thus it was that St. Louis addressed a series of teachings to his daughter Queen Isabella of Navarre, and Durand of Champagne composed the *Speculum dominarum* for Joan of Navarre, wife of Philip the Fair. Queens offered the best example of women's necessary respect for moral values, though their married state and the duties required of them as first ladies of the realm did not spare them the criticism inspired by clerical stereotypes. Privileged by her rank, the queen, like her anonymous sisters, found in marriage the hope of salvation dear to the scholars and an environment of subjection according to which social life was organized and tranquilly perpetuated. Her subjection, however, was moderated in domestic activities by the importance of her role, the feelings she inspired in the king, and the unofficial advice she gave him.

Christine de Pizan denounced male iniquity and proposed a "therapy," but she had no more than an awareness of her own subjection and did not alter the hierarchical difference between the two sexes, which remained closely linked to a social structure in which women, especially the queen, and marriage were constantly reconsidered according to new imperatives of male power. These readjustments led to an unexpected institutional change for the queen.

II. THE QUEEN AS DYNASTIC INSTRUMENT

The evolution of the matrimonial bond and of the real status of women went hand in hand with changes in society, notably the "feudal revolution" of the first half of the eleventh century. Among the ruling classes, marriage gained a key position in the arsenal of domination, for on it depended the control of land and power over men. Its content certified its diplomatic nature; for the monarchy, it was a necessity for the continuation of dynasty and kingship, the repetition of the "Capetian miracle."

The Ties of Blood

In the late ninth century, kinship was bound to a narrow perspective that embraced two or three vertical generations, with no hierarchy between blood relations and allies. The nobility of western France arranged itself in vast clans, *Sippen,* linked by marriage in a horizontal structure. Ancestral glory did not guarantee personal promotion, which depended entirely on direct relationships sustained within and by the group; the pursuit of royal favor required that one be linked to figures influential in the royal circle. In establishing these ties, male and female relationships were of equal weight.

Radical change came about in the tenth century as horizontal organization was succeeded by a vertical, lineal form, the *Geschlecht.* The Robertinians, dukes of *Francia* and forebears of the Capetians, did not escape these changes affecting the aristocracy, and it seems unthinkable that those who raised Hugh Capet to the kingship in 987 did not understand that they were supplanting the Carolingians with a new royal race. Hugh was the head of a powerful dynasty; he calculatedly increased the fortune and power of his son Robert, and married off his daughters advantageously. The ducal line, for whom it was unthinkable that son should not succeed father, thus naturally was changed into a royal dynasty, the *stirps regia,* the royal blood. For this house as for the great principalities and later for feudal domains, only a few instances of father-to-son succession were needed for permanent possession of the *honor* to become established, and the Capetians' feeling of hereditary right became stronger. But appropriation of the royal office and a sense of dynasty were not achieved without a lucky combination of coincidences, biological and political. Despite appearances, elective kingship failed to perpetuate itself in the late tenth century. Long described as a rooted principle based only on Capetian tenacity and luck, and the strategy of anticipatory association of the heir, elections took on a purely formal character from the reign of Robert II. Royalty had no foundation other than birth and if the final designation was election, either divine or by lay or ecclesiastical magnates, the claim of heritage and the right to succeed were founded in blood.

Concentration of power in the hands of the *rex coronatus* and the eldest son as *rex designatus,* replacing division of the inheritance, finds a parallel in the great houses of the aristocracy. The head of the house was thus, like the king, master of lineage and race. Younger sons, ousted from immediate claims to the inheritance, were condemned to celibacy or found their fortunes elsewhere; they often challenged the authority of father or brother — and fate was sometimes on their side. Capetians and magnates alike curbed the natural claims of such excluded descendants. The designation of a single agnate as heir clarified the question of succession and made easier the transfer of the heritage to the firstborn son; but it was implicitly necessary that ambitious younger sons should make no bitter or jealous protest. Thus the institution of apanage was soon adopted to inhibit the greed of these sons. The first Capetians' lack of land limited estates assigned to cadets, but after the dynasty's territorial acquisitions became substantial the apanages assigned to younger sons were generous. The systematic use of testamentary dispositions in favor of cadets arose concomitantly with the abandoning of the practice of anticipatory association of the heir; heredity and primogeniture meant that Philip II could dispense with the strategy of association, and Louis VIII bestowed apanages lavishly on his sons to maintain family peace.

Whether by the authoritarian measure of anticipatory coronation or by more flexible family arrangements, royal succession was ordered around the principal heir, its object to facilitate the perennially delicate transition from one reign to another. Structural changes in the noble family had led to the genealogical tree being pruned of its collaterals, and at the same time the role of women was reduced to the mechanical role of transition between generations. Marriage was ordered round the criteria of succession, which encouraged the preservation of ancestral inheritance and power as well as their prestige and growth (Lewis 1986; Wood 1966).

Marriage and Dynastic Prosperity

In the dominant class, the conjugal tie long based on an equality of inheritance was now concentrated on the new concept of the indivisibility of possessions. In the tenth century, the prenuptial contract (*sponsalicium*) gave the new wife possession of half the husband's inheritance, a sharing that established the couple in landed equality. This dotal regime was altered firstly by a reduction in the wife's share accorded by the *sponsalicium*, and secondly by increasingly rigid supervision by the head of the family over the lands bestowed for life. At the same time, daughters of the lineage saw their rights to inherit family lands reduced to the meanest portion. If the all-important blood may be dispersed by daughters' marriages, the inheritance must escape division; everything argued for the careful control of marriage, which inhibited scattering the family stock and stabilized the movement of lands.

The monarchy preceded the aristocracy in this quest to safeguard the family *honor*. If they had recourse to the Constitution of Domains, the Capetians always matched it with a reversionary clause denying the queen the *abusus*. A precautionary measure, this did not affect the queen's attachment to the royal house that had welcomed her. Conjugal harmony, foundation of family peace, was all the more welcomed since marriage subjected the wife to her husband and cast off the fear of the "sly and scheming" weaker sex, a fear explained by the fact that marriage was now a matter only of rational consideration (Duby 1981: 95ff; Gaudemet 1980; Pernoud 1980: 209-38).

The growth of feudalism sharpened the matrimonial tool and allowed it to prune and enhance the dynastic tree. In a mimetic reaction to the feudal environment, the king used marriage as an instrument of alliance, reinforcing ties of vassalage and sealing alliances with the great families by judicious distribution of the daughters under his authority. Many such treaties of alliance provided for one or more unions in the search for peace, as in the marriages proposed between Capetians and Plantagenets. It was usual that such couples were paired off when young, as with Henry, son of Henry II of England, and Margaret, daughter of Louis VII of France — aged respectively three years, and six months. The children's interests and wishes — when they can be unearthed — could not resist dynastic pressure or political objectives, and despite widely held opinion, sons were disposed of just as peremptorily as daughters. Richard I of England was betrothed to Adelaide, a sister of Philip II, but broke off the marriage and accused her of becoming the mistress of his father, Henry II; after Henry died in 1189 a truce was arranged and a marriage agreed upon between Philip's eldest son and Henry's granddaughter. This led to the union of the future Louis VIII and Blanche of Castile, which affirmed Philip's power, confirmed his recent acquisition of the duchy of Normandy, and dissolved the coalition between King John of England and his nephew Otto of Brunswick (Sivéry 1982: 14ff; Berger 1895). Relations between the two realms were peppered with treaties and the marriages that went with them. After Philip IV's victorious intervention in Flanders, Edward I of England — already expelled from Aquitaine, fighting the Scots and unable to assist his ally Count Guy of Flanders — opted for peace with France. The treaty of Vyve-Saint-Bavon restored Edward to Aquitaine and provided new matrimonial ties between the two houses, but these pacifying arrangements could ill resist the chronic warmongering of Capetian and Plantagenet. It was in virtue of a new treaty reached at Montreuil in June 1299 that Edward I married Philip IV's half-sister

Margaret that autumn; Edward's son by his first queen, until lately affi-anced to Guy of Flanders' daughter, was now betrothed to Philip's daugh-ter Isabella though they married only in 1308 (Favier 1982: 226ff).

Sometimes it was a question of defending hypothetical interests by means of subtle matrimonial manipulation. The marriage of Louis IX and Margaret of Provence was at the center of a complex strategic tangle. The Church sought repression of the Albigensian heresy and the defence of its Provençal ally. Raymond-Berengar IV, the future queen's father, hesitated between a French or an imperial alliance, and as the Capetians surveyed the potential adversary that was Toulouse they worried lest the county rise up too quickly from recent defeat. An ally in the Midi was desirable, and, however tentatively, France turned its attention beyond the Rhône (Sivéry 1987: 27ff). The entry of Isabeau of Bavaria into the Valois *mesnie* was part of a similar if more obvious political strategy, the posthumous conclusion of Charles V's eastern policy, through which he sought security to the East in order to concentrate on the war with England. Faithful to the German alliance prompted by his blood relations—his mother was the emperor's sister—Charles hoped to strengthen it by turning to the house of Wittelsbach. On the eve of his death in 1380, he formed the desire that his son should marry a German princess, and after Philip the Bold of Burgundy was named regent he gladly furthered his own German and Netherlandish policies by seeking Isabeau's marriage to the young Charles VI (Autrand 1986: 151ff). Peace treaty, offensive or defensive alliance—on each of which depended war or peace—involved blood ties.

Outside the capricious field of diplomacy, Capetian matrimonial strat-egy had long-lasting territorial consequences which would not have resulted from war alone. To extend their authority in lands over which they had theoretical suzerainty, or over the vassals of a powerful neighbor, kings did their utmost to obtain the subtle matrimonial ties which often accompanied the exploitation of feudal rules for their own profit, and it was through marriage that many fiefs were united to the domain. Philip II's marriage to a niece of the count of Flanders in 1180 brought to the Crown the Boulenois and Artois; that of St. Louis' brother Alphonse of Poitiers to the count of Toulouse's daughter added that county to the realm, and Philip IV's 1285 marriage to Joan of Champagne and Brie joined her inheritance to the royal domain. The last of the great fiefs united to the realm by marriage was Brittany, through Anne of Brittany's marriages to Charles VIII and then Louis XII.

Over and above strictly diplomatic and territorial interests served by royal marriage, the renown of the bride's family could enhance dynastic prestige. A perfect example is Henry I of France's second marriage (May 1051) with Anne, daughter of Grand Prince Iaroslav of Kiev. The motives that impelled the king to seek a wife on the banks of the Dnieper have excited much curiosity—a crowded marriage market, fear of showing favor to a neighboring rival lineage, or concern that a future wife might resemble his mother, who had wanted to put his younger brother on the throne? None of these explanations seems entirely valid, but a particular circumstance may well have influenced Henry's choice. A Cluniac monk had become king of Poland under the name Casimir, and had married Maria Dobronega, Anne of Kiev's aunt. The relationship between the French king and the great Burgundian abbey perhaps introduced Henry to the Kievan reigning house, its history (particularly the qualities of Anne's ancestress Olga), and its fecundity (her grandfather Vladimir the Great may have fathered two dozen children). In any case, the alliance was attractive enough for it to be successfully concluded. Anne's exotic origins added to the aura already conferred on the Capetian dynasty by coronation (Caix de Saint-Aymour 1896; Pernoud 1980: 281ff). A Russian princess, an Iberian like Blanche of Castile, or a German like Isabeau of Bavaria, gave to Capetian marriages a pronounced exogamic and international character—a source of grandeur.

However great their rank, these foreign princesses were traded as if by mercenary brokers, and upon arrival in France they had to endure both their own disorientation and popular xenophobia. Their lives were thus subordinated to the patrilinear transmission of indivisible ancestral inheritance. In the context of succession, the queen thus served as the instrument not only of dynastic posterity, but of its prosperity.

Marriage and Dynastic Posterity

The choice of a royal wife was bound up with the continuation of the "Capetian miracle"—her ability to provide legitimate male issue capable of assuming the succession. The primary question of the ideally fertile womb thus followed upon diplomatic concerns. The new queen's inborn qualities, physiological and moral, informed her reputation as a wife: she was the passive transmitter of Capetian dynastic success. This supreme generative requirement sometimes led to conflict with the Church, which demanded that the inalterable prescriptions of marriage must take precedence over the demands of dynasty and descent. But if sterility, impotence, adultery, incompatibility, or death threatened to undermine dynastic hopes, repudiation, annulment, and remarriage offered a remedy.

The main threat to a royal couple was a prolonged wait for offspring, an emptiness that menaced the future of the line. Procreation alone could combat a high rate of infant mortality, and a queen thought to be barren was liable to be repudiated. Robert II, according to tradition married by his father to Rosala, daughter of the king of Italy and a Carolingian descendant, quickly repudiated her, either because three years of childless marriage stigmatized her as barren or because Robert wished to assert his freedom by dismissing the wife imposed on him by his father; but his second wife, Berthe of Arles, also barren, was ultimately sent away as well. Robert's third consort, Constance of Arles, was abundantly fertile but still lived with the threat of repudiation (Duby 1981: 82-93). Philip I followed in his grandfather's footsteps, wedding Berthe of Frisia as proof of reconciliation with the count of Flanders. Nine years went by before Berthe gave him an heir, the future Louis VI—nine years of uncertainty that made Philip doubt her fertility; in 1092 he rejected her. It cannot be verified that Philip's love for Bertrade de Montfort, wife of the count of Anjou, lay behind this perilous act, which led to his excommunication; a desire to avoid extinction of the royal line may be as good an explanation. Impious and bigamous, Philip nonetheless persevered. Bertrade had proved her fecundity by bearing the count's children; assailed by powerful neighbors, Philip could not ignore the threat of his brother, guardian of the fortress of Montfort near Normandy (Viard 1920-53, 5: 78, 80; Duby 1981: 7-26).   More surprising is Philip II's repudiation of his second wife, Isambour of Denmark, after a disastrous wedding night (14-15 August 1193) inspired in the mature king a profound aversion to his young wife. Hypotheses abound, none related to the consanguinity alleged in the sentence of annulment (5 November 1193), nor to the real cause of the separation. Chroniclers theorized that Isambour was no virgin, that she was deformed, or that she had bad breath. In fact, Philip developed temporary impotence at the sight of her and his male dignity would thus have suffered. This at least is what he asserted—together with a charge of witchcraft—in 1204 when trying to obtain final separation from this virgin queen whose presence threatened his third marriage, to Agnes of Meran. But Isambour was stubborn in her own defence. The admission of impotence might have been accepted by the Church had it come sooner; defined as the organic impossibility of intercourse, impotence was an impediment like consanguinity, entailing nullity of the *sacramentum* of matrimony which was based upon *fides* and *proles* (Bologne 1988: 81ff). Philip knew and argued both pretexts without success; Isambour triumphed (Pernoud and de Cant 1987). Louis XII was luckier when reasons of state compelled him to separate from his childless cousin Joan of Valois and marry Anne of Brittany, widow of Joan's brother

Charles VIII and, more important, heiress to the duchy of Brittany (Quilliet 1986: 218ff). Louis merely swore he had never known Joan carnally; her alleged deformity was otherwise unconfirmed.

Fertility was the queen's cardinal virtue. When she was weak, slow to provide heirs, or failed or refused to arouse the king's affections, the threat of repudiation hung over her. Sometimes it was a question of abuse; impotence was alleged to avoid a shock to morality. Necessity prevailed. Sterility meant extinction of the royal line; adultery, equally feared, questioned the legitimacy of the queen's issue, and the perpetuated lineage must above all else be pure.

Suspicions that Eleanor of Aquitaine fornicated with her uncle Raymond of Antioch during her husband's crusade thus led to her divorce. Eleanor had given Louis VII only daughters; now doubly tarnished, her fecundity offered compelling dynastic reasons for divorce (Paris 1836-38: iv, 383-85; Duby 1981: 201ff). Adultery was not mentioned during the process for her divorce; it would have justified the decree but would have forbidden remarriage, so Louis relied on claims of consanguinity. More intent on indissolubility than exogamy, the papacy refused to accept the alleged kinship between husband and wife, but a divorce was nonetheless pronounced: Louis lost Aquitaine but kept his honor—and the chance to father a son. After Philip IV's daughters-in-law were convicted of adultery, Joan of Burgundy, absolved of guilt, was taken back by her husband, later Philip V. Margaret of Burgundy, wife of the eldest son, afterwards Louis X, died in Château-Gaillard, freeing him from the irksome need for annulment; Blanche of Burgundy, wife of the youngest brother, later Charles IV, died in a convent (Favier 1982: 527). Louis XI did not stand on his ancestry, which he thought doubtful; he often repeated that his notorious grandmother, Isabeau of Bavaria, was an arrant harlot and a great whore, once even alluding to it when he received the king of Naples' ambassador (Kendall 1974: 398). The women who were to transmit the royal blood could not wrong the dynasty with impunity

Royal marriage was liberticide for women. Moral constraints both lay and ecclesiastical made the queen a mere instrument of dynastic continuity, one whose faults might lead to her prompt replacement. Subject to the interests of lineage and inheritance, she was confined in a genealogical vocation, passive yet indispensable to a system in which power was heredity's corollary.

III. THE QUEEN AND THE CONTINUATION OF THE STATE

Royal blood ordered the right of succession to the throne. Coronation, primogeniture and apanages, factors of hierarchy and family cohesion, and a network of centralizing institutions combined to make the king the essence of power and its natural and legitimate exploiter. In this patriarchal context, the queen acquired a legal status second to the king's though as fundamental: without her, dynastic continuity would cease. Beyond genealogical success, however, the growth of Capetian power presupposed a parallel continuity of state. Appropriate legal structures were indispensable if a tight rein were to be kept on power, especially since social and institutional mechanisms governing the transmission of power could create specific cases in which the royal authority was lacking: thus the minority, a price exacted by hereditary rule, emerged as a constitutional principle. Capetian power could only take root when favored by the fortunate conjunction of an unbroken succession of kings, and rules either enunciated or decreed that compensated for sovereigns' temporary incapacities. The lucky chance of genealogical continuity was therefore carefully reinforced by the will and perspicacity of Hugh Capet's descendants; legislation at first spontaneous and temporary, then anticipatory and permanent, compensated for the natural, accidental or inherent inability to rule, so that an efficient substitute was provided for the minor king or the ailing or absent monarch. Analysis of Capetian regencies and attendant legislation—effected as well as abandoned—reflects like a great polyptych the maturing of royal power and its increasing conceptualization. But such analysis reveals too the genesis of a vocation: the queen's emergence as her husband's legal replacement. The regency, surrogate for royalty, acknowledged her at last. Her original, exclusive role as a womb for monarchy put her in a position to assume this charge; overshadowed by the king, she nonetheless drew from this theoretical inferiority the undeniable arguments for her necessary activity as a personage of state.

A Promising Status

We may deduce that at birth, a daughter was not as happily welcomed as a son. Masculinity triumphed in the aristocracy, more so for royalty. Parents hoped for a male heir and regretted the birth of a girl, especially if a son had not arrived first. Dissymmetry between the sexes at birth was marked in adulthood by marriage, which consecrated the transfer of the role of the daughter's guardian from father to husband. The woman, instrument of all clientelistic politics, became on her wedding day a genealogical instrument, an inferiority sanctioned by private law. The marital guardianship, rooted in almost all legislation, resulted in the strict limitation of a woman's legal capacity. Rare were the women who escaped from male tutelage, be it of the father, the husband, or, as custom required in the absence of these two, of the oldest agnate. The laws of the thirteenth century of course extended freedom of action to single women and widows, but married women, the queen first among them, remained under the tutelage and power of their husbands, a subordination common to all areas of social and legal existence. The queen's dowry, whether in land or money, passed from her control and she could not alienate the dower her husband accorded her, a portion of the domain of varying size depending on the times and the personality of the beneficiary. But the separate management of the goods of husband and wife was customary. The queen had her own funds, staff, and dependents; though this freedom was limited to her dower it infused her with the spirit to command and helped forge her abilities as a manager. In absolute terms she was only following the example of her noble sisters, as a passive vector of the growth and transmission of capital; thus domination and submission combined in a tense if promising combination. Nonetheless the law, prejudices about her intellectual qualities (which argued for her son's early majority), and the feminine role model that she offered her daughters combined to steer the queen towards maternal and domestic tasks (L'Hermite-Leclerq 1991: 217ff; Opitz 1991: 279-81).

The guardianship imposed upon the weaker sex restrained women's access to political, seigniorial, or royal duties to such an extent that royal law took little interest in the question. Because her secondary role effaced her, the queen was not under such limitations as the king, who was subject to rules that guaranteed his power while restricting its extent: the oath he took at his coronation was an effective limitation to his power but did not restrain his wife. From the time of Louis VII, the queen's coronations are reported by contemporary authors. They differed in many ways from the kings' coronations. The queen was not marked by the indelible sign of divine delegation: the celestial oil of the Holy Ampulla was reserved for the king, who was anointed seven times while the queen was anointed with holy oil only on forehead and breast. What is of great importance is that the queen did not swear an oath and made no commitment to Church or "Nation" (Poulet 1989: 66; Jackson 1984: 268-71). Brushed aside by preconceived notions of her incapacities, the queen was helped towards power by her genealogical role—a mechanical one, but an essential one as well, and she was confirmed in her new vocation as regent by the absence of explicit prohibitions and by the particular legal limits that gave her authority its special nature.

An Emerging Vocation

Reproduction was the linchpin of the dynastic principle. When children were slow to arrive, the king became a slave to nature's whims. "The destiny of a race, the future of a kingdom, were at the mercy of an embrace in the folds of a bed" (L'Hermite-Leclerq 1991: 259). It was essential that the lineage be perpetuated by a son, that he be sheltered from the dangers that might threaten him, and that he reach maturity before his father died. She who had borne the future of the dynasty, the closest to her son in blood and rank, was the natural choice to ensure his protection and education. The Capetian dynasty was not perpetuated to the fourteenth century without royal minorities or the abeyance of power caused by the king's absence, but confidence in the queen's ability to fill the vacuum was slow to establish itself. The Merovingians Brunhild and Fredegund, Olga in the principality of Kiev, Ermessinde in Catalonia, vindicated their right to govern sons and family possessions with abilities and vigor traditionally associated only with men; but such examples had little influence on Capetian strategy and ideology.

According to received opinion, before his death on 4 August 1060 Henry I on his own authority designated Count Baldwin V of Flanders to govern France until Henry's son and designated successor Philip came of age. Many chronicles agree that Henry's Russian wife, Anne, was excluded from the regency because her command of politics and the French language was suspect (Bouquet 1738-1904, xi: 161; Hugh of Fleury 1851: 389; Aubri of Troisfontaines 1876: 357; William of Malmesbury 1887-89: ii, 291; Hariulphe 1894: 234; William of Jumièges 1914: 185; Orderic Vitalis 1969-80: iv, 351). The natural moral ascendancy of mother over son, moreover, would be greatly reinforced during a regency by Anne's legal authority, changing the nature and modifying the legal content of an institution based on the protection and advice the guardian owed the pupil; it would become a de facto domination which might retard the king's emancipation, disastrous if he was retained in tutelage beyond the legal limits of minority. There was reason to prevent the ascendancy of a Gertrude whose omnipotence might be bitterly contested by her son. The forces of Count Baldwin, solidly organized, easily surpassed the uncertain authority and charisma of the alien queen who had little organized support; but Anne's royal rank and motherhood allowed her to attain great influence during Baldwin's regency.

Some historians, Fliche among them, wrongly insist upon Anne of Kiev's right to the regency, though it could be only a de facto ascendancy justified by the mother-child relationship (Fliche 1912: 16-17). Berthold of Reichenau (1844: 271) agrees, however, with the author of a royal diploma asserting in similar terms that Philip I and Anne of Kiev took the destiny of the kingdom in hand upon the death of Henry I; this donation for Saint-Germain-des-Près was subscribed by the regent Baldwin, who implicitly recognized the queen-mother's power. In another charter, by Bishop Agobert of Chartres, Philip I and his mother (together called "king") are associated in the direction of affairs without distinction (Prou 1908: 19-20). These documents clarify the regent's absolute power and express the familial nature of royal government in the eleventh century, evident in the so-called Capetian trinity, a dynastic machine formed by the king, the queen, and the designated heir, who shared sovereign authority. Though the status of king's mother did not guarantee any particular legal power beyond her emotional ties with the boy, the queen's sacred nature implied rather her right, theoretical but not prescriptive, to share in the regency council's proceedings and the regent's decisions.

Anne of Kiev initially accompanied Philip I in his peregrinations and thus collaborated in the management of the domain. This is borne out by the numerous diplomas she subscribed during the period preceding her remarriage, doubtless in the summer of 1061, to Raoul de Crépy, count of Valois, among the most powerful lords of Francia (Fliche 1912: 18-19, 21). Coming less than one year after Henry I's death, this marriage greatly affected the young king and troubled his entourage. Like a good politician, Baldwin adopted a benevolent attitude, preferring cooperation with this dangerous rival to the struggle to set him aside. Anne kept her title as queen, though the rare diplomas she so subscribed after 1061 suggest her position was adversely affected by her new marriage (Prou 1908: 53). Count Raoul's heightened prestige meant a decline in Anne's credibility, a transfer of authority from the queen to her husband who thereafter exercised powers with which she was legally invested at her coronation. That Raoul took an active part in the regency council is well attested by the frequency of his subscriptions to royal diplomas after 1061 (Prou 1908: 54, 59, 66, 83); in fact, he effectively controlled the regent's politics until Philip I's emancipation in 1066. Following the slight credence initially given the queen-mother, this first abeyance of royal power showed both the queen's potential and the risks involved, a precedent for the future.

The Capetians' dislike for women in politics was of long duration and deeply rooted. When Louis VII in 1147 went on crusade he passed over his mother Adelaide of Maurienne and his wife Eleanor of Aquitaine (who went with him to the Holy Land), and chose as his substitute Abbot Suger of Saint-Denis, a well-informed adviser of his father's who was assisted by Count Raoul of Vermandois and Archbishop Samson of Rheims. Collegiality and masculinity triumphed (Poulet 1989: 291).

Half a century later, Philip II revived the tradition of the Crusade and remained faithful to the notion of collegial administration, but did not show the same reticence about the queen. In June 1190 he notified his *familiares* of the directives to be observed during his absence. Known as the "Testament of Philip Augustus," this text is the first model for a regency by edict. The king entrusted the regency of the kingdom and guardianship of the future Louis VIII to his mother, Adela of Champagne, and her brother Archbishop William of Rheims (his wife, Isabella of Hainaut, had died earlier that year). Placed under the supervision of a council of whose membership we know only that six bourgeois participated in it, the co-regents had limited power; the edict, which strictly controlled the administrative, financial, and ecclesiastical organization of the kingdom, allowed the council slight room for maneuvering. Institutionally encircled, the dowager was nonetheless officially recognized as the king's replacement; the idyll between queen and regency was beginning, and it would persist (Poulet 1989: 300).

In October 1226, as Louis VIII returned victorious from the near-total defeat of Toulouse, he was stricken at Montpensier by a fatal dysentery; near death, he set about limiting its consequences. He had made in June 1225 a testament that dealt only with his goods; now he provided for the succession and his son's minority. The crown was to go directly to his twelve-year-old son Louis, too young to govern by himself. At the king's request the barons and prelates who were present swore to serve young Louis faithfully and to have him crowned as soon as possible. The only information concerning the regency comes from an anomalous document preserved in the Trésor des Chartes.[1] Issued by the archbishop of Sens and the bishops of Chartres and Beauvais, who testified without any promissory oath, it states that Louis VIII's last wishes concerning the royal government in his son's minority were that in the event of his death his children and the kingdom should be under the trusteeship or the tutelage of his wife, Blanche of Castile, until the children reached their majority. The document's precise terms leave no doubt of Louis' desire that Blanche assume the regency.

When Blanche learned of Louis VIII's death on 8 November 1226, she at once took over the government and tutelage of the kingdom in accordance with his last wishes. He had conceded her unlimited authority, conceived in terms of trusteeship and tutelage (*in ballio sive tutela*), though without qualifying its exercise and placing no restraints on the regent's hypothetical tyranny. Blanche of Castile in theory had more power than the king himself, since the only limit on her authority was time. Until her son's majority she was thus freed from the limitations of power imposed on the king by custom and by his coronation oaths. The theoretical authority confided to her verged on the absolute but this dimension was not preserved in practice, where it differed slightly from that exercised by the late king. As much a sovereign as she was, then, and as was the case with those of her predecessors invested with the same office, Blanche faced the weakness of her coercive powers and the strength of her opposition. In legal terms, the authority of the queen-regent had nonetheless been augmented since Philip I's minority by the coalescence of the tutelage or guardianship of the king himself and the governance of the kingdom (a distinction clearly expressed in the eleventh century, though Baldwin of Flanders took charge of both). This original power, in essence different from that of the regality, imposed a heavy handicap: the regent did not enjoy the king's prestige or legality but had to impose extraordinary authority on the kingdom, and the novelty and fragility of the situation encouraged opposition.

Blanche's governmental activity was placed under the lawful authority of the young king, though the language of official records makes it impossible to discern her real role, discussed only in narrative sources. Most royal acts from Louis IX's minority bear the subscription "Ludovicus Dei gratia Francorum rex," with no reference to Blanche. The fictive presumption of the child-king's capacity to rule was more clearly enunciated in the thirteenth century than during Philip I's minority, when Count Baldwin's status as regent and Anne of Kiev's political role were expressly indicated in many royal acts. In the thirteenth century, the king's de facto incapacity was concealed to such an extent that it is impossible to determine from Louis IX's acts exactly when he attained his majority: the formulaic records of the chancery show no changes, but it was of course Blanche who held real power. Legal fiction was introduced in almost perfect form in the thirteenth century, with the signal exception of one important category of acts where the regent's name appeared next to that of the king: oaths of fidelity to the crown. These acts apart, almost all royal acts from Louis' minority, legislation or treaties, issued in his name even if Blanche was active in the preparatory or editorial phases of the documents.

Though they were overshadowed by the fictive presumption of her son's capacity to reign, the range of the queen-regent's prerogatives attests to her absolute power (Poulet 1989: 69ff). Blanche of Castile legislated, dealt with foreign powers, waged war, arranged marriages — in short, imposed herself as sovereign of the realm. She dealt ably with opponents and availed herself of the advice of counsellors and the Church, that staunch propagandist of the monarchic ideal. Louis IX, who was under her sway far longer than was stipulated by law, respected her command of statecraft and recalled her to affairs of state when he went on crusade in 1248. He did not honor his wife Margaret of Provence with the trust he reposed in his mother; though Margaret remained in France during his last crusade, Louis opted then for a co-regency under Simon de Nesle and Mathieu de Vendôme. Louis and Margaret's son, Philip III, showed a like concern; an intriguer, Margaret was excluded from her son's legislation (Poulet 1989: 321ff, 324ff).

To Philip III's departure from custom succeeded Philip IV's revival of tradition. The orders he promulgated in October 1294 stipulated that in the event of his death before his son was of age, the tutelage of the new king and the government of the realm would devolve upon Queen Joan of Navarre.[2] Philip clarified neither the extent of Joan's powers nor the conditions in which they would be exercised. His silence on an institutional question of such import does not indicate the acts' deficiency but rather their flexibility. Tacitly and voluntarily, Philip entrusted Joan with powers similar to those exercised by Blanche of Castile. Relying on the existing institutions of government, her administration would be free to meet the contingencies of the moment. Philip placed one restriction on her: if she remarried during the minority of their eldest son, she would lose both power and fortune. This encroached on her personal freedom but was not purely gratuitous, for it touched on critical public concerns. The minor king must be protected; Philip hoped to avoid the sudden, dangerous promotion of one who might become a direct competitor of the young king, subjugate him, and even usurp royal power. At a time when the question of a woman succeeding to the throne of France had never been raised, there must be no risk other than a possibly overambitious queen-mother.

The choice of the queen as regent was in fact the least of many evils. To persuade himself of his good sense, Philip IV spoke highly of his wife's qualities, hoping they would not change if she did assume the responsibilities of state: her loyalty, her fidelity, her devotion, and her love for the kingdom and its people. This panegyric contrasted, however, with Joan of Navarre's real situation. Always in her husband's shadow, she had remained absent from the political scene except where her own inheritance, Navarre and Champagne, was concerned. There is no doubt that

Joan would have been able to assume the responsibilities entrusted to her—or at least, her relative anonymity had not revealed (or had served to conceal) any natural ineptitude for command. This was similar to Blanche of Castile's situation while Louis VIII was alive. Philip IV doubtless had discerned in his wife gifts similar to those of his grandmother, qualities indispensable for her destined role.

For political ends, the natural ties that united the queen to her son were thus institutionalized, even if the legitimate, beneficial influence of mother upon child could be colored by authoritarianism and turned to decision-making after a young king reached his majority. Philip IV did not, moreover, consider his decision to be contrary to his predecessors' practice, though Henry I did not entrust Anne of Kiev with the guardianship of their son, and Philip III took precautions against any possible influence by his mother or wife on a boy-king. Placing the queen-mother atop the state pyramid when the continuity of the Capetian dynasty was most threatened was seen as the most sensible solution, even if mother-love was a fragile notion in public law.

Since Anne of Kiev's day the female presence in the regency had been greatly reinforced. Apart from Blanche of Castile, twice invested with absolute power, the few queens authorized to assume the regency (Adela of Champagne and, in theory, Joan of Navarre) were recognized as tutors and regents, but under conditions that suggest the ancestral disdain for women. The collegiality of interim power lessened possibilities of usurpation and tyranny; prohibiting remarriage avoided risky transfers of authority which could traverse the principle of inheritance. The dowager queen was preferred to the wife. Trust in the mother, distrust of the wife — an idea close to the contradictory theological image of femininity that opposed Mary to Eve; blood ties—descendance is a guarantee of the honesty that widowhood reinforces—and emotional ties were seen as a shield against all attacks that might lead the king astray from his royal destiny. The mother shared the son's success, but an intriguing and authoritarian parent like Margaret of Provence emphatically remained a personage to be avoided. The regency, born second like woman in Genesis, guaranteed the continuation of the royal office, a temporary monarchy serving an everlasting monarchy. The procedure whereby the queen replaced her husband received legal definition in the fourteenth century when the "Capetian miracle" had burnt out; in the sixteenth it would become common practice.

A New Aptitude Becomes Customary

From 1314 to 1328 the three sons of Philip IV succeeded each other upon the throne, all well-known for their matrimonial problems and none leaving surviving male issue. The absence of a king wounded the dynasty that had always produced a viable successor and put to the test a successional system that remained elementary and incomplete. The lack of a male heir necessitated exhaustive redefinition of that successional law. The exclusion of women from the succession in 1316 was confirmed in 1322, and in 1328 relatives through female descent were barred, meeting both national and dynastic expectations. The path from the relegation of women to the role of successional accessory, to their final eviction therefrom, had been marked out for a long time. The disinheritance of women reinforced male primogeniture and reaffirmed the superiority of the patrilineage; exclusion of in-laws prevented the crown's exportation and gave a strictly national character to the succession. The heir from then on could only be Capetian and French. The queen, excluded from inheritance, from then on offered all the legal guarantees to allow her triumph in the regency (Poulet 1989: 348ff).

The tension between Philip VI, the first Valois, and his English rival Edward III led to the first organization of the regency after the innovations in successional law. The rivalry between France and England reached its peak in 1338: unlucky claimant to the French crown and a vassal humiliated by the confiscation of his Aquitanian fief in 1337, Edward III was busily preparing large-scale diplomatic and military actions. In August 1338 Philip, certain that war was unavoidable, felt it well to provide a substitute against the day when he must devote himself entirely to the struggle against his adversary.

By orders given at Clermont-en-Beauvaisis, Philip designated his wife, Joan of Burgundy, to look after the government of the realm "for existing needs and those which may arise" (Poulet 1989: 348ff). The choice of a relative was in conformity with the tradition of a royalty based on blood ties; the role of the king's relatives in the affairs of the realm had never declined, and the role of women, ever more specialized, had become clearer. If on occasion royalty had turned to the acuity and authority of mothers, the credibility once accorded the queen-mother was now extended to the wife. How to justify this choice, which no other king had previously made? Diplomatic language, ceremonious and impenetrable, is on rare occasions interspersed with more human comments. Thus, after a barren and commonplace ritual formula there appears "our dearly beloved companion, the queen," unambiguously conveying the import that of all mortals, Joan was the one Philip could trust. Philip was a "found king," enthroned by common consent and not without opposition. He had learned to mistrust his entourage and not to bestow his trust unthinkingly. His wife was raised with him and must fall with him; who better to entrust with the dynastic heritage?

Joan of Burgundy thus obtained all the powers exercised by her husband. Philip's orders insist first of all upon the ordering of public finance, his greatest concern that in his absence the treasury be supplied and sensibly managed. He then stressed the extent of Joan's judicial powers; her right of reprieve is clearly expressed, and she had the right to revoke banishments, reduce sentences, and pronounce amnesties. If thoroughly applied these letters would result in a splitting of royal power: to the king would fall the duties of war, to the queen the duty of guaranteeing their financing. An absence of unequivocal archival sources does not exclude Joan of Burgundy's involvement in shaping these provisions; her discretion need not imply her silence.

The institutional and political crises that peppered the fourteenth and fifteenth centuries were accompanied by enactments intended to safeguard the continuity of the state, which unintentionally guaranteed the continuity of the dynasty as well. Next after Philip VI it was Charles V who continued this judicial crusade most carefully. After the English captured his father John II in September 1365, Charles learned the delicate job of king, which drove home for him the meaning of the state and the necessity of its continuation (Poulet 1989: 374ff). In 1374, his poor health obliged him to guarantee an institutional system which would meet the demands of state in the event of his death. After some hesitation, his first outline provided that his queen, Joan of Bourbon, would assume guardianship of their children and would govern the realm with the support of the dukes of Burgundy and Bourbon. This enactment, with its intermingling of powers, was scarcely viable, and nothing justified the return to earlier models except apprehension that the widowed queen might become so powerful that when the time came, her son would not be able to free himself from her control. But the fact remains that definitive legislation had now separated guardianship of the royal children from the government of the realm, and the essence of these dispositions was spread over two further enactments. Joan of Bourbon was not to exercise the regency itself; she retained only the guardianship of her children until they reached the age of fourteen.[3]

Charles V explained at length the reasoning that led him to choose his wife for this responsibility. Following the example of Philip the Fair, he

explained that "a mother loves her children more tenderly and has a gentler and more feeling heart to look after them carefully than any other person, however closely related to them." The choice of the queen was all the
more sensible given that the exclusion of women and their issue from the
French throne protected the king from attempts by his mother to usurp
royal power. Her exclusion from the succession was the ultimate guarantee of her integrity, making her in practice the person most capable of
assuming the guardian's role. But the priority thus accorded her did not
prevent others from coming to share her tutelary authority or to assist the
queen in her duties; thus, Charles V nominated his brother Duke Philip of
Burgundy and Joan's brother Duke John of Bourbon as co-guardians
and governors of his children. This collegiality and hierarchy of guardianship controlled the queen's actions and ensured faithful guardianship.
Another precautionary measure was that Joan was prohibited from
remarrying until her eldest son reached his majority, as had been provided
in Philip the Fair's case to make sure that no new husband would automatically become co-guardian of the minor king. This would have gravely
altered the organization of the guardianship by raising to that critical position someone not legally designated to share it. This union would not in
itself constitute a political risk for the young sovereign, though the harmful influence of an education supervised by an unscrupulous stepfather
might well be feared. Anne of Kiev's second marriage perfectly illustrates
what could happen; Charles V preferred security and renewed the link
with the earlier Capetians, and in so doing slowed the growth of female
power by declining to invest his wife with sovereign authority.

In 1393, Charles VI barely escaped a fiery death in the hideous incident
known to history as the "Bal des ardents." On the day following this
tragedy Charles sought to avert the difficulties his death would have produced, and perpetuated the separation of powers introduced by his father.
Charles' wife Isabeau of Bavaria would become the principal guardian of
their year-old son Charles, but in keeping with the collegiality enunciated
in 1374, she would be assisted as regent by an advisory council of relatives
and intimates.[4] The queen's institutional and political role was, however,
strengthened after Charles VI felt himself free of his father's posthumous
influence, and after he began to suffer periodic attacks of madness he
went back on the enactments of 1393. New ordinances in April 1403
affirmed the principle of immediate succession and the fiction of the king's
capacity to reign regardless of his age at accession. The queen's influence
was expanded: Isabeau was to have charge of her children and would govern the realm seconded by her husband's relatives and advisors. In 1407

new laws of regency took on an abstract form in order to withstand the test of time; while not formally nominated, the queen would nonetheless assume power according to the conditions of 1403.[5] The effects of this incontestable institutional progression were overshadowed by the "Passion of Charles VI": foreign war; internal rivalry and civil war; ruptures within the royal family as the princes of the blood formed their own foreign alliances; a queen greedy for power. Benefiting from the upheavals, the opportunistic Isabeau increased her wealth and power but preferred a life of entertainment and celebration to the establishment of political domination. According to the drift of the moment, she allied herself with whomever seemed likely to triumph: first her brother-in-law Duke Louis of Orléans, and after his assassination, his murderer Duke John the Fearless of Burgundy. Isabeau's misbehavior did not bring the queen's constitutional vocation into question. The institution itself was blameless: the law is a mere tool in skilled or unskilled hands, and the queen either worked with or against it.

Isabeau's grandson Louis XI expanded the range of family members who might be recruited as regent. The dowager queen was the first enlisted, then the wife; now it was the eldest sister of the minor king. On the eve of his death, Louis confided the destiny of the realm to his elder daughter Anne and consequently to her husband Louis of Bourbon, lord of Beaujeu. Designated verbally by the dying king, the couple wrested from the States-General of 1484 a guarded national recognition of their authority. The difficulties they encountered were identical to those of most regencies, if not all changes of reign—natural outlets of accumulated tensions. Pragmatic and lucid, Anne preserved royal power so well that after attaining his majority, Charles VIII called upon her again when he launched his Italian invasion (Poulet 1989: 186ff, 335ff).

Over five centuries, the regency had become a complex and efficient institution that complemented and completed royalty. Analyzing its maturation reveals the gradual emancipation of the queen from legal and ideological constrictions. Instrument of posterity and dynastic prosperity, she became guarantor of the continuity of the state; it was thus incumbent upon Capetian wives, least visible and prestigious of the royal blood, to support masculine power and to perpetuate the dynasty by supplying successive incarnations. The dialectic between a modest if encouraging status and the weaknesses of royal law amidst transformation formalized her authority in the specific context of the abeyance of kingly power. This evolution took place in two phases, easily distinguished. Under the Capetians, mistrust of women was a keynote: temporary exclusion from the regency, interim collegial power and prohibition of remarriage, a restriction of choice for the queen-regent. The vocation of regency was consolidated with the exclusion of women from the succession, and under the Valois the tasks at the heart of the dynasty became specialized: the king to reign, the queen to second him and substitute for him if he was a minor, absent, or incapacitated; his relatives to assist, or to assume the government if need be. On the eve of the sixteenth century this institutional genesis was complete; Louise of Savoy, Catherine de Médici, and Anne of Austria would officiate with full legal rights over the fundamental laws of the monarchy, among which the regency now took its proper place.

Relegated to second rank like most of the female sex, Capetian women emerged from anonymity through the regency, though not without resistance. Like other women in warfare, medicine, and the Church, they successfully asserted themselves and assured their place in a society that persisted in trying to mask them. Without reaching equality with men, these women showed that femininity was not an eternal symbol of weakness.

Strasbourg

CHAPTER 8

The King's Mother and Royal Prerogative in Early-Sixteenth-Century France

ELIZABETH MCCARTNEY

Upon the premature death of her son Francis II of France on 5 December 1560, Catherine de Médicis became the first queen in French history to succeed to the regency without prior royal designation. She acted simply as mother of the young new king Charles IX and her regental prerogative was later confirmed by a meeting of the Estates General (Barry 1964: 350, 407-08; Mattei 1978; Lightman 1981; Hanley 1983). The regency of 1560 is rightly seen as a significant point in the history of French fundamental law, but while much attention has been given to the historical evolution of regental prerogative (particularly within the context of French public law regulating succession to the Crown), little recognition has been given significant developments in this area during the earlier sixteenth-century regencies of Louise of Savoy, mother of King Francis I. The omission is understandable, for Louise's authority as regent was unusual: as the king's mother but not an anointed queen, she was the first "royal" mother to exercise regental prerogative independently of ceremonial investiture. As a result, modern scholars have overlooked how contemporary writers emphasized the dynastic, mother-son bond between Louise and Francis to support her right to act as Francis' guardian and later regent of the realm. This chapter considers several manuscripts, most of them from 1505 and 1506, that addressed the juridical and dynastic nature of regental authority within the context of royal succession, French public law, contemporary political concerns and legal scholarship.

I. A "ROYAL" MOTHER AND SON

Neither the marriage of Charles of Valois, count of Angoulême, to Louise of Savoy, nor the birth of their son Francis was hailed as a significant event for the royal house of Valois. Initially, Charles' kinsman King

Louis XI had encouraged the marriage to secure the border between France and Italy; after Louis' death the acting regent, his daughter Anne of Beaujeu, supported the marriage to assure that Louise (her orphaned niece) would be provided for by the aging count (de Maulde La Clavière 1895; Mayer 1966; Paris 1970; D. Mayer 1966; Knecht 1982: ch. 1; Castelot 1983). When Charles and Louise married in 1488, the dynastic future of the French monarchy seemed secure. Negotiations were underway for the young King Charles VIII to marry Anne, duchess of Brittany, a union as noteworthy for securing the last great independent fief to the royal domain as for Valois dynastic fortunes. Little over a year passed between their marriage in 1491 and the birth of a dauphin, and by 1494, the year of Francis of Angoulême's birth, the royal court was celebrating Charles VIII's military victories in Italy (Godefroy 1684: 628; Scheller 1981-82: i, 5-69). But recognition that Francis of Angoulême would be king had been voiced by Francis de Paula, whom Louise (following Anne of Brittany's example) consulted to assure the birth of a son; in gratitude, she named her second child and only son after the mystic (De Costé 1643: 9; Guichenon 1660: i, 602).[1] Then the divine providence guiding royal succession abandoned the reigning Valois. The dauphin died in 1495, and despite processions and prayers none of Queen Anne's children by Charles VIII survived infancy (Le Boterf 1976: 258-59).

Charles' unexpected death in 1498 thus elevated to the crown his cousin Louis, duke of Orléans. Among those who counted on royal favors from the new king was the now-widowed Louise of Savoy; shortly after Louis' accession she petitioned him to grant the duchy of Orléans to her son, hoping that as both a cousin and her family's designated guardian, Louis would be especially keen to help Francis. But he was unwilling to part with any portion of his patrimony and reluctant to grant Louise full authority over her children. Instead of recognizing her right to act as guardian and tutor, he tightened his control over her family by appointing a privileged (and ambitious) courtier, Pierre de Rohan, seigneur de Gié, to serve as Francis' guardian (de Maulde La Clavière 1895: introduction; Knecht 1982: 7-8). Louis' decision was largely inspired by the ongoing politics at the royal court that often involved Gié's ambition, and by dynastic concern for the future of the French royal house. Thirty-six and in poor health in 1498, Louis was childless and there was much anxiety for the direct succession to the throne. To preserve the union of France and Brittany, Louis divorced his wife, Louis XI's daughter Jeanne, to marry Charles VIII's widow (Molinet 1828: 101; Pélissier 1890: nos. 2-3, 47-110; Drèze 1991: 91). When in 1499 Anne became pregnant by Louis, the royal court hoped for a son; but with the birth of a daughter, Claude, attention focused on the status of Louis' nearest male relative, the boy Francis of Angoulême.

After a serious illness that coincided with an episode at the royal court whereby Gié's personal ambition allegedly transgressed his authority as either guardian or minister of the realm, Louis XII moved to allay uncertainty over the designation of his successor.[2] In 1505 the king drew up a royal testament that recognized Francis as successor to the Crown, provided he married Louis' daughter Claude. Louis also stipulated that if he died before Francis reached fourteen, the recognized legal age for royal majority, a regency would be established whereby Queen Anne and Louise of Savoy would share authority as guardians of the royal children (Isambert 1822-33: xi, 443-45; Knecht 1982: 6-9).[3] Louise was thus recognized as the legal guardian of her two children, but the greater significance lay with her designation as regent. Her duty to oversee Francis' health, welfare, and education assured her a privileged status at the royal court, where she was able to influence certain policies such as Louis XII's decision to reconvene in Lyon the interdicted Council of Pisa (Trebuchet 1822: 49; Mignet 1895: i, 36-57). One snag remained: Queen Anne might yet bear a son. But again divine providence deserted the Valois, and of Anne's children by Louis XII only Claude and a second daughter, Renée, survived (Godefroy 1615: i, 125; de Saint Gelais 1622: 98; Terrasse 1945: i, 46-49; Le Boterf 1976: 258-59).[4]

In 1506, the manuscript *Le Compas du Dauphin*[5] was presented to Louise in recognition of her new status as a "royal" mother. Several references in this text refer to Louis XII's formal designation of Francis as his successor in 1505. Louise is praised as mother and regent, and Francis is called "royal prince" and "dauphin"; the work stresses the need to assure public welfare and prevent instability of government, issues that the delegates to the Estates General addressed when it convened in Tours to ratify King Louis' testament. A specific reference to "the sorrow of a father without a son" implied that *Le Compas'* author may have been influenced by a 1503 edition of Petrarch's *Les Remedes de L'Une et L'Autre Fortune,* which Louise possessed.[6]

In rhymed verse, the anonymous *Compas* outlines Louise's duty to teach Francis the moral virtues and intellectual pursuits necessary to rule wisely; emphasis is laid on his piety and his knowledge of Holy Scripture, law, and science. Only under his mother's aegis will Francis become the most "virtuous among men," able to rule with the compassion and wisdom of his Biblical predecessors.[7] Throughout the text, Louise is encouraged to apply her customary care and devotion to her son's intellectual development (though as the work centers on her maternal rights to act as Francis' guardian, the reader might miss the fact that *Le Compas* was meant to promote the appointment of Francis Du Moulin as her son's tutor). Finally, the author addresses the divine providence guiding the dynastic fortunes of French rulers, noting that without devotion to God a king would fall prey to flattery and be unable to execute the responsibilities of his office, particularly the right to pass sentence and uphold justice.[8]

When this treatise is compared with those that addressed the political, spiritual, and moral education of French kings in late- thirteenth-, fourteenth-, and fifteenth-century France, *Le Compas* seems rather ordinary. Neither its discussion of the future king's education nor the accompanying miniature is exceptional. The anonymous author, a good Aristotelian, echoes the works of Giles of Rome, Jean Gerson, Philippe Mézières, and Philippe de Commynes (Giles of Rome 1966: book 1 parts 1, 2; Keohane 1980: part 1, ch. 1 [for Commynes]; Ranum 1980: introduction and ch. 1; Krynen 1981). But while *Le Compas* is a *livre du circonstance* inspired by political and dynastic crises at the royal court around 1505, it merits closer scrutiny. Two themes in the discussion of Louise's maternal devotion address constitutional principles regulating royal succession. The first centers on the dynastic basis of French rulership that emphasized the "seminally transmitted nature of French rulership"; the second established the basis of an argument grounded in notions of blood ties and lineage to support the queen's right as a royal mother to act as guardian of the royal children and regent of the realm.

That *Le Compas* is inherently concerned with issues of royal succession is evident in its discussion of kingship. As Louise is praised for her maternal devotion and urged never to let her responsibilities be preempted, exemplary models of Biblical kingship are cited: Francis is exhorted to emulate David and Solomon, each of whom had a special distinction in regard to the Christian tradition of rulership and the hereditary nature of kingship (Du Moulin 1561: 29-32; Giesey 1961: 8 [note 19], 25; Scheller 1983: 75-151 [esp. 94 note 77]; Poulet 1989: i, ch. 1).[9] The dynastic basis of French rulership is further stressed through the motif of Louise's role in assuring the perpetuity of the dynasty by transmitting French kings' *bon sang* (good blood) to her son so he may succeed to the throne.[10]

The dynastic interests of *Le Compas* are enhanced by a miniature honoring Louise's preeminence as a royal mother (Fig. 8.1). She is depicted standing at her son's side, holding over him a large golden compass which, according to the narrative, is a symbol of her maternal obligations.

Fig. 8.1. Louise of Savoy as guardian and educator of her son the future Francis I. *Le compas du Dauphin* (Paris B.N. Fr. 2285, fol. 5r)

The dolphin Francis holds directs attention to his royal status. The unique dynastic bond between mother and son is realized in gesture: Louise inclines her head toward her son as he raises his face towards hers, and she firmly—if not commandingly—grasps his hand (Le Coq 1987: 74-77).[11] That this is a liminal moment for both is emphasized by the compositional arrangement. The scene occurs in a room that serves as a passageway to an adjacent one, and architectural details heighten the sense of transition. A door stands open in the background as Louise and Francis join hands; an inscription attesting to the divine providence that guides mortal affairs extends over the frame of the entire miniature.[12] Moreover, the supporting columns are asymmetrical. To the right are two rounded gold columns, while to the left (adjacent to the open door) is a single rectangular column in black and gold. Whether the visual reference is meant as an architectural trope for Louise's singular role as mother and guardian is uncertain, though in the circumstances it does seem appropriate. The reader recognizes that the two wills of mother and son are, in effect, one; that both enjoy divine protection, and that neither Gié's political ambition nor Louis XII's reluctance to recognize Louise's right to act as guardian could break the bond that unites mother and son. In turn, there emerges from *Le Compas* an implicit recognition of a dynastic component of a royal mother's right to act as guardian that also touches on a queen's right to act as regent.

An impressive legacy of evidence attests to the preeminence of French queens in the thirteenth and fourteenth centuries. Ceremonial privileges,

Fig. 8.2. Blanche of Castile as regent and educator of
her son Louis IX. Bible moralisé (The Pierpont Library,
New York, MS 240, fol. 8r).

legal and fiscal prerogatives, and diplomatic immunities reflected the
exalted nature of the queen's office (A. Lewis 1981: chs. 4, 5). Among the
distaff honors, one directly touched the government of the realm: the right
to act as regent when the king was absent from the realm or if his death
left a minor on the throne. Although the designation of a regency was a
royal prerogative, the queen's importance as a mother assured her a privileged role in guiding the welfare of her children and, on occasion, the gov-

ernment of the realm. When, just before his death in 1226, Louis VIII granted the regency to his queen, Blanche of Castile, he gave little justification; like most of his contemporaries, he recognized that as a royal mother, Blanche was uniquely qualified to protect the interests of her children (Olivier-Martin 1931: 45; Poulet 1989: i, 67).[13] Several depictions of Blanche attest to the dynastic basis of her regental authority. The best known is found in an illuminated Moralized Bible that belonged to her son, Louis IX (Fig. 8.2).[14] The miniature is divided into two tiers: Blanche and Louis are shown seated side by side in the upper, while in the lower, two scribes work on a folio page of a Bible. As they labor, the regent engages in conversation with her son; since he is shown in royal regalia, the implication is that she is advising him on affairs of state. A slightly later image of Blanche as regent is found in a manuscript by Guillaume de Saint-Pathus, where the subject is her obligation to oversee her son's education: under her watchful eye, the tutor Saint-Pathus instructs his royal pupil (Fig. 8.3). Significantly, this image of Blanche was included in the quasi-official history of France, *Les Grandes Chroniques* (Berger 1895: 104-07; Hedeman 1991: 124-26).

Fig. 8.3.
The regent Blanche of Castile directs the education of her son Louis IX. Guillaume de Saint-Pathus, Vie et miracles de Saint Louis (Paris B.N. Fr. 5716, p. 16).

The most striking difference among the depiction of Louise of Savoy and the two of Blanche of Castile is the compositional arrangement of the former, specifically the avoidance of any impediment either architectural (as in the Moralized Bible, Fig. 8.2) or pedagogical (the tutor in Fig. 8.3). As a result, Louise of Savoy's authority as royal guardian is stressed without drawing attention—at least not directly—to the political and dynastic circumstances that initially eclipsed her legal right and maternal duties. Consequently, both the depiction of Louise of Savoy and Francis I and the praise accorded his "crownworthiness" mark an important step in celebrating the dynastic basis of regental authority.[15]

The powers and authorities Blanche of Castile enjoyed as regent reflected the historical development of a hereditary basis of rulership that eventually evolved into a mystique of royalty (Wright 1974: 224-43; Brown 1980: 174-82; Lewis 1981: chs. 4, 5; Brown 1982: 77-110; Scheller 1983: 91-92; Gousset, Avril, Richard 1990; Hedeman 1991). Late-thirteenth- and early-fourteenth-century Capetian kings celebrated the "seminally transmitted nature" of royal authority either to burnish royal policies or, as in the case of the Valois Charles V, to emphasize dynastic greatness (Giesey 1961; Poulet 1989: part ii; Hedemann 1991: ch. 3). While the queen's bio-genetic importance became a recognized component of this late Capetian rulership propaganda, the dynastic ideas of blood ties and lineage that supported a queen's right to act as guardian and regent were difficult to graft upon public laws regulating succession to the Crown.[16] Neither the hereditary basis of rulership nor belief in the quasi-miraculous nature of royal authority encouraged legists or canonists to develop legal arguments to support this type of public authority (Giesey 1961; A. Lewis 1977: 225). The same reluctance is also found in royal legislation. In 1294, for example, Philip IV addressed forthrightly the possibility that his early death might necessitate a regency. In a royal edict, Philip confided the regency to his queen, Jeanne of Navarre, bestowing upon her virtually the same powers that Blanche of Castile enjoyed as regent. Though Philip cultivated notions of blood ties and lineage that emphasized his dynastic greatness as a descendant of Louis IX, he could not develop a corollary to support directly the queen's regental prerogatives; he justified his decision by citing his faith in the superiority of maternal love. As his declaration was compatible with both natural law and French public law, it was repeated by the Valois Charles V and Charles VI (Isambert 1822-33: vi, 716-26; Olivier-Martin 1931: 104; Lightman 1981: 57; Poulet 1989: i, 89).[17]

The political trauma surrounding the Valois succession in 1328, moreover, encouraged significant developments in both the juristic and dynastic basis in public law regulating succession to the Crown; and this, in turn, discouraged celebrating the dynastic basis of a queen's authority. Of central importance was the promulgation of Salic Law, which posited a queen's lack of juridical capacity. Initial interest at the royal court regarding the queen's preeminence was soon eclipsed as the Valois assured their hereditary right to the throne, and celebrations of dynastic greatness rapidly excluded recognition of enatic contributions. Instead, Valois royal historiography, court ceremony, and regental prerogatives reflected limits on a queen's public authority (Erlande-Brandenburg 1968: 7-36; Sherman 1969: chs. 4-5; Jackson 1969: 113, 309-10; Guenée 1978: 465; Muhlack 1982: 153-97; Krynen 1985: 407; Hedeman 1991: chs. 6-7). Rather than celebrating dynastic ideas underpinning contemporary views of queenship, recognition of the queen's bio-genetic importance was tempered through Marian imagery or examples from classical sources: when Christine de Pizan supported Isabeau of Bavaria's regental prerogative, she allegorically compared Isabeau with Orthéa to address political unrest, the dynastic basis of royal succession, and the superior authority of women (Hindman 1986: 89, 130-37; Chance 1990b: chs. 3-4). But while she urged Isabeau to follow Blanche of Castile's example, Pizan was unable to apply dynastic notions of lineage and blood ties found in feudal law codes to support the queen's regental authority.

Between 1505 and 1515, when Francis of Angoulême acceded to the throne, however, writers at the royal court did celebrate the dynastic basis of royal succession in tandem with Louise of Savoy's preeminence as a royal mother. Among the works that specifically emphasized blood ties and lineage is the manuscript *Vers sur la naissance et le bapteme de Francis I*. Though its title and an accompanying miniature depicting the baptism imply the work dates from the late fifteenth century, several references recall events of 1505-06.[18] As with the anonymous *Le Compas du Dauphin*, the author celebrated Louise's bio-genetic importance, and two other works written late in Louis XII's reign drew specific attention to her own exalted lineage and to her role in transmitting to her son the *bon sang*, explicitly identified as that of Louis IX. In these works Louise is hailed as "Mater Regis" and dynast, honors that continued to be celebrated after Francis' accession.[19]

II. MATERNAL DEVOTION AND REGENTAL AUTHORITY

Louis XII was the first and last Valois-Orléans king. In the last months of his life he remarried and temporarily renewed hopes for a male heir, but died sonless on 1 January 1515; Francis of Angoulême was crowned king on 25 January (Godefroy and Godefroy 1649: i, 245-46; Bryant 1986: 111, 157, 163, 166-67, 172, 191, 193, 195). The new queen Claude missed the coronation because of her pregnancy but attended the ceremonial entry pageantry at Paris; Louise of Savoy was in attendance upon her son at both ceremonies, where she took a privileged position (Godefroy and Godefroy 1649: i, 247, 276; Knecht 1982: 16).

Pope Leo X was among the contemporaries who recognized the significance of Louise's status as "Mater regis." Some months after Francis' accession, Leo sent congratulations to the French royal court, praising Louise's piety, devotion and maternal vigilance; he particularly emphasized her diligence in her "labeurs grant [sic]," noting that her accomplishments provided further testimony of God's omnipotence.[20] Papal praise was timely, as Leo was hoping for several reasons to curry French favor: thwarting the Holy Roman Emperor's influence in Italy, continuing negotiations regarding the Pragmatic Sanction, and obtaining French commitment to a Crusade (Le Coq 1987: 261-69). Ultimately it was Francis' desire to validate French claims to Italian territory that prompted him to mount a military expedition within a year of his accession.

As preparations for the expedition drew to a close, the king confided the regency to his mother. In royal letters dated 15 July 1515, he notified the governmental bureaus as well as cities and towns throughout the realm of his intentions (Bourrilly 1910: 16-17).[21] In a brief prologue Francis echoed many sentiments expressed in Pope Leo's bull. First, he noted that his mother was qualified to act as regent by virtue of her wisdom and prudence, and because of the "great and singular love" that she held for his subjects. Next, he placed in her hands full authority to decide issues of government (including domestic and foreign affairs) as well as security of the realm and judicial matters. And he bestowed on her specific obligations regarding the appointment of royal officers and the right to fill vacant benefices, to grant remissions for crimes, and to confirm privileges of government usually enacted during ceremonial entries into cities. These powers were impressive but not sweeping. Francis affirmed that Louise's regental obligations included consultation with governmental bureaus and, particularly, with ranking members of the Parlement of Paris. He allowed for the possibility that exceptional issues could arise in his absence, but took care to limit them by taking with him to Italy the royal seal needed to affirm important legislation. As a result, royal power effectively remained with him and any pressing concerns must await his return, particularly those regarding royal policy and important matters of justice. Finally, a council composed of important members of the royal court and government was constituted to advise the regent whenever necessary.

The most interesting section of the regency letters dealt with Louise's right to exercise privileges symbolic of her son's sovereign authority. The rights to fill vacant benefices and to grant pardons for crimes recalled the king's obligations to his subjects and since at least the thirteenth century were significant hallmarks of a regent's authority as well. But while the Capetian regent Blanche of Castile enjoyed the right to fill benefices, this prerogative ceased (along with other rights such as pardoning criminals) to be accorded a queen-regent in the course of the fourteenth century (Berger 1895: 407; Olivier-Martin 1931: 40; Secousse 1967-68: vii, 226, 230). When Louis XI's daughter Anne of Beaujeu as regent claimed the pardoning privilege, the Parlement of Paris objected, arguing that since this right was symbolic of the king's sovereign authority, she must obtain his written permission. Citing this precedent, the Parlement successfully restricted Francis I's right to award Louise the rights to pardon criminals and appoint to vacant benefices.[22]

The court's objections were not an auspicious beginning for the regency, but once Francis left for Italy whatever acrimony existed between the royal court and the judicature dissipated. As regent, Louise carefully cooperated with the Parlement of Paris, and according to extant records of the *Chambre des comptes* and the *Hôtel de Ville,* routine affairs of government continued without interference from the regent. On the other hand, Louise diligently attended to matters touching her rights to oversee royal policy. For example, in the south of France, she fulfilled ceremonial roles in renewing the appointment of guilds and supervised the fortification of French borders (Brink 1982: 15-25). Louise's cooperativeness afforded no chance for the Parlement of Paris to overturn royal policies or contest negotiations over the Pragmatic Sanction; unable to press the regent, the court eventually notified her that it would resume discussions regarding the sale of offices and other important matters (such as the return to ecclesiastical elections) once the king returned from Italy.

The impressive victories of the French army meant that Louise's tenure as regent was short, but its brevity did not preclude recognition of the dynastic basis of her regental authority. Louise herself cultivated such discussions. For example, ostensibly to honor the victory at Marignano, she commissioned the manuscript *Dominus Illuminatio Mea.*[23] As the title suggests, the work is a rendition of Vulgate *Ps.* 26, "Dominus inluminatio mea et salus mea quam tenebo," adapted to fit events in Francis' and Louise's lives (Orth 1976: 5; Knecht 1982: 44-47, 66; Le Coq 1987: 220-57, 312-13; Crouzet 1991: 423-34). The choice of psalm was well suited to themes found in the manuscripts noted earlier. Emphasis is placed on the special divine grace accorded to French rulers and, by extension, the realm itself, and on the divine providence guiding the French to victory. There is also an appreciation for the comfort the king's private devotions brought him; his piety and diligence secure God's grace, and an illustration underscores the divine providence guarding him by showing him as a mounted warrior amidst a field of fallen soldiers. Louise, too, is honored for her piety: she secures divine favor for the army by praying on the tomb of Francis' ancestors as he rides off to war, and she offers her heart to members of the Three Estates, implying her willingness to extend God's grace to her subjects.

As the narrative of the French victory at Marignano unfolds, a second theme of devotion—that of mother and son—is discussed. Illustrations in the text encourage the reader to consider Louise's maternal duties to her son in the context of his obligations as king. In one illustration she presents a large cross to a kneeling Francis, recalling not only the pressing religious concerns awaiting him, but also her role in teaching him religious doctrine. The intertwined themes of maternal devotion and duty are underscored in two nearly identical illustrations that portray mother and son standing in front of a cross (Figs. 8.4 and 8.5). Both pictures have a compositional arrangement similar to the *Le Compas* miniature. Louise and Francis are shown arm in arm; the cross recalls the divine providence that has protected them. Text and illustrations evoke the pious, contemplative life necessary if Francis is to govern wisely. Like *Le Compas, Dominus Illuminatio Mea* offers a discussion of French kingship that centers on Francis' duties to assure justice to his subjects and protect the realm. He is again encouraged to emulate Biblical predecessors, especially David and Moses. Finally, both works give obedience to parental authority a higher value than is customarily found in didactic literature recognizing a mother's obligations to her children.[24]

Fig. 8.4. Francis I and his mother Louise of Savoy before the cross. Dominus Illuminatio Mea (Paris B.N. Fr. 2088, fol. 3v)

Fig. 8.5. Francis I and Louise of Savoy. Dominus Illuminatio Mea (Paris B.N. Fr. 2088, fol. 4r).

In *Dominus Illuminatio Mea,* it is Moses who guides the reader's thoughts from the private elements of maternal devotion to Louise's public duties as regent. As the reader contemplates the dynastic bond that unites royal mother and son, Francis declares his devotion to his mother. In one illustration he approaches a temple where Moses holds a tablet reading "Honora Matrem"; the accompanying text is such a free translation of a passage of the psalm that his request to spend his days in the Lord's house is nearly indistinguishable from a wish to reside in his mother's house (Orth 1976: i, 5). Throughout the text, a series of devices is used (or omitted) to effect a subtle blurring of filial and maternal authorities. Although each illustration describes Francis as "Filius" or "Rex," they occur in neither thematic nor chronological order. No distinctions are suggested between Louise's obligations as guardian for her son and as regent, between Francis' status as a royal heir and his assumption of sovereign duties, or Louise's maternal duties and her regental ones.

The intertwining of royal and regental prerogatives also surfaced in public ceremonies held to honor Louise. In 1517 Amiens' annual festival in honor of the Virgin Mary celebrated Louise's preeminence as both royal mother and sometime regent, manifesting the Amienois' understanding that the sanctity and permanence of the dynastic bond uniting mother and son supported Louise's regental prerogatives. The registers of the Hôtel de Ville (the civic bureau in each town that organized such festivities) shows how Amiens prepared for the occasion, including the execution of a present for their honored visitor, a beautifully illuminated manuscript compilation of songs, ballads, and festivities in honor of Louise and the Virgin, *Chants royaux en l'honneur de la Sainte Vierge prononcés au Puy d'Amiens* (Orth 1976: i, 34; Scheller 1983: 117-99; Le Coq 1987: 326-36).[25] Several poems in the manuscript compared the two, noting that Louise ruled on earth as the Virgin did in Heaven. One parallel drawn between the royal and Heavenly mothers is especially noteworthy as it remarked the dynastic basis of regental authority, noting that as regent, Louise was "the royal blood as well as the honorary body of the king."[26]

Louise's importance as royal mother and regent was again honored in the festivities in Paris on 10 May 1517, when Francis' wife Claude was anointed and crowned as queen-consort. Several manuscripts ordered to recount these solemnities afford an unusual depiction of regental authority.[27] The last monument of the entry pageant shifted attention from the dynastic importance of the new queen to that of the king's mother (Fig. 8.6). This monument depicted Francis and Louise in the guise of the great Capetian king and queen-regent, Louis IX and Blanche of Castile. The king is shown in majesty, seated under a canopy that bears an inscription based on the *Song of Songs* (1:16): "Lectulus Nostrae Iusticiae floridus est" (Oulmont 1911: ch. 4; Le Coq 1987: 388-91).[28] To the king's left, Justice holds an upright sword; to his right, his mother Blanche gestures as if encouraging him to consider petitions from three of his subjects. This compositional arrangement pointed with succinct clarity to Louise's ability to influence her son's judicial policies, while attesting to her concern for the welfare of his subjects. Finally, for high-ranking members of the royal administration (especially Parlementaires) in the procession, the message affirmed a tenet of royal policy: justice was a sovereign prerogative that Francis and his mother meant to uphold.[29]

Fig. 8.6.
Counselled by Justice and his mother, Blanche of Castile, Louis IX receives his subjects' petitions. Le sacre [et] couronnement... de Claude de France (1517) (Paris B.N. Fr. 14,176, fol. 41r).

There was a dynastic element in the comparison of Louise to Blanche of Castile. As Claude approached the monument, a drama was performed that told of Louis IX's achievements (Le Coq 1987: 377, 388-91).[30] The cast included Louis, Blanche, and allegorical personifications of Justice, the Church, and Nobility, each of whom praised the king for restoring peace to the realm; Blanche appeared in only the first of the play's eight acts, but her presence set the tone for the rest of the play. The comparison between Louise and her predecessor was significant for a number of reasons. First, it witnessed a renewed interest in Blanche's regental achievements; second, comparison of the two emphasized the role each played as the king's mother. Finally, the drama centered on a discussion of how Louis' wisdom guided the administration of justice and royal government, areas in which Blanche exerted much influence.[31] Within the decade, the comparison was to acquire additional constitutional importance when a privileged member of the royal court used it to defend Louise's right as regent to determine royal policy.

The year 1522 was not auspicious for the French. On 27 April, French troops were defeated by the imperial army at La Bicocca; there followed a second setback, the English invasion of Picardy. To reconquer the Italian territories required a large and well-financed army, and to many Frenchmen (including members of the Parlement of Paris) this threatened to render the Crown insolvent. The king recognized that his absence from the realm might encourage opposition to royal policies on ecclesiastical concerns, religious orthodoxy, and current fiscal strategies such as selling offices (including judicial ones) to raise needed revenues (Major 1980: 54-55, 66-69; Knecht 1982: 113-15, 126-29, 147-49). In royal letters dated 12 August 1523, Francis conferred the regency on his mother (Dupuy 1655: 105-06; Isambert 1822-33: xii, 210-26). The prologue contains sentiments found in the letters of 1515, attesting to the singular devotion and love which Louise held for Francis' subjects, but the tenor of this appointment is more precise. First, the king stated his confidence in his mother's ability to govern wisely. Then, noting that she was experienced in directing the affairs of government, he established the parameters of her authority: she was to enjoy full powers and authority in the administration of the realm (including its defense) and the direction of foreign policy. She was also to be an active partner in any concern touching justice, and had the right to hear requests, receive petitions, and to be informed of issues pending in the various offices of government, including the Parlement of Paris. And she was accorded prerogatives that had earlier provoked the Parlement of Paris: the right to fill vacant benefices and pardon criminals.

Although the Parlement did not oppose Francis' wishes, relations between regent and judicature were noticeably more strained in 1523 than in 1515. Routine matters of government proceeded in due course, though some concerns (especially those touching royal policies regarding heresy and other religious matters) proved to be sources of friction. For example, the Parlement refused consent to Louise's appointment of Chancellor Duprat as archbishop of Sens and abbot of St.-Benoît-sur-Loire, and challenged her decision to continue ecclesiastical elections (Shennan 1968: 199-200; Knecht 1982: 180-83). By far the most testing issues of the regency arose with Francis' defeat and capture at Pavia (24 February 1525). The shock of his captivity prompted members of the Paris Parlement (and civic leaders in the provinces) to contest Louise's right to act as regent by promoting an alternate regent, Charles de Bourbon. For Louise's opponents he was the ideal candidate, since as the king's closest male relative he did not suffer prescriptions on temporal authority imposed by French public law. Ultimately, Bourbon's candidacy never seriously challenged Louise's tenure; as a member of her council, he already enjoyed a privileged and active role in government, and declined the chance to displace her (von Ranke 1853: 95-97, 106-07; Jacqueton 1892; Knecht 1982: chs. 11-12).[32]

The attempt to confer the regency on the king's closest male relative emphasized an anomaly in French public law. Salic Law recognized only a queen's lack of juridical capacity, but her authority as regent embraced an impressive panoply of powers and prerogatives that virtually mirrored the king's sovereign authority. This issue was brought to the fore when Louise invited the Parlement of Paris to submit remonstrances on its displeasure with royal and regental policies (Doucet 1921: ch. 2; Shennan 1968: 198-99; Stocker 1973: 191-212; Griffiths 1979: 29-36; Knecht 1982: 179-80). Following her suggestion, the court presented a list of grievances, divided into two parts. The first outlined the court's discontent, and the occasions on which king and regent had allegedly encroached upon its authority. The second argued the court's right to share in the government and administration of the realm: decisions rendered by the Parlement had superior constitutional status to those of the regent because the judicature's authority derived historically from the king's sovereign power to legislate judicial disputes.

Drawing upon arguments voiced by Chancellor Duprat on previous occasions regarding the exalted nature of royal prerogative, Louise offered a pithy rebuttal: her constitutional rights were superior to any rights of court, since her authority was based in part on her regental prerogatives and in part on her status as the king's mother.[33] After establishing that it was not the court's province to restrict royal authority, she argued that her regental prerogatives were inseparable from the king's will and that her rights as a royal mother to hold the regency were to be honored above law and custom. Her final assertion directed attention to the nub of an unresolved issue when she noted that Salic Law's limitations on her temporal authority as a woman did not apply to her regental rights as the king's mother.[34]

Within the year, two manuscripts were presented to the regent that displayed a historical appreciation for the dynastic importance of regental authority. Initially, Louise had commissioned Etienne Le Blanc (her secretary and a *greffier* in the *Chambre des Comptes*) to chart her ancestry. Her request was motivated by political problems that arose with the death of Charles de Bourbon's wife Suzanne in 1521. According to Suzanne's testament, Charles was to inherit her properties and retain them even in the event of his second marriage. Louise, a relative of Suzanne, sought the inheritance for herself; Francis declared that the estate had escheated to the Crown and that he chose to award it to his mother. By the time the king finished preparations for the Italian campaign in 1523, the dispute over the inheritance had escalated in importance because of Charles de Bourbon's defection to the Imperial cause (Knecht 1982: ch. 10; Hanley 1983: 51). By 1525, Le Blanc had finished tracing the fortunes of the house of Bourbon, or at least those that supported Louise's claims, but when news reached the royal court of Francis' captivity, Le Blanc amended the treatise to include the new issues that now preoccupied the regent. The addendum includes an account of St. Louis' Crusade, which resulted in his captivity, the efforts to raise money for his ransom, discussions of Louis' acts of charity and the relics that were brought back from the Holy Land, and the economic stability of the realm during Louis' captivity.[35] On the whole, Le Blanc's *Genealogie de Bourbon et histoire des accroissemens territoriaux de cette famille*[36] is an impressive piece of historiographical research. Le Blanc exploited with care an abundance of archival sources, including registers from Louis IX's reign in his family's possession; he also consulted letters, royal testaments, and existing charters to support Louise's claims to the Bourbon properties.

Despite his propensity for historical research, Le Blanc's account of Blanche of Castile's regency, *Les Gestes de la reine Blanche de Castille*, is based on chronicles (Delisle 1900: 481-83, 491-92; Orth 1976: i, 149-54; Le Coq 1987: 478-91).[37] This work discusses Blanche of Castile's first regency, emphasizing the years 1226 through (approximately) 1230. Since these years were marked by numerous rebellions against royal and regental authority, the narrative centers upon Blanche's prescient policies in assuring her son's welfare against the ambitions of feudal lords (Berger 1895: chs. 2-5; Olivier-Martin 1931: ch. 3; Jordan 1979: ch. 5; Poulet 1989: i, 67).[38] Throughout the work, Le Blanc praises Blanche's piety, virtue, wisdom, devotion, and, most important of her maternal obligations, the diligence with which she taught her son the precepts that would enable him to rule justly.

As the political history of Blanche's regency unfolds, Le Blanc adduces arguments to support the unique dynastic right of a royal mother to act as regent. First, the superior counsel of women mitigates any prescriptions on their legal rights: because of their innate kindness and virtue, women were superior to men. Next, Le Blanc appeals to natural law to uphold the unique dynastic bond between a mother and her children, invoking the sanctity of the blood tie to affirm the special dynastic relationship that entitled a mother to have "the guardianship and government of her children."[39] In the last portion of the narrative Le Blanc discusses Blanche's achievements during her second regency, which witnessed her love for her people, her charity and religious patronage, and her concern for the enforcement of justice.

The accompanying miniature (Fig. 8.7) is more beautifully executed than those found in most of the sixteenth-century manuscripts in Louise of Savoy's possession. The regent is seated under a canopy, steering a *gouvernail* in a fountain of water. Two details direct attention to the devotional bond that unites mother and son: the canopy's inscription attests to Louise's role in teaching Francis piety, while the wings attached to her shoulders echo Vulgate *Ps.* 90:4 ("Scapulis suis obumbrabit tibi, Et sub pennis eius sperabis"), emphasizing her desire to protect her son.[40] Le Blanc reclines at her feet, hands folded and an expression of concern or anxiety on his face; the gesture is that of a supplicant and the inscription "Verbo dic tum et sanabitur" across the top of the miniature affirms the nature of his petition to the regent. The text from which the passage derives (Luke 7: 1-10) recounts the Roman soldier who invited Christ "to say the word and heal the sick." The illustration thus invokes Eucharistic imagery and is the most compelling request presented to a French regent to direct religious affairs.[41]

As a depiction of regental authority, this miniature is exceptional. The depiction of Louise of Savoy in the guise of Blanche of Castile captured with succinct clarity the pivotal roles both regents played during their sons' absences. It does not detract from the singular importance of either royal mother; it directs attention to the prerogatives of rulership associated with the direct administration of the realm.[42]

Fig. 8.7. Blanche (with Louise of Savoy's features) steers the ship of state.
Les Gestes de Blanche de Castille (Paris B.N. MS Fr. 5715, fol. 14v).

III. THE KING'S MOTHER AND SOMETIME REGENT

Louise's second regency formally ended on 17 March 1526 with
Francis' return from captivity,[43] but interest in the juristic and dynastic
elements of regency rights now continued to attract the interest of contemporaries. The conclusion of a regency customarily invited little discussion of either the juridical or dynastic basis of regental authority; once a
king resumed his sovereign obligations, affairs of state became a royal prerogative, conducted —in theory at least—independently of the sometime
regent. If contemporaries assumed that Francis' return signaled the end to
Louise's participation in government, however, the king's policies (especially those pertaining to the Parlement of Paris) rekindled interest in her
regental powers (Shennan 1968: 200-02; Knecht 1982: 199-200). For
example, Louise's influence was clearly evident in Francis' decision to
restrict the court's authority to intervene in royal policies, particularly
those touching religious matters. The king also upheld Louise's right to fill
vacant benefices, in particular her nomination of Duprat as archbishop of
Sens and abbot of Saint-Benoît. To rebuke the court's attempt to perse-
cute Duprat for allegedly overstepping his authority as chancellor, Francis
followed Louise's suggestion, made during her regency, that the
Parlement of Paris send a delegation to debate the issue before the royal
council, whose delegates strongly favored royal authority.

More significant recognition of Louise's authority as a royal mother and
regent unfolded in 1527. In July, the constitutional assembly known as
the *lit de justice* was convened to hear charges of treason against Charles de
Bourbon. Since Bourbon had committed treason in 1523 when he
defected to the Imperial cause, the trial should have commenced prior to
the king's departure on the Italian campaign; but lengthy preparations for
the campaign required postponing the trial until Francis returned. The
delay did not mitigate the constitutional moment underlying the assembly.
According to French public law, a peer's trial (even a posthumous trial)
required the king's presence which, in turn, assured that the ceremonial
display of majesty would be impressive. Although Louise was not directly
involved in the proceedings, she had contributed considerably to
Bourbon's frustration with royal politics by challenging his right to inherit
his wife's properties. The king's intervention on his mother's behalf
accomplished two things: it placed the dispute within the jurisdiction of
the Parlement of Paris and encouraged Bourbon to defect to the emperor.
The proceedings of this *lit de justice* have considerable importance for the
development of French public law, although not because of the issue of
treason. An eloquent speech delivered by Charles Guillart, president of

the Parlement of Paris, precipitated a two-day rupture in the proceedings, during which Francis issued a royal edict restricting the court's right to meddle in affairs of state — a mandate that touched directly on previous policies and included the authorities of both the regent and the chancellor (Knecht 1982: 200-02).

A second assembly, held in December 1527, dealt with an issue of public law regarding the inalienability of the realm. According to the Treaty of Madrid, which effected Francis' return from captivity, the French agreed to cede the duchy of Burgundy and other properties to Emperor Charles V. At the time, the cession seemed the only way to assure the king's speedy return; Louise noted in a memorandum to a privileged member of the court, Philippe Chabot, that of the two choices — cession of Burgundy or the king's continued detention — the former was the lesser threat to the realm (Knecht 1982: 189; Hanley 1983: 72). In reality, neither Francis nor Louise had any intention of ceding the duchy to the emperor. Consequently, by convening the assembly the king sought, and received, consent to contemporary royal policy on a number of issues. Again, the assembly did as much to affirm royal policy as it did to sanction regental authority. Louise's presence at its opening session served as a timely reminder that it was due to her prescience that Francis was free. In turn, the king honored her in two ways: first, he designated Louise as "guardian and regent" for his eldest son the dauphin, a position that for one later jurist rendered her regent for life (Bouchel 1615: iii, 145).[44] Francis' confidence in his mother also embraced foreign policy, for she was largely responsible for renegotiating the Treaty of Madrid, completed in 1529 (Knecht 1982: ch. 14).

The constitutional assemblies held in 1527 provided a public forum that addressed the juridical basis of both royal and regental authority. Neither the king's sovereign powers, nor the prerogatives of rulership that Louise enjoyed as regent, could be prescribed by the court. In this sense, the *lits de justice* dramatized Louise's stance in 1525 when the Parlement of Paris presented remonstrances to her: that her authority was not enjoined in the court's jurisdiction, but was inseparable from the king's sovereign power and just as inscrutable. In a more subtle way, the solemnity of the proceedings sanctioned regental prerogative by honoring her accomplishments in conjunction with discussions of French public law. As a result, the emphasis on regental authority had shifted somewhat from stressing the lack of juridical capacity inherent in regency appointments to acknowledging that the scope of regental authority was considerable, embracing direct governance of the realm and the right to determine foreign policy as well as important matters of state (even the persecution of heresy). Both assemblies pointed as well to the changing nature of rulership whereby power was centered on the person of the prince and, by extension, his mother.

Among the contemporaries who recognized the dynastic basis of regental authority were two jurists, Barthélemy Chasseneuz and Charles Grassaille. Some years after Louise's death in 1531, Chasseneuz published a compendium of royal prerogative, *Catalogus Gloriae Mundi*, which treated the exalted nature of French rulership, including privileges and prerogatives enjoyed by French queens. In 1538 Chasseneuz' former pupil, Grassaille, published *Regalium Franciae Libri Duo*, as thorough an exposition of the glories, authorities, and preeminence accorded to French kings and queens as that of Chasseneuz. Both recognized that French queens were entitled to privileges that reflected the Crown's immortal *dignitas*; mindful that whatever authorities a queen enjoyed reflected French public law, they advanced arguments that ultimately drew attention to the dynastic basis of queenship.

First, both legists investigated the matrimonial bond, the source of a queen's privileges of office. With an impressive mastery of Roman, canon, and feudal law codes, they created analogies between French queens and Roman and Biblical counterparts to establish a juristic basis for the queens' authority (Chasseneuz 1546: 46-49; Grassaille 1538: 258-67).[45] By examining feudal law and adapting arguments of medieval glossators as well as contemporary legists, Chasseneuz and Grassaille recognized that a woman's authority extended both to the administration of fiefs and to the right to act as her children's guardian (Chasseneuz 1546: part 2, 49-69 [esp. 68-69]; Grassaille 1538: 200-02, 253).[46] Such responsibilities, Chasseneuz argued, reflected the moral superiority of women. In a lengthy discussion he listed the legal privileges accorded women, skirting notions of women's biological and moral inferiority found in popular didactic literature by arguing that a lack of temporal authority did not diminish a woman's virtue, honor, or dignity. Noting that women should be praised for their strength, courage, magnanimity, piety, and above all, wisdom, he raised a related issue: a mother's duty to educate her children (Chasseneuz 1546: part 2, 49-62, 64, 67-69).[47]

Grassaille affirmed Chasseneuz' conclusions on women's moral superiority. Although he did not adumbrate the privileges enjoyed by a wife or mother as carefully as did Chasseneuz, he introduced an argument compatible with French public law to support the privileges accorded women in feudal law (Grassaille 1538: 200-02). Neither the right to act as

guardian nor the right to exercise public authority (such as the administration of fiefs) could conflict with Salic Law: citing a gloss of the canonist
Baldus, Grassaille noted that laws regulating succession and inheritance
were grounded in notions of blood ties and lineage, whereas a woman's
responsibilities to her family were divinely sanctioned. Concluding his discussion on women's legal privileges, Grassaille argued that the Salian
Franks proscribed women's inheritance rights without eclipsing their
importance, or the reverence due them, as mothers (Grassaille 1538: 235-37).
The sanctity of maternal devotion provided the trope necessary for both
jurists to develop legal arguments recognizing the dynastic basis of Louise
of Savoy's authority as regent. Chasseneuz and Grassaille noted that by
virtue of her authority as the king's mother, she was entitled to the highest
honors (Chasseneuz 1546: part 3, 124; Grassaille 1538: 247, 263). Both
writers, moreover, argued that because of this preeminence, Louise's
authority could not be diminished by Queen Claude's stature as both a royal
daughter of France and a crowned queen-consort (Grassaille 1538: 263).

The contributions made by a number of remarkable mothers were illustrated from scriptural and classical sources. Two of the former were particularly important. First, Chasseneuz and Grassaille accorded special
reverence to the veneration Christ bestowed upon his mother. By adapting ideas from Aquinas' discussion of kingship and temporal authority, the
Christological basis of rulership now included the king's mother who, by
virtue of the dynastic tie that bound mother and son, was entitled to enjoy
the privileges and ceremonial honors bestowed upon the Virgin
(Chasseneuz 1546: part 1, 2, and part 3, 115-24).[48] A second appeal to
Scripture emphasized Louise's ceremonial preeminence to support her
public authority as the king's mother. Citing Vulgate *Ps.* 44:10 ("Adstetit
est thronis matris iuxta thronum Regis," modified from "Astitit regina a
dextris tuis [Regina adstat ad dexteram tuam]" and *III Reg.* 2:19, "Positus
est thronis matris iuxta thronum Regis"), both Chasseneuz and Grassaille
noted that as the king's mother, Louise enjoyed the privilege of being
seated to his right (Chasseneuz 1546: part 3, 147; Grassaille 1538: 24, 258-
67). The success of this trope of maternal devotion depended on acquain-
tance with feudal and canon law as well as French royal ceremonial, all of
which recognized that ceremonial seating to the right was a sign of honor
and power. In French feudal law, it symbolized the hereditary right of the
eldest son; in French public law, the dauphin was accorded this ceremonial prerogative. Jacques de Cessoles' *Le Jeu de eschez moralisé* (1504)
cited this ceremonial prerogative in his discussion of Anne of Brittany's
authority as queen-consort (Cessoles 1504: fols. 7v, 9v-10r; Chasseneuz

1529: part 3, 147-48).[49] Whether Chasseneuz and Grassaille were aware that medieval queens and regents (such as Blanche of Castile) were accorded this ceremonial privilege is unclear. Regardless of ceremonial antecedents in French history, both jurists addressed notions associated with the dynastic basis of regental authority more forthrightly than their fifteenth-century predecessors.[50]

Several scholars note that legists of late-medieval and early-sixteenth-century France desired, first and foremost, to preserve the old order of the French monarchy by balancing monarchist and constitutionalist ideas (Church 1941: 43-59; Kelley 1970: 159, 185, 189, 195-200, 212; Franklin 1973: 6-22; Skinner 1978: ii, 259-66, 287). Chasseneuz' *Catalogus* and Grassaille's *Regalium* were impressive compilations of systems of legal thought augmented by scriptural and historical precedent, but by their very natures they ultimately proved to be of limited value; neither embodied a theory of rulership that supported directly the growth of royal power since the late fifteenth century. In the mid-sixteenth century a significant change in legal scholarship almost ended the legist tradition; jurists, Charles Du Moulin among the first, modified constitutionalist arguments to support the growth of royal absolutism (Du Moulin 1561). Recognition of the significance of Du Moulin's works has fostered a lack of interest in Chasseneuz' and Grassaille's discussions of Louise of Savoy's preeminence as a royal mother or her authority as regent. But for several reasons, both merit closer scrutiny.

Chasseneuz' and Grassaille's discussions of the legal and ceremonial prerogatives accorded to French queens echo arguments advanced by a number of jurists in the early sixteenth century who defended Anne of Brittany's rights as queen against the alleged transgressions of a royal minister (see note 2). These writings included a number of concerns, one of which drew attention to the dynastic basis of rulership. According to such jurists as Charles Bonnin and François Marc, a queen's lack of temporal authority did not prevent her enjoyment of privileges symbolic of the king's sovereign authority by virtue of her status as his wife, not ceremonial investiture as queen. Consequently, contemporary legal opinion held that a queen's authority was bestowed on her automatically (Chasseneuz 1546: part 2, 58; Grassaille 1538: 263).[51] Both Chasseneuz and Grassaille extended this argument to apply to Louise of Savoy; neither upheld the importance of ceremonial investiture in bestowing regental authority. Both argued that simply by virtue of her stature as the king's mother, Louise of Savoy should be honored as a "queen" (Chasseneuz 1546: part 1, 69; Grassaille 1538: 262-63). They cited—but did not uphold—an argument by the canonist Baldus, who noted that the title could not be awarded a mother who was not a king's wife. The opinions of a later canonist, Bartolus, and the late-fifteenth-century feudists Antonius Corsettus and Panormitanus were cited to support Louise's preeminence as a "royal" mother, citations illustrative of the manner in which Chasseneuz and Grassaille simultaneously preserved legal tradition while noting variation and circumstances of change.   The same strategy is evident in their discussions of the sanctity of maternal devotion. Recalling notions grounded in medieval political theory that paralleled temporal and celestial spheres of rulership, Chasseneuz and Grassaille adapted Marian imagery to support contemporary politics. Framing their discussions of regental authority in the context of Christ's veneration of his mother, both jurists subtly reworked arguments found in late- medieval writers such as Jean Juvenal des Ursins, who addressed a queen's lack of juridical capacity by evoking Marian imagery. Chasseneuz and Grassaille included the analogy to support Louise's right to privileges symbolic of the king's sovereign authority and her right to act as regent (Chasseneuz 1546: part 1, 2; des Ursins 1985: ii, 48-51; compare Jordan 1990: 24-25).

Nor did Chasseneuz and Grassaille introduce arguments to limit Louise's public authority. Both realized that French public law regulating succession to the throne reflected notions of Aristotelian biology; but their discussions of a mother's right to act as guardian, a prerogative grounded in private law, modified notions of biological inferiority so that the right of guardianship pertained automatically to a mother through the unique dynastic bond between mother and child (Grassaille 1538: 235-45, 250-56).[52] Nor did either jurist accept notions of feminine moral depravity introduced in contemporary popular literature and didactic treatises (Jordan 1990: 2-25, 65-100). Rather, both eschewed recognizing personal ambition as a reason to fear a woman's public authority. In this, Chasseneuz and Grassaille set a standard of scholarship often overlooked by biographers of Louise of Savoy and later queens (Larousse 1873: x, 724; Mayer 1966: introduction; Bordeaux 1971; Freeman 1972: 77-98; Brink 1982: 15-25). In marked contrast to later writers, the concern of both jurists was to introduce discussions of queenship within the context of French rulership, so that the accomplishments of women such as Louise of Savoy were not isolated from the history of the French monarchy. And while the legist tradition proved of limited use to the study of absolutist kingship, Chasseneuz and Grassaille did influence those who addressed the dynastic basis of regental authority that emerged in 1560 (Rubin 1977; Mattei 1978; Lightman 1981; Lightman 1986: 299-312 esp. 308-09).

Iowa City, Iowa

CHAPTER 9

The Portrayal of Royal Women in England, Mid-Tenth to Mid-Twelfth Centuries

PAULINE STAFFORD

etween 950 and 1150 a series of royal women played a prominent part in the political life of England. In the 950s Eadgifu, the mother of King Eadred; in the late tenth century Ælfthryth, wife of Edgar and mother of Æthelred II; in the early eleventh century Emma-Ælfgifu, wife successively of Æthelred and Canute and mother of Harthacanute and Edward the Confessor; in the mid-eleventh century Edith, wife and widow of Edward the Confessor and daughter of Earl Godwine; after the conquest, Mathilda, wife of William the Conqueror, Edith-Mathilda, wife of Henry I, and finally, in the generation of the Conqueror's grandchildren, the empress Mathilda, daughter of Henry I, and Mathilda, wife of the empress' rival and cousin, King Stephen. These women are thrown into relief by a series of royal wives and daughters who did not apparently exercise significant political power, women like Ælfgifu, wife of King Edmund and mother of Edgar, Wulfthryth, that same king's second wife, and Edith, the daughter of Wulfthryth and Edgar. Some of these women achieved another form of power and authority through the religious life, some through posthumous sanctity.

The circumstances that brought power and influence to this succession of women were various (Stafford 1981: 3-27; Stafford 1989: 162-79; Davis 1990: chs. 1-2; Chibnall 1986: 54-104). They fulfilled traditional female family roles magnified by the status of royal dynasties and extended by the fraught politics of succession to the throne. Two foreign conquests produced the sort of dynastic uncertainty that drew women into politics. The importance of marriage alliances with foreign rulers or with powerful nobles contributed to the power of some of them; the development of ecclesiastical reform movements close to the court influenced others. All acted within a tradition of queenly power to which their predecessors in England, or to a lesser extent, in Normandy, had contributed. And with most of them, factors of personality and contingency played their part.

This succession of powerful women allows an examination of the representation of female power in a society like that of the early Middle Ages, where family and Christian attitudes were dominant forces shaping women's lives and the discourses of female power. Insofar as these have remained constants through much of the history of women in the Western world, such examination has wider relevance. But they also show that those discourses were not so monolithic as to preclude a favorable view of female power, especially when we consider the individual circumstances and relationships of writers and subjects. Powerful women may even be able to adapt them to their own use.

The most cursory survey of the imagery employed reveals it as predominantly Christian and familial, but also contradictory and ambiguous. Biblical references included Judith, Esther, Susannah, Rachel, Sarah, Martha, Mary, and Leah as well as Eve, Jezebel, and Delilah; good women and bad, active leaders of their people and long-suffering wives, women as seducers of good men but also Eve as mother of all the living. Early Christian martyrs and virgins like Perpetua and Agnes stood beside widows and great benefactresses like Paula and Helen. Virginity continued to carry charismatic power as well as to mean bodily control. Mary was the impossible virgin mother, but also the queen of Heaven. Familial imagery presented mistresses of households accumulating and dispensing their household wealth, ruling their followers, children, and servants, preserving the dignity and standing of their families, yet also being profligate, oppressive, and partial. It had its influential wives and mothers counselling husbands and sons, but also dominating the uxorious. It spoke of beautiful brides of high lineage and of seductive schemers surrounded by predatory relatives; of dignified female matchmakers, mothers, aunts, and grandmothers, who metamorphose into procuresses. Powerful women became images in themselves, dynastic saints—and sinners.[1]

The representation of royal women was affected not only by the palette of images available to describe them, but more deeply by the nature of the politics and structures that provided them with opportunities: family and its roles, and specifically the pattern of political action and comment on it, which is associated with succession dispute; the court and its brand of intensely personal politics; and finally the power and authority of Christian sanctity and its temporal manifestation in the convent and in virginity.

This is not the place to discuss in detail the circumstances that produced and influenced the power of these women. It arose from two sources: the traditional roles of women in the family, and the court politics that were central to personal monarchies.[2] All of these women played parts in political life that fluctuated considerably during different periods of their lives. These fluctuations reflect the stages of family life, perhaps especially the status of widows and dowagers, and the vagaries of the intensely personal world of court politics. The succession to the throne and the problems that produced provided them with some of their most important, but also most transitory, opportunities.

The imagery already reflects that ragged boundary between public and private which characterizes the dynastic politics of the early Middle Ages. This allowed the public roles of women to emerge from their familial ones,[3] but at the same time constrained the public woman with the idealized behavior of the wife, mother, and daughter. That idealization was conceived from a largely male viewpoint. It failed to recognize, let alone resolve, the contradictory expectations of wife and mother in a patriarchal family, or the specific problems of women as stepmothers and second wives in a polygynous society. It suppressed the tensions of familial and dynastic politics behind images of harmony. Family and court were mythologized, idealized, and paralleled as centers of harmony and consensus.[4] Early medieval writers found it difficult to describe or accept the legitimacy of political conflict, even the conflict of interest that we would now take to be central to much of politics. In such family imagery women pass from the apotheosis of wifely counsel and motherly loyalty to the degradation of sexual seduction and self-seeking ambition. Behind many images lurked the deep-seated fears of the seductive, independent, sexually mature woman, the emasculator of effeminate men, the fear of the sexual and procreative power of women within the family, compounded by Christian distaste for sexuality. These constituted important elements of the discourse on female power.

Power itself, or more correctly, authority and power, had its own language which was not entirely gender specific. Women in general and queens in particular enjoyed little of that "magisterial" authority that was considered legitimate, though they derived some accepted authority from the role of mother and mistress of the household. On the other hand, they exercised much power through influence and counsel. These latter, whether exercised by men or women, were fraught and debatable areas throughout the Middle Ages, open to accusations of abuse and of covert use. Women were especially open to accusations of the abuse of sexual power, of secret murder, witchcraft, and scheming.[5] Their activity in the spheres of court and family politics encouraged suspicion, but also encouraged these types of activities.

The role of wife and especially mother in a dynastic political system draws women into the area of succession; indeed, this becomes a major sphere of acceptable political action. Succession politics show repeated patterns. Political struggle both before and after the death of a king centers on the question of who will succeed him. Factions are built up and support canvassed for rival claimants; the outcome is decided in a form of "election," in the sense that the winner will be he (rarely she) who can convince most of the great nobility (and in this society, churchmen) of the rightness and desirability of his succession. Such politics necessarily involve propaganda and character assassination, both because the question of fitness for rule and legitimacy are central and because the forum is the court itself where the politics of the personal produce a hotbed of gossip, intrigue, and suspicion. Issues of birth, and thus of marriage, are frequently aired, especially at a time when reforming ecclesiastical views are focussing attention on the definition of marriage itself. Women, as the wives and mothers of claimants, are natural targets; occasionally, as in the case of the Empress Mathilda, they are targets as claimants in their own right. As protagonists in such politics, women themselves use and manipulate the arguments.

The pictures that we have of both royal men and women from the tenth to the twelfth centuries have been deeply affected by the prominence of succession as a political issue; witness the picture of the godless Harold Harefoot smuggled into his mother's bed in a warming pan, or of the soft and pliable Stephen, too weak to rule. But our picture of male rule and action is not shaped solely by such images; our sources present us with men acting in a variety of situations. Because royal women often come into prominence in the sources only in such disputes, our view of the active political woman may be unduly colored by the passion of succession politics. Yet, since succession and court *are* major areas of female action we must be aware that they dictate their own patterns of activity.

Court and family gave women both legitimate authority and power, opening them to accusations of the illegitimate use of both. Christianity influenced both, but did not simply provide an extra palette of images. It reinforced some of the secular roles with the authority of divine approbation; it added other roles that carried both power and authority even as it stressed a general view of the feminine that was largely derogatory. Thus the informal and dangerous role of influence and counsel was sanctioned as the Christian wife and mother who led her husband or son to conversion, or by the tenth century, to ecclesiastical patronage or reform. The charismatic authority of virginity was never entirely lost, not even in the midst of reform movements that increasingly stressed the priesthood and its sacramentally sanctioned powers. At its fullest, it expressed itself in the abbess or saint. Such authority might be considered inappropriate and unavailable to most women whose secular roles were created by their position as wife and mother, but even so, it could be adapted. The chaste wife or widow could prophesy.[6] At the same time Christianity possessed its own *ad feminam* image to attack royal women who crossed great ecclesiastics: Jezebel, a wife who opposed prophets.[7] It was a major influence on the increasingly sharp and misogynistic definition of gender during this period (Dalarun 1991: 31-54). But ecclesiastical writers are no simple purveyors of celibate anti-feminism. Centuries of interaction with the powerful had extended and refined their imagery.

Christian writers early found ways of portraying the powerful wealthy women of Christian elites in flattering terms. By the fourth century if not before, the wealthy woman, often a queen or empress, was acceptable when she acted as benefactress of churches and churchmen. Such women played a critical role in the advancement of Christianity; an acceptable image of their behavior was essential. But the ambiguities of a religion committed to humility remained. It was preferable that such a woman exercise her generosity with humility. An image of a queen/empress dispensing charity as a handmaiden became common. The image reversed the status conferred by wealth in its dispensation, recognized and upended the role of household. At first, concern centers especially on the *expenditure* of wealth and its manner, paralleling the concern of early medieval elites with generosity, hospitality, and the proper social use of wealth. But already there were worries about the method of *acquisition*. Powerful women were represented counselling their husbands to mercy, calling for the reduction of taxes or imposts.[8] That worry grew increasingly acute as time went on and by the twelfth century in England had become dominant.

By the eleventh and especially the early twelfth century, Christian writers were experiencing doubt about power and wealth, their exercise and possession. In spite of its accommodation with early medieval society the Christian church never entirely lost its critical relationship with wealth and power. The tenth to twelfth centuries saw a series of reform and renewal movements in the Church, including in England (Stafford 1989). Such movements had the potential to widen the critical distance between ecclesiastical commentators and secular society (Mason 1977). In addition, by the late eleventh century in England, many writers were English monks affected by the outcomes of the Norman Conquest.[9] The experience of that conquest as tyranny and the increasing awareness of, if not actual rises in, taxation, sharpened the critique of power in such men and made them especially sensitive to the acquisition and disposal of wealth by the powerful. It also produced a nostalgia in some of them for an English past. Here reaction to power itself and to the immediate past influenced comment on royal women.

These men underline the need to consider short-term political factors and relationships as well as the longer-term evolution of the nature and portrayal of female power. If any group of women are likely to receive a good press from interested ecclesiastics it is the powerful; if any group is likely to suffer the ultimate denigration of their transgression of the accepted female role, it is the same. The relationship of writer and subject, in time and place, as patron and client, can be critical here. Dead women may be treated differently from the living, more readily sanctified or vilified according to the needs and purposes of the writer; a patroness or powerful queen is treated more circumspectly. A powerful woman filled different roles at different stages of her life, and she learned from experience. Pictures of her created at different times should be separated, not just according to author and intention, but into those produced during and after her lifetime, in her youth, middle, and old age. All this seems obvious. But all too often such disparate sources are used and either reconciled into a composite character, or worse, read in isolation and generalized into a series of contradictory assessments in which the same woman is unrecognizable (Chibnall 1988).

It is the purpose of this chapter to examine the portrayal of royal women in this period as a question of importance in its own right, though it is also a necessary preliminary to understanding and assessing their political action. I have defined my chosen authors as the historians of the period, that is, those producing chronicles and/or saints' lives where the saint is part of the immediate past. Thus, I have included Goscelin, who is still drawing on oral memory and writing a form of recent history, but have excluded Ælfric, whose saints' lives are drawn from a remote past. The scope of the chapter has made it impossible to treat all authors individually, but since historical factors are so important in portrayal I have nonetheless eschewed a general comparative approach for a chronological one. I have concentrated on three periods in particular: the late tenth and early eleventh century, the time that saw a renewed interest in history and in saintly biography; the late eleventh century, namely, the generation living with the aftermath of the Norman Conquest; and the early and mid-twelfth century, a date which allows consideration of the twelfth-century English historical renaissance. The interest and importance of William of Malmesbury and Goscelin of St. Bertin have called for individual treatment. Those authors who worked for royal female patrons in the thick of political events, that is, for politically active women defending or executing their own political roles, seem to me to be of such significance that I have singled them out for special consideration.

The period from about 990 to 1020 saw something of a revival of historical writing in England, prompted by the impact of revived monasticism (Gransden 1974; Stafford 1989: 3-23). A detailed vernacular account of Æthelred's reign was made, now surviving in the *Anglo-Saxon Chronicle* (Keynes 1978: 227-53), and a number of saints' lives were written, two of Dunstan, one of Oswald archbishop of York, and two of Æthelwold of Winchester, all three now acknowledged as leaders of the reform movement. A Life of King Edward the Martyr was produced at Shaftesbury, possibly during this period though as we now have it, it may have been reworked at a later period (Fell 1971; Fell 1978: 1-13). In addition, ecclesiastics like Bishop Æthelwold produced short commentaries on recent history; one of the fullest forms an introduction to his translation of the *Regularis concordia* (Whitelock 1979a: no. 238).

These first constructions of tenth-century history do not, on the whole, accord a large place to royal women, in marked contrast to later writing (see below, especially on Ælfthryth, pp. 202, 209, 211-12). The writers concerned were still close in time to recent events and some of the protagonists were still alive. It is no surprise to find that the saints' lives written during the reign of Æthelred II make little or no reference to any involvement of his mother Ælfthryth in the murder of his brother; indeed the author of the earliest Life of Dunstan, known as "B," omits all reference to the succession dispute that brought Æthelred to the throne and in which his mother was involved. The *Anglo-Saxon Chronicle* has its own version of events from 985 to 1016 in which internal treachery figures prominently.

The first picture of Ælfthryth is thus brief. She appears the favored image of ecclesiastical patroness beside her royal husband Edgar. Æthelwold refers briefly to her as entrusted by her husband with the care of nunneries and exhorted by him "to take thought for the nuns . . . following his example" (Whitelock 1979a: no. 238 [at 922]). But he does not accord her the time-honored role of pious royal counsellor. The Life of Oswald records that it was the nobles and chief men staying with the queen who murdered King Edward (Whitelock 1979a: no. 236 [at 915]). But the circumspect authors of this period go no further in commenting on the mother of the reigning king.

There was greater freedom when commenting on the dead, and especially when dealing with the mid-tenth-century succession dispute, the

brief reign of King Eadwig, and the vicissitudes of Dunstan, a man who
was now presented as a spearhead of the reform movement. Three women
had been involved here: Eadgifu, the mother of King adred and grandmother of Eadwig and Eadgar, and Eadwig's noble wife Ælfgifu and her
mother. All three were cast in already defined roles.

Eadgifu is the benefactress of churches and a pious influence on her
sons. It is at her intercession that Eadred offers a bishopric to Dunstan in
the "B" Life of Dunstan; it is she, the venerable queen, who prevents
Æthelwold from leaving the kingdom in Ælfric's Life of Æthelwold, advising her son what a loss Æthelwold would be to the kingdom and persuad-
ing him to give the abbot Abingdon to revive (Whitelock 1979a: no. 235
[at 905]). What is lacking from all accounts of Eadgifu is any consideration of the role she undoubtedly played at court under her sons or in the
succession dispute after 955.

Hagiographical convention had already determined how political
events and actors were presented. The succession dispute in the lives of
Dunstan is not a political conflict with politically interested actors, but a
moral struggle of a saintly bishop to bring to task a foolish, misled young
monarch. The role of a good woman in such a story is to support the saint,
which Eadgifu duly does. In such a morality tale, however, women who
seem in any way to oppose the saint and his interests can expect very different casting.

The most prominent women in the mid-tenth-century story are Ælgifu,
the wife of Eadwig, and her mother. The most memorable representation
of them is in the "B" Life of Dunstan. "A certain woman, foolish, though
she was of noble birth, with her daughter, a girl of ripe age, attached herself to him [Eadwig], pursuing him and wickedly enticing him to intimacy,
obviously in order to join and ally herself or else her daughter to him."
The king disports himself wantonly with them, even quitting his coronation for the caresses of these "loose women," to "wallow between them in
evil fashion, as if in a vile sty." Dunstan reprimands them, incurring the
enmity of the woman who then schemes for Dunstan's exile (Whitelock
1979a: no. 234 [at 901]). The implicit comparison with Jezebel is made
explicit by Adelard, writing his Life of Dunstan a decade or so later: "This
tortuous snake entered the palace of King Eadwig where, through another
Jezebel and through courtiers whose hearts he knew, with serpentine
words he roused the king to eliminate that column of light [Dunstan]"
(Adelard of Bath 1874: 59). Jezebel is here confounded with Eve as an
agent of the diabolical snake.

Here is the sexual seductiveness of woman as an agent of man's
downfall, using her triumph to oppose the forces of righteousness, her

foolishness casually remarked, her power recognized and condemned. The picture is completely stereotyped. The women are not named, their role merely to fulfill the conventional one of enemy to the saint. But however simplified by the conventions of hagiography, this was a family succession struggle involving women in their legitimate concerns. The development of the image illustrates this. A mother's role in the marriages of her children has become that of a procuress, for herself or her daughter, tarred by association with her own mature sexual desire. Such a reshaping of family roles into a critique of female power is even clearer in the treatment of Ælfthryth in the Passion of Edward the Martyr.

It is this work that first openly accuses Ælfthryth of the murder of Edward. The work cannot be dated with any certainty, though such a denigration of Ælfthryth, and thus through her of the claims of her son Æthelred and his descendants, has a logical place in succession arguments early in the reign of Canute. That king was concerned with his title to the English throne and several of his actions show a desire to cast his predecessor Æthelred and Æthelred's descendants in a bad light.[10]

Ælfthryth is cast as the plotting stepmother, a stock character but also a recurrent reality in family politics. The murder is perpetrated by one of her followers. But the image is extended into the evil mother who beats the young Æthelred with a candlestick when he weeps for his dead brother. The queen is later overcome with remorse, but when she attempts to attend the reburial of her stepson the horse refuses to carry her. She is an evil mother, not merely a jealous stepmother. She is punished by a miracle, but one that may refer to the duty of women to tend to the family dead: the author adds that Edward's sister Edith (see pp. 207-09) was present at the funerary rites, fulfilling the proper female role. The nature of the murder, in the course of a struggle over the throne, called forth imagery appropriate to the family role in which Ælfthryth had acted. The fact that the major protagonists were now all dead, and the climate of political comment perhaps openly hostile to them, allowed blame to be attached to Ælfthryth and the imagery to be elaborated appropriately. The reality of her political activity is now recognized, yet the picture of her career, even of this limited aspect of it, is still woefully inadequate.

This first generation of writers and hagiographers paid relatively little attention to women. When they dealt with them at all, it was to cast them in the stereotyped roles that were already conventional in the hagiographical literature on which they drew. These were already being affected by the political arguments surrounding the succession to the throne. Those who wrote history rather than hagiography, like Æthelwold and the author of the *Anglo-Saxon Chronicle*, worked to some extent outside this framework. But the very purposes that inspired them to undertake the unusual task of history-writing precluded any concern for the role of women or comment on it. To an active bishop like Æthelwold, a stress on kings and their own commitment to reform seemed more important. The chronicler had his own view of England's downfall that did not turn on the wiles of women.[11] Significantly, by the time William of Malmesbury wrote in the early twelfth century, the cycle of disaster that he now saw begin-ning would have a female origin.

It seems, however, that we have lost some of the emerging historical consciousness that characterized the turn of the millennium in England. We have lost the importance of dynastic history that seems to have emerged now. It emphasized the West Saxon dynasty and its exploits as warriors, lawgivers and just rulers, and, apparently, as saints (Barlow 1963: 28 [note 2]; Corbet 1986). Women featured among those saints. Ælfgifu, Eadgar's mother, is called a saint in the *Anglo-Saxon Chronicle*. Like her Ottonian contemporary Mathilda, she was a "mother of the dynasty." If there was a Life of her similar to those of Mathilda it has been lost.[12] But her importance may be indicated by an action of her grandson Æthelred. When Æthelred married Emma of Normandy, Emma changed her name to Ælfgifu. Æthelred showed a marked awareness of the history of his family in the naming of all his children.[13] This unique example of an early English queen changing her name at marriage suggests not only this strong dynastic sense but also perhaps the importance in that sense of a saintly female ancestor.

Another lost voice is that of Queen Ælfthryth herself. In view of what we know of succession politics, Ælfthryth would have used arguments from recent history during the dispute over the throne after 975. An echo of her argument or that of her and her son's supporters may still be heard in post-conquest works. Stories were still circulating after the conquest of Edgar's marriages and even of his lasciviousness (Wright 1939: 74). Some of them cast doubt on Edgar's marriages and their legitimacy. The origins of such stories certainly do not lie in the cult of Edgar that grew up in the eleventh century at Glastonbury (Barlow 1963: 28 [note 2]). They may have been fostered, if not created, in the nunneries associated with the women in Edgar's life, where Goscelin had access to them; it is tempting to see them almost as an alternative "woman's view" of Edgar. But it is probable that their origin lies partly in the arguments about marriage and legitimacy in and after 975. Ælfthryth was a third wife to whom the taint of adultery could cling. That taint affected the claim of her son. In the arguments after Edgar's death, Ælfthryth's concern would have been to stress the legitimacy of her marriage and her consecration as queen, and to cast doubt on Edgar's earlier marriages. If we can hear anything of the picture of herself that Ælfthryth stressed it is this: legitimate wife and queen.[14] Like Emma later vilifying the earlier wife of Canute, Ælfthryth would not have provided a favorable picture of the other women in Edgar's life.

In this first stage the vocabulary for describing women and their power thus remained limited. It was heavily influenced by hagiographical conventions casting women in limited and predictable roles. It already utilized images adapted from women's family roles. It probably included non-virginal dynastic saints. A politically active woman utilized a vocabulary of ecclesiastically legitimated consecrated power, but especially those notions of legitimate marriage and procreation on which secular and ecclesiastical society had converged (Duby 1978, 1984).

By the late eleventh century the faltering reemergence of historical writing of the turn of the millennium had blossomed. Vernacular chroniclers were now producing fuller contemporary history; the first substantial rewriting of pre-1066 history may have already begun by the 1090s at Worcester.[15] A burst of activity in the writing of English saints' lives is associated particularly with the pen of Goscelin of St. Bertin. Much of this is "committed" history, produced if not for a particular political purpose, at least in a climate of strong political feelings. Even the saints' lives are a response to the new circumstances after the Norman Conquest. Nor were the chroniclers little more inclined than their predecessors to draw attention to contemporary female activity. The monastic tradition in which they wrote was fatalistic, laconic, increasingly inclined to be judgmental, on occasion even of kings, but still weak in political analysis and detail, especially of the life of the court. The only references to Edith, Edward the Confessor's widow, and to Mathilda, wife of William the Conqueror, are to their deaths and burial, and to Mathilda's consecration as queen. The MS D of the *Anglo-Saxon Chronicle* proves an important exception.

MS D, the northern version of the *Chronicle*, contains extensive references to Margaret of Scotland. In particular the panegyric entered under 1067, but written later, is our first full and complimentary picture of a powerful woman. Margaret is the ideal Christian wife. For her own part she had shunned marriage, desiring to remain a virgin; but God had foreseen the great things he was to accomplish through the fulfillment of her dynastic role. She was to turn her husband and his people from the path of error. She was an influence for religious good, a divine instrument, and her high birth enabled that position; her lineage went back to Edgar son of Eadred[16] and on her mother's side to the Emperor Henry.

Margaret's actual role in Scotland and its history is far more debatable. This picture is one cultivated in Northern English circles where the link between Scotland and the pre-1066 dynasty was important and at the early twelfth-century English court where it was fostered especially by her daughter Edith-Matilda (Baker 1978b: 119-41; Huneycutt 1990: 81-97). In both cases it is an image cultivated as part of the politics of Anglo-Norman succession. She and her descendants carried the claims of the West Saxon dynasty to the throne. She is a dynastic saint, a mother, however reluctant, a fertile wife who was the agent of God's purpose. This is not hagiography shaped by family roles, as we saw in the surviving saints' lives of *ca.* 1000. This is family politics calling for hagiographical expression. If the tenth century did produce a lost Life of Ælfgifu, this is how she might have looked.

Except, perhaps, for the alleged preference for virginity. By 1100, writers seem rather more worried about the royal bed and its activities. Goscelin writing of Ælfgifu remarks that her miracles show "with what piety and fortitude she occupied Edmund's bed" (Wilmart 1938: 59). Goscelin normally portrayed religious women, a more welcome task for a clerical writer of his day uneasy with the fertile dynastic mothers of the early Middle Ages. His Ælfgifu betrays his unease, which may be a symptom of the growing misogyny and anti-sexuality of many of his northern French contemporaries (Dalarun 1991: 31-54). But in other respects Goscelin is still happy in his portrayal of powerful women, a happiness that may be a result of his position as a travelling hagiographer, his nostalgia for the English past, and his ability to marry their power to virginity.

Goscelin is the most important writer on women in eleventh-century England. A Flemish monk, working in England before the Norman Conquest, he became the major chronicler of the English saints in the decades after that conquest. Among those saints were several women, and particularly two royal women of the recent past: Edith, daughter of King Edgar and a nun at Wilton, and her mother, Edgar's second and discarded wife Wulfthryth, who was abbess there. In assessing Goscelin's picture of these royal women it is important to note his general sympathy with women.[17] Goscelin wrote of powerful women, powerful not merely in virtue of their virginity but also of their wealth and dynastic position. There is little of that anxiety about wealth and power that would so trouble William of Malmesbury a generation later. This may be the contrast between a blinkered hagiographer and one of the greatest historians of the twelfth century, a contrast of date and tradition, or a result of Goscelin's uncomplicated nostalgia for a pre-1066 past that had become more problematic by William's day. But Goscelin's creative use of his imagery suggests that it is more than these. Goscelin sympathized with the women whom he pictured and produced a language in which to describe them.

Not all the words are new, though they can be combined in novel ways. Edith is distinguished by birth and ancestry, but her female ancestors are singled out, especially her grandmother Ælfgifu. Edith and her mother are Paula and Eustochium, that Christian mother and daughter whose religious life Jerome made a type of female piety; but they are also Christian Amazons. Wulfthryth is another Helen, an active holy woman, even after becoming abbess of Wilton. Like Helen, she secures a relic of Christ's passion, and Goscelin likens the silver with which she acquires it to the ointment with which the woman anointed Christ's feet; Christ is served with silver as with that precious ointment that had so embarrassed the disciples (Wilmart 1938: 53-54, 59, 73-75).

His creation of such an image shows Goscelin already aware of those critiques of wealth that would trouble William of Malmesbury. Indeed, elsewhere he uses such discomfort to explain royal patronage of the Church, as when Canute and Emma were moved by the contrast between the poverty of the church of Sherborne and themselves "weighed down by gold and jewelled ornaments" (Talbot 1959: 81). For Goscelin, the gold can still be used, sanctified by its purpose. Women of high status can still exercise traditional patronage. Ecclesiastical expenditure would of course continue to sanctify wealth in the twelfth century and later, though Malmesbury would never use such vivid imagery to justify the women who undertook it.

It is when he comes to describe power itself that Goscelin is most original and, if such a term can be applied to the eleventh century, most "feminist." Edith was the sister of a martyr, sister of Edward briefly king in the 970s. Dynasties liked a little holiness in the blood. But Goscelin claims that during the troubles of the 970s the throne itself was offered to Edith. The great men wanted to make her ruler, preferring a mature woman to an ignorant infant. They even offered their daughters to be consecrated nuns in exchange for her. Like Christ, Edith refuses a kingdom. The question is not of Goscelin's historical accuracy—his is an unlikely interpretation of the 970s—but of his ability to think female rule was acceptable. He confronts the question squarely, and uses the unusual argument that many nations have been ruled by women (Wilmart 1938: 82-83, 84). In the Europe of the late tenth century this was indeed the case: it was an age of female regency, and in Ottonian Germany just such a religious royal woman, Mathilda of Quedlinburg, would rule for her nephew. Rarely, however, is the question of female rule faced and justified as openly as by Goscelin.

Goscelin's pictures of female saints mix existing traditions and images with nostalgia and sympathy in the bowl of patronage. Take out the sympathy and add a good measure of Canterbury partisanship and we have his contemporary Osbern further vilifying those Jezebels who had confronted Dunstan (Stubbs 1874: 100-02). Ingredients mattered. When Goscelin varied his recipe by substituting critical memories of an exploitative Ælfthryth for adulatory ones of Edith, a different dish emerged (Esposito 1913: 10-26). Goscelin was a travelling cook who worked with what he had, as well as a proponent of nouvelle cuisine. The ingredients for Ælfthryth were such as to be readily remixable by twelfth-century writers no longer restrained by her dynastic power. For some she became simply a type of the evil feminine; at Ely, a witch opposing Christian virtue with evil power associated already with sexual excess (Blake 1962: 127-28). For Gaimar she took on a new guise as the seductive, romantic heroine setting out to woo Edgar with her charms (Geffrei Gaimar 1888-89: lines 3975-4075 [at i, 168-72]). Historical distance freed the chef's hand for some creative cooking. Ælfthryth's declining reputation shows a need to be aware of the relationship in time and purpose of the writer to his/her subject. As the woman and her power ceased to be a living reality comment might be more open, but it could also become more stereotyped. Gaimar and the author of the Book of Ely were no longer engaging with a real woman but with a convenient vessel into which to pour those feminine vices required by their story. The emphasis on sexual power, seduction, and witchcraft results from that dehistoricizing process as much as from the developing misogyny of the twelfth century.

Misogyny, or at least a greater attention to the construction of gender, is an increasingly marked feature of twelfth-century writing. It accompanies an increasing awareness of racial characteristics, demarcations of orthodoxy and heterodoxy, and attention to role definition. All this has been explained as a reaction to the proliferating opportunities which the twelfth century provided, as an extension of the Gregorian reform, in general as a drawing and sharpening of social boundaries and the mechanisms of social control (Boswell 1980; Bynum 1982). In England it coincides with a proliferation of historical writing itself, so that the novelty of these attitudes, as opposed to their importance, is unclear. But a century that began with bishops inveighing against effeminate fashions (Orderic Vitalis 1969-80:

vi, 66-68) and in which an English king publicly sheared the long hair of his followers was one likely to prove more sensitive to the differentiation of male and female (Hughes 1991: 147-69). Gender definition that stressed the public, military man appeared to preclude female activity. The increased professionalization of church and state sharpened the public-private distinction which the dynastic kingdoms of the early Middle Ages had blurred. Authority was increasingly located exclusively in the public sphere, though since the dynastic nature of politics remained, power could still be found within the family. As authority became less personal and charismatic so the exercise of power came under more scrutiny. In England, this scrutiny was furthered by the experience of conquest and thus of power and rule as alien and exploitative. The formal role of the queen and her household grew, in England particularly, around the turn of the twelfth century with the need for regency. This caught up royal women even further in the critique of all power, but reinforced that very influence over counsel and patronage which had always softened clerical attitudes toward them. There was no simple unilineal development. If the twelfth century sees a definition of the male as "tough" to the female as "tender," it simultaneously bred a rival definition of the "feminized" chivalric hero and continued to be recorded and deeply influenced by a clerical culture that could never completely embrace such a gender demarcation.[18] When we add to this the influence of individual factors affecting historical writers and their work, it will come as no surprise to find that the representation of powerful women becomes more, not less, complex in the early twelfth century.

William of Malmesbury was certainly affected by common misogynistic stereotypes. He remarks casually that the rule of silence Robert of Arbrissel imposed on his nuns was desirable because "when it is broken, women are prone to vain talk" (William of Malmesbury 1887-89: ii, ch. 440 [at 512]). Such attitudes are sharpest when male writers indulge in generalization. Speaking of individual women William is more thoughtful, though even here misogyny shows through. Ælfthryth, wife of Edgar, is condemned as the murderess of her stepson, scarcely an anti-female remark given the verdict of Malmesbury's sources, but his presentation of the story shows increasing gender-consciousness. Ælfthryth allures Edward with "female blandishments" and her crime, the violence of a woman, the "sin of an abandoned mother," becomes the cause of that cycle of punishment of the English who now groaned under the yoke of barbarian servitude (William of Malmesbury 1887-89: i, ch. 162 [at 183-84]). She did penance, "clothing her pampered body in hair cloth."

William's picture of Ælfthryth was contradictory, a fact he openly acknowledges. She is praised as Edgar's faithful wife, but condemned as her stepson's murderess. Unlike some modern historians, William does not feel it is necessary to reconcile the contradictions. He faced the same opposing pictures with Emma. He writes, "Edward's mother Emma had for a long time mocked at the very needy state of her son, nor ever assisted him; she transferred her hereditary hatred of the father to the child, for she had loved Canute more when living and more commended him when dead; besides accumulating money by every method she had hoarded it, regardless of the poor, to whom she would give nothing for fear of diminishing her heap"; ". . . and yet, though much credit is to be attached to those who relate these circumstances, I find her to have been a religiously-disposed woman and to have expended her property on ornaments for the church of Winchester and probably upon others" (William of Malmesbury 1887-89: i, ch. 196 [at 237-38]). Edith, wife of Edward the Confessor, was a woman "whose breast was the school of every liberal art, though skilled little in earthly matters; when you saw her if her learning amazed you, you must languish at the purity of her mind and at her beauty." Yet he found that in her husband's time and after, she was suspected of adultery, a charge from which she had finally to clear herself on her deathbed (William of Malmesbury 1887-89: i, ch. 197 [at 239]). Most of this imagery is now familiar, as are the sources of its contradictions, those rival portrayals of great benefactresses, dynastic saints, and the character assassinations of succession politics which William had read. His unease about wealth is a more recent complication.

William accepts the powerful women in the story he is telling and the connection between their power and wealth. Ælfgifu, mother of Edgar, dresses in rich clothing, but such wealth is a means to liberality. But William is aware that liberality can be prodigality, recognizes the problems of patronage, and criticizes the means of gaining wealth. William is ready to criticize power itself, in men and women. William Rufus is condemned for his acquisitiveness; Robert of Normandy exhibits a weakness defined as a desire to be nice to everyone, which results in profligacy. Malmesbury's pictures of the powerful women whom he himself knew must be read against this background.

William commented on a living powerful woman, the Empress Mathilda, and for him she was a virago (William of Malmesbury 1955: 24). This is the first English example I have found of a term that shows the difficulty in describing an active female except as a pseudo-male. This may relate to the fact that William is one of the first male authors whose sympathetic comment on a living powerful woman has survived; it is also a sign of sharper gender-definition. Mathilda was a woman always inclined to good, a daughter, granddaughter, and niece of kings whose mother's ancestry went back to Egbert through fourteen kings (William of Malmesbury 1955: 3, 43). High lineage was an established way of complimenting a woman in the dynastic politics of succession in which Mathilda was involved.

There is another image of Mathilda in the pages of William's contemporary, the anonymous author of the *Gesta Stephani*. His Mathilda is arrogant, proud, arbitrary, threatening; her look is "grim . . . her forehead wrinkled into a frown, every trace of a woman's gentleness removed from her face, blazing into unbearable fury," yet she can use all a woman's waxing allurements and endearments (Potter 1955: 122, 178). She exhibits both the abuses of power in general and the abuses of power particularly expected from a woman; she is both unfeminine in the expected graces of woman, and utterly female in the weaknesses possessed by a woman. She is haughty, overbearing, with an imperious voice and harsh and insulting language. Her followers are effeminate men whose chief aim is "wanton delight rather than resolution of mind" (Potter 1955: 116).

William and the author of the *Gesta Stephani* were on opposite sides during the twelfth-century civil war between Stephen and Mathilda. They were on opposite sides in a succession dispute that involved Mathilda as a major protagonist. Both writers make it clear to what extent we should always bear in mind the simple criteria of historical source criticism. Malmesbury wrote to some extent as a partisan of the empress,[19] the author of the *Gesta Stephani* as an enemy. Both wrote during the lifetime of their subjects, indeed, in the thick of civil conflict whose outcome was as yet uncertain. Both described Mathilda at a difficult and relatively early stage of her career. We would not expect the same reactions to Mathilda as we might get from writers remote in time and space, uncommitted, writing when victory for one side or the other was assured. We would not expect the same sort of assessments as we might get from those who wished to gain her patronage in the less fraught circumstances of her early life in Germany or of her later position as countess of Anjou and duchess of Normandy (Schnith 1976: 135-57; Chibnall 1988). All this warns that neither is a full picture of Mathilda, nor can they simply be tacked together to produce one.

William deployed the largely traditional language of favorable succession argument, arguably tinged with the new misogyny. The *Gesta Stephani* retaliated with traditional character assassination, though now cast in more misogynistic terms. Mathilda's haughtiness may be no more than an inversion of the traditional dignity of earlier queens, a virtue become a vice, just as the matchmaker became the procuress. But his effeminate men and verbally abusive women are not familiar from the immediately preceding centuries (though these have been seen to be very restricted in their comment on powerful women), and may point to a sharper definition of gender and an association of women and speech that will be familiar to later historians.[20] But it is also important that Mathilda was the first woman to claim the throne in her own right and not merely to act for a son. Accusations of immorality and promiscuity are less relevant in arguments against her: she must be attacked for her exercise of power itself. It may be this novel situation as much as twelfth-century misogyny that calls forth a new style of abuse.

In contrast with his picture of the living Mathilda, Malmesbury's portrait of her mother, Edith-Mathilda, the wife of Henry I, is nuanced and sophisticated. Edith-Mathilda was the woman to whom his work was dedicated, though she was dead by the time he reached Book V and wrote an assessment that is also an obituary (William of Malmesbury 1887-89: ii, ch. 418 [at 493-95]). He begins with those virtues that traditionally distinguished a royal wife and mother in a Christian society; she was of high birth, beautiful but chaste, satisfied with only two children. She was not wanting in royal magnificence, but beneath her royal habit was clad in hair cloth. Thus far she might be one of Goscelin's queens, recognizably a dynastic saint in the mold of the Ottonian Mathilda, portrayed by a grateful client. But times have moved on, and back. She visited churches barefoot in Lent, washed the feet of the diseased, handled ulcers dripping with corruption, pressed the hands of the sick to her lips. Such extravagant role reversal recalls the lives of the Merovingian queens Radegund and Balthild, which drew on ascetic ideals of earlier Christianity. Extravagant asceticism had proved inappropriate to the dynastic women of the early Middle Ages and disappears from their lives between the eighth and eleventh centuries. Its reemergence in the twelfth is part of a general restressing of asceticism, especially for women. Mathilda loved to hear divine service, as had so many of her predecessors, but unlike most of them she is singled out for being prodigal to clergy with good voices. And this prodigality prompts William to embark on a critique of her expenditure. She attracted scholars, versifiers, and singers to her court, she was lavish with foreigners and rewarded them too much. She fell into the error of prodigal givers, bringing claims on her tenants, taking away their property, thinking little of them as she took the credit as a liberal benefactress.

The real culprits, Malmesbury hastens to add, were her servants, but she cannot be wholly absolved. She was too influenced by them. Yet, he ends, she was in other ways holy, her death was a great loss, and her spirit manifested "by no trivial indications" that she was a resident in Heaven. The tone of the client writing the pious obituary finally triumphs.

Malmesbury's picture of Mathilda is influenced by his criticism of all the Norman kings for their acquisitiveness. It is influenced by his obvious feeling that 1066 had produced an influx of foreigners who took the places and patronage that should have gone to the native English. It is probably influenced by such practical developments as the growth of the queen's court and household between the tenth and twelfth centuries.[21] But for whatever reason, he has produced not necessarily a more rounded picture of Mathilda, but certainly a more rounded picture of the nature and exercise of power by a medieval queen.

The twelfth century had begun to produce a language of politics, a way of talking about the problems of power. The early Middle Ages had in many respects lacked such a language. It presented rulers in black-and-white stereotypes, political action as treachery or loyalty. Opposites and contradictions were recognized. The queen in her household dispensing hospitality was the antithesis of the monstrous mother of Grendel, a *femme sole* defending her hall as a woman alone (Chance 1990a: 248-61). But writers still lacked a conceptual framework to recognize those contradictions in particular situations, in the very exercise of power itself, in conflicting or changing motivations of individuals. Malmesbury's picture of a queen who is good and bad, his recognition of the problem of wealth, its acquisition and distribution, is not self-evident. It is a new and significant attempt to speak about a queen's power in the royal court, a shift toward a language of politics that will allow the chroniclers of the twelfth and later centuries to draw a fuller picture than their predecessors could ever attempt. The familiarity of such language in later sources must not mislead us into failing to recognize the importance of its first appearance. William is in this, as in so many ways, a founder of English historical writing. But the first signs of that groping toward a new way of talking about politics are found in England not in William of Malmesbury, but in two eleventh-century works, the *Encomium Emmae Reginae* and the *Vita Ædwardi Regis qui apud Westmonasterium requiescit*. It is no accident that both works were produced for and in close collaboration with two of the active political women of that century.

Between 950 and 1150 three royal women close to the center of power commissioned historical works. In 1041 the *Encomium Emmae* was produced for Emma, widow of Æthelred the Unready and Canute; mother of Harthacanute, the reigning king; and of Edward, the future Confessor, Harthacanute's half-brother and the man designated in that year as regent or future ruler (Campbell 1949; Stafford 1989). In 1066-67, during the process of the Norman Conquest, the *Vita Ædwardi Regis* was written for Edith, that same Confessor's widow (Barlow 1962). At some less determinate date early in the twelfth century a Life of Queen Margaret of Scotland was composed for Margaret's daughter Edith-Matilda, by that time wife of Henry I (Pinkerton 1889; Huneycutt 1990). The first two in particular were commissioned by women in the thick of political events in which their political survival was at stake; both are designed to promote that survival. The third has no such dramatic context. All three are concerned to some extent with the question of succession, an issue which we have seen was of central significance in drawing women into politics and in affecting the image drawn of them that survives. The *Encomium* is concerned to justify and bolster a family trinity of power in which mother and two sons rule together. The *Vita Ædwardi* aims to secure Edith's future in a succession crisis whose outcome is still not clear. By contrast the Life of Margaret is a less urgent work, in some respects a Mirror of Princesses for a ruling queen, in others a dynastic work securing the line of succession for a daughter's children by stressing the lineage and virtues of her mother.

The Life of Margaret is the only work for which it is easy to find parallels in England or on the Continent. It recalls the Lives of Mathilda, the Ottonian queen, produced for her male descendants to bolster respective claims to the throne. It is the production of a dynastic saint, of relevance to her offspring. It recalls the cult of Ælfgifu in the late tenth century. Margaret becomes the pious queen, a fitting mother and grandmother of ruling children. More than the Ottonian Mathilda, however, she is a pious queen in her household, a role model for her daughter Edith-Matilda (Huneycutt 1990) as well as a conduit of virtue and blood to her descendants. William of Malmesbury was conscious of the problems and contradictions of exercising power through the royal household; Edith-Matilda herself felt the need for a model in her situation as queen-in-the-household. Given the purposes of the work, it is not surprising that it provides a classic restatement of the acceptable face of female power that had evolved in the early Middle Ages: wife, mother, household manager, patroness of churchmen, active within the limits that such statuses defined. Margaret's image has its own ancestry, which stretches back to Helen; as so often, it is an image manipulated and drawn for the benefit of others. It is not a biography of a powerful woman and her problems, but its production for such a woman and its presentation of another shows the continued existence and acceptance of such a sphere of female power even as it hints at its increasing problems.

The *Encomium* and the *Vita Ædwardi* are different. As early examples of secular biography they have few parallels in England or among its immediate neighbors.[22] It is in their direct engagement with contemporary politics and efforts to describe and discuss them that their great novelty lies. Is it accidental that such new ground is broken by two works produced for royal women faced with the peculiar insecurity of female political actors? Since this chapter is concerned with the portrayal of women these questions are not central to it; yet in their content, in their motivation, and even in their silences these texts portray the actions and situation of powerful women more graphically than most of the detailed descriptions with which I have so far been concerned. Although commissioned by women, neither work places a woman center stage. Edith is a peripheral character in a story dominated by her father, husband, and brothers.[23] Emma's actions are discussed more directly in the *Encomium*, but well over half the work is concerned with the accession and rule of her second husband Canute. This is no accident. For both women their own survival depended on the claims that derived from the male members of their families. The legitimacy of male power, whether as saintly rulers, conquering kings, or chief royal advisers, affected the chances of their womenfolk. The precariousness and dependence of female power is graphically illustrated.

In the first book of the *Encomium*, Emma is described in one of the most traditional of female images as a woman whose marriage binds peace, whose birth and connections are the key to her choice. To justify Emma's position the author resorts to the most uncontroversial of female roles. Throughout Book I, the author maintains his stated intention to praise Emma through praise of her family, in particular her husband, Canute. This is more than an affirmation of the basis of her power in his. In the succession dispute after his death she had to make difficult choices among sons of two royal fathers. To justify her support for Harthacanute, her son by the conqueror Canute, that conquest had to be legitimized. So too did her failure to support or secure a division of the kingdom between her sons. The undesirability of division is a recurring theme in the story of the takeover; the contents of Book I are Emma's arguments.

It is in the second book, as Emma plunges into the turmoil of the succession dispute itself, that she emerges as a central figure. The complex marriage practices of the early Middle Ages presented Emma with a rival wife after 1035. She shows herself ready to utilize the arsenal of anti-female imagery in her own struggle. She accuses her rival wife of being a concubine whose son is not really the son of Canute. Dynastic politics may create opportunities for women but they provide little space for sisterhood. She presents herself as the faithful mother who worked for the good of all her sons. But the imagery that had described the ideal household of early medieval dynastic politics was ill suited to the real situation of an Emma. Faithful mothers should not find themselves with children by two husbands. The faithful mother is an image beloved of male writers, lovingly developed for the Virgin Mary (Dalarun 1991). Its ideological nature is betrayed by the contradictions that emerge when it is applied to the actual situation of many women in a society whose use of marriage for dynastic and political ends produced serial monogamy if not polygamy. The image was a particular problem for Emma since the struggle that followed 1035 resulted in the murder of one of her sons and the choice of another in preference to his brothers. Emma felt herself accused by the image, whether openly or implicitly. She answers those accusations, and in doing so she relates the details of discussions and events. She describes herself negotiating with her sons in a way we see few early queens doing. Her difficulty in talking her way out of an ideological contradiction inscribed in the imagery of her own society takes us closer to a discussion of politics than any other eleventh-century English source. But she never denies or repudiates the image itself. She justifies herself within it. A woman trapped by a patriarchal ideology and its imagery? But also a woman exploiting it. It is only as the faithful mother that she can now claim her position alongside both sons in power. To repudiate the image would be not merely to justify herself by showing the impossibility of her situation in 1036, but to lose the claim to power in 1041.

Emma is rarely described; she is portrayed through her actions, and it is an active woman who is presented in the *Encomium.* When we do see her it is as a proud and generous queen. In her exile in Flanders she receives aid from Count Baldwin, but she lives off her own income and provides for her alms and patronage. The emphasis is the recurrent one on the dignity of royal power, expressed in the ability to give. It is also on the good queen's ability to manage her own household. That management does not mean, as in the ninth-century pictures of the Empress Judith, her ability to manage its personal and sexual relations,[24] but her ability to manage its finances. Is this a response to a growing eleventh-century emphasis on wealth and its management, to Emma's awareness of the developing critique of royal and queenly power that William of Malmesbury would later articulate so clearly? Or is it the difference between a queen's own defense of herself on ground of her own choosing, as opposed to the more normal reply to an attack by enemies not only on herself as a royal woman but also on her son?

Even more than Emma, Edith is presented almost entirely in relation to men, as daughter, sister, and wife/daughter. The latter is a particularly interesting image. The established idea of the chaste wife is adapted to suit the circumstances of a barren marriage. A saintly husband needs such a wife; Edith was constructing her husband's claim to sanctity, and thus her own claim to survival, on his chastity. Edith's humility is not the more traditional humility of the handmaiden who serves the poor; that image was inappropriate for a still-living woman who aspired to retain her position. It is the humility of the daughter who sits at her husband/father's feet, but whom he is careful to raise to a throne beside him. Here is no role reversal, but a confounding of two familial roles which avoid any abdication of power. Her humility is that of the patroness who does not aspire beyond the attainable. Her building work at Wilton emulates that of the king, but is completed before it. By implication he has sought fame through overambitious projects, while she has humbly confined herself to the possible. There are interesting fore-echoes of William of Malmesbury's strictures on those who seek fame through patronage, if not of his awareness of the human costs of all such action.[25]

Edith is not center stage, but she is the counsellor who is ever present when things go well. Her exile in the 1051 crisis is more insupportable than that of Godwine her father himself (Barlow 1962: 23). But in the end she is confounded precisely because of her secondary situation. She weeps when the husband and brothers whose concord has been a source of her power are divided. Her tears are not merely for herself, but also for the realm. That realm and Edith are inextricably bound together. She is a gem on the kingdom's breast, she foresees its future, she and it are handed by the dying Edward to Harold for safekeeping (Barlow 1962: 15, 54, 79). Is Edith claiming an identity beyond the overt ones of wife and daughter, an identification with the political fate of England, the ultimate argument for political survival?

I have ended with three women using, manipulating, and reshaping the imagery of powerful women. How far that was a personal reshaping in any of these cases must, of course, be debatable. All three works were written by clerics for patronesses. Edith and especially Emma must have worked closely with their writers to have provided the sort of detail that is given; but in both cases we have the voice of a woman mediated through the clerical, dynastic, and male culture of the early Middle Ages. That culture recognized and produced an imagery to describe powerful women that was by no means entirely pejorative. It was arguably shifting in a more misogynistic direction by the late eleventh century, though this often appears less important than the specific circumstances of writers still working with an old-established palette of colors. It is often at its most stereotyped when describing dead women. The harshest criticism and the most fulsome adulation are often reserved for such women; living patronesses are treated with respect. The imagery did not encourage or facilitate the description of the politically active woman. To some extent this is not a gender-specific problem; early medieval writers found "politics," as we might understand the word, "unthinkable." The eleventh-century women I have discussed in fact extended the political vocabulary of contemporary writing because of the peculiar demands and needs that they, as politically active women, imposed.

Throughout the period women were seen constantly in the midst of, and as a result of, succession politics. The resulting picture of female political action is thus in many ways partial. Such action, however, is more central to dynastic politics than to other systems, and its personal familial nature creates opportunities denied to women in other systems. Women's activity at court, as advisers, patronesses, and centers of faction is poorly represented in the imagery, which rarely goes beyond the most general and long-standing of stereotypes. But their management of the household and its finances was becoming an issue by the twelfth if not by the eleventh century. This allows us to see more of the activity of a queen, albeit usually only through criticism. The criticism is in some ways gender specific; queens were more likely to be attacked through their management of the household, kings for their general taxation. But the two converge in a generally greater critique of power and wealth, in a shift from criticism of the powerful for not giving, to an awareness of the cost of giving. Attitudes remained ambiguous here. The late eleventh century did not witness a sea-change so much as an uneasy recognition of contradictions. Goscelin could still find acceptable defenses of the wealth from which powerful women at this date derived their status.

One conclusion of this discussion must be the constraints that the imagery of power imposed on women. Emma held to a maternal image that was inappropriate to her situation, and even if her tenacity is to be seen as proof that that image had something to offer her, it suggests that she was caught in its contradictions. But Emma reminds us that another conclusion is called for. The imagery was sufficiently extensive and flexible to be used by, or on behalf of, powerful women. Goscelin could argue for female rule itself. Edith, the humble daughter/wife, turned humility into a virtue of power and identified her survival with that of the English. Here is no Angel of the Hearth.

This leaves me with an open question. Tenth-century Ottonian kings certainly, and West Saxon kings possibly, used the picture of their female ancestors. Is it going too far to suggest that Emma and Edith used the portrayal of the men of their families to their own ends? To consideration of the portrayal of royal women by royal women should we not add the portrayal of royal men by royal women? And in so doing should we recognize the active role such women were playing, and rescue them from a too-condescending picture as eternal victims? How completely were they trapped within an ideology fraught with contradictions and counter-images? Should we not be wary of reducing an Emma or an Edith by denying that they were themselves able to manipulate images, and, within limits, successfully?

The Polytechnic, Huddersfield

CHAPTER 10

Reigning Queens in Medieval Europe: When, Where, and Why

ARMIN WOLF

Europe still has seven monarchies. Today four of them have kings and three have reigning queens: the Netherlands, Denmark, and the United Kingdom of Great Britain and Northern Ireland. But what of reigning queens in medieval Europe? Reigning queens are distinct from queens-consort, whose rights as the wife of a king are based on marriage while the rights of a reigning queen depend upon birth. Here I shall not consider consorts, no matter how much de facto influence they might have had; I also exclude queens who governed a kingdom temporarily as regents for their minor sons or absent husbands. Such cases happened fairly often and are examples of effective government by women. These regents would be a very good topic for another study,[1] but this chapter is restricted to queens who reigned in their own right, although I shall include cases of failed claims to queenship. Such failures will help to answer the question with which my chapter begins: Reigning queens: when, where, and why?

Let me first draw up a table of such queens in medieval Europe (see table on page 170, in which the names in brackets are those of failed claimants). Between 1100 and 1600, we count altogether 20 reigning queens. If we add the sixteenth century to the Middle Ages, we can make the following observations.

Apart from France, with her interpretation of the Salic Law to exclude female succession, and the Empire, with its elected rulers who were always male, all other European kingdoms had the possibility of installing a reigning queen—not very often, but nonetheless in a considerable number of cases. This study on reigning queens is part of a more extensive study on medieval successions in general (Wolf 1987, 1991).[2] In order to find out when, where, and why women did succeed to European thrones, we have to go into more detail; this compels me to restrict myself

France:	Mallorca:
None	(Isabella, 1375)
England:	Sicily:
(Matilda the Empress, 1135-1154)	Constance, 1194-98
(Jane Grey, 1553)	Maria, 1377/92-1401
Mary Tudor, 1553-58	
Elizabeth Tudor, 1558-1603	Naples:
(Mary Stuart, 1558-1587)	Giovanna I, 1343-82
	Giovanna II, 1414-35
Scotland:	
Margaret of Norway, 1286-90	Hungary:
Mary Stuart, 1542-1567	Maria, 1382-95
	(Elisabeth, 1437-42)
Portugal:	
(Beatrix, 1383-85)	Bohemia:
	(Elisabeth, 1437-42)
León-Castile:	
Urraca 1109	Poland:
(Constança, 1369-87)	Jadwiga, 1382-99
Isabella I, 1474-1504	
Juana (the Mad) 1504-1516/55	Sweden:
	Margarethe I, 1389-1412
Navarre:	
Juana I (of Champagne), 1274-1303	Norway:
Juana II (of France), 1329-49	Margarethe I, 1380-1412
Leonor, 1479	
Caterina, 1484-1516	Denmark:
Juana III, 1555-72	Margarethe I, 1375-1412
Aragón:	Holy Roman Empire:
Petronilla, 1137-62	None
Juana (the Mad), 1516-55	

to the century between 1350 and 1450. In this time period I have studied every succession in the eighteen European kingdoms. In these kingdoms from 1350 to 1450 exactly 100 successions took place, including those of so-called anti-kings and pretenders who failed. And among these 100 successions we find no fewer than twelve successions of women who became reigning queens—that is, 12 percent. Daughters succeeded fathers seven times, mothers followed sons twice, sisters succeeded childless brothers twice, and one granddaughter followed her grandfather. Let us discuss these 12 cases one by one, comparing the different situations with the help of the tables of succession that I have prepared. My tables are arranged country by country; the blocks show those who became or claimed to be kings or queens between 1350 and 1450. The names of women are always encircled to emphasize the often unrecognized importance of female lines in determining successions. The different lines framing the blocks indicate different families.

I start in Western Europe with the case of Beatrix of Portugal, whose bid for queenship failed. After King Fernâo died in 1383 a sequence of eight father-to-son successions ended in Portugal, for Beatrix was the only surviving child of the deceased king. Shortly before this, the eleven-year-old girl had been married to Juan I, the king of Castile. After the death of her father, Beatrix was proclaimed queen of Portugal by her followers, and her husband added the words "king of Portugal" to his title. The Portuguese, however, disliked the idea of having a foreign king, and King Fernâo's illegitimate brother Joâo of Aviz was declared king of Portugal. The question was decided by war; the Castilians invaded Portugal and besieged Lisbon, but lost the battle of Aljubarotta in 1385. John of Aviz was victorious, and though Beatrix did not resign her rights in Portugal she never reigned there.

More successful was Blanche of Navarre, who became the heiress to that kingdom in 1425. Unlike the child Beatrix of Portugal, Blanche was a thirty-four-year-old adult when her father died, and as a widow after her first marriage to Martin of Sicily she had gained some experience in governing a kingdom. By 1425 she had taken as her second husband a near relative, Juan of Aragon, with whom she ruled Navarre in common. Unfortunately for her son Carlos of Viana, Blanche died before her husband; that she had been regarded as the reigning queen is shown by Carlos' claims to the kingdom after his mother's death. But Juan of Aragon was unwilling to turn over the kingdom to Carlos, who was supported by part of the population in a tragic uprising against his own father. As Juan had become king of Aragon in the meantime, he had the means to suppress his unlucky son's uprising.

When Emperor Sigismund, also king of Hungary and Bohemia, died in 1437 he provided in his last will that the estates of the kingdom of Bohemia should accept his daughter Elisabeth and his son-in-law Albert of Austria for the government and administration of the realm, in accordance with the written law of Bohemia, which provided that females inherited as well as males (Palacky 1844-65: iii part 3, 295; Hödl 1978: 127). A fortnight after Sigismund's death, Albert and Elisabeth were elected king and queen of Bohemia on condition that they took up their residence in that country. Albert came to Prague and was crowned king; Elisabeth had been invited to come and be crowned as well but was unable to do so, for as the heiress to two kingdoms she was then in Hungary taking part in the government of that realm. While her husband too was elected and crowned king of Hungary, Elisabeth was recognized as regent there without being crowned. After Albert's early death in 1439, she gave birth to his son, Ladislas, in February 1440; by a *coup d'état* she got hold of St. Stephen's crown and had the baby crowned king of Hungary when he was less than five months old. Though another party of the Hungarian estates two months later elected and crowned the Polish king Wladyslaw (without St. Stephen's crown), Elisabeth claimed to rule the kingdom until her death in 1442 (Hödl 1978: 6). Unlike Blanche of Navarre, Elisabeth outlived her husband, claiming to reign in her own right, and fighting for the succession of her son.

What these first three cases have in common is that the heiresses Beatrix of Portugal, Blanche of Navarre, and Elisabeth of Hungary and Bohemia were married before their fathers died. In other cases the heiresses had not yet been married.

When Pedro the Cruel, king of Castile, was deposed, murdered, and replaced by his illegitimate brother Henry of Trastámara in 1369, Pedro's two unmarried daughters fled to England. There the elder of them, Constanca, married John of Gaunt, duke of Lancaster, the third son of King Edward III. The Trastámara kings were allied to France; to support the English possessions in Aquitaine, John of Gaunt used his wife's claim to the Castilian throne to declare them king and queen of Castile. He invaded Spain in 1386, but the campaign was unsuccessful and ended with a diplomatic solution: John and Constanca gave up their claims to Castile and their only child, Catarina, married the son and heir of Henry of Trastámara, uniting the claims of both lines.

In the following cases, young unmarried heiresses really did become queens. In 1377, Maria of Sicily inherited that kingdom from her father, a member of the dynasty of Barcelona. The fifteen-year-old girl was put under the guardianship of a Sicilian noble, but it was planned that she should marry Galeazzo Visconti, later the duke of Milan. This might have led to a union of Milan and Sicily, endangering the Sicilian claims of Maria's agnatic relatives in Catalonia. To avoid this, she was kidnapped by a Catalonian noble and taken to Barcelona, where she was married to her nephew Martin the Younger of Aragon. Both returned to Sicily in 1392 and were crowned together; documents were issued by "Martinus et Maria dei gratia Rex et regina Siciliae" (Testa 1741-1743: i, 151, 161). Their only son died young in Maria's lifetime, and she herself died before her husband; Martin became sole ruler after her death.

When Louis the Great, king of Hungary and Poland, died in 1382 he left two daughters, Maria and Jadwiga, both betrothed but unmarried. Maria was to marry Sigismund of Luxembourg-Bohemia, mentioned above, and was to inherit Poland; Jadwiga, engaged to a Habsburg, was to inherit Hungary. The idea was to bring the neighboring countries together, but the plan failed because both daughters lived with their mother at the Hungarian court and shortly after Louis' death the elder, Maria, was proclaimed queen of Hungary though she was originally intended for the throne of Poland. The Polish nobility, moreover, wanted to end the personal union of the two kingdoms and have a queen of their own. Hence they demanded of the queen-mother Elisabeth that she send one of her daughters to reside in Poland, and since she hesitated, they delivered an ultimatum that if no princess was sent, they would freely elect a king after a certain date. So the younger daughter Jadwiga, aged nine, was crowned queen in Krakow in 1384, in opposition to a remote male cousin, Ziemowit of Masovia, who was proclaimed king by a noble faction in 1383, but who was compensated and resigned his claims in 1385.

The young queen Jadwiga was then urged to break her engagement to William of Habsburg and to marry instead Jagiello, the ruler of neighboring Lithuania. He was elected king of Poland in absentia, on the condition that he take up residence in Poland. Four years after Jadwiga's coronation, Wladyslaw-Jagiello was crowned king in Krakow, and the couple governed the country together until Jadwiga's early death in 1399 or 1400. Since no children had survived, the king's legitimacy was contestable, but he remained on the throne after marrying Anne of Cilly, one of the closest relatives of the former reigning house.

A very similar case was that of Jadwiga's elder sister Maria of Hungary. Six days after the death of her father Louis the Great, the twelve-year-old girl was crowned at Szekesfehervar by the archbishop of Esztergom as if she were a king, not by the bishop of Veszprem as if a queen-consort. The queen-mother, Elisabeth of Bosnia, was her guardian. Three years later Maria was married at fifteen to Sigismund of Luxembourg-Bohemia, who received only the title "regni Hungarie tutor," not "rex," nor was he crowned in 1385 (von Aschbach 1838-45: i, 25 [note 11]). While Sigismund travelled to Bohemia, some Hungarian nobles, especially from Croatia, summoned Charles of Durazzo, the nearest male cousin of the deceased Louis the Great, to become king of Hungary; Charles was crowned king of Hungary on 31 December 1386. Queen Maria and the Queen-Mother Elisabeth were compelled to be present at Charles' coronation, but only seven weeks later Elisabeth managed to have Charles murdered. In revenge, the Croatian nobles seized the two queens and kept them in prison, where Elisabeth was drowned; the nobles then offered the crown to Ladislas, Charles' ten-year-old son and successor in the kingdom of Naples. Now the Republic of Venice saw the danger in a union of the kingdoms of Hungary and Naples on both sides of the Adriatic Sea, and allied herself with Maria's husband, Sigismund of Bohemia. While Venetian troops besieged the castle in which Maria had been held for about a year, Sigismund returned to Hungary and was crowned king. After his queen was freed by the Venetians the couple was reunited and Maria ceded to Sigismund the *ius regni et diadema,* though this did not mean that she totally resigned the queenship. Since documents were issued in both their names, she was still regarded as the reigning queen while Sigismund was co-regent and commander-in-chief of the army (von Aschbach 1838-45: i, 75). The marriage was without issue, and after Maria's death in 1392 (or 1395) Sigismund's title to the throne was contested by 32 nobles. Sigismund condemned them to death; they were publicly beheaded in Ofen. He then legitimized his kingship by marrying Barbara of Cilly, one of the nearest relatives of the old Hungarian kings.

The parallels between the queenships of Maria of Hungary and her sister Jadwiga of Poland are obvious. In both cases the queens died without surviving issue, and their husbands remained in power by marrying other cognates, i.e., relatives through female lines, of the old dynasty. We now turn to two different cases, Giovanna I and Giovanna II, queens of Naples. Giovanna I was proclaimed queen after the death of her grandfather, Robert the Wise, as his nearest living kin. Shortly before, she had been married to Andreas, younger brother of Louis the Great of Hungary. Her sixteen-year-old husband represented the elder line of the same dynasty of Anjou to which Giovanna herself belonged. Andreas made himself unpopular in Naples, however, by bringing foreigners from Hungary to the Neapolitan court. It was provided that Giovanna should become the reigning queen while Andreas should be prince-consort with a royal title. This agreement, however, was endangered when the pope named Andreas "king" without Andreas's having been crowned. Possibly a co-regency with the queen could have been declared, but before that could happen, Andreas was murdered.

A reigning queen who survived her husband was a new phenomenon in the history of female successions in medieval Europe. Louis of Hungary, brother of the murdered Andreas, accused Giovanna of the crime. She fled to the papal court at Avignon, while Louis invaded Naples on behalf of Charles, Giovanna's infant son by Andreas. After Charles' death at the age of three, however, Louis resigned his claim to the throne of Naples and Giovanna returned. As the estates of Naples wanted a male presence in the government, Giovanna was soon married to Luigi of Taranto, another cousin from the younger line of her Angevin dynasty. As prince of Taranto, he was no foreigner. They were crowned together in 1352 and governed the country as king and queen. During this period we see a situation corresponding to that of Blanche of Navarre, Maria of Sicily, Jadwiga of Poland, and Maria of Hungary, as we have discussed. Contrary to these cases, however, Giovanna did not die before her husband; in 1362 she was left a widow at thirty-six, and she remained reigning queen until her death twenty years later. Though she was married for a third and fourth time — to King Jayme of Mallorca and to Otto of Brunswick — neither of these later husbands became king of Naples; they remained consorts only.

A comparable case is that of Giovanna II of Naples. When she succeeded her brother, King Ladislas, in 1414, she was a forty-one-year-old widow; in the following year she married Jacques de Bourbon. Like the Angevins of Naples, the Bourbons were a branch of the French Capetian dynasty, but — and this is an important difference to the case of Giovanna I — Jacques de Bourbon did not descend from the former kings of Naples, either through male or female lines. Thus he had no personal claim to the throne of Naples in right of his own birth. Nevertheless, some nobles recognized the queen's husband as king, and he held Giovanna as though she were a prisoner. Bringing foreigners from France to Naples made him unpopular, and this led to a turn-around: one year later the imprisoned queen, in alliance with Italian nobles, succeeded in taking Jacques prisoner, excluding him from the government, and sending him back to France, where he lived for twenty-odd years as a monk in Besançon. In 1419 Giovanna was crowned queen and remained sole ruler until her death sixteen years later. She had no children, but played her possible testamentary heirs against each other—Alfonso of Aragon and Sicily, Louis III of Anjou, and René of Lorraine.

My last case is Margarethe of Denmark. When her father, Waldemar Atterdag, the last male of the old royal line in Denmark, died in 1375, Margarethe at twenty-three was his only surviving daughter; her elder sister Ingeborg had not lived to fight for the succession of her son Albert of Mecklenburg, then aged ten. Instead Margarethe fought to secure the Danish succession for her own son, the five-year-old Olaf of Norway. As nearest in degree to the dead King Waldemar, Margarethe used the titles "regina Daciae" and "filia et heres Waldemarii" (Hoffmann 1976: 149). In exchange for royal property, she obtained support for Olaf to be elected king of Denmark in 1376.

Before her father's death Margarethe had been married to Haakon of Norway. Her situation was thus like that of Blanche of Navarre, but while Blanche succeeded together with her husband Juan, Margarethe did not succeed together with Haakon. She took over the government alone, as guardian of the boy-king. How is this difference to be explained? The reason might have been that her husband Haakon was the reigning king of Norway. As we have seen, the estates generally did not like a foreign king; thus, they preferred only Margarethe to represent the kingdom of Denmark. In Navarre, however, Juan, when prince but not king of Aragon, could reside with Blanche in Navarre and become king of that country. Juan also had his own claim to Navarre, but Haakon had no claim to Denmark. I think these two reasons explain how Margarethe was able to rule on her own without her husband although in the beginning the other way might have been chosen: the first constitution of the boy-king Olaf (1376) was issued in the name of both parents: "Nos quoque Haquinus dei gracia rex Suecie et Norwegie et Margareta eadem gracia regina ibidem una cum dicto domino Olauo rege Dacie filio nostro karissimo." In 1377, however, the second constitution was issued by Olaf and his mother alone: "Olauus dei gracia Danorum Slauorum Gothorum rex, Margareta eadem gracia Swecie et Norwegia regina" (Wegener 1856-60: ii, 24).

The two important steps on Margarethe's way to becoming a reigning queen were the deaths of her husband in 1380 and of her son in 1387. Margarethe did not marry again and had no further issue. Her deceased son Olaf had been elected king of Denmark, was hereditary king of Norway, and possessed claims upon the kingdom of Sweden. At his death we find the unique situation of a mother becoming heiress of her childless son, since she was nearest in degree of consanguinity to him. Indeed, with the argument that Margarethe was the nearest kin of the last two kings, her father Waldemar and her son Olaf, she was recognized in Denmark "in veram suorum Dominam (husbunde) principem et plenipotentem totius regni Daciae tutricem" (Hoffmann 1976: 153). This means that Margarethe had changed from being the guardian of King Olaf to being the guardian of Denmark, from the guardian of a boy to the guardian of a kingdom. It must be pointed out that Margarethe's claims in Denmark on the one hand, and in Norway and Sweden on the other, were based on different genealogical situations. But the result was the same: after the death of Olaf she was recognized as the guardian not only of the kingdom of Denmark but of Norway and Sweden too.

In Sweden she succeeded only after a military conflict in which King Albert of Mecklenburg-Sweden was taken prisoner. He was only freed after six years, under the condition that he resign his claims. In the meantime Margarethe took control of the next heir of the three kingdoms, her great-nephew, the eight-year-old Erik of Pomerania. Under her guardianship Erik was recognized as hereditary king of Norway and, after Albert's forced resignation, of Denmark and Sweden. Although Erik was sixteen years of age at his coronation, Margarethe gave up neither her guardianship nor her government before her death fifteen years later. Erik had only the title of a king, but she was "höghborne förstynne, nadighe fru drotning"—highborn princess, gracious lady and queen (Wegener 1856-60: ii, 28; Christensen 1980: 28).

I want to conclude with some remarks of a systematic nature. We have observed the following conditions under which a woman could become a reigning queen:

- If she was nearer in degree of consanguinity to the late king than the nearest male (e.g., Jadwiga of Poland, not Ziemowit of Masovia; Maria of Hungary, not Charles of Durazzo).
- If she outlived her husband naturally (Margarethe in Norway), murdered him (as Giovanna I of Naples perhaps killed Andreas), or chased him out of the country (as Giovanna II did Jacques de Bourbon).
- If she was an adult while the nearest male was a minor (like Margarethe of Denmark against Albert of Mecklenburg).
- If she was the native representative of the country, while the competitor was a foreigner, as happened in several cases examined here.

In the general study on successions mentioned above (Wolf 1991), I have shown which principles in the law of succession were observed in late-medieval European monarchies. One of these rules, it is true, was that males were preferred to females. But this rule was not the only principle. The others were as follows:

- The successor had to be a descendant of the first king of the land, and within the group of descendants of that first king.
- The closest in degree of consanguinity was preferred to more distant relatives.
- Agnates were preferred to cognates (the distaff line); older individuals to younger ones, those of full age to minors; lines of descent reckoned according to primogeniture to cadet lines;
- legitimate descendants to illegitimate ones;
- natural heirs to adopted heirs;
- healthy individuals to the handicapped or insane;
- natives to foreigners.

With the exception, however, of the single principle that males were preferred to females, all the other rules were valid for both sexes. In fact, these principles were able to decide several successions in favor of women, and they thus answer the questions where, when, and why queens could reign in medieval Europe.

Max-Planck-Institut für Europäische Rechtsgeschichte
Frankfurt-am-Main

PORTUGAL
Succession in:
1383/85

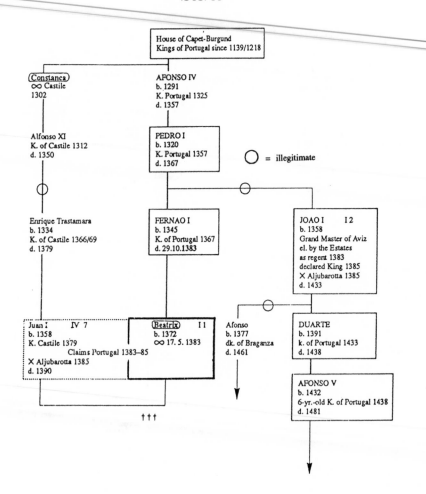

House of Capet-Burgund
Kings of Portugal since 1139/1218

(Constanca)
∞ Castile
1302

AFONSO IV
b. 1291
K. Portugal 1325
d. 1357

Alfonso XI
K. of Castile 1312
d. 1350

PEDRO I
b. 1320
K. Portugal 1357
d. 1367

○ = illegitimate

Enrique Trastamara
b. 1334
K. of Castile 1366/69
d. 1379

FERNAO I
b. 1345
K. of Portugal 1367
d. 29.10.1383

JOAO I   I 2
b. 1358
Grand Master of Aviz
el. by the Estates
as regent 1383
declared King 1385
X Aljubarotta 1385
d. 1433

Juan :   IV 7
b. 1358
K. Castile 1379
        Claims Portugal 1383–85
X Aljubarotta 1385
d. 1390

(Beatrix)   I 1
b. 1372
∞ 17. 5. 1383

Afonso
b. 1377
dk. of Braganza
d. 1461

DUARTE
b. 1391
k. of Portugal 1433
d. 1438

AFONSO V
b. 1432
6-yr.-old K. of Portugal 1438
d. 1481

† † †

© 1986 Armin Wolf

NAVARRE
Succession in:
1425

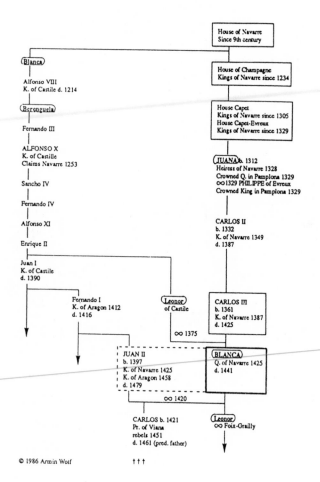

© 1986 Armin Wolf   † † †

CASTILE
Succession in:
1369

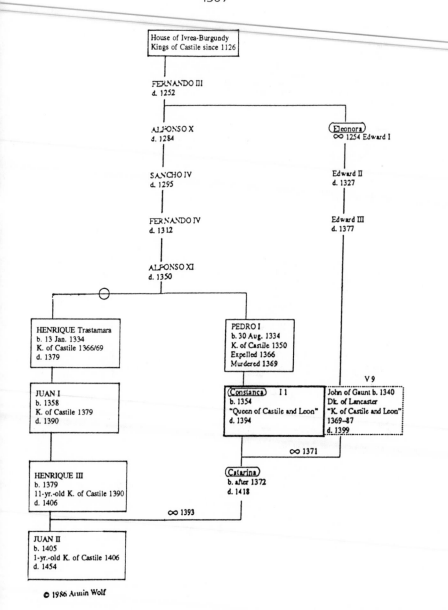

House of Ivrea-Burgundy
Kings of Castile since 1126

FERNANDO III
d. 1252

ALFONSO X
d. 1284

Eleonora
∞ 1254 Edward I

SANCHO IV
d. 1295

Edward II
d. 1327

FERNANDO IV
d. 1312

Edward III
d. 1377

ALFONSO XI
d. 1350

HENRIQUE Trastamara
b. 13 Jan. 1334
K. of Castile 1366/69
d. 1379

PEDRO I
b. 30 Aug. 1334
K. of Castile 1350
Expelled 1366
Murdered 1369

V 9

JUAN I
b. 1358
K. of Castile 1379
d. 1390

Constanca   I 1
b. 1354
"Queen of Castile and Leon"
d. 1394

John of Gaunt b. 1340
Dk. of Lancaster
"K. of Castile and Leon"
1369–87
d. 1399

∞ 1371

HENRIQUE III
b. 1379
11-yr.-old K. of Castile 1390
d. 1406

Catarina
b. after 1372
d. 1418

∞ 1393

JUAN II
b. 1405
1-yr.-old K. of Castile 1406
d. 1454

© 1986 Armin Wolf

SICILY
Succession in:
1377/92

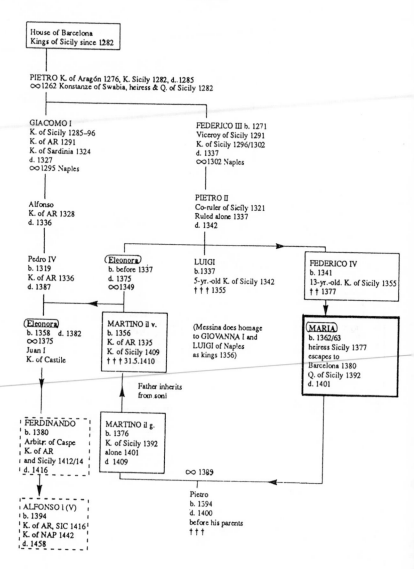

←↓↑→ Direction of inheritance

© 1986 Armin Wolf

POLAND
Succession in:
1382/84

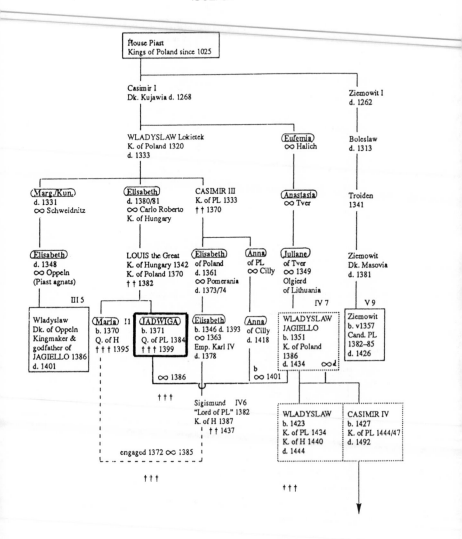

© 1986 Armin Wolf

HUGARY

Successions in:
1382

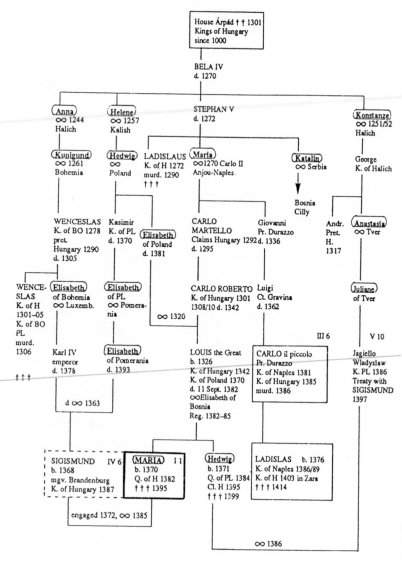

House Árpád † † 1301
Kings of Hungary
since 1000

BELA IV
d. 1270

Anna
∞ 1244
Halich

Helene
∞ 1257
Kalish

STEPHAN V
d. 1272

Konstanze
∞ 1251/52
Halich

Kunigund
∞ 1261
Bohemia

Hedwig
∞
Poland

LADISLAUS
K. of H 1272
murd. 1290
† † †

Maria
∞1270 Carlo II
Anjou-Naples

Katalin
∞ Serbia

George
K. of Halich

Bosnia
Cilly

WENCESLAS
K. of BO 1278
pret.
Hungary 1290
d. 1305

Kasimir
K. of PL
d. 1370

Elisabeth
of Poland
d. 1381

CARLO
MARTELLO
Claims Hungary 1292
d. 1295

Giovanni
Pr. Durazzo
d. 1336

Andr.
Pret.
H.
1317

Anastasia
∞ Tver

WENCE-
SLAS
K. of H
1301–05
K. of BO
PL
murd.
1306

Elisabeth
of Bohemia
∞ Luxemb.

Elisabeth
of PL
∞ Pomera-
nia

∞ 1320

CARLO ROBERTO
K. of Hungary 1301
1308/10 d. 1342

Luigi
Ct. Gravina
d. 1362

Juliane
of Tver

III 6

V 10

Karl IV
emperor
d. 1378

† † †

Elisabeth
of Pomerania
d. 1393

LOUIS the Great
b. 1326
K. of Hungary 1342
K. of Poland 1370
d. 11 Sept. 1382
∞Elisabeth of
Bosnia
Reg. 1382–85

CARLO il piccolo
Pr. Durazzo
K. of Naples 1381
K. of Hungary 1385
murd. 1386

Jagiello
Wladyslaw
K. PL 1386
Treaty with
SIGISMUND
1397

d ∞ 1363

SIGISMUND   IV 6
b. 1368
mgv. Brandenburg
K. of Hungary 1387

MARIA   I 1
b. 1370
Q. of H 1382
† † † 1395

Hedwig
b. 1371
Q. of PL 1384
Cl. H 1395
† † † 1399

LADISLAS   b. 1376
K. of Naples 1386/89
K. of H 1403 in Zara
† † † 1414

engaged 1372, ∞ 1385

∞ 1386

† † †   † † †

NAPLES
Succession in:
1343/52

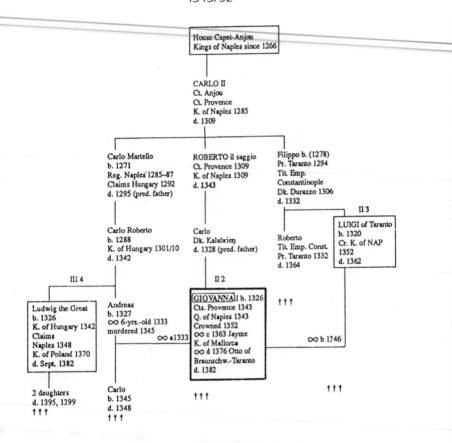

House Capet-Anjou
Kings of Naples since 1266

CARLO II
Ct. Anjou
Ct. Provence
K. of Naples 1285
d. 1309

Carlo Martello
b. 1271
Reg. Naples 1285–87
Claims Hungary 1292
d. 1295 (pred. father)

ROBERTO il saggio
Ct. Provence 1309
K. of Naples 1309
d. 1343

Filippo b. (1278)
Pr. Taranto 1294
Tit. Emp.
Constantinople
Dk. Durazzo 1306
d. 1332

II 3

LUIGI of Taranto
b. 1320
Cr. K. of NAP
1352
d. 1362

Carlo Roberto
b. 1288
K. of Hungary 1301/10
d. 1342

Carlo
Dk. Kalabrien
d. 1328 (pred. father)

Roberto
Tit. Emp. Const.
Pr. Taranto 1332
d. 1364

III 4

Ludwig the Great
b. 1326
K. of Hungary 1342
Claims
Naples 1348
K. of Poland 1370
d. Sept. 1382

Andreas
b. 1327
∞ 6-yrs.-old 1333
murdered 1345
∞ a1333

II 2

GIOVANNA I b. 1326
Cts. Provence 1343
Q. of Naples 1343
Crowned 1352
∞ c 1363 Jayme
K. of Mallorca
∞ d 1376 Otto of
Braunschw.-Taranto
d. 1382

†††

∞ b 1246

2 daughters
d. 1395, 1399
†††

Carlo
b. 1345
d. 1348
†††

†††

†††

© 1986 Armin Wolf

NAPLES
Succession in:
14 14/19

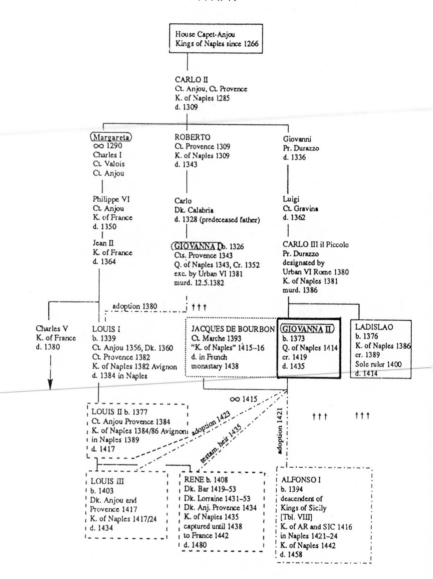

House Capet-Anjou
Kings of Naples since 1266

CARLO II
Ct. Anjou, Ct. Provence
K. of Naples 1285
d. 1309

(Margareta)
∞ 1290
Charles I
Ct. Valois
Ct. Anjou

ROBERTO
Ct. Provence 1309
K. of Naples 1309
d. 1343

Giovanni
Pr. Durazzo
d. 1336

Philippe VI
Ct. Anjou
K. of France
d. 1350

Carlo
Dk. Calabria
d. 1328 (predeceased father)

Luigi
Ct. Gravina
d. 1362

Jean II
K. of France
d. 1364

(GIOVANNA I) b. 1326
Cts. Provence 1343
Q. of Naples 1343, Cr. 1352
exc. by Urban VI 1381
murd. 12.5.1382

CARLO III il Piccolo
Pr. Durazzo
designated by
Urban VI Rome 1380
K. of Naples 1381
murd. 1386

adoption 1380   † † †

Charles V
K. of France
d. 1380

LOUIS I
b. 1339
Ct. Anjou 1356, Dk. 1360
Ct. Provence 1382
K. of Naples 1382 Avignon
d. 1384 in Naples

JACQUES DE BOURBON
Ct. Marche 1393
"K. of Naples" 1415–16
d. in French
monastary 1438

(GIOVANNA II)
b. 1373
Q. of Naples 1414
cr. 1419
d. 1435

LADISLAO
b. 1376
K. of Naples 1386
cr. 1389
Sole ruler 1400
d. 1414

∞ 1415

LOUIS II b. 1377
Ct. Anjou Provence 1384
K. of Naples 1384/86 Avignon
in Naples 1389
d. 1417

adoption 1423

adoption 1421

† † †   † † †

LOUIS III
b. 1403
Dk. Anjou and
Provence 1417
K. of Naples 1417/24
d. 1434

testam. heir 1435

RENE b. 1408
Dk. Bar 1419–53
Dk. Lorraine 1431–53
Dk. Anj. Provence 1434
K. of Naples 1435
captured until 1438
to France 1442
d. 1480

ALFONSO I
b. 1394
descendent of
Kings of Sicily
[Tbl. VIII]
K. of AR and SIC 1416
in Naples 1421–24
K. of Naples 1442
d. 1458

© 1986 Armin Wolf

DENMARK
Succession in:
1375

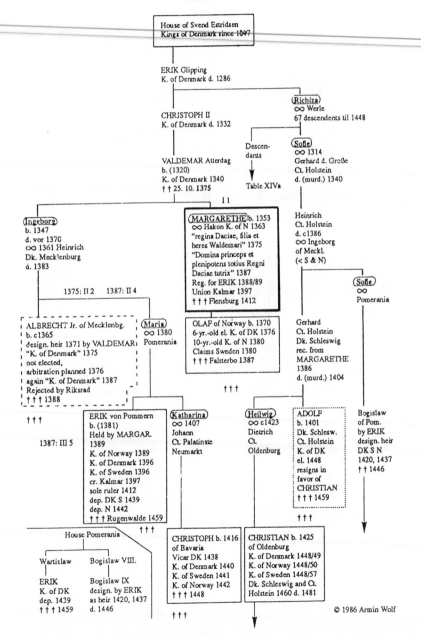

© 1986 Armin Wolf

NORWAY   SWEDEN
Succession in:
1380/97   1389/97

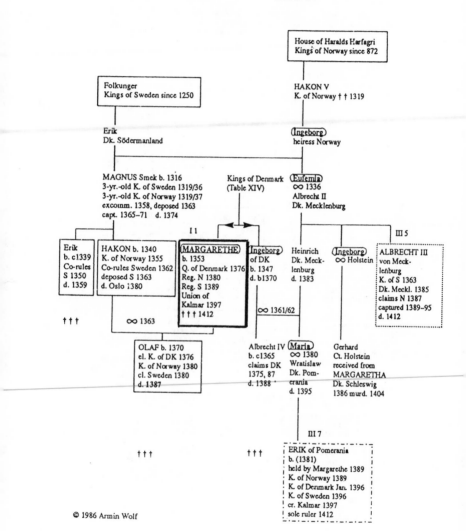

House of Haralds Harfagri
Kings of Norway since 872

Folkunger
Kings of Sweden since 1250

HAKON V
K. of Norway †† 1319

Erik
Dk. Södermanland

Ingeborg
heiress Norway

MAGNUS Smek b. 1316
3-yr.-old K. of Sweden 1319/36
3-yr.-old K. of Norway 1319/37
excomm. 1358, deposed 1363
capt. 1365–71   d. 1374

Kings of Denmark
(Table XIV)

Eufemia
∞ 1336
Albrecht II
Dk. Mecklenburg

I 1   III 5

Erik
b. c1339
Co-rules
S 1350
d. 1359

HAKON b. 1340
K. of Norway 1355
Co-rules Sweden 1362
deposed S 1363
d. Oslo 1380

MARGARETHE
b. 1353
Q. of Denmark 1376
Reg. N 1380
Reg. S 1389
Union of
Kalmar 1397
††† 1412

Ingeborg
of DK
b. 1347
d. b1370

Heinrich
Dk. Meck-
lenburg
d. 1383

Ingeborg
∞ Holstein

ALBRECHT III
von Meck-
lenburg
K. of S 1363
Dk. Meckl. 1385
claims N 1387
captured 1389–95
d. 1412

†††   ∞ 1363

∞ 1361/62

OLAF b. 1370
el. K. of DK 1376
K. of Norway 1380
cl. Sweden 1380
d. 1387

Albrecht IV
b. c1365
claims DK
1375, 87
d. 1388

Maria
∞ 1380
Wratislaw
Dk. Pom-
erania
d. 1395

Gerhard
Ct. Holstein
received from
MARGARETHA
Dk. Schleswig
1386 murd. 1404

III 7

†††   †††

ERIK of Pomerania
b. (1381)
held by Margarethe 1389
K. of Norway 1389
K. of Denmark Jan. 1396
K. of Sweden 1396
cr. Kalmar 1397
sole ruler 1412

© 1986 Armin Wolf

CHAPTER 11

Female Succession and the Language of Power in the Writings of Twelfth-Century Churchmen

Lois L. Huneycutt

The complex question of the relationship of women to power has been a vexed one for historians and feminist theorists for what is beginning to seem like a very long time. Approaching the question becomes more complicated when scholars investigate eras and cultures far removed from our own, when even basic assumptions about gender roles and differences often vary widely from ours. These complications are evident from the results of recent studies on women and power in the Middle Ages that have revealed an often puzzling picture (Erler and Kowaleski 1988: 1-17). Certainly medieval medical and scientific views of women, mainly inherited from antiquity, were extremely misogynistic (Bullough 1973). In addition, medieval Christian theologians accepted and furthered the patristic view of woman as the cause of original sin and portrayed women as having special barriers to overcome before they could achieve salvation (Børrenson 1981). But when it comes to relationships between actual men and women, the situation becomes ambiguous. For instance, even the most misogynistic of male theorists sincerely respected individual female friends and relatives (d'Alverny 1970; Ruether 1979). At the same time, some who professed respect and even reverence for the female sex as a whole maintained troubled relationships with actual women (McLaughlin 1975; Muckle 1955). Another paradox is that while theoretical writings on gender attributed qualities such as capriciousness, physical weakness, lust, instability, lack of intelligence, irrationality, and a tendency toward duplicity to the female sex, men of the feudal nobility routinely expected women to occupy positions requiring grave judgement and responsibility. Men expected their female relatives to be able to manage and defend their estates, raise their children, and further their familial goals while they fought or crusaded in distant lands, often for years at a time. Royal and noble women were present at and expected to participate in political councils, and their advice was often sought and considered in planning familial strategies and alliances (LoPrete 1990). Most medieval chroniclers casually accepted the fact that individual women could be learned or pious, and that women often displayed exceptional bravery or ability, even in the waging of war (Bandel 1957). Indeed, despite the supposed "marginality" of medieval women, literary and record sources alike show that females of the noble class were fully integrated into the family structure (Gold 1985: 1-18, 116-52).

This integration of women into the family is particular important because, at least until the middle of the twelfth century, the medieval world drew little distinction between "public" and "private" spheres of life and authority, or between public and private rights. Thus, despite the misogyny of the age, a female member of an economically or politically powerful family often enjoyed considerable authority and freedom of movement in what we today would consider the "public sphere." Although the intellectual, cultural, and social changes that characterize the "second feudal age" took their toll on the ability of married noblewomen to act autonomously, some women did continue to manage and inherit fiefs, counties, and sometimes even kingdoms (McNamara and Wemple 1973, rpt 1988; Huneycutt 1989b). Widows often administered properties for their minor sons. Less frequently, women inherited in their own right, although often they did not gain control of their realms without controversy, up to and including actual warfare. Part of their struggles involved the production of polemic literature, most of it by churchmen who found themselves in the sometimes troubling position of supporting female candidates to the throne.

Two of the medieval world's best-known instances of females claiming the right to rule on their own, that is, as reigning queens rather than as regents or consorts, occurred at a crucial point in the mid-twelfth century, when the rise of professional administrative bureaucracies, coupled with changes in inheritance patterns and marriage customs, were combining to erode women's freedom to act in the public sphere. In both cases, prominent churchmen chronicled the struggles of females to claim the thrones that they had inherited. Since considerations of space must confine analysis to just a few of these writers, I have chosen to concentrate on several well-known commentators whose views on women have recently been explored by other scholars. These scholars tend to acknowledge the inconsistencies in the thought of chroniclers who accepted the public status of royal and noble women, but who nonetheless were apt to repeat stereotypical and conventional moral judgements dismissing women as fickle or unfaithful daughters of Eve, as bad influences on their husbands, as shrews, or even worse, to see women as "domestic tyrants" who sapped the prowess of fighting men. The main thrust of current scholarship has been to demonstrate the casual and natural way in which even the most misogynistic of chroniclers accepted the public role of the royal or noble woman. Several scholars have posited that, because of this acceptance, medieval chroniclers were generally silent about the possibility or consequences of female rulership (Chibnall 1990; Nederman and Lawson 1987). My intent here is to probe the limits of the twelfth-century acceptance of the exercise of public authority by women and to consider in some detail how several medieval thinkers conceived of the problem of female succession and the possibility of a reigning queen. I believe that a careful study of the language and the omissions of the thinkers in question shows that, while they were quite comfortable with the idea of females as regents or transmitters of power, their tolerance did not often extend to acceptance of a female exercising authority in her own name.

I begin with the caveat that I have only recently begun to explore this subject, and that the conclusions I present herein are open to discussion and revision. My eventual goal is to explain or perhaps even reconcile the theoretical, often misogynistic, positions of high-medieval churchmen with their support of actual women in public roles. In this preliminary study, I can only point to the apparent contradictions in their thinking and speculate how twelfth-century polemicists could justify placing women in positions of public authority while at the same time denying the abilities of the female sex as a whole. I am concentrating on the mid-twelfth century primarily because it is the era with which I am most familiar. I am convinced that similar comparisons throughout the Middle Ages would be fruitful and might add much to our understanding of the medieval concept of "power" as well as the history of gender constructs. A second reason for choosing to begin with this period is that the twelfth century has long been accepted as a time in which western Europeans displayed a new interest in many forms of subjectivity, an interest that led to both the "discovery of nature" and the "discovery of the individual" (Chenu 1968; Morris 1972; Bynum 1982: 82-109). Newer work has indicated that these years also witnessed a heightened awareness of gender differences as new roles for both men and women opened up with the urbanization of Europe, changes in monastic expressions of spirituality, and changes even in the structure and function of the noble family (Bloch 1991; McLaughlin 1991). Thus, one can expect to find, and indeed there are, many extant works from the era relating to the topic of gender roles and the exercise of public power.

The first case of female succession I will consider is that of Maud or Matilda, daughter and designated heir of King Henry I of England. Also known as "the Empress," because of her early marriage to Emperor Henry V, Matilda fought for her inheritance with her cousin Stephen from 1135 until Stephen's death in 1154. She came close to defeating him several times, but never gained the crown. She did, however, negotiate an agreement that allowed her son to take the throne upon Stephen's death (Chibnall 1991: 64-176). The second, possibly less familiar example is that of Melisende, who inherited the kingdom of Jerusalem upon the death of her father, Baldwin II, in 1131. Melisende overcame two challenges to her rule, first from her husband and later from her son, but except for a brief period of exclusion, participated in ruling Jerusalem until her death in 1161 (Mayer 1972; Hamilton 1978).[1] In both cases, the diplomatic evidence shows that the women in question saw themselves as true heirs and rulers in their own right, but the narrative evidence from chronicles, letters, and other expository prose shows that the idea of a female wielding power in her own right was literally inconceivable to many twelfth-century commentators.

One of the most important chroniclers for the study of the Anglo-Norman era is Orderic (or Ordericus) Vitalis, an English monk who lived in the monastery of St. Evroul in Normandy during the middle years of the century. His misleadingly titled *Ecclesiastical History of England and Normandy* is in fact an attempt at a universal history, and for the events of the eleventh and twelfth century, he provides an invaluable and usually trustworthy source (Chibnall 1984; Gransden 1974: 151-65). Orderic displayed strong views on human folly and the tendency toward vice. In his view, women were capable of both great virtue or great evil, and were much more likely than men to achieve either extreme.[2] He was quite willing to attribute male weakness or vacillation to the negative influence of women (Farmer 1986: 522-23). Orderic blamed the wantonness and lewdness prevalent in the courts of William Rufus and Robert Curthose on the natural male desire to please foolish women (Orderic Vitalis 1969-80: iii, 186-91, and vi, 308-09). He also believed that the company of women was bad for men, and that female influence emasculated warriors. For instance, after the Battle of Hastings, many Normans left England before their terms of service were complete. Orderic blamed their desertion not on the soldiers themselves, but on their lustful wives, who had supposedly sent messages announcing that they were sexually starved and would take lovers unless their husbands returned immediately (Orderic Vitalis 1969-80: i, 218-20).

Orderic's treatment of the story of Adelaide, countess of Sicily and later queen-consort of Jerusalem, shows his willingness to use female wickedness as an explanatory device. According to other sources, Adelaide, who had successfully administered Sicily for many years as regent for her minor son, was lured to Jerusalem in 1113 to marry King Baldwin I. The alliance was attractive to Baldwin because Adelaide brought with her a huge dowry and the promise of much-needed naval aid. Upon her arrival in the kingdom, she found that Baldwin already had a wife, who had retired to a nunnery. The marriage went ahead despite the irregular situation, but later, when the patriarch of Jerusalem was forced to annul the marriage or face excommunication, Adelaide found herself penniless, friendless, and in disgrace. By late 1117 she had no choice but to return to Sicily, where she died the following year (Hamilton 1978: 145-47; William of Tyre 1943: i, 489, 514). Orderic, who knew little of the situation, supplied his own interpretation of Adelaide's plight. According to him, she had been successful in Sicily only because she had exploited a male protector whom she poisoned as soon as her son came of age. Orderic depicted Adelaide as insatiably greedy for worldly pomp and honors, lusting after the crown of Jerusalem. Baldwin, on the other hand, comes off remarkably well. Orderic portrayed him gaining control of Adelaide's dowry, happily distributing it among the soldiers who were "suffering against the pagans for the sake of Christ". After using all her money, he naturally "repudiated the woman who was wrinkled with age and notoriously stained with many crimes" (Orderic Vitalis 1969-80: vi, 429).

Adelaide was not the only woman who resorted to poison in Orderic's writings (Orderic Vitalis 1969-80: ii, 79-80, 122-25; iii, 28-31; vi, 50-55; discussed in Chibnall 1990: 108-09). Like many of his Norman contemporaries, Orderic was obsessed with the idea and regarded poison as a likely female weapon (Douglas 1964: 408-15; Russell 1973b: 73-83). But, as Marjorie Chibnall has pointed out, Orderic overall portrayed women more as companions and helpmates to their husbands than as bad influences (Chibnall 1990: 111). In fact, Orderic's chronicle, above all else, is the story of the rise, fall and struggles among the great families of England and Normandy. He naturally included noblewomen in his account, recognizing that they helped govern their realms during minorities or periods of war and that they were influential in the family's decisions to found or patronize monasteries. His own feelings on the English succession are difficult to discern from his chronicle, but the language he uses to refer to the Empress and her status makes it clear that he never considered her apart from her relationship to her father, her husband, and her son.[3] If Orderic had a blind spot, it is that he never came to terms with the unusual situation of a female claimant to the throne. He had been a strong supporter of King Henry I and recognized that the king had designated his daughter as his successor. Commenting on the 1133 birth of Matilda's son, later King Henry II, Orderic implied that he was destined to be king.[4] But once Stephen had seized the throne, Orderic became coolly neutral as he chronicled the events of the English civil war. He saw it as natural that Stephen's queen (also named Matilda), who was countess of Boulogne in her own right, would use her property and influence on behalf of her husband, and that she would call upon her vassals for aid. When Stephen was captured by the Empress' forces, Orderic accepted without comment Queen Matilda's role as a military strategist and leader of her own and her husband's forces (Orderic Vitalis 1969-80: vi, 520-21, 546-47, discussed in Chibnall 1990: 113).

But while Matilda of Boulogne played a role traditional for medieval wives, the Empress' role was extraordinary because she claimed the right to rule by inheritance and in her own name. When describing events in which both Matildas were involved, Orderic did not explicitly acknowledge this difference. He expressed no opinion on the possibility or suitability of female succession, always referring to Henry's daughter as countess of Anjou, the title she had gained upon her second marriage.[5] Likewise, in his brief comments on events in the Holy Land, he writes that Fulk of Anjou "married Melisende, daughter of Baldwin II, and received the kingdom with her" (Orderic Vitalis 1969-80: v, 128-29). Later, commenting more fully on Fulk's troubles in the Holy Land, Orderic claims that Fulk had been offered the crown during Baldwin II's lifetime but refused to wear it until the old king died, at which time he assumed full (and presumably sole) authority (Orderic Vitalis 1969-80: vi, 390-92). Nowhere does he mention the possibility of Melisende as a reigning queen.

The silence of the chroniclers as to the constitutional position of both Melisende and Matilda is striking. Also striking is the lack of reference to the sex of either claimant. Although many commentators writing since the Middle Ages have attributed Matilda's failure to gain the throne to the fact that she was a woman, gender does not appear to have been an overt issue in the twelfth-century succession debate. Among all the extant writings of the contemporary and near-contemporary partisans of both Stephen and the Empress, never once is the Empress' sex given as a direct reason for barring her from the throne. Is Orderic's failure to comment on a female candidate to the throne due not to any reluctance to accept a ruling queen but rather because the possibility seemed less unusual to him than it does to modern minds? Newer studies have done much to counter the view, prevalent until quite recently, that the feudal nobility of England and Normandy rejected Matilda primarily because of her sex (Davis 1990: 14, 36; Schnith 1976: 136-37). This older view cannot be supported from the sources (Gunn 1990; Nederman and Lawson 1987). The silence of Orderic and his fellow chroniclers does not, however, negate the fact that they recognized special problems concerning a female candidate to the throne, nor does it mean that anyone welcomed the situation. It is quite clear that Henry I expected that his daughter's accession might not happen smoothly. In order to secure his succession plans, Henry took the unusual step of requiring a public oath of support for Matilda during an 1127 court gathering. The hostile author of the *Gesta Stephani* pointed out that, even in 1127, many in the kingdom doubted whether the Empress would ever succeed (Potter and Davis 1990: 10-12). Some of the barons who later repudiated their oath claimed that their promises had been contingent upon acceptance of any husband Henry chose for his then-widowed daughter. Since they had not agreed to the choice of Geoffrey of Anjou, they felt free to withdraw their support for Matilda. Others claimed that their oaths had been forced and were therefore invalid or that Henry had changed his mind at the last minute and nullified their oaths (John of Salisbury 1986: 83-85; Potter and Davis 1976: 10-12; Davis 1967: 15-18). But when Matilda's right to succeed was formally challenged at the papal court, Stephen's adherents chose to argue the case on its feudal merits, claiming that the marriage of Matilda's parents had been unlawful and that Stephen was therefore Henry's true heir.[6] The emphasis and insistence upon hereditary principles is unmistakable. Most commentators, even those with some personal animosity toward the Empress, agreed that she possessed the most legitimate hereditary claim to the throne but that Stephen's anointing and coronation should not be undone (Nederman and Lawson 1987: 85). Indeed, in both cases of female succession under consideration here, contemporaries took great pains to enunciate and emphasize the hereditary principles involved. Both kingdoms were emerging from long periods of uncertain and disputed succession (Mayer 1985; Williams 1978). Both women were married and mothers of sons with clear legal rights of succession, and in both instances, contemporaries were willing to admit the right of women to hold power and to transmit that power to their sons. In both cases, I believe that contemporaries reluctantly overlooked the sex of the lawful candidate in order not to sacrifice the larger principles of hereditary right. The need to establish a hereditary monarchy in the Latin kingdom of Jerusalem was so strong that authors of the latest study on William of Tyre have argued that William exaggerated Melisende's actual power in relationship to her husband and son. Despite the fact that William elsewhere indicated that he did not consider women fit to rule, he was forced to accept Melisende in order to emphasize the legitimacy of the line of kings descended from Baldwin II (Edbury and Rowe 1983: 80-83). Medieval thinkers did not need to reject explicitly the misogyny they inherited from antiquity in order to construct a legal framework centered on the family. With few exceptions, these commentators never viewed Melisende and Matilda as "female claimants" or as women exercising power in their own right. Rather, they were portrayed as representatives of their families, agents for their fathers, husbands, and sons. The issue of gender was defused when chroniclers could fit female claimants into the "regent" mold that medieval women traditionally occupied. As long as women in positions of public authority could be seen as acting for another, they posed no threat to the feudal order.

This acceptance of women as regents is consistent even among those who most strongly feared the influence of women upon the chivalric order. My second commentator, John of Salisbury, was an Englishman trained at the school of Chartres. A pupil of Abelard and a member of the circle of Thomas à Becket, he served the papal *curia* in Rome for several years and ended his days as bishop of Chartres. He is known both for his legal defense of the claims of the Empress expressed in his *Historia pontificalis* (John of Salisbury 1986: 83-86) and for the anti-feminine views expressed in his *Policraticus*. In the latter, John chastised the knightly order of his day for abandoning martial virtues in favor of the frivolities of courtly life. He saw court life and the constant presence of females in the court as the major cause for the loss of knightly virility he believed to be rampant (John of Salisbury 1990: 89-91, 131, 184-85). Women, according to John, were "clinging, wily, deceptive, and demanding." At one point he characterized wives as "domestic tyrants" (Nederman and Lawson 1987: 87).

In 1987, Nederman and Lawson argued that there is another side to John's view of women, one that allowed for the possibility of female rule. In the *Policraticus*, John used Dido as an exemplum of a queen who ruled wisely and well until she succumbed to her desire for Aeneas. Thus, according to Nederman and Lawson, John showed that women could wield power if they overcame their passionate natures and the demands of their bodies. While John did not prohibit women from positions of authority on principle, it is clear that he believed they must take pains not to exhibit their characteristic vices. And while this concession does not excuse John from his misogynistic stance, it did allow the authors to reconcile his political support of the Empress with his fear and hatred of women (Nederman and Lawson 1987: 88, 92-93).[7] But while Nederman and Lawson were successful in showing that John "was sufficiently realistic to recognize that women cannot reasonably be prohibited from involvement in the public affairs of the twelfth century," I am not willing to go so far as to believe, as they did, that John also "was quite willing to let a woman govern so long as she does not interfere with that proper and exclusive realm of masculine identity, warfare" (Nederman and Lawson 1987: 93). A closer look at John's treatment of the English succession is in order.

Like Orderic, John never commented directly on the sex of the Empress. But unlike those of the monk of St. Evroul, John's views on the English succession are quite clear. According to John, "everyone knew" that Stephen had usurped the kingdom despite his oath to King Henry and the fact that he had sworn fealty to the Empress (John of Salisbury 1986: 83). In his description of the case heard in Rome on whether Stephen or Matilda had the better claim to rule, John presented the case solely on its feudal merits. He emphasized Matilda's hereditary right and took pains to show the ludicrous nature of Stephen's claims that Matilda was not Henry's true heir. The papal court decided not to interfere, believing that it would be more harmful to "undo" Stephen's coronation than it was to disallow Matilda's hereditary claims (John of Salisbury 1986: 84-86). But John saw Henry II, not the Empress, as the injured party in Stephen's usurpation. This view is made manifest in the *Policraticus* (John of Salisbury 1990: 119-20):

> For indeed God, desiring to punish the malice of a people, had broken the promise which the nobility had confirmed by oath to the daughter of the Lion of Justice; new men were conceded favour to be raised to power and a foreign man [Stephen] was allowed to rule over the kingdom in contempt for goodness and equity. . . . Therefore, invading the kingdom, he disinherited and excluded the lord [Henry II] for whom, if there was loyalty in the man, he was sworn to die both because of the merits of his predecessors in the office and by necessity of his oath. He was devoted to corrupting neighboring nations, he contracted marriages and alliances with their princes, lest by the intercession of God the child who was still crying in his cradle might undertake the claim of his inheritance.

John's interpretation here was by no means unique. The author of the *Gesta Stephani* claims that when Robert earl of Gloucester, a natural son of Henry I, was urged to take the throne in 1135, he yielded his claim not to his sister, but to his sister's son (Potter and Davis 1976: 10).

As recent studies (Chibnall 1990; Nederman and Lawson 1987) have shown, John, Orderic, and their contemporaries indeed realized and accepted that the political and social realities of their day inevitably meant that women, acting to secure familial claims, would sometimes exercise public authority. Most commentators agreed that women had a definite and valuable role to play within the public sphere, and praised them when they took on strong and active roles. The possibility exists that Orderic and his fellow historians were so used to seeing females in positions of authority that they saw nothing to comment upon during the succession struggles of Melisende and the Empress. I believe it is more likely the case that, with few exceptions, both Matilda and Melisende were regarded simply as regents ruling for their minor sons than as queens in their own right. Indeed, Matilda may also have ultimately viewed herself in the same manner. In her recent biography of the Empress, Marjorie Chibnall has argued that, after the Empress' party lost the 1141 campaigns, Matilda changed her focus from securing the throne for herself to working for the succession of her son (Chibnall 1990: 205-06).

The distinction between a woman ruling in her own right and ruling as a regent for a minor son leads me to my final writer, Bernard, abbot of the Cistercian monastery of Clairvaux. As the head of the rapidly expanding Cistercian order, Bernard was in a position to comment on nearly every noteworthy occurrence in twelfth-century Europe. He was a passive supporter of the Empress, more out of dislike for Stephen than out of enthusiasm for Matilda. But it is in his role as adviser to Queen Melisende that we can really begin to discern his attitude toward females and the exercise of public authority. In Melisende's case, the evidence distinctly shows that she, at least, saw herself not as a mere transmitter of royal blood, but as a queen in her own right. Even before her father's death she began signing charters with formulae such as "daughter of the king and heir to the kingdom of Jerusalem" ("filia regis et regni Hierosolimitani haeres" [Kohler 1900: 128]). Fulk, count of Anjou, came to the Holy Land to marry Melisende and share in ruling the kingdom, although it is not clear from the sources exactly what kind of power-sharing the barons and the royal family originally envisioned (Mayer 1972, 1985; Edbury and Rowe 1983: 80-83). William of Tyre, admittedly one of Melisende's partisans, believed that she ruled the kingdom by hereditary right. His description of the power struggle between the royal couple emphasizes Melisende's status as heir of her father, and ends with Fulk's total capitulation to Melisende and her party. According to his account, Melisende was so angry at those who had sided with Fulk that they were forced to take measures for their own safety. Even the king feared her wrath, "finding no place was entirely safe among the kindred and partisans of the queen." The two were finally reconciled, but Fulk had learned his lesson. From this time forward, William contended, Fulk became so uxorious that "not even in unimportant cases did he take any measures without [Melisende's] knowledge and assistance" (William of Tyre 1943: ii, 220-21). Despite modern skepticism about the extent of Melisende's power, William's contention seems to be borne out by diplomatic evidence (Edbury and Rowe 1983: 81-82; Mayer 1972; Mayer 1988: 84-85). All the surviving royal charters that Fulk issued after their reconciliation bear the phrases "consensu Milisendis uxoris," "assensu uxoris Milisendis," or "consensu Milisendis reginae" (Röhricht 1893-94, rpt 1960: nos. 163, 164, 174, 179, 181, 210). In charters in which Fulk acts solely as count of Antioch, concerning his own lands, he does not mention Melisende. The most telling evidence of Melisende's determination to rule came in 1145, when her son came of age and she refused to relinquish the throne. She clearly saw herself as a ruler for life rather than as a regent for her son, a possibility that seems not to have occurred in the thinking of many medieval churchmen. Bernard provides a vivid example of this "blind spot." He viewed even the strongest women as part of a royal or noble lineage. In one letter, written to Melisende shortly after her husband died, Bernard exhorted her thus:

> Now that your husband the king is dead, and the young king as yet unfit to discharge the affairs of state and fulfill the duty of a king, the eyes of all will be on you and the entire burden of the kingdom will fall on you alone. You must set your hand to great things and, although a woman, you must act as a man by doing everything you have to do "in a spirit prudent and strong." You must arrange all things prudently and discreetly so that all may judge you from your actions to be a king rather than a queen and so the Gentiles may have no occasion for saying "Where is the king of Jerusalem?" But you will reply, "Such things are beyond my power; they are great matters which far exceed my strength and my knowledge; they are the duties of a man, and I am only a woman, weak in body, changeable of heart, not far-seeing in counsel nor accustomed to business."

Bernard went on to assure the queen that she should rely on the strength of the Lord to assist her in ruling (Migne, *PL* clxxxii: 557).

In a second letter, Bernard praised Melisende for ruling herself and her kingdom with the advice of wise men, and for "providently and wisely meeting the dangers which threatened the Holy Land according to the wisdom God gave you, with sound counsels and help. These are actions which become a strong woman, a humble widow, a great queen" (Migne,

PL clxxxii: 495). Bernard's letters reveal two important points about his conception of Melisende and her position. First, he, like other twelfth-century thinkers, is unable to consider her outside her familial relationships or, failing that, apart from the "wise" males who are giving her counsel. And second, when Bernard considers secular power, it is entirely in masculine terms. In order to succeed, even as a regent, Melisende must become a "king" rather than a "queen." She must also somehow overcome the handicaps of her female sex and acquire the "masculine" virtues of strength, steadfastness, and wisdom. But these "masculine" qualities are not available to males alone. Bernard realizes that, under certain circumstances, women were perfectly capable of assuming qualities that otherwise might be considered foreign to their nature.

Bernard was not alone in urging or praising women in positions of authority to exercise what are normally thought of as masculine qualities. During the English Civil War, both Matildas were described in masculine terms. The *Gesta Stephani* praised Stephen's wife for the "manly courage" she exhibited during Stephen's captivity (Potter and Davis 1976: 27). At one point the chronicler described her as having "a manly heart in a woman's body" (Potter and Davis 1976: 122; Bandel 1957: 117). The Empress was similarly referred to as having "masculine courage in a female body" and as being "an example of fortitude and patience" (Ralph of Diss, quoted in Chibnall 1991: 194). Modern scholars have sometimes been troubled by the tendency of medieval commentators to use such gendered language in describing or praising noblewomen. It does seem as if these male commentators only approved of women when they were acting against their essential female nature and taking on masculine characteristics. I do not believe, however, that this is necessarily the case. While medieval chroniclers definitely disapproved of some of the vices they associated with the female nature, they also approved of some feminine characteristics and even urged males to develop them. For instance, in the Cistercian literature of the twelfth century, we see many instances of male religious authority being compared to nurturing mothers (Bynum 1982: 110-69). Bernard himself spoke of the relationship of an abbot to his congregation in terms of nurturing and dependence, and both in his letters and his spiritual writings, he described himself as a "bride" and a "mother" (ibid., 115-18). It appears that the twelfth-century writers under consideration here interpreted the exercise of secular power as an activity calling for what we see as active, vigorous, and "masculine" virtues, while the exercise of authority in monastic life called mainly for passive, contemplative, nurturant, predominantly "female" qualities. According to their world view, God placed persons in positions of authority according to his plans, and he also provided humanity with a range of behaviors appropriate to those positions. The successful wielding of power called for many qualities, both "male" and "female" in nature. Feminine virtues such as prudence, wisdom, patience, and compassion often were as critical as the masculine qualities of strength, bravery, resolve, and fidelity. Twelfth-century writers called upon persons in authority to exercise whatever virtues were appropriate to their station in life without regard to their sex.[8]

While it is clear that medieval thinkers were not able or even willing to exclude women from sharing in public authority, it is not so clear that their tolerance extended to accepting a female ruler in her own right. Matilda enjoyed the approbation of French and German chroniclers who could fit her into the familiar patterns of female intercessor or regent, but the English chroniclers who saw her claiming power in her own right often saw her as haughty, arrogant and unwomanish (Chibnall 1988: 107-08). Few general conclusions about the "status of women" in the turbulent twelfth century can be drawn from the way in which the succession of Melisende and Matilda were presented in the chronicles, but it certainly seems that contemporaries were not willing to surrender authority to a female acting on her own behalf. To modern eyes, these chroniclers seem to have avoided an obvious problem by seeing powerful females as members of noble or royal families rather than as individuals. But it would be unfair to accuse them of deliberate evasion. In both of the cases I have considered, polemicists were unusually concerned with establishing the principle of hereditary succession after long periods of disorder. In addition, medieval writers always tended to see people not as individuals but as representatives of groups, types, or families (Bynum 1982). I am reminded of the admonition given by a pioneer scholar in the field of medieval women's history. Half a century ago, Eileen Power warned against trying to find something so elusive as a definition of the "status" of medieval women. There are, she wrote, inherent problems in trying to determine what in any age constitutes the "position of women," and it will always be "one thing in theory, another in legal position, and yet another in everyday life" (Power 1975: 9).

Department of History
The University of California, Hayward

NOTES 2

1. The few older biographies in Hungarian yield little, as the records are insufficient to reconstruct the lives of early-medieval queens. References to eleventh- to thirteenth-century queenship in general histories of Hungary are equally rare, with the exception of the "famous queens" such as Gisela and the hapless Gertrudis. Pioneering exceptions include Gábor Klaniczay's studies on the saintly princesses of the Árpád dynasty (1990: 95-128), and a recent popular history by Erik Fügedi (1986a), as yet untranslated, on the tragic fate of the late-fourteenth-century Angevin queens. For those fluent in Hungarian, bio-bibliographical references can be found in Kenyeres 1967-81. In general, reference to Hungarian literature will be omitted here, as these works can be easily found in bibliographical handbooks.

2. Based mainly upon Schwennicke 1980-84: i, tables 153-55.

3. Dau. of Theodul Synadenos by a sister of Emp. Nicephoros III Botoniates, who hoped to make the Hungarian queen's brother his heir (Sturdza 1983: 425).

4. Dau. of the *sebastocrator* Isaac Komnenos, s. of John II and br. of Emp. Manuel II, for whom see following note (Sturdza 1983: 276-77).

5. Dau. of Emp. Manuel II by Anne of Sulzbach; the div. may have been imposed, as Manuel's mother was Irene of Hungary, dau. of Ladislas I (Schwennicke 1980-84: i, tables 153-54; Sturdza 1983: 277).

6. Dau. of Constance, hss. to the principality of Antioch, by Renaud of Châtillon (Gabriel 1944: 122).

7. Dau. of Peter II, titular emp. of Constantinople (Schwennicke 1980-84: i, table 155).

NOTES 3

1. We have no sources describing the crowning of Danish queens in the Middle Ages apart from a fourteenth-century chalk painting on the wall of a village church (Jørgensen and Skovgaard 1910); see fig. 3.2. See also Vestergaard 1990; Hoffmann 1990: 131-37.

NOTES 4

Earlier versions of this paper were read at the Conference on "Medieval Women" at the University of York (September 1990), and at the Women's History Seminar at the University of London (November 1990). To the audiences on both occasions, I owe thanks for many searching questions and comments. I should also like to thank Rosamund McKitterick for further constructive criticism, and John Parsons for editorial support and patience.

1. For depiction of myths on Roman sarcophagi from the second century A.D. as "a way of aestheticizing death," Veyne 1987a: 232-33; for the *quadriga* as symbol of the virtues in Carolingian thought, Mähl 1979.

2. Aurelius Augustinus 1972: 143-52, 239-42, 255-60, 239-42, 273-742 and 278, where Proserpina's name is derived from *proserpere*, "to creep forth" (compare Varro, "because like a serpent she sways now to the right, now to the left," quoted in Aurelius Augustinus 1972: 145 [note 20]).

3. The later history of the sarcophagus has its own interest. When Frederick Barbarossa in 1165 had Charlemagne canonized and wished to transfer his bones to a more elaborate tomb, the sarcophagus was thought unsuitable and the remains, still wrapped in Byzantine silk, were put in an oakwood coffin until 1215, when Frederick II got them into the silver-gilt reliquary known as the *Karlsschrein*. The sarcophagus remained at Aachen in the octagon church till the 1790s when French revolutionary armies took it to Paris; it was returned to Aachen after the Congress of Vienna.

4. Einhard 1911: ch. 30 (at 34-35), ch. 32 (at 36-37), depicts Charlemagne as ailing, and describes portents of his death in the three years preceding 814.

5. No such "rereading" was necessary for Louis the Pious' sarcophagus, which dated from the late fourth or fifth century and depicted a Christian theme, the crossing of the Red Sea (Melzak 1990: 630-32; compare Dierkens 1991: 166-68).

6. Aurelius Augustinus 1972: 294. Compare responses to the statue of Theodoric in the Aachen courtyard: it may have been set up "simply . . . as an enhancement of the magnificence and display appropriate to a great ruler" (Bullough 1991a: 62), but shortly after Charlemagne's death it was denounced as an abomination by one who saw the Arian king as the epitome of tyranny (Godman 1986: 134-37).

7. The absence of direct evidence for a female gaze in the Carolingian period does not, of course, mean that no such gaze existed. For gender-differentiated views of rape in late-medieval pastoral poetry, see Gravdal 1991.

8. Paris, BN, MS lat. 1 fol. 3v; color reproduction in Mütherich and Gaehde 1977: 76 (plate 21), black-and-white in McKitterick 1990: 83.

9. McKitterick's illustration does not show the female scribe's pen very clearly; in the drawing based on this miniature on the dust jacket of Wemple 1981, reprinted from a woodcut in Lacroix 1963, the female scribe's pen has completely disappeared, and her right hand appears to be *holding* the scroll! Among connections between scholars and Carolingian women listed by McKitterick 1990: 85-86, that linking Alcuin to Charlemagne's sister Gisele and her niece Rotrude seems especially important: it leads straight to Tours, and the two women themselves invoke the Jerome-Paula-Eustochium model.

10. Now in the museum of Meaux, it was kept in a reliquary until 1792 when it was thrown out and buried in earth. Exhumed in 1803, it was again put in a reliquary which was not opened until 1985. The design came from a Sassanid Persian model. Other examples are from Maastricht, Belgium, and St.-Maurice d'Agaune, Switzerland (Laporte 1989: 47; Laporte and Boyer 1991: 58 [color photo]). My thanks are due to J.-P. Laporte for generously supplying information about the fragment, and for permission to reproduce his black-and-white illustration of it.

11. I am grateful to Marian Archibald of the British Museum for help with Irene's coins and for providing photographs, which the B.M. kindly gave permission to reproduce.

12. For the tradition of scattering largesse, Hendy 1985: 192-201 (esp. 196).

13. Miller 1971: 639-52 argues that Byzantine monarchy was, in a symbolic sense, sexually ambiguous, hermaphroditic; an interesting interpretation, which could be applied elsewhere in early-medieval Europe. But misogyny seems to have been as prevalent in Byzantium (Theophanes is a case in point) as in Francia.

14. Citing Luke 10:39-42, and then Luke 7:38.

15. Wallach 1977: 207-08 suggests, not wholly convincingly, an additional "sarcastic" (*sic*) touch in what he took to be a deliberate alteration to a passage quoted from Isidore's *Etymologies*, where "unmarried women even of marriageable age [*perfectae aetatis*] should remain in tutelage because of their lightmindedness [*levitas animi*] is altered to "of advanced [*provectae*] age. . . ."

16. Arguing that the source of this notice, in a Cologne computistical MS written up in 805, was a contemporary annal from St.-Amand.

17. Now in the New York Metropolitan Museum of Art. Its thickness and unusually large size, 22 x 14.5 cm (9" x 6") suggested to S. Lewis (1980: 92) that it was originally intended to be fixed to a door rather than a bookcover (though Rosamund McKitterick kindly tells me that covers can be still larger than 9" x 6"); Lewis recalls that Mary was acclaimed in the Akathistos hymn as "Thou through whom Paradise is opened." I am grateful to the Metropolitan Museum for permission to reproduce this photograph.

18. On Lewis' interpretation of the image, Irene would have risked causing offence in the west at an exceptionally dangerous time.

19. Kurze 1895: 31 records what may be a mission of conciliation to Carloman, but Bertrada can equally well be seen as Charlemagne's agent.

20. The fact that his nephew Tassilo of Bavaria and Duke Arichis of Benevento were also married to daughters of King Desiderius spelled further dangers for Charlemagne. Both women were credited with important political roles that deserve further study.

21. For Adalard, son of Bernard, "nullo negotio persuaderi posset . . . ut, ei [Hildegarde] quam vivente illa [Desiderius' daughter] rex acceperat, aliquo communcaret servitutis obsequio" (Paschasius 1879: col. 1511). For Benedict of Aniane the evidence is less explicit, but he had been handed over as a boy by his father to Bertrada *inter scholares nutriendum*, to be brought up among the young men at the palace, and would have been placed in a very awkward position when her protégée was divorced and supplanted (Ardo 1887: 201).

22. Listing (at 502) Charlemagne's blessings, among them "quod Deus transtulit illum [Carloman] de regno ad alterum et exaltavit te super omne hoc regnum sine sanguinis effusione." Thanks were also due for receipt of the Italian *regna*, "com [*sic*] omnibus praeciosis."

23. Hildegard *∂*. 30 April, Bertrada 12 July, 783.

24. If he was writing the *Vita Karoli* for Louis the Pious in the 820s or 830s, Einhard may have intended to contrast, not compare, Louis' wife Judith with Fastrada.

25. This letter survives in a unique MS which seems to have associations with St.-Denis in the period of Fardulf's abbacy (*ca.* 793-806).

26. The Psalter is now Montpellier, Bibliothèque Universitaire MS 409.

27. Charlemagne may have had sexual relations with one or more of these women before 800, that is, during Liutgard's lifetime, but available evidence leaves this unclear. Only three concubines were named in the original version of Einhard's text, but in Class C MSS (which also have Walahfrid's preface) the fourth, Madelgard, is added. Werner 1967: 443 suggests Walahfrid may have made the addition; if so, this was presumably because he, or his patron, was interested in Madelgard's daughter Ruothild, for whom as abbess of Chelles see above, pp. 45-46.

28. Among Charlemagne's descendants, however, a ninth-century Hugh very nearly succeeded in claiming a kingdom, and a tenth-century Hugh did so (Werner 1967: table, generations V and VI).

29. Alcuin 1895: letters 15, 32, 72, 84, 154, 195, 213, 214, 216, 228, 279 are addressed to them; they are mentioned in letters 88, 150, 153, 177, 244, 262.

30. Astronomer 1829: ch. 21 (at 618); a messenger was sent to Louis "ab eis qui sepulturam eius [i.e., Charlemagne] curarunt, liberis scilicet et proceribus palatinis." A glance at the family tree reveals that the only "children" capable of taking such action at this point were daughters. Astronomer further singles out for mention Wala, Charlemagne's cousin and brother of Gundrada, for whom above, ibid. pp. 56-57.

31. For eunuchs in Late Antiquity, Hopkins 1978: 172-96, esp. 196: "The violent criticism directed against eunuchs diverted dissatisfaction which might otherwise have been aimed at the emperor . . . [Eunuchs] were used as lubricants for the system." Charlemagne also employed eunuchs in his palace, apparently in imitation of Byzantine practice (Theodulf 1881: 493 [lines 87-92]; McCormick 1986: 364).

NOTES 5

An earlier version of this paper was presented at the International Congress on Medieval Studies at Western Michigan University, May 1991. I am grateful for audience reaction and for generous comments by Judith Bennett, E. A. R. Brown, Margaret Howell, Lois Huneycutt, Jacqueline Murray, and the late Michael M. Sheehan CSB, without, of course, implying that they share responsibility for any oversights.

Unless otherwise indicated all MS material is in the Public Record Office, London (S.C. 1 = Ancient Correspondence; C 47/ = Chancery miscellany; JUST 1/ = Justices Itinerant [formerly cited as J.I. 1/]); *CPR* = *Calendar of Patent Rolls, CClR* = *Cal. of Close Rolls, CLR* = *Cal. of Liberate Rolls* (all ed., P.R.O).

1. If Edward merely sought a polite excuse, surely one queen's objection would have sufficed. Compare, too, Nicholas Trevet's account of Eleanor of Castile's objection to enclosing her six-year-old daughter in a convent—for which that daughter was Trevet's likely source—and the fact that Edward I kept all his daughters single until they were past fourteen (both points discussed below, pp. 75, 77).

2. Walker sees Furnivall 1897 as important in shaping the popular image. As influential, however, is the frequently cited eleventh-century marriage of the duke of Gaeta to the prince of Capua's daughter, " . . . infantulam nolentem, flentem, et pro viribus renitentem, non assientibus sed valde dolentibus matre et parentela . . . ." (Noonan 1973: 419-20).

3. For methodology, Parsons 1984: 250-56. The compilation's length precludes printing it here. Lack of documentation compelled omission of the first house of Lancaster descended from Henry III's younger son, the Staffords of Buckingham descended from Edward III's last son, and the Beauforts descended from John of Gaunt (though mentioned here, Margaret Beaufort is not part of the numerical evidence, as she is the only female of that family whose age at first childbirth can be accurately calculated).

4. Walker 1982: 125 cites *Cal. Fine Rolls 1327-1337*, 82, 96, showing a fourteenth-century official attitude that marriageable age was around fifteen; see also Herlihy 1985: 103-07.

5. The seven: the Lord Edward married Eleanor of Castile just before her thirteenth birthday; she perhaps had a short-lived daughter seven months later (J. Parsons 1984: 248, 257). Eleanor dau. of Edw. II, *b.* June 1318, *m.* May 1332 Reinald, count of Gueldres, first child *b.* May 1333 (Isenburg-Büdingen 1953: i part 2, table 2; Lane 1910: i, 222). John of Gaunt, duke of Lancaster *m.* May 1359 Blanche of Lancaster *b.* 25 Mar. 1345, first child *b.* Mar. 1360 (Lane 1910: i, 160-61, 248-49). Henry of Bolingbroke's marriage to Mary de Bohun is discussed below, p. 75. Blanche dau. of Henry IV, *b.* 1392 *m.* July 1402 Ludwig III, Count Palatine; first child *b.* May 1406 (Isenburg-Büdingen 1953: i part 1, table 31; Lane 1910: i, 307-08). Margaret *b. ca.* 1385, dau. of Thomas Holand, earl of Kent, *m.* bef. 28 Sept. 1397 John Beaufort, earl of Somerset; eldest son (qy if first child) *b.* Nov. 1401 (Cokayne 1910-40: vii, 156 [note "e"], and xii part 1, 44-45); her sister Elizabeth *b. ca.* 1393 was m. *ca.* 29 Aug. 1394 to John, lord Neville, only child *b.* Sept. 1406 or Sept. 1407 (Cokayne 1910-40: vii, 156 [note "e"], and xii part 2, 548-49).

6. Walker 1982: 125 cites *Cal. Close Rolls 1369-1374*, 246-47, a non-royal case in which a couple were to live apart until the nine-year-old bride reached thirteen.

7. They were cohabiting by Sept. 1238 (Luard 1890: ii, 228); that November it was feared she was barren (Paris 1872-84: iii, 518). Anxieties were perhaps high as Eleanor's sister Margaret, married to Louis IX of France in 1234, remained childless until 1240.

8. Isabella had four children between Nov. 1312 and 1321 and at least one miscarriage or stillbirth in 1313 (Trease 1959: 46 [note 184, where "Edmund" should read "Edward"]). On Edward's bastard, Blackley 1964: 76-77; Gaveston's wife was *b.* 1292, their daughter in Feb. 1312 (Lane 1910: i, 182-84).

9. Few English royal daughters took the veil; for the Hungarian royal house, Vauchez 1977: 400-402 and Klaniczay 1990: 95-128, and for the potential influence of professed royal virgins in tenth-century León, see Roger Collins' essay, pp. 98-119. See also Janet Nelson's comments on the cloistered and professed women of the Carolingian house, pp. 43-70.

10. Except for Henry VIII (and presumably Katherine of Aragon and Anne Boleyn) there is little evidence that English royal parents reacted to the births of daughters as

implied by Bullough 1973: 496-97 or Haskell 1973: 469-70; the well-known anecdote told of Elizabeth of York's birth (1466) says less about the reactions of Edward IV and his wife than of the fatuous courtier who had predicted a son. Elizabeth's baptism and her mother's churching followed the elaborate prescriptions of the *Liber Regie Capelle* (1445-49), which does not indicate that such celebrations were differentiated according to a newborn royal's sex (Scofield, 1923: i, 393-96; Ullmann 1961: 72-73; Staniland 1987).

11. Born late in 1241, Eleanor of Castile wed on 1 Nov. 1254 (J. Parsons 1984: 248-49). Eleanor of Provence, likely born in 1223, married in Jan. 1236 (Paris 1872-84: iii, 335; Isenburg-Büdingen 1953: i part 2, tables 45, 110; Cox 1974: 7-9, 20-21; Sivéry 1987: 11).

12. Howell 1990 suggests Eleanor interrupted her travels with Henry to stay at Windsor with her children for extended periods of time. I am most grateful for generous suggestions and references from Miss Howell, whose monograph on Eleanor of Provence is nearing completion.

13. Mary's letter is S.C. 1/19/111 ("envoy ioe ore a vous et vous prie et requer humblement que pleysir vous seit par tous les entrevenantz a moy mander, pur laese de mon cuer, vostre estat" [Woodstock, Sunday after St. Bartholomew, 1291 or later as she calls herself "humble nonayn du covent Dambr'"]).

14. Green 1859-69, as cited above for Edward I's daus.; for a pilgrimage by Charlemagne's wife and daughters to a convent associated with his family, see Nelson's essay in this volume, p. 56.

15. E.g., *Cal. Patent Rolls 1301-1307*, 36, 37, 38, 65, 102, 254, 313, 389; Green 1859-69: ii, 298-99, 300; J. Parsons 1991, and forthcoming; Huneycutt, forthcoming. On cultivating royal daughters' patronage, see Nelson's essay above, p. 60.

16. Griffiths 1979: 13-36; Allen 1979: 171-92. A commonplace book from Henry IV's reign (1399-1412) includes excerpts from Nicholas Trevet's Anglo-Norman chronicle (*ca.* 1320?) giving the issue of Edward I's daughters, in Henry IV's day the nearest kin to Edward III's descendants as the issue of Edward II's younger children was extinct ("Del engendrure de les ffillez de Roy Edward ffitiz le Roy Henry terce de sa primer femme Alianore ffille au Roy despayne," London, BL, Harl. 2386, fols. 33r-34v; Dean 1976: 345-46). For a 1425 claim to parliamentary precedence among earls, involving descents from Plantagenet women, see Record Commission 1783-1832: iv, 268.

17. Edward I's gddaus. Joan of Bar (dau. of the Eleanor of the 1282 incident, *m.* 1293 Henry III of Bar) *m.* Earl John de Warenne; Mary de Monthermer, dau. of Joan "of Acre" (1272-1307, *m.* 1290 Earl Gilbert de Clare of Gloucester, and then *m.* 1295 Ralph de Monthermer), *m.* Earl Duncan of Fife. Edward III's gddau. Philippa de Coucy, dau. of Isabella (1332-1379, *m.* 1366 Enguerran de Coucy), *m.* Earl Robert de Vere of Oxford. Henry I's patronage of his nephew Stephen of Blois may be recalled here, as may John's selection of a Castilian niece to marry Louis of France in 1200.

18. With the knights and ladies listed in J. Parsons 1977: 155-57, compare the queen's grants to: John and Christiana de Weston (*CChR*: ii, 234), William and Iseult le Bruyn (Francisque-Michel and Bémont 1885-1906: ii, nos. 1569-71), and John and Joan Ferré (*CChR*: ii, 188, 256). It is not certain that the short-lived first wife of Eleanor's steward Guy Ferré, Jr. ever was the queen's attendant, but Eleanor almost

certainly arranged the marriage and provided for them (*CChR*: ii, 330; Kirk *et al.* 1899-1964: ii, 53). A similar pattern is noted for Isabella of France's women in 1311-12 (Blackley and Hermansen 1971: xiii-xiv).

19. The friars are noted in the king's wardrobe book for 1289-90 (C 47/4/5 fols. 13r, 29r). Eleanor of Provence's daughters shared her Franciscan sympathies (*CLR*: vi, no. 409; Stevenson 1839: 97; Kingsford 1915: 70-71).

20. These points are developed further in J. C. Parsons, "Of Queens, Courts and Books: Reflections on the Literary Patronage of Thirteenth-Century Plantagenet Queens," forthcoming in J. H. McCash, ed., *The Literary and Artistic Patronage of Medieval Women* (University of Georgia Press).

21. Bourdieu 1977: 62-63, feels Kabyle women play little part in such accumulation.

22. Compare the formulations in Ruddick 1984. Only superficially does this reflect the idea that mothers seek to spare daughters their female destiny but force it on them by training them for nothing else (de Beauvoir 1952: 578-80).

23. Daughters' training itself would presumably instill a perception that they were future actors of some importance; protective protests like that of 1282, Eleanor of Castile's exception to Mary's enclosure, or Margaret Beaufort's plea (assuming daughters were aware of them, as Mary seems to have been) would give them some indication of their importance to their parents.

24. Beardwood 1969: 106-08; *CPR 1281-1292*, 417-18. JUST 1/542 m. 1r identifies Eleanor de Ewelle as dau. of Richard de Ewelle, wardrobe buyer to Henry III, who in 1265 gave Ewelle the marriage of Edmund de Hemmegrave (*CPR 1258-1265*, 451). In 1291 Hemmegrave claimed that after he refused to marry Ewelle's dau., the queen exacted from him £200 as the value of his marriage. This was unquestionably the money the queen seized from the Lombards; in Feb. 1292 Hemmegrave quitclaimed the identical sum to Eleanor de Ewelle (JUST 1/542 m. 3r).

25. We may never know the truth behind accounts of the projected marriage of Edward III's daughter Isabella to the lord of Albret's son, which claim that Edward allowed Isabella the freedom to refuse the marriage, which she did when just about to take ship for Gascony (Green 1859-69: iii, 164-228).

NOTES 6

1. For the role of siege warfare in eighth-century Spain see Collins 1989: 135-37.

2. Her mother first appears in a Leonese document of 21 February 934 (Rodriguez 1972: 606-08).

3. Better documented is the foundation of the *Infantado* of Covarrubias by Count García Fernàndez of Castile and his wife Ava for their daughter Urraca (Garrido Garrido 1983: documents 4, 9). A section of the original church of San Salvador survives inside a later rebuilding, but the site is extremely difficult of access due to the apparent impossibility of finding the current key-holder! On the church, Gómez Moreno 1919: i, 253-59; the royal burials are noted in two slightly later recensions of the eleventh-century *Chronicle of Sampiro*, the only Leonese narrative history of this period (Pérez de Urbel 1952: 332, 334, 339).

4. Some forty royal documents survive from the reign of Ordoño III, of which only one was certainly witnessed by Elvira. Her appearance at the judicial assembly of which that document is a record may have been prompted by the role of the Infantado of San Salvador as the depository of the authoritative text of the *Forum Iudicium* (Rodríguez 1982: 159, 165 [note 14]; Collins 1985: 498-502).

5. Documents of Sancho I are relatively rare. They are listed in the appendix to Rodríguez 1987, but without full witness lists; they may be found in the editions of charter collections cited by Rodríguez. A document of 23 May 962 is confirmed by Elvira together with the bishop of León and some of his clergy (Saéz and Saéz 1990: no. 354).

6. This cult has not been much studied. The Spanish *vita* is to be found only in Florez 1747-1879: xxiii, 23-31, Hrothswitha's version in Migne, *PL* 137: cols. 1093-1102.

7. Vermudo's legitimacy has been much debated (Saéz 1946: 58-65). Rodríguez 1982: 103-05, advances strong arguments against the presumed existence of a first wife of Ordoño III called Elvira Peláez; but his inference that this makes Vermudo a son of Ordoño's one and only wife, Urraca Fernández, must be resisted (see note 15).

8. Vermudo II married first the Portuguese Velasquita Ramírez (dissolved *ca.* 991) and then (before December 994) Elvira Garcés, daughter of Count García Fernández of Castile (Ruben 1960; Sánchez Candeira 1950: 449-503).

9. This conclusion is based primarily upon tabulation of witness lists of the charter collections of León cathedral and the monastery of St. Facundus at Sahagún. One or two additional texts can be found in such collections as the Cartulary of Samos. For Navarrese preeminence in León at this time, Pérez de Urbel 1969-70: ii, 249-50; Rodríguez 1987: 127.

10. Madrid, Archivo Historico Nacional, sección de códices, 986B fols. 20v-21r; Viñayo 1982: 128.

11. The only known document of King Jimeno Garcés uses the dating formula "regnante Scemeno Garsianes cum suo creato domno Garsea in Pampilona . . ." (Ubieto Arteta 1962: document 14). This implies that while the infant García was not called king, he was seen as exercising formal royal authority alongside his uncle. The earliest document referring to García as king is dated 26 June 933 (Ubieto Arteta 1981: document 7). Interestingly, Jimeno's sons were never expected to inherit their father's status.

12. The index to Ubieto Arteta 1981 prefers the former, but it is only ten to fifteen kilometres from Pamplona, which would seem strangely close for the centre of a subkingdom. The upper Araquil valley would make a more comprehensible unit, and its Lizárraga is 45 to 50 kilometres from Pamplona by road.

13. The only partial exception is Sancho II as subking in Aragón (948-70), for whom Collins 1986b: 101.

14. Sancha Sánchez married three times: to Ordoño III of León, to Alvar Harraméliz, lord of Alava, and to Fernán González of Castile (Lacarra 1945: 237). She is another good example of the Navarrese traditions typified by her daughter Urraca.

15. It is improbable, contrary to Rodriguez' views referred to above (note 7), that Urraca was the mother of Vermudo II (r. 984-999); for her to be queen of Navarre while he

was king of León would surely have aroused some comment in the kingdoms' limited historiography. To be accurate, Uracca appears in two illuminations, one a copy of the other; she features together with her husband and his brother King Ramiro of Viguera in the Codex Vigilano of 976 (MS Escorialensis d.1.2), and the Codex Aemilianensis of 992 (Escorialensis d.1.1). See de Silva y Verástegui 1984: 419-21 and plates 26-27.

NOTES 7

1. Paris, AN, J 401, no. 1.

2. Paris, AN, J 401, nos. 4-5.

3. The perpetual edict establishing the age of majority for French kings is Paris, AN, J 401 a-c; ordinance of October 1374 on guardianship of the children of France and the regency of the kingdom, J 401 no. 8, and J 402 no. 7. As Joan predeceased Charles V, these provisions never actually came into effect in her case. See Poulet 1989: 130ff.

4. The January 1393 ordinance on the guardianship is Paris, AN, J 402 no. 10; the ordinance on the regency of the same date is J 402, no. 11.

5. The ruling of April 1403 is Paris, AN, J 402 no. 12; that of December 1407 (following the murder of Charles VI's only brother, Duke Louis of Orléans) is J 402 no. 14.

NOTES 8

This chapter is a revised version of a conference paper presented at the Twenty-Sixth International Congress on Medieval Studies at Western Michigan University, May 1991. It is also a portion of my forthcoming doctoral dissertation, "French Queens in the Cult of the Renaissance Monarchy," University of Iowa, Department of History. Research was supported by doctoral fellowships from my department; by The Ada L. Ballard Dissertation Fellowship in the Humanities, Graduate College, University of Iowa; and an AAUW Dissertation Year Fellowship. The Iowa Renaissance Studies group funded research and participation in NEH seminars at the Newberry Library in Chicago. Finally, I would like to thank Ralph E. Giesey, Richard A. Jackson, John C. Parsons, and Constance H. Berman for invaluable tips and encouragement. I have also profited from conversations with a number of scholars, notably Chris Africa, Joseph A. Bergin, Joan A. Holladay, William C. Jordan, and Donovan Ochs.

1. Louise kept her faith in relics and pilgrimages to assure a male heir (Baux 1902: 447-464; Baux, Bourrilly, Mabilly 1904: 31-64; Bourrilly 1910).

2. Queen Anne petitioned for Gié's dismissal; charges of treason were brought against him, but he was ultimately acquitted (Knecht 1982: 7-8 notes Louise of Savoy's involvement in the incident; the introduction to de Maulde La Clavière 1885 gives a thoughtful assessment of the personalities and issues involved).

3. A copy of Louis' testament is Paris, AN, KK 1438, 191-92. The right to guardianship of royal children was the basis for a queen's regental authority; for constitutional and historical foundations of that prerogative see Olivier-Martin 1931; Mattei 1978; Lightman 1981; Poulet 1989: i, and above, ch. 7.

4. Marot's "Prières sur la restauration de la santé de Madame Anne de Brétaigne, royne de France," (Paris, BN, Fr 1539 fols. 6v, 10r) reveals hopes for an heir; Paris, Bibliothèque de l'Arsenal 791, fol. 1r-v has copies of Louis XII's royal letters on a procession to pray for an heir. *Odos Monocolos* (Paris, BN, Lat. 8396) depicts Louise of Savoy as St. Agnes bearing a banner dated 1512; the year and the date of St. Agnes' feast recalled 21 January, when the last son died, virtually guaranteeing Francis' succession to Louis XII. Louise noted the significance of St. Agnes in her journal (Savoy 1838: 434; le Boterf 1976: 259; Orth 1976: i, 93-98 and Le Coq 1987: 127-38 discuss the miniature; see also Knecht 1982: 8-10). These MSS derive from royal treatises praising the king's exalted lineage, e.g., Paris, BN, Fr. 2222 ("La nativité du Roy Charles VIIIᵉ").

5. Now Paris, BN, Fr. 2285.

6. Paris, BN, Fr. 2285, fols. 5v, 6r, 7v, 8r-v, 12v, and 13v refer to Francis as heir; fols. 5v, 6v, 7r, and 12v honor Louise as princess, mother, guardian, and regent; fols. 15r-16v discuss the Estates General at Tours and the sorrows of king and realm without an heir, a lament eloquently developed by the anonymous translator of *Les Remèdes* (Paris, BN, Fr. 225), dialogues lxxciii ("Du Roy sans filz"), and lxxix ("Du Royaullme perdu"). I do not consider here themes found in allegorical treatises, for which see Le Coq 1987: 74-77, ch. 3, and 161.

7. Paris, BN, Fr. 2285, fols. 7r-v, 10r-v, 11r, 13r-v.

8. Ibid., fols. 6v, 9v, 13v-15v.

9. Paris, BN, Fr. 2285, fols. 13r-v, 15r.

10. Paris, BN, Fr. 2285, fols. 5v, 6r, 16v-17r. Reference to blood lines derived from thirteenth-century royal historiography celebrating alleged Capetian descent from the Merovingians (Spiegel 1978: 129-48; Wood 1966: ch. 1). *Le Compas* stresses Francis' descent from the sainted Louis IX; on the dynastic basis of late-medieval royal succession and Louis IX as "sub genearch" for Valois and Bourbon, Giesey 1961: 25-37; Joinville 1668: 121; Gousset, Avril, Richard 1990: 9-16; and on the use of *reditus* legends in late-medieval France as contrasted to the thirteenth century, Poujol 1977: 259-69 (esp. 266-67). Celebrations of the dynastic basis of royal succession and divine favor guiding the births of royal heirs were part of the dynastic mystique of late-medieval French rulership (as discussed further, below); such works as those cited in note 3 do not, however, recognize the enatic component to royal succession.

11. Le Coq 1987 analyzes text and miniature without noting dynastic concerns; ibid., ch. 3 (esp. 161) notes other MSS hailing Louise as Francis' mother, but those allegorical works do not treat *Le Compas'* dynastic ideas. The closest model for the arrangement is the Psalter of Queen Emma, in which the Carolingian regent holds her son's hand as Christ blesses the royal family (Cahn 1985: 72-85)—a miniature unknown to the late-medieval French royal court. Simons 1988: 4-30 stresses the 1506 miniature's novelties by comparing Renaissance portraiture of women in profile with passive gazes. The frontispiece to Nicole de La Chesnaye's *La Nef de Santé avec le gouvernail du corps humain* of 1508 (Paris, BN, Vélins 1105) shows the author presenting his work to Louise and Francis; as in the 1506 miniature Louise faces the reader, stressing her importance in Francis' life.

12. In truth, translation of the inscription defies resolution, but it reveals both the juristic and dynastic bases of late-medieval kingship, which inspired celebration of the exalted stature of the French royal house. Late-fifteenth- and early-sixteenth-century MSS and printed books based on MSS in King Charles V's possession celebrated the education of French rulers in the context of the divine providence that oversaw their welfare; a notable example is Barthélemy de Glanville's *Le Propriétaire en francoys* (Paris, BN, Impr. Rés. R.219), translated from a work presented to Charles V, which extolled the importance of studying Holy Scripture. Celebration of the divine protection accorded a queen-regent, moreover, was often connected with her authority as mother.

13. A queen did not exercise temporal authority in her own right; her ability to act as regent derived from feudal and customary law practices touching succession to fiefs (in addition to works cited, see above discussion of the influence of private law concepts of guardianship and rights of minors in succession, below, pp. 180-81). While a mother was usually preferred as guardian, concern that queenly ambition could hinder succession to the Crown surfaced in early regencies: after Louis IX's death his wife did not become regent in part because suspicion of her personal ambition never abated (Boutaric 1867: 417-58; Olivier-Martin 1931: i, 95; Poulet 1989: i, 101).

14. New York, Pierpont Morgan Library MS 240. I must thank the Registrar of the Pierpont Morgan Library, Mr. David Wright, and Professor Anne Roberts, Department of History, University of Iowa, both of whom helped me immeasurably regarding my interest in this miniature.

15. On Francis' "crownworthiness," see Giesey 1961: 25-37.

16. I take the term "bio-genetic" from Bedos-Rezak 1988.

17. The interest these edicts held for sixteenth- and seventeenth-century jurists is affirmed by many MS copies, e.g., Paris, BN, Fr. 15527, fols. 95r-103r, 158r-v; Paris, AN, KK 1438, fols. 181r-184v has copies of regency legislation, 1409 to 1417; Paris, BN, Fr. 16630 has royal edicts and other documents on the appointment of a regent. Celebration of lineage was not absent in legislation instituting a regency or pertaining to the regent's powers (Saenger 1977: 17).

18. Paris, BN, Fr. 2275, the miniature on fol. 4; textual references are fols. 3r, 4r, 5v, 6v.

19. Paris, BN, Fr. 2472, *Discours ou Panegyrique Moral. . . Louise de Savoy*, esp. fols. 5r, 8r. Vatican, Ottob. Lat. 2720, *Recognitiones Loyse de Sabaudia*, celebrates her role in transmitting the "bon sang." Fifteenth-century England had two "royal" mothers—Cecily, duchess of York, and Lady Margaret Beaufort were both "the king's mother" (Armstrong 1983: xii-xiii).

20. Paris, BN, Fr. 20055, fols. 95v-97v.

21. Paris, AN, Xia 1517, fol. 292.

22. A copy of the *arrêt* of 28 April 1483, by which the Parlement restricted Anne's right to pardon, is in a seventeenth-century collection of documents relating to regental authority in Paris, BN, Fr. 16630, fol. 117r. Paris, AN, Xia 1517 (Register of the Parlement of Paris), fol. 292r, shows the court preoccupied with limiting Louise's right to fill vacant benefices; Paris, BN, Dupuy 85, fol. 48r-v, has a copy of Louise's agreement renouncing privileges conferred on her by Louis XII, including the right

to release prisoners. The court's actions were grounded in kingship's changing nature, which stressed the king's sovereign authority (especially in matters of justice) and extended to royal policies, e.g., the king's decision to create and sell offices including judicial ones (issues covered by Doucet 1921: i, 60; Shennan 1968: ch. 6; Knecht 1982: 19-22; Descimon 1991: 455-73; Jackson 1984: ch. 7).

23. Now Paris, BN, Fr. 2088.

24. These themes surface in other MSS commissioned to celebrate the French victories, e.g., New York, Pierpont Morgan Library, M.147, fol. A5, which shows Louise presenting the allegorical figure of Poetry to her armored and mounted son, who is accompanied by three other allegorical figures. The accompanying text discusses Louise's maternal zeal, which apparently extends to teaching her son the finer rhetorical arts. See also Sabatier 1991: 407.

25. Now Paris, BN, Fr. 145. Archives départmentales, Somme, Registre des Comptes CC 95 (1518), fol. 151, records that the council of Amiens ordered Le Chant Royal and gives a description of the council's wishes that corresponds with the finished MS; the artist was Jacques Platel.

26. Paris, BN, Fr 145, fol. 2r ("Tu as porte comme mere et regent/ Le Royal Sang Le corps honorifique/ Du Roy François qui les Françoys regente"). Comparison of royal and divine mothers appears in François Du Moulin's "Petit Livret faict à Madame Sainte Anne et de la Royne, sa fille, vierge pure, mere de Jesu Christ" (Paris, Bibliothèque de l' Arsenal 4009), apparently written in Louise's first regency and dedicated to her (fol. 34v) who, Du Moulin hopes, will intervene on behalf of his friend accused of heresy. Orth 1976: i, 127 treats the work in relation to contemporary religious issues, noting the passage "As the Virgin Mother of God was fifteen years old when she conceived the Prince of Life by the Holy Ghost, so were you, Madame, when you conceived the King of France by Your late Husband." Le Coq 1987: 278-79 cites another example.

27. Several such MSS survive, e.g., Paris, BN, Fr. 5750 and 14116; Paris, École des Beaux Arts 491; London, BL, Cott. Titus A xvi and Stowe 582. Le Coq 1987: 378, studies Bibliothèque de Nantes 1337. See also Hindman and Spiegel 1981. Comparison reveals minor variations in details but the composition and thematic interest of the miniatures does not vary.

28. Other writers incorporated dynastic notions in discussions of the king's obligation to render justice, e.g., Alain Chartier's "La Prenosticacion dy Roy Charles VIII de ce nom" (Paris, BN, Fr 20055, fol. 13r), which celebrated Charles' exalted lineage while praising the powers accorded French kings.

29. Studies on Blanche of Castile discuss her influence on matters of justice (Berger 1895: 328-29; Olivier-Martin 1931: 65-68; Jordan 1979: ch. 5; Poulet 1989: i, 70-76). Emphasis on the king's ceremonial presentation witnesses contemporary notions of immortality of the royal office that influenced late-fifteenth-century politics, propaganda, and constitutional discussion on "twin bodied Majesty" (Kantorowicz 1957). While the king's ceremonial presentation was cultivated at this period (Scheller 1983: 8), the mixture of ceremonial and dynastic themes in this miniature is unusual though not unique. In 1516, Symphorien Champier completed "Les grans croniques des gestes et vertuex faictz des très excellens . . . ducs . . . des pays de Savoye et Piemont," which included a depiction of Francis and Louise accepting a copy of the work, she in

widow's garb while he holds a prominent *main de justice* (Paris, BN, Vélins 1517, fol. 1r). The 1517 coronation book miniature also attests to the ongoing debate between the royal court and the Parlement of Paris over the king's right to intervene in affairs of justice (as Hanley 1983: 52 notes for a later period in Francis' reign, the depiction of the king in Majesty is an important element of early modern constitutional assemblies).

30. Le Coq sees this as homage to Louise; as Gringoire devised the spectacles for Claude's entry, the emphasis was hardly coincidental. More than one MS has survived —Le Coq used Paris, BN, Nouv. Acq. Fr. 794; I note Paris, BN, Fr. 17511, fol. 1r.

31. See note 24.

32. In March 1525 an attack portraying Louise as "Lady Ambition" was widely distributed in churches, but on the whole opposition to her regency dissipated during Francis' captivity. The contemporary writer François Belleforest was critical of her, but other contemporaries lauded her wisdom and prescience in foreign and domestic affairs (Dolet 1540; Paradin 1573).

33. Duprat had a vested interest in the nature of Louise's regental authority; Paris 1970: i, 68 notes that in 1520, Duprat granted his approval before Jean Thenaut's *Le Triomphe des Vertues* (Paris, BN, Fr. 144) was presented to Louise. *Le Triomphe* was one of many MSS allegorically celebrating Louise's authority as the king's mother and regent, to the point that the recent birth of a royal heir was rendered into the "crown jewel" of Louise's regency. See also Doucet 1921: 49-74; Buisson 1935: 118.

34. Register of the Parlement of Paris, Conseil, 14 November 1525 (Paris, AN, Xia 1529, fol. 4): "Mais qu'elle est trop puissante pour s'en venger . . . . Ce qu'elle n'avoit voullu qu'il y a eu d'autres qui disoient qu'elle n'estoit que une femme. Et qu'elle savoit bien qu'elle n'estoit le Roy mais femme. Touteffoys qu'elle savoit bien qu' elle estoit mere du Roy et qu'elle estoit Regente Et que ce n'estoit a La Court a retraindre et limiter sa regence comme elle se seoit efforce faire." Griffiths 1979: 33-36 consulted this register, but stressed only Louise's frustration that "she was but a woman," without noting her argument regarding her maternal rights.

35. Fol. 5r assigns the work to Louise's request; the accompanying miniature shows the author presenting the work to her and attests that it was finished prior to her regency. The defence of her legal claims occupies fols. 1-22, the discussion of Louis IX's crusade and his good works fols. 23-30. Le Coq 1987: 478 dates the work to 1521-22; Le Blanc discusses Louis IX's ransom and grasps the constitutional importance of Francis I's captivity (Major 1980: 53-55). Jordan 1979: ch. 7 discusses Louis' and Blanche of Castile's charity and devotion, including the need to reform royal coinage.

36. Now Paris, BN, Fr. 5719.

37. Now Paris, BN, Fr. 5715. Le Blanc was well suited to compare Louise and Blanche, his interest perhaps inherited; his father Louis le Blanc was responsible for splendid depictions of Charles VIII and Louis XII commissioned to celebrate dynastic links between those late Valois kings and Louis IX (François 1946: 367-82).

38. Paris, BN, Fr. 5715, fols. 2v-6v.

39. Paris, BN, Fr 5715, fols. 6v-7v. Emphasis on the superior counsel of women echoes the writings of Christine de Pisan, on the influence of whose works at the Valois

court see Willard 1991, Sommers 1991. Le Blanc's interest in the dynastic basis in feudal law for a mother's right to act as her children's guardian could reflect legal curiosity perhaps nourished by his kinship to the jurist Guillaume Budé (I owe to Myra D. Orth the information, discovered by her, that Le Blanc was Budé's nephew).

40. The *gouvernail* as an attribute of regental authority is singular, though Tervarent 1958 has classical examples. For the wing motif, well known to contemporaries, Le Coq 1987: 470-74; two extant *médailles* honor Louise with this device (Pradel 1936: nos. 215-16), as does a *jeton* (Van Gennep 1897: 63-64).

41. Le Blanc knew of Louise's interest in religious concerns, which surfaced in MSS commissioned in her honor (Orth 1976 and 1982: 55-66; Griffiths 1979: 29-36; Knecht 1982: 179-83; Doucet 1921: ii, ch. 2). The contemporary *Journal d'un Bourgeois* (Bourrilly 1910: 187) assesses Louise's preoccupation with such issues; see also Isambert 1822-33: xii, 231-32.

42. Lunenfeld 1981: 157-62 and Hindman 1983: 102-10 discuss contemporary artists' difficulties in depicting distaff authority as they were hampered by notions of feminine inadequacy or depravity; Jordan 1990 emphasizes limitations on any woman's public power in this period. Given these factors, Le Blanc's treatise and his depiction of Louise as regent are even more remarkable. His work was copied into seventeenth-century collections on regental prerogative, e.g., Paris, BN, Fr. 15534, Fr 2830; neither depicts Louise as Blanche, but even without the visual attribution Le Blanc's ideas were clearly of interest to later writers.

43. Louise's role in negotiating Francis' release (Knecht 1982: 172-91; Jacqueton 1892) was noted by jurists and historians of the *ancien régime* interested in political powers of queens-regent (e.g., Goesman 1725: 115-16).

44. Royal processions prior to the assembly also emphasized Louise's preeminence; Paris, AN, KK 1437, fols. 35v *et seq.*, describes processions to the abbey of St.-Denis which both Francis and Louise attended. Paris, AN, Xia 1531, fols. 26v-38v, is an account of the *lit de justice* in the registers of the Parlement of Paris; Louise is (fol. 38r) acknowledged as "selle gouvernante et Regente de la personne du dauphin" (Bouchel 1615: iii, 145).

45. I do not develop here arguments by either Chasseneuz or Grassaille on queens' privileges of office, the symbolism of their regalia, or their exalted status as *uxor regis;* these points are treated in my dissertation.

46. Grassaille places the greater emphasis on rights of administration and guardianship. Both note that a mother's authority cannot interfere with her children's inheritance rights. Both are based on opinions of medieval canonists, particularly Baldus and Bartolus.

47. Many of Chasseneuz' claims had been voiced by Benedict 1521, qu. 27, fol. 423v, and Corsetti 1512, who held that women's rights to act as tutor were naturally bestowed on them by their virtue despite biological inferiority. These arguments were worked into treatises such as S. Champier's *Le `Regime' . . . d'un Jeune Prince* (Paris, BN, Fr 1959), presented to Louise of Savoy in honor of her appointment as Francis' guardian.

48. Both jurists echo fifteenth- and sixteenth-century writers, e.g., J. Textor, who evoked Marian imagery to praise maternal responsibilities, and St. Anthony of Florence (1506), ch. 20, who discusses privileges accorded the Virgin and stresses her dynastic importance in transmitting the *stirps divina* (compare the festival at Amiens when Louise was honored with the Virgin, above, p. 169). Béguin 1988: 7-16, and Grodecki 1988 extend discussion of Marian iconography to include the contemporary cult of kingship.

49. The fifteenth-century jurist Jean de Terrevermeille (1536) discussed the seating to the right as a sign of hereditary right (for analysis in terms of public law, Giesey 1961). Cessoles' use of the privilege in the context of queenship reflects a certain dogmatic ambivalence: he accords Anne the ceremonial prerogative of seating to the right but also notes that virtue and goodness notwithstanding, women were less capable of ruling well, especially because of their penchant to gossip (Paris, B.N. Rès, R. 251).

50. Many of Chasseneuz' and Grassaille's arguments derived from the works of legists and feudists interested in women's rights to succeed to fiefs. In turn, both used feudal and customary law to address questions of public law relating to royal and distaff authority. But while such notions, particularly the dynastic basis of rulership, were of paramount importance to fifteenth-century writers, their interest had not extended to the queen.

51. Both emphasize that the queen's regalia and her right to privileges associated with rulership are attributes of office. Citing Guillaume Benedict and Lucas de Penna, Chasseneuz notes that privileges such as the right to grant clemency did not bestow powers of administration on the queen.

52. Here I differ from Kelley 1970: 199, who holds that the discussion of Salic Law was partly inspired by political troubles during Catherine de Médicis' regencies. In my view Grassaille does not seem to be troubled by regental prerogatives, and his work, published in 1538, clearly preceded Catherine's regental declaration of 1560. Chasseneuz 1546: part 2, 68, adeptly supports maternal authority by reworking Aristotelian notions of biological inferiority; his arguments were largely based on two medieval legists, Lucas de Penna and Guillaume Benedict.

NOTES 9

1. English history at this period has no equivalent, however, of the images of Brunhild and Fredegund, which Merovingian and early Carolingian writers employed to such effect.

2. These circumstances are discussed in a broad comparative framework in Stafford 1978: 79-100, Stafford 1981: 3-27, and Stafford 1983. For the French context, see e.g., Verdon 1973: 108-19; Facinger 1968: 3-48. For Ottonian Germany, Corbet 1986; Leyser 1979.

3. On this intrusion of the private into the public, this same lack of rigid boundaries, and the parallel situation this created for women in the Hellenistic period, see van Bremen 1983: 223-42. The familial imagery noted there is present in early-medieval sources, e.g. Krusch 1888: ch. 4 (at 485-86), where Balthild is *mater* to the king and princes, *filia* to the priests, and *optima nutrix* to the young men.

4. One of the clearest examples is in the arguments mounted in the 830s against Empress Judith, second wife of Louis the Pious. The dissension that Judith allegedly raised within the family is paralleled by accusations of her mismanagement of the household, and both are linked to the wider troubles of the realm (Agobard of Lyons 1887: 274-79 and Paschasius Radbertus 1967: book 2, ch. 7 [at 158-60]). Her enemies made her a Jezebel, the dominant and evil wife, but in court eyes she was Esther, the ideal wifely counsellor of the Old Testament.

5. Goody 1970, and Harris 1973: 145-59 make clear the link between legitimate sanctioned power and the expression of legitimate aggression, but also link women's domestic roles with their exclusion from such expression. The mother, within the family a figure of authority, is a particular focus for conflicts between feelings and demands of kinship and those of political life. She is faced with the reality of such conflicts and is likely to be accused of generating the problems they produce.

6. For continental examples, see the acceptably political prophetic utterances of Mathilda, widow of Henry the Fowler (Pertz 1841: 296-97; Koepke 1852: 578; Corbet 1986). As with Mathilda, who fulfilled her marital duties before widowhood and as will be seen for English royal women, ecclesiastical writers could stretch their definitions of chastity generously if they so wished.

7. Chibnall 1988: 107-30 comments interestingly that this image is not used of Mathilda the Empress, and links this with the fact that she never incurred the hatred of powerful prelates. It should also be noted that much comment on Mathilda was contemporary, in the context of a civil conflict that she stood a chance of winning, or during the reign of her son Henry II. The influence of such factors on the representation of women is an important element in this chapter.

8. This imagery is discussed in Holum 1982, the link between women as patrons and their role in families by van Bremen 1983: 223-42. The images created now continued in use and development throughout the early Middle Ages, as in the lives of Radegund and Balthild, in Gregory of Tours' treatment of powerful women, and in the tenth-century lives of Mathilda, wife of Henry the Fowler.

9. On the nostalgic view of the Old English past this could produce see, e.g., Gransden 1974; Mason 1990. On the increased criticism of kings and potentially of all power to which it contributed, Clanchy 1983: 52-6, more fully discussed in Stafford 1989.

10. See, e.g., Wormald 1978: 54, and Rollason 1983: 1-22; for general early comment on the early stages of Canute's reign, Stafford 1989.

11. The only implication of a woman's involvement is a 1003 reference to the betrayal of Exeter by Emma's reeve, a French ceorl, Hugh. The chronicler's concern with the treachery of *English* nobles means that he passes over the incident with little comment, though his criticism is clear in emphasis on the man's French birth and low status. This is the only hint in English sources of that theme of the alien princess with her alien followers, which was an important theme in criticism of eleventh-century Capetian queens such as Constance.

12. Whitelock 1979b: 224 (MS D, *s.a.* 955). That it is the post-conquest MS D that makes the comment may relate to the D writer's interest in the Old English dynasty and its female members. But the cult is unlikely to have been post-conquest, and Ælfgifu is already important as the mother of Edgar and the recipient of prophecies

about him in the early Life of Dunstan. Here we might note that 1066 in some ways cuts off many possible cultic developments of the tenth and eleventh centuries at the same time it encourages others. Specifically, West Saxon royal family cults may have been a prime example.

13. Barlow 1970: 28. Æthelred named his children after kings of the tenth century in turn, beginning in his first marriage with Athelstan, and in the children of his second marriage to Emma returning to Alfred and Edward the Elder. He had at least three daughters by his first marriage: another Ælfgifu, Eadgyth and Wulfhild, the last a surprising departure from the dynastic name-giving which characterized this king, perhaps taken from her mother's family. The name is known, however, from the family of his half-sister Edith. Does its use suggest an attempt at reconciliation with that family? Edith and her mother Wulfthryth were still alive at Wilton during his reign.

14. Ælfthryth and her ecclesiastical supporters may have been partly responsible for the growing iconography of Mary Queen of Heaven at this date (see Deshman 1976, 1988).

15. Probably the chronicle later known under the name of Florence of Worcester was begun now.

16. *Recte* son of Edmund. The mistake in an English vernacular chronicle is significant; it may underline the increasing irrelevance of the detailed history and cult of the West Saxon dynasty after 1066, though this is hard to reconcile with the obvious interest of the D writer in that history.

17. Apparent in the number of female saints' lives he wrote, in his relations with the community at Wilton and especially in his autobiographical *Liber Confortatorius* (Talbot 1955: 1-117). Here Goscelin speaks passionately of his feelings for Eve, a young nun of Wilton; he provides for her in her new life as an anchorite a guide which shows his familiarity with a range of positive Christian female imagery. And he sometimes speaks of his own experience in ways which compare it to that of women, e.g., when he likens his own exile to that of a young princess married into a foreign court where she does not even know the language.

18. Caroline Walker Bynum's work is essential on this latter point. 19. Thompson 1987: 35-36, however, notes that William was aware of the problems of writing contemporary history; Thompson feels that we should not overstress the extent of William's political commitment.

20. The analysis of this point offered in Bloch 1987: 1-24 has been much questioned, e.g., by discussion in *Medieval Feminist Newsletter* 6 (fall 1988).

21. I hope to say more of the development of the queen's household in these centuries in my forthcoming book on Emma and Edith.

22. Helgaud's Life of Robert the Pious is the closest comparison for the *Vita Ædwardi*, but it is far more a saint's life than either of the works in question. The biographies of the Ottonian women, Mathilda and Adelaide, are similarly hagiographical. We have to return to the ninth-century lives of Charlemagne and Alfred to match the secular emphasis, and in neither case will we find the attempts to discuss political situation and actions which we find in the two later works. It may be no coincidence that it is in Normandy, in the works of Dudo of St.-Quentin, William of Jumièges, and

William of Poitiers, that we find the closest contemporary attempts to write secular biography. But what is most significant about both works is the production of secular, political works for living protagonists, both of them women.

23. The lost portion of the work contained a portrayal of Edith alongside that of her brothers, but there is nothing to suggest that this was of central significance to the plot.

24. For such accusations against Judith see Agobard and Paschasius Radbertus. The nature of those accusations was appropriate to a succession issue that involved the claims of her son and the fitness of her husband to rule, both of which were impugned by a sexually promiscuous wife and mother. The management of royal finance and the methods of its acquisition were, however, a growing obsession in eleventh- and early-twelfth-century English writers.

25. The contrast with Helgaud's presentation of the relationship between Robert and Constance is interesting, and yet another proof that Edith, for all her absences, is the heroine of this work.

NOTES 10

1. Such as the essays by Roger Collins, André Poulet, and Elizabeth McCartney in this volume — Ed.

2. Citations here are generally restricted to references to literal quotations from sources. For further sources and authorities, see Wolf 1987 and 1991.

NOTES 11

A preliminary version of this paper was presented at the 1992 Missouri Conference on History, and I would like to thank the chairman and organizer of the session, Professor A. Mark Smith, for his helpful comments. A glance at the bibliography shows my intellectual debt to Professor Marjorie Chibnall, who generously shared her insights with me during the 1990 and 1991 Battle Conferences and while I visited Cambridge in 1991. Finally, I would like to thank John Parsons both for his patience and for his encouragement throughout my graduate career.

1. There is some reason to believe that the succession details worked out in Jerusalem were modeled on, or at least influenced by, the agreements negotiated in England. After the English barons swore allegiance to Matilda as Henry I's heir, she was married to Geoffrey of Anjou, son of Count Fulk, who shortly afterward was called to Jerusalem to marry Melisende. See Mayer 1985.

2. For instance, paraphrasing *Ecclesiasticus* 25: 26, Orderic commented that "there is nothing so bad as a bad woman" (non est malicia super maliciam mulierem) (Orderic Vitalis 1969-80: vi, 213).

3. See Orderic Vitalis 1969-80: vi, xxv-xxvii for a discussion of Orderic's likely loyalties.

4. "Rex anglorum pater eius Ioffredo Andegauorum comiti eam in coniugem desponsavit, quae marito suo filium nomine Henricum anno dominicae $M^oC^oXXX^oIII^o$ peperit, quem multi populi dominum expectant si Deus omnipotens in cuius manu sunt omni concesserit" (Orderic Vitalis 1969-80: v, xii, 200-21, 228 [and note 2]).

5. Chibnall notes that Orderic once did, at least implicitly, recognize that the Empress had some independent claim to Normandy. He described military action in the duchy, led by Geoffrey of Anjou, and referred to him as the "stipendiary commander" of his wife's forces ("stipendiarius coniugi suae factus") (Orderic Vitalis 1969-80: vi, xxvi, 482).

6. The Empress' mother, Queen Matilda II, had been reared and educated in the monasteries of Romsey and Wilton. Although she never took monastic vows, and her parents never intended her to do so, she had been seen wearing the veil. Archbishop Anselm ordered an inquiry into her status before he would perform her marriage to Henry in 1100. The council found her free to marry, but long after the deaths of Queen Matilda and Anselm, rumors surfaced about her status, and King Stephen's adherents were not slow to take advantage of these rumors. The story is most fully narrated by Eadmer of Canterbury; for modern discussion see Chibnall 1991: 7-8. John of Salisbury and Gilbert Foliot provided separate accounts of the hearings at the papal court (Eadmer of Canterbury 1866, rpt 1964: 121-26; Brooke, Morey and Brooke 1967: 60-66; Morey and Brooke 1965: 118-21).

7. John's treatment of Dido is somewhat more negative than Nederman and Lawson indicate, since he uses Dido to show "the end of rulership by women and the effeminate" (John of Salisbury 1990: 131).

8. Bynum's warning about the difference between confusing feminine imagery with improvements in the status of women is worth repeating. "It seems," she wrote, "that the somewhat sentimentalized maternal imagery of the twelfth- to fourteenth-century religious writing does not tell us—at least not primarily—about the lives of (or even attitudes toward) real women" (Bynum 1982: 169).

B·I·B·L·I·O·G·R·A·P·H·Y

Adelard of Bath (1874). *Epistola Adelardi ad Elfegum Archiepiscopum de Vita Sancti Dunstani.* In Stubbs, W., ed. (1874): 53-68.

Adrevald of Fleury (1879). *Miracula sancti Benedicti patrata in Gallia post translationem ad medium usque saeculum IX.* Migne, *PL* cxxiv: 910-48. Paris: Garnier.

Affeldt, W. (1980). Untersuchungen zur Königserhebung Pippins. *Frühmittelalterliche Studien* xiv: 95-187.

Agobard of Lyons (1887). *Agobardi archiepiscopi Lugdunensis libri duo pro filiis et contra Judith uxorem Ludovici Pii.* Waitz, G., ed. MGH, SS: xi part 1, 274-79. Hannover: Hahn.

Albert-Buisson, F. (1935). *Le Chancelier Antoine Duprat.* Paris: Hachette.

Alcuin (1881). *Alcuini Carmina.* Dümmler, E., ed. MGH, Poetae latini aevi karolini: i, 160-351. Berlin: Weidmann.

Alcuin (1895). *Alcuini Epistolae.* Dümmler, E., ed. MGH, Epistolae: iv, 1-481. Berlin: Weidmann.

Alexander, J. J. G., and Gibson, M. T., eds. (1976). *Medieval Learning and Literature: Essays Presented to Richard William Hunt.* Oxford: Clarendon Press.

Allen, A. (1979). Yorkist Propaganda: Pedigree, Prophecy and the "British History" in the Reign of Edward IV. In Ross, C., ed. (1979): 171-92.

Amundsen, D. W. (1973). The age of menarche in medieval Europe. *Human Biology* xlv: 363-69.

Andrieu, M., ed. (1938-41). *Le pontifical romain au moyen âge.* 6 vols. Studi e testi lxxxviii, lxxxix. Vatican City: Biblioteca Apostolica Vaticana.

Angilbert (1881). *Angilberti Carmina.* Dümmler, E., ed. MGH, Poetae latini aevi karolini: i, 355-65. Berlin: Weidmann.

Anonymous (1738-1904). *Ex Historiae Franciae Fragmento.* In Bouquet, M., ed. (1738-1904): xi, 160-62.

Anthony of Florence, St. (1506). *Prima-Quarta Pars Totius Summe Majories Beati Antonin.* Lyon: J. Cleyn, vulgo Schuab.

Ardo (1887). *Vita Benedicti abbatis Anianensis et Indensis.* Waitz, G. ed. MGH, SS: xv part 1, 198-220. Hannover: Hahn.

Ariès, P., and Duby, G., eds. (1988). *A History of Private Life, II: Revelations of the Medieval World.* Cambridge, MA: Harvard University Press.

Armstrong, C. A. J. (1983). *England, France and Burgundy in the Fifteenth Century.* London: Hambledon.

Aschbach, J. von (1838-45, rpt 1964). *Geschichte Kaiser Sigmunds.* 4 vols. Hamburg: F. Perthes (rpt Aalen: Scientia).

Astronomer (1829). *Vita Hludowici Imperatoris.* Pertz, G., ed. MGH, SS: ii, 604-48. Hannover: Hahn.

Attreed, L. (1983). From *Pearl* Maiden to Tower Princes: towards a new history of medieval childhood. *JMH* ix: 43-58.

Aubri of Troisfontaines (1876). *Chronicon ab O. C.-MCCXLI.* In Bouquet, M., ed. (1738-1904): xi, pp. 349-63.

Aurelius Augustinus (1972). *On the City of God against the Pagans.* Bettenson, H., trs., Knowles, D., ed. Harmondsworth: Penguin.

Autrand, F. (1986). *Charles VI: la folie du roi.* Paris: Fayard.

Bak, J. M. (1973). *Königtum und Stände in Ungarn im 14.-16. Jahrhundert.* Quellen und Forschungen, hrsg. M. Hellmann, vi. Wiesbaden: Steiner.

Bak, J. M., ed. (1990). *Coronations. Medieval and Early Modern Monarchic Ritual.* Berkeley: University of California Press.

Bak, J. M. (forthcoming). A kingdom of many languages: the case of medieval Hungary. In Boglioni, P., and Hasenohr, G., eds. (forthcoming).

Baker, D., ed. (1978a). *Medieval Women. Essays Presented to R. M. T. Hill.* SCH subsidia 1. Oxford: Basil Blackwell, for the Ecclesiastical History Society.

Baker, D. (1978b). "A Nursery of Saints": St. Margaret of Scotland reconsidered. In Baker, D., ed. (1978a): 119-41.

Baliñas, C. (1988). *Defensores e traditores: un modelo de relación entre poder monáriquico e oligarquía na Galicia altomedieval.* Santiago de Compostela: Xunta de Galicia.

Banani, A., and Vyronis, S., eds. (1977). *Individualism and Conformity in Classical Islam.* Wiesbaden: Otto Harrassowitz.

Bandel, Betty (1957). The English chroniclers' attitude toward women. *Journal of the History of Ideas* 16: 113-18.

Bard, I. N. (1978). *Aristocratic Revolts and the Late Medieval Hungarian State, A.D. 1382-1408.* (Ph.D. diss., University of Washington).

Barlow, F., ed. (1962). *Vita Ædwardi Regis qui apud Westmonsterium requiescat.* London: Nelson.

Barlow, F. (1963). *The English Church, 1000-1066: A Constitutional History.* London: Longmans.

Barlow, F. (1970). *Edward the Confessor.* London: Eyre and Spottiswoode.

Barlow, F. (1980). The king's evil. *EHR* xcv: 3-27.

Barry, F. (1964). *La Reine de France.* Paris: Éditions du Scorpion.

Bastgen, H., ed. (1924). *Libri Carolini.* MGH, Concilia: ii, supplement. Hannover: Hahn.

Bautier, R.-H., ed. (1982). *La France de Philippe Auguste: le temps des mutations.* Actes du colloque international. Paris: Éditions du Centre National de la Recherche Scientifique.

Baux, E. (1902). Louise de Savoy et Claude de France à Lyon. Étude sur la première régence, 1515-1516. *Revue d'histoire de Lyon* i: 447-64.

Baux, E., Bourrilly, V.-L., and Mabilly, P. (1904). Le voyage des reines et de François I en Provence et dans la vallée du Rhône (Decembre, 1515-Fevrier, 1516). *Annales du Midi* xvi: 31-64.

Beardwood, A., ed. (1969). *Records of the Trial of Walter Langeton, bishop of Coventry and Lichfield 1307-1312.* Camden Society, 4th ser., iv.

Beauvoir, S. de (1952). *The Second Sex.* Parshley, H. M., trs. New York: Knopf.

Bedos-Rezak, B. (1988). Women, Seals and Power in Medieval France, 1150-1350. In Erler, M., and Kowaleski, M., eds. (1988): 61-82.

Béguin, S. (1988). Un project de Rosso pour le chapitre de Notre-Dame de Paris. *Bulletin de la Société de l'Histoire de l'Art français* (Société de l'Histoire de l'Art français) s.n., 17-24.

Beitscher, J. (1976). "As the twig is bent . . .": Children and their parents in an aristocratic society. *JMH* ii: 181-91.

Bell, S. G. (1988). Medieval Women Book Owners: Arbiters of Lay Piety and Ambassadors of Culture. In Erler, M., and Kowaleski, M., eds. (1988): 149-87.

Benedict, G. (1521). *Solennis ac perutilis repetitio, C. Raynutius.* Lyon, n.p.

Bennett, J. M., Clark, E. A., O'Barr, J. F., Vilen, B. A., and Westphal-Wihl, S., eds. (1989). *Sisters and Workers in the Middle Ages.* Chicago: University of Chicago Press.

Benson, R. L., and Constable, G., eds. (1982). *Renaissance and Renewal in the Twelfth Century.* Cambridge, MA: Harvard University Press.

Benton, J. F. (1961). The court of Champagne as a literary center. *Speculum* xxxvi: 551-91.

Benton, J. F. (1977). Individualism and Conformity in Medieval Western Europe. In Banani, A., and Vyronis, S., eds. (1977): 145-58.

Benton, J. F. (1982). Consciousness of Self and Perceptions of Individuality. In Benson, R. L., and Constable, G., eds. (1982): 263-95.

Berger, E. (1895). *Histoire de Blanche de Castille, reine de France.* Paris: Fontemoing.

Bernard of Clairvaux. *Opera omnia.* Migne, *PL* clxxxii-clxxxvi.

Bernath, M., and von Schroeder, F., eds. (1974-81). *Biographisches Lexikon zur Geschichte Südosteuropas.* 4 vols. Munich: Oldenbourg.

Berthold of Reichenau (1844). *Annales de rebus post Hermanni Contracti gesta ab anno 1054 usque ad ejus seculi finem.* Pertz, G. H., ed.. MGH, SS: v, 264-326.

Bezzola, R. R. (1944-63). *Les origines et la formation de la littérature courtoise en Occident (500-1200).* 3 vols. in 5 folios. Paris: Champion.

Binski, P. (1990). Reflections on *La estoire de Seint Aedward le rei*: hagiography and kingship in thirteenth-century England. *JMH* xvi: 333-50.

Blackley, F. D. (1964). Adam, the bastard son of Edward II. *BIHR* xxxvii: 76-77.

Blackley, F. D., and Hermansen, G., eds. (1971). *The Household Book of Queen Isabella of England for the Fifth Regnal Year of Edward II.* Edmonton: University of Alberta Press.

Blake, E. O., ed. (1962). *Liber Eliensis.* Camden Society, 3rd ser., xcii.

Bloch, R. Howard (1987). Medieval misogyny. *Representations* xx: 1-24.

Bloch, R. Howard (1991). *Medieval Misogyny and the Invention of Western Romantic Love.* Chicago: University of Chicago Press.

Boglioni, P., and Hasenohr, G., eds. (forthcoming). *Variis loqui linguagiis: Le pluralisme linguistique dans la société médiévale.* Montréal: Institut d'études médiévales.

Bologne, J. C. (1988). *La naissance interdite: stérilité, avortement, contraception au moyen âge.* Paris: Orban.

Bónis, G., Bak, J. M., and Sweeney, J. R., eds. (1988). *Decreta regni mediaevalis Hungaria. The Laws of the Mediaeval Kingdom of Hungary,* Volume I: 1000-1301. Irvine, CA: Schlacks.

Bordeaux, P. H. (1971). *Louise de Savoie, "Roi de France".* Paris: Perrin.

Borgolte, M. (1987). *Die Grafen Allemanniens im merowingischer und karolingischer Zeit.* Sigmaringen: J. Thorbecke.

Børreson, Kari (1981). *Subordination and Equivalence: The Nature and Role of Women in Augustine and Thomas Aquinas.* Talbot, C. H., trs. Washington, D.C.: Catholic University of America Press.

Boswell, J. (1980). *Christianity, Homosexuality and Social Tolerance.* Chicago: Chicago University Press.

Botfield, B., and Turner, T., eds. (1841). *Manners and Household Expenses of England in the Thirteenth and Fifteenth Centuries.* Cambridge: Roxburghe Club.

Bouchel, L. (1615). *La Bibliothèque ou trésor du droict français.* 5 vols. in one folio. Paris: D. Langlois.

Boulding, E. (1976). *The Underside of History: A View of Women Through Time.* Boulder, CO: Westview Press.

Bouquet, M., ed. (1738-1904). *Recueil des historiens des Gaules et de la France.* Nouvelle édition, 24 vols. Paris: Libraries associés, L. F. Delatour, Desaint, Imprimerie royale, Imprimerie impériale, Imprimerie nationale.

Bourdieu, P. (1977). *Outline of a Theory of Practice.* Nice, R., trs. Cambridge: Cambridge University Press.

Bourrilly, V.-L., ed. (1910). *Journal d'un Bourgeois de Paris sous le règne de François Ier (1515-36).* Société de l'Histoire de France. Collection de textes pour servir à l'étude et à l'enseignement de l'histoire, xliii. Paris: A. Picard.

Boutaric, E. (1867). Marguerite de Provence, femme de Saint Louis. Son caractère, son rôle politique. *Revue des questions historiques* iii: 417-58.

Brandenburg, E. (1935). *Die Nachkommen Karls des Grossen.* Frankfurt-am-Main: Zentralstelle für deutsche Personen- und Familiengeschichte (Genealogie und Landesgeschichte, bd. 10).

Braunfels, W., ed. (1965-68). *Karl der Grosse, Lebenswerk und Nachleben.* 4 vols. Düsseldorff: L. Schwann.

Bremen, R. van (1983). Women and Wealth. In Cameron, A., and Kurht, A., eds. (1983): 223-42.

Bréquigny, L. G. de, and Champollion-Figéac, J. J., eds. (1839-47). *Lettres des rois, reines, et autres personnages des cours de France et d'Angleterre depuis Louis VII jusqu'à Henri IV.* 2 vols. Paris: Imprimerie Royale.

Bricka, C. F. (1979-84). *Dansk biografisk leksikon*. 3rd edn. 16 vols. Copenhagen: Gyldendal.

Brink, J. E. (1982). Louise de Savoie, "King" of France, 1525-26. *Proceedings of the Ninth Annual Meeting of the Western Society for French History*: 15-25.

Brooke, Z. N., Morey, A., and Brooke, C. N. L. (1967). *The Letters and Charters of Gilbert Foliot*. Cambridge: Cambridge University Press.

Brown, E. A. R. (1976). Eleanor of Aquitaine: Parent, Queen and Duchess. In Kibler, W. W., ed. (1976): 9-34.

Brown, E. A. R. (1980). Philippe le Bel and the remains of Saint Louis. *Gazette des Beaux Arts* xcv: 174-82.

Brown, E. A. R. (1982). La Notion de la Légitimité et la Prophétie à la cour de Philippe-Auguste. In Bautier, R.-H., ed. (1982): 77-110.

Brown, E. A. R. (1985). Burying and Unburying the Kings of France. In Trexler, R., ed. (1985): 241-66.

Brown, E. A. R. (1987). The prince is father to the king: the character and childhood of Philip the Fair of France. *Mediaeval Studies* xlix: 282-334.

Brown, E. A. R. (1988). The political repercussions of family ties in the early fourteenth century: the marriage of Edward II of England and Isabelle of France. *Speculum* lxiii: 573-95.

Buisson, A. (1935). *Le chancelier Antoine Duprat*. Paris: Hachette.

Bryant, L. (1986). *The King and the City in the Parisian Royal Entry Ceremony*. Geneva: Librarie Droz.

Bullough, D. (1991a). *Imagines rerum* and their Significance in the Early Medieval West. In Bullough, D., ed. (1991b), 39-96.

Bullough, D., ed. (1991b). *Carolingian Renewal, Sources and Heritage*. Manchester: Manchester University Press.

Bullough, V. L. (1973). Medieval medical and scientific views of women. *Viator* iv: 485-501.

Byerly, B. C., and Byerly, C. R., eds. (1977). *Records of the Wardrobe and Household 1285-1286*. London: H. M. Stationery Office.

Bynum, C. W. (1982). *Jesus as Mother: Studies in the Spirituality of the High Middle Ages*. Berkeley: University of California Press.

Bynum, C. W. (1987). *Holy Feast and Holy Fast: The Religious Significance of Food to Medieval Women*. Berkeley: University of California Press.

Cabaniss, A. (1967). *Charlemagne's Cousins*. Syracuse, NY: Syracuse University Press.

Cahn, W. (1985). The psalter of Queen Emma. *Cahiers archéologiques* xxxiii: 72-85.

Caix de Saint Aymour, A. (1896). *Anne de Russie, reine de France et comtesse de Valois au XIᵉ siècle*. 2nd edn. Paris: Honoré Champion.

Cameron, A. (1978). The Theotokos in sixth-century Constantinople: a city finds its symbol. *Journal of Theological Studies*, n.s. xxix: 79-108.

Cameron, A., and Kurht, A., eds. (1983). *Images of Women in Antiquity*. London: C. Helm.

Campbell, A., ed. (1949). *Encomium Emmae reginae*. Camden Society, 3rd ser. lxxii.

Carle, B., Damsholt, N., Glente, K. and Trein Neilsen, E., eds. (1980). *Aspects of Female Existence: Proceedings of the First St. Gertrud's Symposium (1978)*. Copenhagen: Gyldendal.

Castelot, A. (1983). *Francois Ier*. Paris: Perrin.

Cathwulf (1892). *Epistola*. Dümmler, E., ed. MGH, Epistolae: iv, 501-05. Berlin: Weidmann.

Centre Nationale de la Recherche Scientifique (1975). *Peter Abelard, Pierre le Vénérable: les courants philosophiques, littéraires, et artistiques en occident au milieu du XIIe siècle*. Colloques internationaux du Centre National de la Recherche Scientifique, 546. Paris: Centre National de la Recherche Scientifique.

Cessolis, Jacobus de (1504). *Le Jeu des Eschez Moralisé*. Paris: Antoine Verart.

Chance, J. (1990a). The Structural Unity of *Beowulf*: the Problem of Grendel's Mother. In Damico, H., and Hennessey, A., eds. (1990): 248-61.

Chance, J., trs. (1990b). *Christine de Pizan's "Letter of Orthea to Hector"*. Newburyport: Focus Information Project.

Chasseneuz, B. de (1546). *Catalogus gloriae mundi*. Lyon: Regnault.

Chaves de Almeida, L. (1944). *Os tumulos de Alcobaça e os artistas de Coimbra*. Lisbon: Ramos de Ramos Afon.

Chenu, M. D. (1968). *Nature, Man and Society in the Twelfth Century: Essays on New Theological Perspectives in the Latin West*. Taylor, J., and Little, L. K., ed. and trs. Chicago: University of Chicago Press.

Cherniavsky, M., and Giesey, R., eds. (1965). *Selected Studies by Ernest H. Kantorowicz*. Locust Valley: J. J. Augustin.

Chibnall, M. (1984). *The World of Orderic Vitalis*. Oxford: Clarendon Press.

Chibnall, M. (1986). *Anglo-Norman England*. Oxford: Basil Blackwell.

Chibnall, M. (1988). The Empress Mathilda and church reform. *TRHS*, 5th ser. xxxviii: 107-30.

Chibnall, M. (1990). Women in Orderic Vitalis. *The Haskins Society Journal* ii: 105-21.

Chibnall, M. (1991). *The Empress Matilda: Queen Consort, Queen Mother, and Lady of the English*. Oxford: Basil Blackwell.

Chodorow, N. (1974). Family Structure and Feminine Personality. In Rosaldo, M. Z., and Lamphere, L., eds. (1974): 43-66.

Christensen, A. E. (1980). *Kalmarunionen og nordisk politik 1319-1439*. Copenhagen: Gyldendal.

Christensen, A. E., Ellehøj, S., Clausen, H. P., and Mørch, S., eds. (1977-90). *Danmarks historie*. 9 vols. Copenhagen: Gyldendal.

Christine de Pizan (1986). *Le livre de la Cité des Dames*. Hicks, E., and Moreau, T., trs. Paris: Stock Moyen Age.

Church, W. F. (1941, rpt 1969). *Constitutional Thought in Sixteenth-Century France*. New York: Octagon Books.

Clanchy, M. (1983). *England and its Rulers, 1066-1272*. London: Fontana.

Classen, P. (1965). Karl der Grosse, der Papsttum und Byzanz. In Braunfels, W., ed. (1964-68): i, 537-608.

Classen, P. (1971-72). Karl der Grosse und der Thronfolge im Frankenreich. In Fleckenstein, J., Krüger, S., and Vierhaus, R., eds. (1971-72): iii, 109-34.

Clayton, M. (1990). *The Cult of the Virgin Mary in Anglo-Saxon England.* Cambridge: Cambridge University Press.

Cokayne, G. E. (1910-40). *The Complete Peerage.* 2nd ed. 13 vols. London: St. Catherine Press.

Collins, R. (1983). *Early Medieval Spain: Unity in Diversity, 400-1000.* London: Macmillan.

Collins, R. (1985). *Sicut lex Gothorum continet:* law and charters in ninth- and tenth-century León and Catalonia. *EHR* c: 489-512.

Collins, R. (1986a). *The Basques.* Oxford: Basil Blackwell.

Collins, R. (1986b). Visigothic Law and Regional Custom in Disputes in Early Medieval Spain. In Davies, W., and Fouracre, P., eds. (1986): 85-104.

Collins, R. (1989). *The Arab Conquest of Spain, 710-797.* Oxford: Basil Blackwell.

Corbet, P. (1986). *Les saints ottoniens. Sainteté royale et sainteté féminine autour de l'an mil.* Beiheft der Francia, 15. Sigmaringen: J. Thorbecke.

Corsetti, A. (Panormitanus) (1512). *Repertorium veridicum aureum ac preclarissimum excellentissimi juris.* Lyon: Nicolaus de Benedictis.

Cosneau, E. (1889). *Les grands traités de la Guerre de Cent Ans.* Paris: Picard.

Cox, E. L. (1974). *The Eagles of Savoy: the House of Savoy in Thirteenth-Century Europe.* Princeton, NJ: Princeton University Press.

Crouzet, D. (1991). Désir de mort et puissance absolue de Charles VIII à Henri IV. *Revue de Synthèse* cxii: 423-32.

Dahlhaus-Berg, E. (1975). *Nova Antiquitas et Antiqua Novitas.* Cologne: Böhlau.

Dalarun, J. (1991). Regards de Clercs. In Duby, G., Perrot, M., and Klapisch-Zuber, C., eds. (1991): 31-54.

d'Alverny, M. T. (1970). Comment les théologiens et les philosophes voient la femme. *Cahiers de civilisation médiévale* xx: 105-29.

Damico, H., and Hennessey, A., eds. (1990). *New Readings on Women in Old English Literature.* Bloomington, IN: Indiana University Press.

Damsholt, N. (1984). The role of Icelandic woman in the sagas and in the production of homespun cloth. *Scandinavian Journal of History* ix: 75-90.

Damsholt, N. (1985). *Kvindebilledet i dansk højmiddelalder.* Copenhagen: Borgen.

Damsholt, N. (1987). War, Woman and Love. In McGuire, B. P., and Reitzel, C. A., eds. (1987): 56-66.

Davies, W., and Fouracre, P., eds. (1986). *The Settlement of Disputes in Early Medieval Europe.* Cambridge: Cambridge University Press.

Davis, N. (1976). Women's history in transition: the European case. *Feminist Studies* iii: 83-103.

Davis, N. (1986). Boundaries and the Sense of Self in Sixteenth-Century France. In Heller, T. C., Sosna, M., and Wellbery, D. E., eds. (1986): 53-63.

Davis, R. H. C. (1990). *King Stephen*. 2nd edn. London: Longmans.

Dean, R. J. (1976). Nicholas Trevet, Historian. In Alexander, J. J. G., and Gibson, M. T., eds. (1976): 328-52.

De Costé, H. (1643). *Les Elogies de Nos Rois et des 'Enfans de France*. Paris: S. Cramoisy.

Déer, J. (1966). *Die Heilige Krone Ungarns*. Osterreisches Akademie der Wissenschaft, Phil.-hist. Kl., Denkschriften 91. Vienna: Böhlaus Nachfolge.

Delisle, L. (1900). Traductions d'auteurs grecs et latins offertes à François Ier et à Anne de Montmorency. *Journal des Savants*, 23rd sér., n.v.: 476-92.

Descimon, R. (1991). La royauté française entre féodalité et sacerdoce. Roi seigneur ou roi magistrat? *Revue de synthèse* cxii: 455-73.

Deshman, R. (1976). *Christus Rex et Magi Reges*: kingship and Christology in Ottonian and Anglo-Saxon Art. *Frühmittelalterliche Studien* x: 367-405.

Deshman, R. (1988). *Benedictus Monarcha et Monachus*: early medieval ruler theology and the Anglo-Saxon reform. *Frühmittelalterliche Studien* xxii: 204-40.

Dierkens, A. (1991). Autour de la tombe de Charlemagne. *Byzantion* lxi: 156-80.

Doherty, P. C. (1975). The date of the birth of Isabella, queen of England (1308-1358). *BIHR* xlviii: 246-48.

Dolet, É. (1540). *Les Gestes de Françoys de Valois, Roy de France*. Lyon: É. Dolet.

Doucet, R. (1921). *Étude sur le Gouvernement de François Ier*. 2 vols. Paris: E. Champion.

Douglas, D. (1964). *William the Conqueror. The Norman Impact upon England*. Berkeley: University of California Press.

Douglas, M., ed. (1970). *Witchcraft Confessions and Accusations*. ASA monographs, 9. London: Tavistock.

Drèze, J.-F. (1991). *Raison D'État, Raison de Dieu*. Paris: Beauchesne.

Duby, G., and Le Goff, J., eds. (1977). *Famille et parenté dans l'occident médiéval. Actes du colloque de Paris, 6-8 juin 1974*. Rome: École française de Rome.

Duby, G. (1978). *Medieval Marriage. Two Models from Twelfth-Century France*. Forster, E., trs. Baltimore: Johns Hopkins University Press.

Duby, G. (1981). *Le chevalier, la femme et le prêtre*. Paris: Hachette.

Duby, G. (1984). *The Knight, the Lady and the Priest*. Bray, B., trs. New York: Pantheon.

Duby, G., and Perrot, M., eds. (1991a). *Histoire des Femmes en Occident*. 5 vols. Paris: Plon.

Duby, G. (1991b). Le modèle courtois. In Klapisch-Zuber, C., ed. (1991): 261-76.

Duchesne, L., and Vogel, C., eds. (1886-1957). *Le Liber Pontificalis. Texte, Introduction et Commentaire*. 3 vols. Paris: Ernest Thorin.

Dulac, L., and Dufournet, J. (1988). Christine de Pizan (études recueillies par L. Dulac et J. Dufournet). *Revue des langues romanes* xcii: 237-380.

Dümmler, E., ed. (1895). *Caroli Magni Epistolae*. MGH, Epistolae: iv, 528-32, 546-48, 555-66. Berlin: Weidmann.

Dupuy, P. (1655). *Traité de la Majorité de nos Rois, et des Regences dy Royaume.* Paris: Veuve M. Dupuy.

Durán Gudiol, A. (1988). *Los Condados de Aragón y Sobrarbe.* Zaragoza: Guara.

Eadmer of Canterbury (1884). *Historia novorum in Anglia.* Rule, M. ed. RS lxxxi. London: HMSO.

École française de Rome (1985). *Culture et idéologie dans la genèse de l'état moderne. Actes de la table ronde organisée par le Centre national de la recherche scientifique.* Rome: École française de Rome.

Edbury, P. W., and Rowe, J. G. (1983). *William of Tyre: Historian of the Latin East.* Cambridge: Cambridge University Press.

Einhard (1911). *Vita Karoli Magni.* Pertz, G. H., Waitz, G., and Holder-Egger, O., eds. MGH, SSRG separatim editi, vi. Berlin: Weidmann.

Elias, N. (1983). *The Court Society.* Jephcott, E., trs. Oxford: Basil Blackwell.

Engel, P. (1990). The Age of the Angevins, 1301-1342. In Sugar, P., Hanák, P., and Frank, T., eds. (1990): 34-53.

Enright, M. J. (1988). Lady with a mead-cup. Ritual, group cohesion and hierarchy in the Germanic warband. *Frühmittelalterliche Studien* xxii: 170-203.

Erlande-Brandenbourg, A. (1968). Le tombeau de Saint Louis. *Bulletin monumental* 126: 7-36.

Erler, M., and Kowaleski, M., eds. (1988). *Women and Power in the Middle Ages.* Athens, GA: University of Georgia Press.

Esposito, M. (1913). La vie de S. Wulfhilde par Goscelin de Cantorbéry. *Analecta Bollandiana* xxxii: 10-26.

Facinger, M. (1968). A study of medieval queenship: Capetian France 987-1237. *Studies in Medieval and Renaissance History* 5: 3-48.

Farmer, Sharon (1986). Persuasive voices: clerical images of medieval wives. *Speculum* lxi: 517-43.

Favier, J. (1982). *Philippe le Bel.* Paris: Fayard.

Féjer, G. (1829-44). *Codex diplomaticus Hungariae ecclesiasticus ac civilis.* 11 vols. in 44 folios. Buda: Royal University of Hungary.

Fell, C. (1971). *Edward, King and Martyr.* Leeds: University of Leeds School of English.

Fell, C. (1978). Edward King and Martyr and the Anglo-Saxon Hagiographic Tradition. In Hill, D., ed. (1978): 1-13.

Ferdinandy, M. (1972). Ludwig I. von Ungarn. *Südost-Forschungen* xxxi: 41-80.

Fernandes, A. (1972). *Portugal no período vimaranense.* Guimaraes: Barcelos.

Fernández Conde, F. J. (1978). *El monasterio de San Pelayo de Oviedo.* Oviedo: C.S.I.C.

Fichtenau, H. (1963). *The Carolingian Empire.* Munz, P., trs. Oxford: Basil Blackwell.

Fleckenstein, J., and Schmid, K., eds. *Adel und Kirche. Festschrift für Gerd Tellenbach.* Freiburg-Basel-Vienna: Herder.

Fleckenstein, J., Krüger, S., and Vierhaus, R., eds. (1971-72) *Festschrift für Hermann Heimpel zum 70. Geburtstag.* 3 vols. (Veroffentlichen des Max-Planck-Instituts für Geschichte, 36). Göttingen: Vandenhoeck and Ruprecht.

Fliche, A. (1912). *Le règne de Philippe I*ᵉʳ, *roi de France*. Paris: Société française d'imprimerie et de librarie.

Florez, H. (1747-1879). *España sagrada*. 51 vols. Madrid: M. F. Rodriguez.

Fradenburg, L., ed. (1991a). *Women and Sovereignty*. Edinburgh: University of Edinburgh Press.

Fradenburg, L. (1991b). Sovereign Love: The Wedding of Margaret Tudor and James IV of Scotland. In Fradeburg, ed. (1991a): 78-100.

Francisque-Michel, M., and Bémont, C. (1885-1906). *Rôles gascons*. 4 vols. Paris: Imprimerie Nationale.

François, M. (1946). Les Rois de France et les traditions de Saint Denis à la fin du XVᵉ siècle. *Mélanges dédiés à la Mémoire de Félix Grat*. 2 vols. Paris: Chez Mme Pecqueur-Grat.

Franklin, J. H. (1973). *Jean Bodin and the Rise of Absolutist Theory*. Cambridge: Cambridge University Press.

Freccero, C. (1991). Marguerite de Navarre and the Politics of Maternal Sovereignty. In Fradenburg, L., ed. (1991): 133-49.

Freeman, A. (1957). Theodulf of Orléans and the *Libri Carolini*. *Speculum* xxxii: 663-705.

Freeman, A. (1965). Further studies in the *Libri Carolini*. *Speculum* xl: 203-89.

Freeman, A. (1971). Further studies in the *Libri Carolini III*. *Speculum* xlvi: 597-612.

Freeman, J. F. (1972). Louise of Savoy: a case of maternal opportunism. *The Sixteenth Century Journal* iii: 77-98.

Froissart, J. (1867-77). *Oeuvres: Chroniques*. Kervyn de Lettenhove, J. M. B. C., ed. 25 vols. Brussels: Academie Royale de Belgique/V. Devaux.

Fügedi, E. (1982). *Ispanok, bárok, kiskirályok*. Budapest: Müvelt Nép.

Fügedi, E. (1974). Das mittelalterliche Königreich Ungarn als Gastland. In Schlesinger, W., ed. (1974): 471-507; rpt in Fügedi (1986), as ch. VIII.

Fügedi, E. (1986a). *Könyörulj, bánom, könyörulj*. Budapest: Helikon.

Fügedi, E. (1986b). *Kings, Bishops, Nobles and Burghers in Medieval Hungary*. Bak, J., trs. London: Variorum.

Furnivall, F. J. (1897). *Child marriages, divorces, and ratifications in the diocese of Chester, A.D. 1561-1566*. London: Early English Text Society, Original series, cviii.

Gabriel, A. L. (1944). *Les rapports Dynastiques Franco-Hongrois au Moyen-Age*. Budapest: Imprimerie de l'Université.

Gaehde, J. (1971). The Turonian sources of the San Paolo Bible. *Frühmittelalterliche Studien* v: 359-400.

Ganshof, F. L. (1970). *The Middle Ages. A History of International Relations*. Hill, R. I., trs. New York: Harper and Row.

Galbraith, V. H. (1935). The literacy of the medieval English kings. *Proceedings of the British Academy* xxi: 201-35.

García Alvarez, R. (1960). La reina Velasquita. *Revista de Guimaraes* lxx: 1-27.

García Gomez, E., trs. (1967). *Anales palatinos del Califa de Córdoba Al-Hakam II, por 'Isa ibn Ahmad al-Razi (360-364 H)*. Madrid: Sociedad de Estudios y Publicaciones.

García Larragueta, S. (1983). *Los documentos de los reyes de Pamplona en el siglo XI* (Folia Budapestina). Zaragoza: Catedra "Zurita," Institución "Fernando el Católico."

Garrido Garrido, J. M., ed. (1983). *Documentación de la Catedral de Burgos (804-1183)*. Burgos: Ediciones Garrido Garrido.

Gaudemet, J. (1980). *Sociétés et mariages*. Strasbourg: Cerdic.

Geffrei Gaimar (1888-89). *Lestorie des Engles solum Maistre Geffrei Gaimar*. Hardy, T. D., and Martin, C. T., eds. 2 vols. RS xci. London: HMSO.

Genet, J.-P., ed. (1991). *L'historiographie médiévale en Europe*. Paris: CNRS.

Gibson, M., Nelson, J., and Ganz, D., eds. (1981). *Charles the Bald: Court and Kingdom*. Oxford: British Archaeological Reports, International Series 101.

Giesey, R. E. (1961). *The Juristic Basis of Dynastic Right to the French Throne*. Transactions of the American Philosophical Society. Philadelphia: American Philosophical Society.

Giles of Rome (1966). *Li Livres du Gouvernement des Rois*. Molenaer, S. P., trs. New York: AMS.

Glente, K., Winther-Jensen, L., and Reitzel, C. A., eds. (1989). *Female Power in the Middle Ages*. Proceedings of the Second St. Gertrud's Symposium 1986. Copenhagen: Reitzel.

Godefroy, T. (1615). *Histoire de Louis XII*. Paris: A. Pacard.

Godefroy, T., and Godefroy, D. (1649). *Le cérémonial françois*. 2 vols. Paris: S. et G. Cramoisy.

Godefroy, T., and Godefroy, D. (1684). *Histoire de Charles VIII*. Paris: S. Mabre-Cramoisy.

Godman, P. (1985). *Poetry of the Carolingian Renaissance*. London: Duckworth.

Godman, P. (1986). *Poets and Emperors. Frankish Politics and Carolingian Poetry*. Oxford: Clarendon Press.

Godman, P., and Collins, R., eds. (1990). *Charlemagne's Heir: New Perspectives on the Reign of Louis the Pious (814-840)*. Oxford: Clarendon Press.

Goesman, M. (1725). *Essais historiques sur le Sacre et Couronnement des Rois de France, Les Minorités et Régences*. Paris.

Goetz, H.-W. (1980). *Die Geschichtstheologie des Orosius*. Darmstadt: Wissenschaftliche Buchgesellschaft.

Goetz, H.-W., ed. (1991). *Weibliche Lebensgestaltung im frühen Mittelalter*. Cologne and Vienna: Böhlau.

Gold, P. S. (1985). *The Lady and the Virgin: Image, Attitude and Experience in Twelfth-Century France*. Chicago: University of Chicago Press.

Gómez Moreno, M. (1919). *Iglesias Mozárabes: arte español de los siglos IX a XI*. 2 vols. Madrid: Centro de Estudios Historicos.

Goñi Gaztambide, J. (1963). *Catálogo del Becerro antiguo y del Becerro menor de Leyre*. Pamplona: Institución Príncipe de Viana.

Goñi Gaztambide, J. (1979). *Historia de los obispos de Pamplona*. 2 vols. Pamplona: Ediciones Universidad de Navarra.

Gonzalez, J. (1960). *El Reino de Castilla en la Epoca de Alfonso VIII*. 3 vols. Madrid: Consejo superior de investigaciones cientificas.

Goody, E. (1970). Legitimate and Illegitimate Aggression in a West African state. In Douglas, M., ed. (1970): 207-44.

Goody, J., ed. (1973). *The Character of Kinship*. Cambridge: Cambridge University Press.

Goody, J. (1983). *The Development of the Family and Marriage in Europe*. Cambridge: Cambridge University Press.

Gousset, M.-Th., Avril, F., and Richard, J. (1990). *Saint Louis, Roi de France*. Paris: Bibliothèque Nationale.

Gransden, A. (1974). *Historical Writing in England, c. 550-1307*. London: Routledge and Kegan Paul.

Gransden, A. (1982). *Historical Writing in England, c. 1304 to the Early Sixteenth Century*. London: Routledge and Kegan Paul.

Grassaille, C. de. (1538). *Regalium Franciae libri duo*. 2 parts in 1 vol. Lyon: apud haeredes S. Vincentii.

Gravdal, K. (1991). *Ravishing Maidens: Writing Rape in Medieval French Literature and Law*. Philadelphia: University of Pennsylvania Press.

Green, M. A. E. (1859-69). *Lives of the Princesses of England from the Norman Conquest*. 6 vols. London: H. Colburn.

Grierson, P. (1966-73). *Catalogue of the Byzantine Coins in the Dumbarton Oaks Collection*. 5 vols. Washington, D.C.: Dumbarton Oaks Center for Byzantine Studies.

Griffiths, G. (1979). Louise of Savoy and reform of the church. *The Sixteenth Century Journal* x: 29-36.

Griffiths, R. A. (1969). The trial of Eleanor Cobham: an episode in the fall of Duke Humphrey of Gloucester. *Bulletin of the John Rylands Library* li: 381-99.

Griffiths, R. A. (1979). The Sense of Dynasty in the Reign of Henry VI. In Ross, C., ed. (1979): 13-36.

Grodecki, C. (1988). Le bâton cantoral de Notre-Dame de Paris. *Bulletin de la Société de l'Histoire de l'Art français* s.n.: 17-32.

Guenée, B. (1978). Les généalogies entre l'histoire et la politique: la fierté d'être Capétien, en France, au moyen âge. *Annales E.S.C.* xxxiii: 450-77.

Guichenon, S. (1660). *Historie généalogique de la Royale Maison de Savoye*. 2 vols. in 1 folio. Lyon: G. Barbier.

Guillaume de Jumièges (1914). *Gesta Normannorum Ducum*. Marx, J., ed. Paris-Rouen: Picard-Lestringant.

Gundlach, W., ed. (1892). *Codex Carolinus*. In MGH, Epistolae: iii, 469-657. Berlin: Weidmann.

Gunn, Victoria (1990). Women, Character and Sovereignty in Civil War: A Tale of Two Matildas. Presented at "Women and Sovereignty," annual meeting of the Traditional Cosmology Society, St. Andrews, Scotland (unpublished).

Halecki, O. (1991). *Jadwiga of Anjou and the rise of east central Europe.* Gromada, T. V., ed. Boulder, CO and Highland Lakes, NJ: Social Science Monographs/Atlantic Research.

Hallam, E. (1991). The Eleanor Crosses and Royal Burial Customs. In Parsons, D., ed. (1991): 9-21.

Halphen, L., and Poupardin, R., eds. (1913). *Chroniques des comtes d'Anjou et des seigneurs d'Amboise.* Collection de textes pour servir à l'étude et à l'enseignement de l'histoire. Paris: Picard.

Hamilton, Bernard (1978). Women in the Crusader States: the Queens of Jerusalem (1100-1190). In Baker, D., ed. (1978a): 143-74.

Hamilton, J. S. (1988). *Piers Gaveston, Earl of Cornwall, 1307-1312: Politics and Patronage in the Reign of Edward II.* Detroit: Wayne State University Press.

Hampe, K., ed. (1899). *Epistolae selectae pontificum Romanorum Carolo Magno et Ludowico Pio regnantibus scriptae.* MGH, Epistolae: v, 1-84. Berlin: Weidmann.

Hanawalt, B. (1988). Lady Honor Lisle's networks of influence. In Erler, M., and Kowaleski, M., eds. (1988): 188-212.

Hanley, S. H. (1983). *The Lit de Justice of the Kings of France.* Princeton, NJ: Princeton University Press.

Hanning, R. W. (1977). *The Individual in Twelfth-Century Romance.* New Haven: Yale University Press.

Hariulphe of Oudenbourg (1894). *Chronique de l'abbaye de St-Riquier.* Lot, F., ed. Paris: Picard.

Harris, G. (1973). Furies, Witches and Mothers. In Goody, J., ed. (1973): 145-59.

Haskell, A. S. (1973). The Paston women on marriage in fifteenth-century England. *Viator* iv: 459-71.

Hauck, K. (1968). Paderborn, das Zentrum von Karls Sachsen-Mission 777. In Fleckenstein, J., and Schmid, K., eds. (1968): 92-140.

Hedeman, A. D. (1991). *The Royal Image. Illustrations of the Grandes Chroniques de France, 1274-1422.* Berkeley: University of California Press.

Hehl, E.-D., ed. (1987). *Deus qui mutat tempora. Menschen und Institutionen im Wandel des Mittelalters.* Festgabe für A. Becker. Sigmaringen: Thorbecke.

Helmholz, R. (1974). *Marriage Litigation in Medieval England.* Cambridge: Cambridge University Press.

Hendy, M. (1985). *Studies in the Byzantine Monetary Economy, c. 300-1450.* Cambridge: Cambridge University Press.

Herlihy, D. (1975). The natural history of medieval women. *Natural History* lxxxvii: 56-67.

Herlihy, D. (1985). *Medieval Households.* Cambridge, MA: Harvard University Press.

L'Hermite-Leclerq, P. (1991). L'ordre féodal. In Klapisch-Zuber, C., ed. (1991): 217-60.

Herrin, J. (1987). *The Formation of Christendom.* Princeton, NJ: Princeton University Press.

Hill, D., ed. (1978). *Ethelred the Unready: Papers from the Millenary Conference.* Oxford: British Archaeological Reports, British series lix.

Hincmar of Reims (1980). *De Ordine Palatii.* Gross, T., and Schieffer, R., eds. MGH, Fontes iuris germanici antiqui in usum scholarum separatim editi, iii. Hannover: Hahn.

Hindman, S., and Spiegel, G. M. (1981). The *fleur de lis* frontispieces to Guillaume de Nangis's *Chronique Abrégée*: political iconography in late fifteenth-century France. *Viator* 12: 381-408.

Hindman, S. (1983). The iconography of Queen Isabeau de Bavière (1410-1415): an essay in method. *Gazette des Beaux Arts* cii: 102-10.

Hindman, S. (1986). *Christine de Pizan's "Epistre Orthéa:" painting and politics at the court of Charles VI.* Studies and Texts lxxvii. Toronto: Pontifical Institute of Mediaeval Studies.

Hlawitschka, E. (1965). Die Vorfahren Karls des Grossen. In Braunfels, ed. (1965-68): i, 51-82.

Hlawitschka, E. (1985). Zu den grundlagen des Aufstiegs der Karolinger. *Rheinische Vierteljahresblätter* xlix: 1-61; also in Hlawitschka, E. (1988), 72-100.

Hlawitschka, E. (1988). *Stirps Regia. Forschungen zu Königtum und Führungsschichten im früheren Mittelalter.* Frankfurt-am-Main: Peter Lang.

Hödl, F. (1978). *König Albrecht II. Königtum, Reichsregierung und Reichsreform 1438-1439.* Vienna: Böhlau.

Hoffmann, E. (1976). *Königserhebung und Thronfolgerordnung in Dänemark bis zum Ausgang des Mittelalters.* Berlin: de Gruyter.

Hoffmann, E. (1990). Coronations and Coronation Ordines in Medieval Scandinavia. In Bak, J., ed. (1990): 125-51.

Holum, K. (1982). *Theodosian Empresses, Women and Imperial dominion in Late Antiquity.* Berkeley: University of California Press.

Hopkins, K. (1978). *Conquerors and Slaves.* Cambridge: Cambridge University Press.

Hørby, K. (1977). *Status regni Dacie. Studier i Christofferlinjens ægteskabs- og alliancepolitik 1252-1319.* Copenhagen: Dansk historisk Forening.

Horvath, J., and Székely, G., eds. (1974). *Középkori kútföink kritikus kérdései.* Memoria saeculorum Hungariae, i. Budapest: Akadémiai Kiadó.

Howell, M. (1987). The resources of Eleanor of Provence as queen consort. *English Historical Review* cii: 372-93.

Howell, M. (1990). Eleanor of Provence: *generosa et religiosa virago.* Presented at the Institute for Historical Research, University of London (unpublished).

Hugh of Fleury (1851). *Historia Nova Francorum.* Pertz, G. H., ed. MGH, SS: ix, 376-95. Hannover: Hahn.

Hughes, D. O. (1991). Les Modes. In Duby, G., et al., eds. (1991): 147-69.

Huneycutt, L. (1989a). The idea of the perfect princess: the life of Saint Margaret in the reign of Matilda II, 1100-1118. *Anglo-Norman Studies* xii: 81-97.

Huneycutt, L. (1989b). Images of queenship in the high middle ages. *The Haskins Society Journal* i: 61-71.

Huneycutt, L. (1989c). Medieval queenship. *History Today* xxxix: 16-22.

Huneycutt, L. (1990). Public lives, private ties: St. Margaret of Scotland as queen and mother. Presented at "Women and Sovereignty," annual meeting of the Traditional Cosmology Society, St. Andrews, Scotland (unpublished).

Huneycutt, L. (forthcoming). Intercession and the High Medieval Queen: the *Esther* Topos. In MacLean, S. B., and Carpenter, J., eds. (forthcoming).

Isembart, Decrusy, Jourdain (1822-33). *Recueil général des anciennes lois françaises, depuis l'an 420 jusqu'à la révolution de 1789*. 29 vols. Paris: Plon Frères.

Isenburg-Büdingen, W. K. von (1953). *Stammtafeln zur Geschichte der Europaïschen Staaten*. 2nd edn. 4 vols. in 3 folios. Marburg: J. A. Stargardt.

Jackson, R. A., ed. (1969). The Traité du Sacre of Jean Golein. *Proceedings of the American Philosophical Society* cxiii: 305-24.

Jackson, R. A. (1984). *Vivat Rex! Histoire des sacres et couronnements en France (1364-1825)*. Strasbourg: Associations des publications près les Universités de Strasbourg.

Jacqueton, G. (1892). *La Politique extérieure de Louise de Savoie; relations diplomatiques de France et de l'Angleterre pendant la captivité de François Ier (1525-1526)*. Paris: E. Bouillon.

John of Marmoutier (1913). *Gesta Consulum Andegavorum*. In Halphen, L., and Poupardin, R., eds. (1913): 25-74, 135-71.

John of Salisbury (1986). *The Historia Pontificalis of John of Salisbury*. Chibnall, M., ed. and trs. 2nd ed. Oxford: Oxford University Press.

John of Salisbury (1990). *Policraticus: Of the Frivolities of Courtiers and the Footprints of Philosophers*. Nederman, C. J., trs. Cambridge: Cambridge University Press.

Johnstone, H. (1923). The wardrobe and household of Henry, son of Edward I. *Bulletin of the John Rylands Library* vii: 384-420.

Johnstone, H. (1931). *Letters of Edward Prince of Wales 1304-1305*. Cambridge: Roxburghe Club.

Johnstone, H. (1946). *Edward of Carnarvon*. Manchester: Manchester University Press.

Joinville, J. de (1668). *Histoire de S. Louis, IX*. Du Fresne du Cange, C., ed. Paris: Nouvelle collection des mémoires pour servir à l'histoire de France, n.p.

Jones, M. K., and Underwood, M. G. (1992). *The King's Mother. Lady Margaret Beaufort, Countess of Richmond and Derby*. Cambridge: Cambridge University Press.

Jordan, C. (1990). *Renaissance Feminism. Literary Texts and Political Models*. Ithaca, NY: Cornell University Press.

Jordan, W. C. (1979). *Louise IX and the Challenge of the Crusade. A Study in Rulership*. Princeton, NJ: Princeton University Press.

Jørgensen, E., and Skovgaard, J. (1910). *Danske Dronninger*. Copenhagen: Hagerup.

Kantorowicz, E. H. (1957). *The King's Two Bodies. A Study in Medieval Political Theology*. Princeton, NJ: Princeton University Press.

Kantorowicz, E. H. (1965). The Carolingian King in the Bible of San Paolo Fuori le Mura. In Cherniavsky, M., and Giesey, R., eds. (1965): 82-94.

Kardos, T. (1941). *Középkori kultúra, középkori költészet*. Budapest: Franklin.

Kelley, D. R. (1970). *Foundations of Modern Historical Scholarship*. New York: Columbia University Press.

Kendall, P. M. (1974). *Louis XI, l'universelle araigne*. Paris: Fayard.

Kenyeres, A., ed. (1967-81). *Magyar Életrajzi Lexikon*. 3 vols. Budapest: Akadémiai Kiadó.

Keohane, N. O. (1980). *Philosophy and the State in France*. Princeton, NJ: Princeton University Press.

Kerbl, R. (1979). *Byzantinische Prinzessinen in Ungarn zwischen 1050-1200 und ihr Einfluss auf das Arpadenreich*. Dissertationes der Universität Wien, cxliii. Vienna: Verband der Wissenschaftlichen Gesellschaften Österreichs.

Kessler, H. (1977) *The Illustrated Bibles from Tours*. Princeton, NJ: Princeton University Press.

Keynes, S. (1978). The declining reputation of King Æthelred. In Hill, D., ed. (1978): 227-53.

Kibler, W. W. (1976). *Eleanor of Aquitaine: Patron and Politician*. Austin: University of Texas Press.

King, M. L. (1991). *Women of the Renaissance*. Chicago: University of Chicago Press.

King, P. D. (1972). *Law and Society in the Visigothic Kingdom*. Cambridge: Cambridge University Press.

Kingsford, C. L. (1915). *The Grey Friars of London*. Aberdeen: Aberdeen University Press.

Kirby, J. L. (1970). *Henry IV of England*. London: Constable.

Kirk, R. E. G., et al., eds. (1899-1964). *Feet of Fines for Essex*. 4 vols. Colchester: Essex Archaeological Society.

Klaniczay, G. (1990). *The Uses of Supernatural Power: The Transformation of Popular Religion in Medieval and Early-Modern Europe*. Singermann, S., trs., and Margolis, K., ed. Princeton, NJ: Princeton University Press.

Klapisch-Zuber, C., ed (1991). *Le moyen âge*. Duby, G., and Perrot, M., eds. (1991), ii. Paris: Plon.

Klauser, R. (1957). *Der Heinrichs- und Kunigundenkult im mittelalterlichen Bistum Bamberg*. Bamberg: Selbstverlag des Historischen Vereins.

Knecht, R. J. (1982). *Francis I*. Cambridge: Cambridge University Press.

Knox, J. (1558). *The First Blast of the Trumpet against the Monstrous Regiment of Women*. Geneva: Crespin.

Koepke, R., ed. (1852). *Vita Mahthildis Reginae Antiquior*. MGH, SS: x, 573-82. Hannover: Hahn.

Kohler, Charles, ed. (1900, rpt 1964). Chartes de l'abbaye de Notre-Dame de la Vallée de Josaphat en Terre-Sainte, 1108-1291. *Revue de l'orient latin* vii: 108-22.

Konecny, S. (1976). *Die Frauen der karolingischen Königshauses*. Vienna: VWGÖ.

Korrodi, E. (1929). *Alcobaça: estudio historico-archeologico e artistico da Real abbad de Santa Maria de Alcobaça*. Oporto: Litografica nacional.

Kovács, É. (1985). Casula Sancti Stephani Regis. *Acta Historiae Artium Academiae Scientiarum Hungariae* v: 181-221.

Krusch, B., ed. (1888). *Vita Balthildis*. MGH, SSRM: ii, 475-508. Hannover: Hahn.

Krynen, J. (1981). *Idéal du prince et pouvoir royal en France à la fin du moyen âge*, 1380-1440. Paris: A. et J. Picard.

Krynen, J. (1985). Genèse de l'état et histoire des idées politiques en France à la fin du moyen âge. In École française de Rome (1985): 395-412.

Kunisch, J., ed. (1982). *Der Dynastische Fürstenstaat zur Bedeutung von Sukzessionsordnungen für die Entstehung des frühmodernen Staaten*. Berlin: Dunker & Humblot.

Kuper, H. (1950). Kinship Among the Swazi. In Radcliffe-Brown, A. R., and Forde, D., eds. (1950): 86-110.

Kurze, F., *post* Pertz, G. H. eds. (1891). *Annales Fuldenses sive Annales Regni Francorum Orientalis*. MGH, SSRG separatim editi, vii. Berlin: Weidmann.

Kurze, F., ed. (1829). *Gesta abbatum Fontanellensium*. MGH, SS: ii, 270-300. Hannover: Hahn.

Kurze, F., ed. (1895). *Annales regni francorum*. MGH, SSRG: vi, 1-178. Berlin: Weidmann.

Labande, E.-R. (1986). Les filles d'Aliénor d'Aquitaine. *Cahiers de civilisation médiévale* xxix: 101-12.

Lacarra, J. M. (1945). Textos navarros del códice de Roda. *Estudios de Edad Media de la Corona de Aragón* i: 193-275.

Lacarra, J. M., ed. (1965). *Colección diplomática de Irache*. Zaragoza: Consejo Superior de Investigaciones Cientificas, Instituto de Estudios Pirenaicos.

Lacroix, P. (1963). *France in the Middle Ages*. New York: Frederick Ungar.

Lambert of Ardres (1879). *Lamberti Ardensis Historia Comitum Ghisnensium*. Heller, I., ed. MGH, SS: xxiv, 550-642. Hannover: Hahn.

Lane, H. M. (1910). *The Royal Daughters of England and their Representatives*. 2 vols. London: Constable.

Laporte, J.-P. (1988). *Le trésor des saints de Chelles*. Chelles: Ville de Chelles.

Laporte, J.-P. (1989). Tissues provenant des reliquaires de Faremoutiers. *Pharanae. Histoire et archéologie du Moustier de Sainte Fare et de son village* i: 46-51.

Laporte, J.-P., and Boyer, R. (1991). *Trésors de Chelles: Sépultures et Reliques de la Reine Bathilde et de l'Abbesse Bertille*. Catalogue de l'exposition organisée au Musée Alfred Bonno. Chelles: Ville de Chelles.

Lappenberg, I. M., ed. (1859). *Annales Mosellani a. 704-797*. In MGH, SS: xvi, 491-99. Hannover: Hahn.

Larousse, P. (1873, rpt 1982). *Grand Dictionnaire Universel du XIXᵉ Siècle*. Paris-Genève: Administration du Grand Dictionnaire Universel, rpt Slatkine.

Le Boterf, H. (1976). *Anne de Bretagne*. Paris: Éditions France-Empire.

Le Coq, A.-M. (1987). *François Iᵉʳ Imaginaire*. Paris: Éditions Macula.

Legge, M. D. (1986). La littérature anglo-normande au temps d'Aliénor d'Aquitaine. *Cahiers de civilisation médiévale* xxix: 113-18.

Le Goff, J. (1990). A Coronation Program for the Age of Saint Louis: the Ordo of 1250. In Bàk, J., ed. (1990): 46-57.

Lejeune, R. (1958). Rôle littéraire de la famille d'Aliénor d'Aquitaine. *Cahiers de civilisation médiévale* i: 319-37.

Lerner, G. (1986). *The Creation of Patriarchy.* Oxford: Oxford University Press.

Levin, C. (1986). John Foxe and the Responsibilities of Queenship. In Rose, M. B., ed. (1986): 113-34.

Levin, C., and Watson, J., eds. (1987). *Ambiguous Realities: Women in the Middle Ages and Renaissance.* Detroit: Wayne State University Press.

Lewis, A. W. (1977). Dynastic structures and Capetian throne-right: the views of Giles of Paris. *Traditio* xxiii: 225-52.

Lewis, A. W. (1981). *Royal Succession in Capetian France. Studies in Family Order and the State.* Harvard Historical Studies. Cambridge, MA: Harvard University Press.

Lewis, A. W. (1986). *Le sang royal. La famille capétienne et l'État, France Xᵉ-XIVᵉ siècles.* Paris: Gallimard.

Lewis, I. M. (1962). *Marriage and the Family in Northern Somaliland.* Kampala: East African Institute of Social Research.

Lewis, S. (1980). A Byzantine *"Virgo militans"* at Charlemagne's court. *Viator* xi: 71-93.

Leyser, K. (1979). *Rule and Conflict in an Early Medieval Society. Ottonian Saxony.* Oxford: Basil Blackwell.

Lightman, H. (1981). Sons and Mothers: Queens and Minor Kings in French Constitutional Law. (Ph.D. diss., Bryn Mawr).

Lightman, H. (1986). Political power and the queen of France: Pierre DuPuy's treatise on regency government. *Canadian Journal of History* xxi: 299-312.

Lincoln, B. (1989). *Discourse and the Construction of Society.* Oxford: Oxford University Press.

LoPrete, K. (1990). The Anglo-Norman card of Adela of Blois. *Albion* xxii: 569-89.

Löwe, H. (1949). Ein Kölner Notiz. *Rheinische Vierteljahresblätter* iii: 6-34.

Luard, H. R., ed. (1890). *Flores historiarum.* 3 vols. RS xcv. London: HMSO.

Lunenfeld, M. (1981). The royal image: symbol and paradigm in portraits of early modern female sovereigns and regents. *Gazette des Beaux Arts* xcvii: 157-62.

Macfarlane, K. B. (1972). *Lancastrian Kings and Lollard Knights.* Oxford: Clarendon Press.

MacLean, S. B., and Carpenter, J., ed. (forthcoming). *Power of the Weak. Essays in the History of Medieval Women.* Champaign: University of Illinois Press.

McCash, J. H. (1979). Marie de Champagne and Eleanor of Aquitaine: a relationship reconsidered. *Speculum* liv: 698-711.

McCormick, M. (1986). *Eternal Victory.* Triumphal Rulership in Late Antiquity, Buzantium and the early Middle Ages. Cambridge: Cambridge University Press.

McGuire, B. P., and Reitzel, C. A., eds. (1987). *War and peace in the Middle Ages.* Copenhagen: Reitzel.

McKitterick, R. (1989). *The Carolingians and the Written Word.* Cambridge: Cambridge University Press.

McKitterick, R. (1990). Women in the Ottonian church: an iconographic perspective. *SCH* xxvii: 79-100.

McKitterick, R. (1991). Frauen und Schriftlichkeit im frühen Mittelalter. In Goetz, H.-W., ed. (1991): 65-118.

McKitterick, R. (1992). Nuns' scriptoria in Francia and England in the early Middle Ages. *Francia* xix (forthcoming).

McLaughlin, M. M. (1975). Peter Abelard and the Dignity of Women: Twelfth-Century "Feminism" in Theory and Practice. In Centre National de la Recherche Scientifique (1975): 287-333.

McLaughlin, M. M. (1991). Gender paradox and the otherness of God. *Gender and History* iii: 147-59.

McLeod, G. K., ed. (1991). *The Reception of Christine de Pizan From the Fifteenth Through the Nineteenth Centuries.* Lewiston: The Edwin Mellen Press.

McNamara, J., and Wemple, S. F. (1973, rpt 1988). The power of women through the family in medieval Europe, 500-1100. *Feminist Studies* i: 126-41, rpt in Erler, M., and Kowaleski, M., eds. (1988): 83-101.

Makk, F. (1989). *The Árpáds and the Comneni. Political Relations between Hungary and Byzantium in the Twelfth Century.* Budapest: Akadémiai Kiadó.

Mähl, S. (1969). *Quadriga Virtutum.* Cologne-Vienna: Böhlau.

Major, J. R. (1980). *Representative Government in Early Modern France.* New Haven: Yale University Press.

Marczali, H. (1911). Le procès de Félicien Záh. *Revue historique* cvii: 43-58.

Marou, H. I. (1971). *Les troubadours.* Paris: Seuil.

Marsh, P. (1985). Identity: an Ethogenic Perspective. In Trexler, R., ed. (1985): 17-30.

Martín Duque, A. J., ed. (1983). *Documentación medieval de Leire (siglos IX a XII).* Pamplona: Diputación foral de Leire.

Mason, E. (1977). William Rufus, myth and reality. *JMH* iii: 1-20.

Mason, E. (1990). *Saint Wulfstan of Worcester, ca. 1008-1095.* Oxford: Basil Blackwell.

Mattei, G. (1978). Les régences françaises pendant la minorité ou démence du roy (fin de XIV - XVIIIe siècles). 2 vols. (Thèse de droit, Université de Paris).

Maulde La Clavière, R. de (1885). *Procédures Politiques du Règne de Louis XII.* Collection de Documents Inédits sur L'Histoire de France. Paris: Imprimerie Nationale.

Maulde La Clavière, R. de (1895). *Louise de Savoie et Francois Ier.* Paris: Perrin.

Mayer, D. M. (1966). *The Great Regent: Louise of Savoy.* London: Wiedenfeld and Nicolson.

Mayer, H. E. (1972). Studies in the history of Queen Melisende of Jerusalem. *Dumbarton Oaks Papers* xxvi: 93-182.

Mayer, H.E. (1985). The succession to Baldwin II of Jerusalem: English impact on the East. *Dumbarton Oaks Papers* xxxix: 139-47.

Mayer, H. E. (1988). *The Crusades.* Gillingham, J. trs. 2nd ed. Oxford: Oxford University Press.

Melzak, R. (1990). Antiquarianism in the Time of Louis the Pious and its Influence on the Art of Metz. In Godman, P., and Collins, R., eds. (1990): 629-40.

Menache, S. (1984). Isabelle of France, queen of England: a reconsideration. *JMH* x: 107-24.

Mertes, K. (1988). *The English Noble Household, 1250-1600*. Oxford: Basil Blackwell.

Migne, J.-P., ed. (1844-64). *Patrologia cursus completus, series latina*. 221 vols. Paris: Garnier.

Mignet, A.-M.-A. (1895). *Rivalité de Francois Ier et de Charles V*. 2 vols. Paris: Didier.

Miller, D. A. (1971). Royauté et ambiguité sexuelle: symbolique de la monarchie à Byzance. *Annales ESC* xxvi: 639-52.

Mínguez Fernández, J. M., ed. (1976). *Collección diplomática del Monasterio de Sahagún (siglos IX y X)*. León: Centro de estudios y investigaciones "San Isidoro."

Mitterauer, M., and Sieder, R. (1982). *The European Family. Patriarchy to Partnership from the Middle Ages to the Present*. Oosterveen, K., and Hörzinger, M., trs. Oxford: Blackwell.

Molinet, J. (1828). *Chroniques de Jean Molinet*. Buchon, J. A., ed. Paris: Verdière.

Morey, A., and Brooke, C. N. L. (1965). *Gilbert Foliot and His Letters*. Cambridge: Cambridge University Press.

Morris, C. (1972). *The Discovery of the Individual, 1050-1200*. New York: Harper and Row.

Du Moulin, C. (1561). *La Première Partie du Traicte de L'origine, Progres et Excellence au Royaume et Monarchie des Françoys*. Lyon: à la Salamandre.

Muckle, J. T., ed. (1955). The letter of Heloise on religious life and Abelard's first reply. *Mediaeval Studies* xvii: 240-81.

Muhlack, U. (1982). Thronfolge und Erbrecht in Frankreich. In Kunisch, J., ed. (1982): 173-97.

Mütherich, F., and Gaehde, J. (1977). *Carolingian Painting*. London: Chatto and Windus.

Myers, A. R. (1940). The captivity of a royal witch: the household accounts of Queen Joan of Navarre, 1419-1421. *Bulletin of the John Rylands Library* xxiv: 263-84.

Nederman, C. J., and Lawson, N. E. (1987). The Frivolities of Courtiers Follow the Footprints of Women: Public Women and the Crisis of Virility in John of Salisbury, In Levin, C., and Watson, J., eds. (1987): 82-98.

Nees, L. (1991). *A Tainted Mantle. Hercules and the Classical Tradition at the Carolingian Court*. Philadelphia: University of Pennsylvania Press.

Nelson, J. L. (1978). Queens as Jezebels: the Careers of Brunhild and Balthild in Merovingian History. In Baker, D., ed. (1978a): 31-77.

Nelson, J. L. (1986a). *Politics and Ritual in Early Medieval Europe*. London-Ronceverte: Hambledon Press.

Nelson, J. L. (1986b). Inauguration Rituals. In Nelson (1986a): 283-307.

Nelson, J. L. (1990). Women and the Word. *SCH* xxvii: 53-78.

Nelson, J. L. (1991). Gender and genre in women historians of the early Middle Ages. In Genet, J.-P., ed. (1991): 149-63.

Newman, W. M. (1971). *Les seigneurs de Nesle.* 2 vols. Philadelphia: American Philosophical Society.

Niermeyer, J. F. (1976). *Mediae Latinitatis Lexicon Minus.* Leiden: Brill.

Noble, T. F. X. (1984). *The Republic of St. Peter.* Philadelphia: University of Pennsylvania Press.

Noonan, J. T., jr. (1973). Power to Choose. *Traditio* iv: 419-34.

Notker Balbulus (1962). *Gesta Karoli Magni.* Haefele, H. F., ed. MGH, SSRG N.S. xii. Berlin: Weidmann.

Olivier-Martin, F. (1931). *Les Régences et la Majorité des Rois.* Paris: Librairie du Recueil Sirey.

Olsen, O., ed. (1988-90). *Danmarkshistorie.* 14 vols. Copenhagen: Gyldendal.

Opitz, C. (1991). Contraintes et libertés, 1250-1500. In Klapisch-Zuber, C., ed. (1991): 277-335.

Orderic Vitalis (1969-80). *Historia Ecclesiastica.* Chibnall, M., ed. 6 vols. Oxford: Clarendon Press.

Orlandis, J. (1957-58). La reina en la monarquía visigoda. *Anuario de Historia del Derecho español* xxvii-xxviii: 109-35.

Orosius (1889, 1964). *Historiarum adversum paganos libri VII.* Zangemeister, C., ed. (Leipzig: Teubner Library), Deferrari, R. J., trs. (Washington: Catholic University of America [Fathers of the Church, l] as *The Seven Books of History against the Pagans.*

Orth, M. D. (1976). *Progressive Tendencies in Manuscript Illumination.* 2 vols. (Ph.D. diss., Institute of Fine Arts, New York University).

Orth, M. D. (1982). Francis Du Moulin and the journal of Louise of Savoy. *Sixteenth Century Journal* xiii: 55-66.

Ortiz-Osés, A., and Mayr, F. K. (1980). *El matriarcalismo vasco.* Bilbao: Universidad de Deusto.

Osgyányi, V. (1985). Beobachtungen des restaurators am Gertrudis-grabmal. *Studia Comitatensia. Régészeti Tanulmányok Pest megyéböl* 17: 603-20.

Oulmont, C. (1911). *Pierre Gringoire.* Paris: H. Champion.

Palacky, F. (1844-65). *Geschichte von Böhmen.* 5 vols. Prague: Tempsky.

Paradin, G. (1573). *Mémoires de l'histoire de Lyon.* Lyon: A. Gryphius.

Paris, M. (1866-69). *Historia Anglorum.* Madden, F., ed. 3 vols. London: HMSO.

Paris, M. (1872-84). *Chronica Majora.* Luard, H. R., ed. 7 vols. RS lvii. London: HMSO.

Paris, P., ed. (1936-38). *Les Grandes Chroniques de France.* 6 vols. Paris: Techener.

Paris, P. (1885, rpt 1970). *Études sur Francois Premier.* 2 vols. Paris: L. Techener, rpt Slatkin Reprints.

Parsons, D., ed. (1991). *Eleanor of Castile, 1290-1990: Essays to Commemorate the 700th Anniversary of her death: 28 November 1290.* Stamford, UK: Paul Watkins.

Parsons, J. C. (1977). *The Court and Household of Eleanor of Castile in 1290.* Studies and Texts, xxxvii. Toronto: Pontifical Institute of Mediaeval Studies.

Parsons, J. C. (1982). Eleanor of Castile and the Countess Margaret of Ulster. *Genealogists' Magazine* xx: 335-40.

Parsons, J. C. (1984). The year of Eleanor of Castile's birth and her children by Edward I. *Mediaeval Studies* xlvi: 245-65.

Parsons, J. C. (1988). The beginnings of English administration in Ponthieu: an unnoticed document of 1280. *Mediaeval Studies* l: 371-403.

Parsons, J. C. (1989). Eleanor of Castile and the Viscountess Jeanne of Châtelleraut. *Genealogists' Magazine* xxiii: 141-44.

Parsons, J. C. (1991). Ritual and symbol in the English queenship to 1500. In Fradenburg, L., ed. (1991a): 60-77.

Parsons, J. C. (1992). Piety, power, and the reputations of two thirteenth-century English queens. *Women of Power* i (forthcoming).

Parsons, J. C. (forthcoming). The Queen's Intercession in Thirteenth-Century England. In MacLean, S. B., and Carpenter, J., eds. (forthcoming).

Paschasius Radbertus (1879). *Vita Adalhardi*. In Migne, *PL* cxx: cols. 1507-57. Paris: Garnier.

Paschasius Radbertus (1967). *Epitaphium Arsenii seu vita venerabilis Walae*. In Cabaniss (1967): 83-204.

Paul the Deacon (1829). *Gesta Episcoporum Mettensium*. Pertz, G. H., ed. MGH, SS: ii, 260-68. Hannover: Hahn.

Pélissier, L.-G. (1890). Documents sur la première année du règne de Louis XII, tirés des archives de Milan. *Bulletin historique et philologique* ii-iii: 47-110.

Pérez de Urbel, J. (1952). *Sampiro, su Crónica y la monarquía leonesa en el siglo X*. Madrid: Consejo superior de Investigaciones Científicas.

Pérez de Urbel, J. (1969-70). *Historia del Condado de Castilla*. 2nd edn. 3 vols. Madrid: Siglo Illustrado.

Pérez de Urbel, J. (1979). *García Fernández*. Burgos: Ediciones de la Excellentísima Diputación Provincial.

Pernoud, R. (1980). *La femme au temps des cathédrales*. Paris: Stock.

Pernoud, R., and Cant, G. de (1987). *Isambour: la reine captive*. Paris: Stock.

Pertz, G. H., ed. (1826). *Annales Laureshamenses*. MGH, SS: i, 19-39. Hannover: Hahn.

Pertz, G. H., ed. (1829). *Gesta Abbatum Fontanellensium*. MGH, SS: ii, 270-301. Hannover: Hahn.

Pertz, G. H., ed. (1841). *Vita Mahthildis Reginae*. MGH, SS: iv, 282-302. Hannover: Hahn.

Phillipps, J. R. S. (1990). Review of Hamilton, J. (1988). *American Historical Review* xcv: 1180-81.

Pinet, M. J. (1927). *Christine de Pisan*, 1364-1430. Paris: H. Champion.

Pinkerton, J., ed. (1889). *Lives of the Scottish Saints. Revised and Enlarged by W. M. Metcalf*. Paisley: Alexander Gardner.

Pinoteau, H. (1982). *Vingt-cinq ans d'études dynastiques*. Paris: Éditions Christian.

Post, J. B. (1971). Ages at menarche and menopause: some medieval authorities. *Population Studies* xxv: 83-87.

Post, J. B. (1974). Another demographic use of inquisitions post mortem. *Journal of the Society of Archivists* v: 110-14.

Potter, K. R., and Davis, R. H. C., eds. (1976). *Gesta Stephani*. Oxford: Clarendon Press.

Poujol, J. (1977). 1515. Cadre Idéologique du développement de l'Absolutisme en France à l'avènement de François Ier. In *Théorie et Pratique Politiques à la Renaissance* (XVIIe Colloque International de Tours): 259-69. Paris: Librarie Philosophique J. Vrin.

Poulet, A. (1989). *La régence et la majorité des rois au moyen âge: histoire de la continuité monarchique et étatique sous les Capétiens et les Valois directs*. Thèse, Faculté des Sciences Historiques, Université des Sciences Humaines de Strasbourg.

Power, E. (1976). *Medieval Women*. Cambridge: Cambridge University Press.

Pradel, P. (1936). *Catalogue des Jetons des Princes et Princesses de la Maison de France*. Paris: Bibliothèque Nationale.

Prestwich, M. (1988). *Edward I*. Berkeley: University of California Press.

Prou, M. (1908). *Recueil des actes de Philippe Ier (1059-1108)*. Paris: Académie des Inscriptions, Chartes et Diplômes.

Quilliet, B. (1986). *Louis XII, père du peuple*. Paris: Fayard.

Radcliffe-Brown, A. R., and Forde, D., eds. (1950). *African Systems of Kinship and Marriage*. Oxford: Oxford University Press.

Ranke, L. von (1853). *Civil Wars and Monarchy in France*. Garvey, M. A., trs. New York: Harper.

Ranum, O. (1980). *Artisans of Glory: Writers and Historical Thought in Seventeenth Century France*. Chapel Hill: University of North Carolina Press.

Ramos Loscertales, J. M. (1961). *El Reino de Aragón bajo la dinastía pamplonese*. Salamanca: Universidad de Salamanca.

Record Commission 1783-1832. *Rotuli parliamentorum*. 7 vols. London, n.p.

Riché, P. (1975). *Dhuoda, Manuel pour mon fils*. Paris: Éditions du Cerf.

Riley, H. T., ed. (1865). *Johannis de Trokelowe et Henrici de Blaneford Chronica et Annales*. RS xxviii part 3. London: HMSO.

Robertson, A. J., ed. (1956). *Anglo-Saxon Charters*. 2nd edn. Cambridge: Cambridge University Press.

Rodolf Glaber (1989). *Historiarum Libri Quinque*. Bulst, N., ed. Oxford: Clarendon Press.

Rodríguez, J. (1972). *Ramiro II Rey de León*. Madrid: Consejo superior de Investigaciones Científicas.

Rodríguez, J. (1982). *Ordoño III*. León: Ediciones Leonesas.

Rodríguez, J. (1987). *Sancho I y Ordoño IV, Reyes de León*. León: Centro de estudios y investigaciones "San Isidoro".

Röhricht, R., ed. (1893-94, rpt. 1960). *Regesta regni Hierosolymitani, MXCVII-MCCXCI*. 2 vols. Burt Franklin Bibliographical and Reference Series, xxiv. New York: Burt Franklin.

Rollason, D. (1983). The cults of murdered royal saints in Anglo-Saxon England. *Anglo-Saxon England* xi: 1-22.

Rosaldo, M. Z. (1974). Woman, Culture and Society: a theoretical overview. In Rosaldo, M. Z., and Lamphere, L., eds. (1974): 17-42.

Rosaldo, M. Z., and Lamphere, L., eds. (1974). *Woman, Culture and Society*. Stanford: Stanford University Press.

Rose, J. (1986). *Sexuality in the Field of Vision*. London: Verso.

Rose, M. B., ed. (1986). *Women in the Middle Ages and the Renaissance. Literary and Historical Perspectives*. Ithaca, NY: Syracuse University Press.

Rosenthal, J., ed. (1990). *Medieval Women and the Sources of Medieval History*. Athens, GA: University of Georgia Press.

Ross, C., ed. (1979). *Patronage, Pedigree and Power in Later Medieval England*. Gloucester: A. Sutton.

Rossiaud, J. (1988). *La prostitution médiévale*. Paris: Flammarion.

Rubin, E. R. (1977). The Heroic Image: Women and Power in Early Seventeenth Century France, 1610-61. (Ph.D. diss., The Graduate School of Arts and Sciences, The George Washington University).

Rudolf of Fulda (1887). *Vita Leobae Abbatissae Biscofesheimensis auctore Rudolfo Fuldensi*. Waitz, G., ed. MGH, SS: xv part 1, 118-31. Hannover: Hahn.

Ruether, R. R. (1979). *Religion and Sexism: Images of Women in the Jewish and Christian Traditions*. New York: Simon and Schuster.

Ruiz, T. F. (1985). Unsacred Monarchy: The Kings of Castile in the Late Middle Ages. In Wilentz, S., ed. (1985), 109-44.

Runciman, S. (1978). The Empress Irene the Athenian. In Baker, D., ed. (1978a): 101-18.

Russell, J. C. (1948). *British Medieval Population*. Albuquerque: University of New Mexico Press.

Russell, J. C. (1973a). *Twelfth Century Studies*. New York: AMS Press.

Russell, J. C. (1973b). Accusations of Poisoning in the Norman World. In Cox (1973a): 73-83.

Rutherford, A. (1932). *The Anglo-Norman Chronicle of Nicholas Trivet: Text, with historical, philological and literary study*. (Ph.D. diss., University of London).

Rymer, T. (1816-69). *Foedera, conventiones, literae. . . .* 4 vols. in 7 folios. London: Record Commission.

Sabatier, G. (1991). Les rois de représentation. Image et pouvoir (xvie - xviie siècles). *Revue de synthèse* cii: 387-422.

Saenger, P. (1977). Burgundy and the inalienability of apanages in the reign of Louis XI. *French Historical Studies* x: 1-26.

Saéz, E. (1946). Notas al episcopología minduniense. *Hispania* vi: 3-79.

Saéz, E. (1949). Sancho Ordoñez, rey de Galicia. *Cuadernos de Historia de España* xi: 25-104.

Saéz, E., and Saéz, C., eds. (1990). *Colleción documental del Archivo de la Catedral de León*, ii. León: C.S.I.C./C.E.C.E.L.

Saint Gelais, J. ed (1622). *Histoire de Louis XII*. Paris: A. Pacard.

Sánchez Candeira, A. (1950). La reina Velasquita. *Hispania* x: 449-503.

Savoy, Louise of (1838). *Journal de Louise de Savoie*. Michaud, J.-F., and Poujoulat, J.-J.-F., eds. Nouvelle collection des Mémoires pour servir à l'histoire de France, Premier série, xvi. London-Paris, n.p.

Scheller, R. W. (1981-82). Imperial themes in art and literature of the early French Renaissance. *Simiolus* i: 5-69.

Scheller, R. W. (1983). Ensigns of authority: French royal symbolism in the age of Louis XII. *Simiolus* ii: 75-141.

Schieffer, R. (1990a). Väter und Söhne im Karolingerhause. In Schieffer, R. ed. (1990b): 149-64.

Schieffer, R., ed. (1990b). *Beiträge zur Geschichte des Regnum Francorum*. Beihefte der *Francia*, xii. Sigmaringen: Thorbecke.

Schieffer, T. ed. (1966). *Die Urkunden Lothars I*. MGH, Diplomata Karolinarum: iii, 1-365. Berlin: Weidmann.

Schlesinger, W., ed. (1974). *Die deutsche Ostsiedlung des Mittelalters als Problem der europäischen Geschichte*. Vorträge und Forschungen xviii. Sigmaringen: Thorbecke.

Schmitz-Cliever-Lepie, H. (1986). *The Treasury of the Cathedral of Aachen*. Aachen: Chapter of the Cathedral of Aachen.

Schneider, R., ed. (1987). *Das spätmittelalter Königtum im europäischen Vergleich*. Vorträge und Forschungen xxxii. Sigmaringen: Thorbecke.

Schnith, K. (1976). *Regni et pacis inquietatrix*: Zur Rolle der Kaiserin Mathilde in der "Anarchie." *JMH* ii: 135-57.

Schramm, P. E. (1968-71). *Kaiser, Könige und Päpste*. 4 vols. Stuttgart: Hiersemann.

Schramm, P. E., and Mütherich, F. (1981). *Denkmale der deutschen Könige und Kaiser*. 2nd ed. Munich: Prestel Verlag.

Schwennicke, D. (1980-84). *Europäische Stammtafeln. Stammtafeln zur Geschichte der europäischen Staaten*, Neue Folge. 2 vols. Marburg: Stargardt.

Scofield, C. L. (1923). *The Life and Reign of Edward the Fourth, King of England and of France and Lord of Ireland*. 2 vols. London: Longmans, Green.

Sears, E. (1990). Louis the Pious as *Miles Christi*: the Dedicatory Image in Hrabanus Maurus's *De laudibus sanctae crucis*. In Godman, P., and Collins, R., eds. (1990): 605-28.

Secousse, C. (1967-68). *Ordonnances des Roys de France de la troisième race*. Farnborough, Hants.: Gress.

Shennan, H. (1968). *The Parlement of Paris*. Ithaca, NY: Cornell University Press.

Sheehan, M. (1971). The formation and stability of marriage in fourteenth-century England: evidence of an Ely register. *Mediaeval Studies* xxxiii: 228-63.

Sherman, C. R. (1969). *The Portraits of Charles V of France, 1338-1380*. New York: New York University Press.

Sherman, C. R. (1977). The queen in Charles V''s 'Coronation Book': Jeanne de Bourbon and the 'Ordo ad reginam benedicendam'. *Viator* viii: 255-98.

Shirley, W. W., ed. (1862-66). *Royal and other Historical Letters of the Reign of Henry III.* 2 vols. RS xxvii. London: HMSO.

Silva y Verástegui, S. de (1984). *Iconográfia del Siglo X en el Reino de Pamplona-Nájera.* Pamplona: Institución Príncipe de Viana.

Simons, P. (1988). Women in frames: the eye, the gaze, the profile in Renaissance portraiture. *History Workshop* xxv: 4-30.

Sivéry, G. (1982). *Blanche de Castille.* Paris: Fayard.

Sivéry, G. (1987). *Marguerite de Provence, une reine au temps des cathédrales.* Paris: Fayard.

Skinner, Q. (1978). *The Foundations of Modern Political Thought.* 2 vols. Cambridge: Cambridge University Press.

Skovgaard-Petersen, I. (1988). Saxo's History of the Danes: an interpretation. *Journal of Scandinavian History* xiii: 87-93.

Skyum-Nielsen, N. (1981). Estonia under Danish Rule. In Skyum-Nielson, N., and Lund, N. eds. (1981): 112-35.

Skyum-Nielsen, N., and Lund, N., eds. (1981). *Danish Medieval History. New Currents.* Copenhagen: Museum Tusculanum Press.

Sommers, P. (1991). Marguerite de Navarre as Reader of Christine de Pizan. In McLeod, G. K., ed. (1991): 71-82.

Spiegel, G. (1978). The *Reditus Regni ad Stirpem Karoli Magni:* a new look. *French Historical Studies* xvii: 129-48.

Stafford, P. (1978a). Sons and Mothers: Family Politics in the Early Middle Ages. In Baker, D., ed. (1978a): 79-100.

Stafford, P. (1978b). The Reign of Aethelred II: A Study in the Limitations on Royal Policy and Action. In Hill, D., ed. (1978): 15-46.

Stafford, P. (1981a). The king's wife in Wessex 800-1066. *Past and Present* xci: 3-27.

Stafford, P. (1981b). Charles the Bald, Judith and England. In Gibson, M., Nelson, J., and Ganz, D., eds. (1981): 137-51.

Stafford, P. (1983). *Queens, Concubines and Dowagers. The King's Wife in the Early Middle Ages.* Athens, GA: University of Georgia Press.

Stafford, P. (1989). *Unification and Conquest.* London: E. Arnold.

Staniland, K. (1987). Royal Entry into the World. In Williams, D., ed. (1987): 297-313.

Stevenson, J., ed. *Chronicon de Lanercost, MCCI-MCCCXLVI. E codice Cottoniano nunc primum typis mandatum.* Edinburgh: Bannatyne Club.

Stocker, C. R. (1973). The politics of the Parlement of Paris in 1525. *French Historical Studies* viii: 191-212.

Stoclet, A. (1986). Gisèle, Kisyla, Chelles, Benediktbeuren et Kochel. Scriptoria, bibliothèques et politique à l'époque carolingienne. Une mise au point. *Revue Bénédictine* xcvi: 250-70.

Strand, B. (1980). *Kvinnor och män i Gesta Danorum.* Göteborg: University of Gothenburg, Department of History.

Strohm, P. (1992a). *Hochon's Arrow. The Social Imagination of Fourteenth-Century Texts.* Princeton, NJ: Princeton University Press.

Strohm, P. (1992b). Queens as Intercessors. In Strohm (1992a): 95-120.

Stuard, S. M., ed. (1976). *Women in Medieval Society*. Philadelphia: University of Pennsylvania Press.

Stuard, S. M., ed. (1987a). *Women in Medieval History and Historiography*. Philadelphia: University of Pennsylvania Press.

Stuard, S. M. (1987b). Fashion's Captives: Medieval Women in French Historigraphy. In Stuard (1987a): 59-80.

Sturdza, M.-D. (1983). *Dictionnaire historique et généalogique des grandes familles de Grèce, d'Albanie et de Constantinople*. Paris: Chez l'auteur.

Stubbs, W., ed. (1874). *Memorials of Saint Dunstan*. RS lxiii. London: HMSO.

Sturler, J. (1936). *Relations politiques et les échanges commerciales entre le duché de Brabant et l'Angleterre au moyen âge*. Paris: E. Droz.

Sugar, P., Hának, P., and Frank, T., eds. (1990). *A History of Hungary*. Bloomington, IN: Indiana University Press.

Szekfü, L. (1974). Sarolta. In Horváth, J., and Székely, G., eds. (1974): 239-52.

Szentpétery, I. (1930). *Magyar oklevéltan*. Budapest: Magyar Tudományos Akadémia.

Szentpétery, I. (1937). *Scriptores rerum Hungaricarum tempore ducum regumque stirpis Árpádianae gestarum*. 2 vols. Budapest: Academia Litterarum.

Szentpétery, I., and Borsa, I., eds. (1923-87). *Regesta regum stirpis Árpádianae critico-diplomatica*. 2 vols. in 4 folios. Budapest: Academia Litt.

Talbot, C. H. (1955). The Liber Confortatorius of Goscelin of Saint Bertin. *Studia Anselmiana* xxxvii (= *Analecta Monastica*, 3rd. ser. fasc. 37): 1-117.

Talbot, C. H. (1959). The life of St. Wulsin of Sherborne by Goscelin. *Revue Bénédictine* lxix: 68-85.

Terrasse, C. (1945). *François Iᵉʳ*. 2 vols. Paris: B. Grasset.

Terrevermeille, J. de. (1526). *Contra Rebelles suorum Regum*. Lyon: Joannis Crespin.

Tervarent, G. ed (1958). *Attributs et Symboles dans L'Art Profane, 1450-1600*. 3 vols. Paris: Droz.

Testa, F., ed. (1741-43). *Capitula Regni Siciliae quae ad hodiernum diem lata sunt*. Palermo: A. Felicella.

Thegan (1829). *Vita Hludowici Imperatoris*. Pertz, G. H., ed. MGH, SS: ii, 585-603. Hannover: Hahn.

Theodulf of Orléans (1881). *Theodulfi carmina*. Dümmler, E., ed. MGH, Poetae latini aevi karolini: i, 437-568. Berlin: Weidmann.

Theophanes (1982). *Chronicle*. Turtledove, H., trs. Philadelphia: University of Pennsylvania Press.

Thietmar of Merseberg (1955). *Thiethmari episcopi Merseburgensis Chronica*. 2nd edn. Holtzmann, R., ed. MGH SSRG, N.S. 9. Berlin: Weidmann.

Thomasset, C. (1991). De la nature féminine. In Klapisch-Zuber, C., ed. (1991): 55-81.

Thompson, E. A. (1969). *The Goths in Spain*. Oxford: Clarendon Press.

250   MEDIEVAL QUEENSHIP

Thomson, R. M. (1987). *William of Malmesbury*. Woodbridge, NJ: Boydell.

Traill, D. A. (1974). *Walahfrid Strabo's "Visio Wettini": Text, Translation and commentary*. Lateinische Sprache und Literatur des Mittelalters, ii. Berne-Frankfurt: Lang.

Trease, G. E. (1959). The spicers and apothecaries of the royal household in the reigns of Henry III, Edward I and Edward II. *Nottingham Medieval Studies* iii: 19-52.

Trebuchet, A.-M.-J. (1822). *Anne de Bretagne, Reine de France*. Paris: Paynel.

Trevet, N. (1845). *Annales*. Hog, Th., ed. London: English Historical Society.

Trexler, R. C., ed. (1985). *Persons in Groups. Social Behavior as Identity Formation in Medieval and Renaissance Europe*. Binghamton, NY: Medieval and Renaissance Texts and Studies.

Turner, R. V. (1988). Eleanor of Aquitaine and her children: an inquiry into medieval family attachment. *JMH* xiv: 321-35.

Turner, R. V. (1990). The children of Anglo-Norman royalty and their upbringing. *Medieval Prosopography* xi: 17-52.

Ubieto, A. (1950). Monarcas navarros olvidados: los reyes de Viguera. *Hispania* x: 3-24.

Ubieto Arteta, A., ed. (1962). *Cartulario de San Juan de la Peña*. 2 vols. Valencia: Anubar.

Ubieto Arteta, A. (1972a). *Trabajos de Investigación*. Valencia: Anubar.

Ubieto Arteta, A. (1972b). Doña Andregoto Galíndez, reina de Pamplona y condesa de Aragón. In Ubieto Arteta, A. (1972a): 113-28.

Ubieto Arteta, A., ed. (1976). *Cartulario de San Millán de la Cogolla (759-1076)*. Valencia: Anubar.

Ubieto Arteta, A., ed. (1981). *Cartulario de Albelda*. Zaragoza: Anubar.

Ullmann, W., ed. (1961). *Liber regie capelle: A Manuscript in the Biblioteca Publica, Evora*. Henry Bradshaw Society, xcii. Cambridge: Cambridge University Press.

Ursins, J. J. des (1985). *Écrits Politiques de Jean Juvénal des Ursins*. Lewis, P. S., ed. 2 vols. Paris: Société de l'Histoire de France.

Van Gennep, A. Raugé (1897). Jetons de Savoie. *Revue Numismatique* i: 63-64.

Vauchez, A. (1977). "Beata stirps": sainteté et lignage en occident aux XIIIe et XIVe siècles. In Duby, G., and Le Goff, J., eds. (1977): 395-406.

Verdon, J. (1973). Les femmes et la politique en France au Xe siécle. In *Économies et sociétés au moyen âge. Mélanges offerts à Édouard Perroy*: 108-19. Paris: Publications de la Sorbonne, Série Études, v.

Vestergaard, E. (1990). A Note on Viking Age Inaugurations. In Bak, J. M., ed. (1990): 119-24.

Veyne, P. (1987a). The Roman Empire. In Veyne, P. ed. (1987b), 5-233.

Veyne, P., ed. (1987b). *A History of Private Life*, i (Duby, G., general ed.). Goldhammer, A. trs. Cambridge, MA: Belknap Press (Cambridge University Press).

Viard, J., ed. (1920-53). *Les grandes chroniques de France*. 10 vols. Paris: Société de l'Histoire de France.

Viguera, M. J., and Corriente, F., trs. (1981). *Crónica del Califa 'Abdarrahman III an-Nasir entre los años 912 y 942 (al-Muqtabis V)*. Zaragoza: Anubar.

Viñayo, A. (1982). Reinas e Infantas de León, abadesas y monjas de San Pelayo y San Isidro. *Semana de Historia del monacato cántabro-astur-leonés*, 123-35. León: Monasterio de San Pelayo.

Vives, J., ed. (1963). *Concilios visigóticos e hispano-romanos*. Barcelona-Madrid: Consejo superior de investigaciones científicas.

Waitz, G., ed. (1841). *Vitae Heinrici et Cunegundis Impp*. MGH, SS: iv, 787-828. Hannover: Hahn.

Walahfrid Strabo (1985). *Visio Wettini*. In Godman, P. (1985): 214.

Walker, S. S. (1976). Widow and Ward: the Feudal Law of Child Custody in Medieval England. In Stuard, S. M., ed. (1976): 159-72.

Walker, S. S. (1982). Free consent and marriage of feudal wards in medieval England. *JMH* viii: 123-34.

Wallace-Hadrill, J. M., ed. (1960). *The Fourth Book of the Chronicle of Fredegar with its Continuations*. London: Nelson.

Wallach, L. (1977). *Diplomatic Studies in Latin and Greek Documents from the Carolingian Age*. Ithaca, NY: Cornell University Press.

Ward, E. (1990a). Caesar's Wife: The Career of the Empress Judith, 819-29. In Godman, P., and Collins, R., eds. (1990): 205-27.

Ward, E. (1990b). Agobard of Lyons and Paschasius Radbertus as critics of the Empress Judith. *SCH* xxvii: 15-26.

Warren, W. (1977). *Henry II*. Berkeley, CA: University of California Press.

Wegener, C. F., ed. (1852-83). *Aarsberetninger fra det kongelige Geheimarchiv*. 7 vols. in 6 folios. Copenhagen: C. A. Reitzel.

Weightman, C. (1989). *Margaret of York: Duchess of Burgundy 1446-1503*. New York: St. Martin's Press.

Weinrich, L. (1963). *Wala: Graf, Monch und Rebell*. Lübeck: Matthiesen.

Wells, R. H. (1983). *Spenser's Faerie Queene and the Cult of Elizabeth*. Totowa, NJ: Barnes and Noble.

Wemple, S. (1981). *Women in Frankish Society*. Philadelphia: University of Pennsylvania Press.

Werner, K. F. (1967). Die Nachkommen Karls des Grossen. In Braunfels, W., ed. (1965-68): iv, 403-83.

Werner, K. F. (1980). Gott, Herrscher und Historiograph. Der Geschichtsschreiber als Interpret des Wirkens Gott in der Welt. In Hehl, E.-D., ed. (1980): 1-31.

Westphal-Wihl, S. (1989). *The Ladies' Tournament*: Marriage, Sex and Honor in Thirteenth-Century Germany. In Bennett, J., et al., eds. (1989): 162-89.

Whitelock, D., ed. (1979a). *English Historical Documents*, I. 2nd. edn. London-New York: Eyre Methuen-Oxford University Press.

Whitelock D., ed. (1979b). *The Anglo-Saxon Chronicle (60 B.C.-A.D. 1042)*. In Whitelock, D., ed. (1979a): 146-261.

Wilentz, S., ed. (1985). *Rites of Power. Symbolism, Ritual and Politics Since the Middle Ages*. Philadelphia: University of Pennsylvania Press.

Willard, C. C. (1991). Anne de France, Reader of Christine de Pizan. In McLeod, G. K., ed. (1991): 59-70.

William of Jumièges (1914). *Gesta Normannorum Ducum.* Marx, J., ed. Paris-Rouen: Picard-Lestringant.

William of Malmesbury (1887-89). *Willelmi Malmesbiriensis de Gestis Regum.* Stubbs, W., ed. 2 vols. RS xc. London: HMSO.

William of Malmesbury (1955). *Historia Novella.* Potter, K., ed. and trs. London: Nelson.

William of Tyre (1943). *A History of Deeds Done Beyond the Sea.* Babcock, E. A., and Krey, A. C., ed. and trs. 2 vols. New York: Columbia University Press.

Williams, A. (1978). Some notes and considerations of problems connected with the English royal succession, 860-1066. *Anglo-Norman Studies* i: 144-67.

Williams, D., ed. (1987). *England in the Fifteenth Century: Proceedings of the 1986 Harlaxton Symposium.* Woodbridge, NJ: Boydell and Brewer.

Wilmart, A. (1938). La légende de Ste Édithe en prose et vers par le moine Goscelin. *Analecta Bollandiana* lvi: 5-101.

Wilson, J. (1980). *Entertainments for Elizabeth I.* Woodbridge and Totowa, NJ: Brewer.

Wolf, A. (1987). Prinzipien der Thronfolge in Europe um 1400. Vergleichende Beobachtungen zur Praxis des dynastischen Herrschaftssystems. In Schneider, R., ed. (1987): 233-78.

Wolf, A. (1991). The family of dynasties in medieval Europe: dynasties, kingdoms and *Tochterstämme. Studies in Medieval and Renaissance History* N.S. xii: 193-268.

Wood, C. T. (1966). *The French apanages and the Capetian Monarchy,* 1224-1328. Cambridge, MA: Harvard University Press.

Wood, C. T. (1988a). *Joan of Arc and Richard III: Sex, Saints and Government in the Middle Ages.* Oxford: Oxford University Press.

Wood, C. T. (1988b). Queens, Queans and Kingship. In Wood (1988a): 13-28.

Wood, C. T. (1991). The First Two Queens Elizabeth. In Fradenburg, L., ed. (1991a): 121-31.

Wormald, P. (1978). Æthelred the Law Maker. In Hill, D., ed. (1978): 47-80.

Wright, C. E. (1939). *The Cultivation of Saga in Anglo-Saxon England.* Edinburgh: Oliver and Boyd.

Wright, G. S. (1974). A royal tomb program in the reign of Saint Louis. *Art Bulletin* lvi: 224-43.

Wroth, W. (1908). *Catalogue of the Imperial Byzantine Coins in the British Museum.* 2 vols. London: British Museum.

Zanger, A. (1991). Fashioning the Body Politic: Imagining the Queen in the Marriage of Louis XIV. In Fradenburg, L., ed. (1991a): 101-20.

Zeumer, K., ed. (1886). *Formulae imperiales.* MGH Formulae. Hannover: Hahn.

About the contributors:

János M. Bak, Professor Emeritus of Medieval History at the University of British Columbia, is now Professor in the Medieval Studies program at the Central European University, Budapest. After studies at Budapest and Oxford, he obtained his doctorate at Göttingen, and has published widely on the history of medieval Hungary and on the symbology of rulership. He has edited *Coronations. Medieval and Early Modern Monarchic Ritual* (University of California Press); with James R. Sweeney and the late György Bónis, is co-editor and translator of *The Laws of the Medieval Kingdom of Hungary*, 2 vols. to date (Bakersfield, CA, 1989, 1992), and, with Paul Hollingsworth, translator of Aron Gurevich's *Medieval Popular Culture* (Cambridge, 1988).

Roger Collins, D. Litt. (Oxon.), F.R.H.S., has been a Lecturer in Medieval History, a Leverhulme Senior Research Fellow and a Vicente Cañada Blanch Senior Research Fellow. He is the author of *Early Medieval Spain: Unity in Diversity, 499-1000* (1983), *The Basques* (1986), *The Arab Conquest of Spain, 710-797* (1989), *Early Medieval Europe, 300-1000* (1991), and *Law, Culture and Regionalism in Early Medieval Spain* (1992); with Peter Godman, he has co-edited *Charlemagne's Heir: New Approaches to the Reign of Louis the Pious* (1989).

Nanna Damsholt, D. Phil, Docent at the Centre for Female Studies in the University of Copenhagen, is the author of *Kvindebilledet i dansk højmiddelalder* (1985, with English summary) and several studies of medieval women.

Lois L. Huneycutt received her Ph.D. in 1992 from the University of California at Santa Barbara. Currently Assistant Professor of History at California State University, Hayward, she has previously published articles on the Anglo-Norman queens of England in *The Haskins Society Journal* (1990) and in *Anglo-Norman Studies* (1990).

Elizabeth McCartney, doctoral candidate in the Department of History at the University of Iowa, is completing her dissertation on "French Queens in the Cult of the Renaissance Monarchy," under the supervision of Ralph E. Giesey. Her article on the juristic and dynastic precepts of public law supporting distaff privileges of office in early modern France will appear in *Power of the Weak: Essays in the History of Medieval Women*, eds. S. B. Maclean and J. Carpenter (University of Illinois Press).

Janet L. Nelson is Reader in History at King's College, London, where she has taught since 1970. A volume of her collected papers, *Politics and Ritual in Early Medieval Europe*, was published by Hambledon in 1986, her translation of *The Annals of St-Bertin* by Manchester University Press in 1991, and her biography of *Charles the Bald* by Longman in 1992. A second volume of papers, *The Frankish World in the Ninth Century*, is to appear in 1993.

John Carmi Parsons, Senior Fellow at the Centre for Reformation and Renaissance Studies, Victoria University (Toronto), is a former Junior Fellow of the Pontifical Institute of Mediaeval Studies in Toronto. He is the author of *The Court and Household of Eleanor of Castile in 1290* (1977), and a series of articles on thirteenth-century English queenship. His study of Eleanor of Castile, wife of Edward I of England, will be published by St. Martin's Press.

Inge Skovgaard-Petersen, D. Phil, Lecturer at the Institute of History in the University of Copenhagen, studies the history of the viking Age and the chronicle of Saxo Grammaticus. She is the author of *Da Tidernes Herre var Nær. Studier i Saxos historie-syn* (1987, with German summary).

Born in Germany, **André Poulet** defended his doctoral thesis in medieval history at the Université des Sciences Humaines at Strasbourg, France in 1989. He has worked on the reign of John II of France and medieval regencies; his research concentrates on the institutional history of fourteenth- and fifteenth-century France. He is currently an instructor in history and in French at the secondary and adult levels.

Pauline Stafford is Lecturer in History in the Department of Humanities, University of Huddersfield. She is the author of *Queens, Concubines and Dowagers: the King's Wife in the Early Middle Ages* (1985), *The East Midlands in the Early Middle Ages* (Leicester, 1985), and *Unification and Conquest: a Political and Social History of England in the Tenth and Eleventh Centuries* (London, 1989). Her forthcoming publications include a *Bibliography of British Women's History* and a biography of the eleventh-century English queens Emma and Edith.

Armin Wolf, Senior Research Fellow at the Max-Planck-Institut für Europäische Rechtsgeschichte in Frankfurt-am-Main, teaches medieval history at the University of Heidelberg; he was Visiting Fellow at The Pennsylvania State University in 1983, and at the University of Kyoto in 1992. His recent English publications include "The Family of Dynasties in Medieval Europe: Dynasties, Kingdoms and *Tochterstämme*," in *Studies in Medieval and Renaissance History*, 12 (1992), and "What can the History of Historical Atlases Teach?: some lessons from a century of Putzger's *Historischer Schul-Atlas*," in *Cartographica*, xxviii part 2 (1991).

I·N·D·E·X

the
opposite
of
music

the
opposite
of
music

janet ruth young

atheneum books for young readers
new york   london   toronto   sydney

Atheneum Books for Young Readers * An imprint of Simon & Schuster
Children's Publishing Division * 1230 Avenue of the Americas, New
York, New York 10020 * This book is a work of fiction. Any references
to historical events, real people, or real locales are used fictitiously. Other
names, characters, places, and incidents are products of the author's
imagination, and any resemblance to actual events or locales or persons,
living or dead, is entirely coincidental. * Copyright © 2007 by Janet
Ruth Young * All rights reserved, including the right of reproduction in
whole or in part in any form. * The text for this book is set in Sabon. *
Manufactured in the United States of America * First Edition *
10 9 8 7 6 5 4 3 2 1 * Library of Congress Cataloging-in-Publication
Data * Young, Janet Ruth, 1957– * The opposite of music / Janet Ruth
Young.—1st ed. * p.   cm. * Summary: With his family, fifteen-year-old
Billy struggles to help his father deal with a debilitating depression. *
ISBN-13: 978-1-4169-0040-5 * ISBN-10: 1-4169-0040-3 * [1. Depression,
Mental—Fiction. 2. Family problems—Fiction. 3. Fathers—Fiction.]
I. Title. * PZ7.Y86528Opp 2007 * [Fic]—dc22 * 2005037122

To my parents, Mildred and George Young

ACKNOWLEDGMENTS

Thanks to Lois Lowry and the PEN New England Children's Book Discovery Committee for first seeing the potential of this book; to Jen Hirsch, formerly of Brookline Booksmith, and Lorraine Barry of the Reading Public Library, as well as Charline Lake, Janine O'Malley, Sandy Oxley, Lincoln Ross, Jan Voogd, and Diane Young, for their comments at various stages of the manuscript; and to my editors at Atheneum, Caitlyn Dlouhy and Susan Burke, for their superb guidance and warm support.

part one

HANDS ACROSS THE SEA

Resting one hand on the corner mailbox, I balance different ways on my bike. A stream of cars goes by before I see the school bus.

Our town has changed in the last five years. Some of the new kids from other places think they're too upscale for Hawthorne. When I tell Mom this, she thinks I'm misinterpreting the signals. She says I should be attuned to regional differences, that in other parts of the country people have different ways of approaching one another and making new friends. She says I should think of myself as an anthropologist, studying various subcultures of the United States and never forming a value judgment that says my way is better. But I think that if someone sits next to you in class for three weeks and never says anything, the message isn't regional boundaries. The message is they don't want to know you.

Gordy is the big exception. When I wave to the bus driver, Gordy hops down the steps with his jacket over his

shoulder, his backpack and music case in the other hand. I don't have much planned. We're going to practice for a vocabulary test, but that won't take long.

"So that's your bike," he says.

"Want to ride it? I could carry your stuff."

"No, thanks."

I like to watch and evaluate the new people who come into town. I've been watching Gordy. In my eyes he is royalty. He is always in his element. He absorbs goings-on without alarm. His hair is always exactly the same length, as if he gets it cut every Tuesday and Thursday. I like to look for people to admire. Otherwise, how will you know who to become?

While Gordy is outstanding in the good sense of the word, I sometimes wonder whether I stand out in the bad sense. My arms and legs seem to grow longer every week, and I am starting to suspect that I may bob up and down excessively when I walk. I say this because a few days ago there was an incident in which I was passing a group of new kids on my way to class and without saying anything they all started bobbing, as if on a prearranged signal. And some of the kids have started calling me Bob.

I wonder what Gordy will think of the house. Our front

door is bright orange, with a brass door knocker in the shape of a salamander. On the door we have an artist's palette dotted with hard, shiny puddles of tint, which my sister Linda made from wood scraps. She also painted our name and house number—Morrison 32—in medieval letters on a white rock at the foot of the driveway. Members of my family try hard to be distinctive.

Dad's Neon is in the driveway. The palette clatters when I open the door.

"Hey, Dad?" I call. "What are you doing home?" Mom is still out. It's two-thirty and she usually doesn't get home from work until four.

But Dad doesn't come to the door as he normally would if I brought someone home. We hear his footsteps at the far end of the house.

"Dad," I say again. Then I see him go by, looking straight ahead, like he needs something from the other end of the house. He's rubbing his hands and whistling between his lower teeth.

"Hi, Mr. Morrison," Gordy says. Dad sees us but doesn't acknowledge us in any way. Gordy and I have stopped within two feet of the door. Something tells me not to go farther. Lately Dad has seemed worried. But he looks

even worse than when we left him this morning. I realize, without entirely knowing what it means, that he probably never left for work.

"Dad, I'm home. Gordy's here."

Dad passes by again. The whistling is not like he's enjoying whistling but like he has to whistle. I don't detect a tune.

"I'm sorry, Gord, I guess my father isn't—"

Gordy steps into the living room, into the square of white couches and chairs Mom calls the conversation area. "Mr. Morrison, did you lose something?"

Dad doesn't acknowledge him.

"I can help you look. You know," Gordy continues, "sometimes when you lose something, you keep looking in the same places over and over again, and a stranger can be the best person to help you find it."

"I'll—" I move past Gordy into the hall to see if I can intercept Dad. Dad is known for riddles and charades. It looks like he's pantomiming "chase," "mechanical," or "shooting gallery."

"Dad," I plead, "stop! Talk for a few minutes. Gord, I don't think my father feels like talking. Maybe we should turn around and . . ."

But just as I suggest going, Gordy stops watching Dad and turns to me. Gordy, so superb in ways both like and unlike me, youngest co-captain ever of the All-State Band. Who has performed twice on the White House lawn, and who I hoped to make into a friend.

"Is that Sousa he's whistling?" Gordy asks. "'Hands Across the Sea'?"

I had expected both Dad and Mom, when they got home from work, to greet Gordy the way they greet my friend Mitchell. Dad usually has a joke, a riddle, a quote of the day, or a piece of music that he wants Mitchell to hear. Of course, my parents have known Mitchell for fifteen years, and they don't know Gordy at all, so it wouldn't be the same. And they might sense how exceptional Gordy is (champion French horn player, youngest co-captain ever of the All-State Band, two-time performer on the White House lawn), and that could make them, especially Mom, eager to impress.

But walking away?

At breakfast this morning, whenever Mom spoke to Dad, it took him a few seconds to answer. It seemed his mind was chasing something. And now it seems his body is following his mind. Whatever his mind was chasing was

so important that he stayed home from work and chased it all day.

"Sorry, Gord," I say. "I guess my father is a little . . ."

Gordy nods before I even say the word "preoccupied."

"I guess we should just be alone right now."

I hand him his coat and backpack. "See you tomorrow?"

"Sorry if I've upset anyone. I didn't mean to." Paralyzed by politeness, he doesn't want to leave without saying—even shouting—good-bye to Dad.

I close the door behind Gordy. Sandbagged by embarrassment. Could someone have prepared me for this? Like Mom? Sometimes she goes on about a topic until you could strangle yourself. Other times she says nothing when it could be important.

Or does she even know? I sit in the chair nearest the door and wonder what in the world I'm going to say to Dad.

DO NO HARM

A few days later Mom calls Dad's office to negotiate some sick time. Then she schedules a physical exam for Dad.

"I hope this guy knows what he's doing," she says.

Mom has hated doctors ever since what happened to her mother, Grandma Pearl. Grandma thought she had the flu. Her face turned the color of driftwood. Cancer was spreading under the whimsical picture sweaters Grandma always wore.

Mom wanted to bring Grandma Pearl to our house. There Mom could set up a hospital bed in the living room, stroke Grandma's hand, spoon-feed her fruit cocktail, and play easy-listening jazz at low volume. But the doctors kept devising new treatments.

I visited the hospital as often as I could. Zonked on painkillers, she still knew who I was. I read aloud from her collection of back issues of *Ladies' Home Journal*. "Here are the Fourth of July centerpieces, Grandma. Which one

do you like the best?" She said that she saw Grandpa Eddie on the ceiling, repairing a carburetor in the nude. "Tell him to put some clothes on, Billy," she said. "He's going to injure himself." The other woman who shared her room coughed so hard I thought she would turn herself inside out like a rubber glove.

A few weeks after the funeral there was a parents' meeting at my school. Sympathetic adults gathered around Mom. Some had also lost their mothers or fathers to cancer. They agreed with Mom about never knowing whether medical treatments were the right decision. Then one woman said to Mom, "Do you know why they put nails in coffins?" When Mom said no, the woman answered, "To keep the oncologists out," and went to get more coffee.

"I'd like to punch that Mrs. Rojas," Mom said in the car on the way home.

Although few people speak about it, the end of life, as I learned in Grandma Pearl's hospital room, is as definite and concrete as the beginning. It is as real an experience as your first day of preschool, for instance. What is the point of living all that time to come to such a wretched end? A science teacher might say that the whole point of Grandma's life was to reproduce, and after that was done, nothing really

mattered. But that hospital room remade my grandmother for me against my wishes. For a long time it was impossible to think of her in her own home, doing a mundane, painless thing. Then months later she came back to me, running water over a package of frozen strawberries.

TREATMENT REPORT: DAY 1

Dad's regular doctor said he has to make an appointment with a psychiatrist. Apparently the psychiatrist will perform the necessary repairs on Dad and he will be normal again.

Although Dad has been worrying, pacing, and not eating, nothing showed up in his physical but weight loss and what you would expect from not getting much sleep. So apparently there is some problem with his head. Or mind. Whatever you would call it.

Mom and Dad had an argument about this. "I don't need a headshrinker," Dad said, "I just need some rest!" But the doctor said he has to go.

Mom will take the morning off to drive Dad to the psychiatrist because he's too sleep deprived to get behind the wheel.

CRAZY PEOPLE

We don't know many people who've been to psychiatrists, and when they did it didn't turn out well.

UNCLE JACK

Grandpa Eddie's brother Jack came home nutty from World War II and had to go right into a veterans' hospital, where he stayed until his death, never getting married or having a family. During the war a lot of people visited him, but afterward he was all but forgotten. The only people who continued to visit were Grandpa Eddie and Grandma Pearl, and they said it made them very uncomfortable. "Jack didn't look well," Grandma would reminisce. "God knows what they were doing to that poor boy."

EDIE SARNOFF

My father's brother Marty, before he got married, was dating a woman who went to a psychiatrist. Edie was on

medication for extreme mood changes. Sometimes she felt so down that she didn't answer the phone when Marty wanted to check on her, and he would go and bang on her door or throw rocks at the window to get her to let him in. Another time she cleaned out her bank account and dragged Marty on a white-water expedition in the Grand Canyon. There she threw herself off the raft and tried to swim, and Marty and the guide pulled her back in. That night she proposed to Marty at the edge of the canyon. (She had already bought diamond rings for both of them.) The one time she came over for dinner she talked so much no one else could say anything. Marty stopped seeing her when he met Aunt Stephanie. Mom and Dad both felt that Edie was a knockout but more trouble than she was worth.

OTHERS

You hear around school that someone is seeing a psychiatrist or on medication. This often occurs at the time of a mysterious absence. Sometimes people behave differently when they get back. Mostly it's been new kids. They never confide in me.

WHAT'S WRONG WITH DAD?

Two nights after the psychiatrist visit, Mom has finished all her work business, and Dad is trying to nap. I'm at my desk staring at my homework. The house is too quiet. Dad used to blast arias all the time, but now no music is allowed because it irritates Dad's mind. Mom comes to my room.

"Make some space. We need to talk."

I move my bike so Mom and Linda can step inside. Mom sits on my bed. Linda sits in my beanbag chair. I'm in an old office chair, although with the three of us here, it's too crowded for me to spin.

I'd have more space if I moved my bike to the shed, but the shed is leaky and the bike will rust. Instead, I carry the bike morning and night across the off-white carpet in the living room. I can't roll it because it would make tracks. These are the constraints under which I live.

"Don't you look nice, Linda," Mom says.

"Do I?" Linda responds. Linda is almost thirteen. Mom

chastised her once for leaving the house in an outfit that was too tight. Now Linda wears the most voluminous things she can find, just to guilt Mom into taking it back. She would go to school looking like a member of a religious farming sect rather than make things easy for Mom. "It's a matter of principle," she says. She and her friend Jodie find old clothes in the attic crawlspace. Today's look is a ponytail on top of her head and a mechanic's coverall of Grandpa's that says "Eddie" on the pocket. Mom never lets Linda know how annoying this is. They're alike in that way.

Mom is assistant director of our local museum, which is all about the leather industry. There's more to leather history than you would think, she tells people. Often these are people who, she says, are trying to decide her social status. So: Indian techniques for tanning leather. The astonishing range of animal hides used to make leather. The barter value of leather in the colonial period. Mom beats people with this information until they soften up from boredom.

But knowledge is not the whole job. She keeps up the collections and the bookshop. Manages the paid staff and the volunteer docents. Oversees maintenance of "the physical plant." The trickiest part is managing her boss, Pudge. He

likes to phone after dinner about museum business while Mom contorts her face into a mask of agony. "Was that the mercurial Pudge?" Dad will usually ask when Mom hangs up the phone. "Was that the irascible Pudge?"

Mom not only works in a museum, she kind of is a museum. She has stick-straight black hair and wears red lipstick. She wears bizarre necklaces, each of which has a story. This one she bought in Mexico when she lived there for a year in college. This one was designed for her by an artist who photographed her wearing it. She stands taller than most men. She is like a museum because she never wants to be forgotten.

"We have a diagnosis," Mom says. "According to the psychiatrist, Dr. Gupta, your father is depressed. Everything he's experiencing—insomnia, anxiety, loss of appetite, tiredness—supports this diagnosis."

Linda wraps her arms around her middle, clutching the extra cloth of Grandpa's overalls.

"I'm not surprised," Mom continues. "Something kept telling me depression, but I refused to accept it. I accept it now. Your father is depressed."

Linda snuffles and pushes her knuckles into her mouth.

"What's wrong, Linda?"

"I know what happens to people who are depressed. They kill themselves!"

"Now where did you get that from?" Mom asks. She reaches down and clasps Linda's ankle.

"We saw a video about it at school. They kill themselves. Sometimes alone, and sometimes in groups, in a suicide pact. One kid even shot himself right in the cafeteria during lunch period!"

"Oh, no," Mom says. "No, Linda, this isn't anything like that. Nothing in that video is going to happen to Dad."

"I saw the movie too," I say. "One teenager intentionally drove into a brick wall with a car full of passengers." The video said not "teenager," but "teen." This was like calling a middle-aged person a "middle." It showed footage from the accident scene—sirens blazing, parents wailing as bodies were removed. I covered my eyes for part of the video, but it was the talk of school that week. The video also discussed copycat suicides, in which a musician or other celebrity kills himself and adolescents duplicate the act, choosing the same date and same method of death, or when one student in a town kills himself and others decide to do the same. While the video played I wondered, *If copycat suicide is such a problem, aren't they worried about giving us ideas?*

But everyone was so excited afterward, talking about this scene or that, that the teachers decided to dismiss us without a question-and-answer period. Among the student body it was universally agreed that the soundtrack was excellent.

"None of that will happen to Dad," Mom says again. Linda climbs on the bed beside Mom, and Mom strokes her hair. "Those kids in the movie, most likely no one cared about them. No one noticed that they were sick. No one tried to help them. In our case, Linda, we have the support we need, and we haven't missed our opportunity. Dad's being treated in plenty of time. And I honestly believe Dr. Gupta knows what she's doing.

"Dr. Gupta says that this kind of illness can come from a change in brain chemistry or from a loss or from a change in living situation that the patient has trouble adjusting to. It's like they're going through a crisis. So Dad will be taking medicine to help his brain, and he's also going to get talk therapy to find out what's going on."

"I have one question."

"What is that, Billy?"

"When will he be better?"

"The medicine should start working in about two weeks."

Linda has curled up under Mom's hand, until she's practically in the fetal position.

"What I need from you right now is input about any problems or difficulties that could be causing stress in Dad's life. Any possibility, Dr. Gupta says, even if it appears unrelated. Let your minds run free. Brainstorm. Think outside the box. Don't censor yourselves."

I turn to a fresh page in my history notebook.

Linda snuffles again. "You're not gonna like what I have to say, Mom."

"That's okay, honey, just go ahead. This is the time to speak freely."

"Maybe he feels *trapped*," Linda says. "Maybe he *never really wanted* a wife and kids. Maybe he'd rather have a totally different life—like be an actor or a race car driver or something."

It's typical that, right after a weepy outburst, Linda is becoming critical again. But Mom's accustomed to Linda's moods. Mom slides the wooden beads along the cord of her necklace, and they make a sound like bones clacking. "Let me reassure you of something, Linda: Your father loves this family more than anything on earth. You should have seen him the day you were born. He said, 'A boy and

a girl. Now I have everything I could ever have wanted from life.'"

I look sideways at Mom. "I thought you said not to censor ourselves."

"Well, censor a *tad*. Use your judgment. Linda, I know you wouldn't say something like that unless you were worried and upset. But maybe we can pursue the possibility that he's dissatisfied with *some area* of his life."

I write "dissatisfied," followed by a question mark.

"You know," I point out, "maybe Linda's onto something. What about the fact that Dad never finished art school? Perhaps he thinks of himself as a failure. It isn't anything like those people in the video, but just, you know, a little unhappy, like something is missing. Like things could be better."

"Dad really isn't what you would call successful," Linda agrees. "I mean, compared to some of the other dads, like Jodie's dad. Not that I'm criticizing him or anything."

"Well, he chose his own path," I offer. I heard this once and liked the sound of it.

"That raises some interesting questions," Mom says. "What is success? Perhaps Jodie's dad did build a second garage for his collection of Italian sports cars, and he takes

his family on expensive vacations every year, but does he feel successful inside? Is he truly happy with his life?"

"*I* think so," Linda says.

"Well, you just don't know, do you? You can only discover the truth by probing beneath the surface."

In fact, Dad *is* kind of unsuccessful compared to other adults. But he didn't seem to want to climb the ladder of success. He got a job as a draftsman in a company that manufactures store fixtures. He opposed overtime as a matter of principle, tore off his necktie when he stepped into the house, and preferred to spend his extra hours playing tennis, drawing cartoons, and listening to opera.

"Mom, are we poor?" Linda asks.

"No, Linda, not poor, just lower middle class. But we're well educated. I have a master's degree and your father attended one of the most prestigious art schools in the country. That's more important than money."

I suggest a different angle. "Mom, the important point is: Does Dad *think of himself* as successful?"

"He is definitely more successful than Uncle Marty," Linda points out. Marty keeps starting businesses with people, but it seems like either the businesses flop or he gets cheated.

"But possibly less successful than other people he knew in college," I add.

"Well, what do you think they're all doing now?" Mom asks. "I met some of them about ten years back. They were in their late thirties and living in divey apartments with six roommates, eating Beefaroni out of the can. They couldn't even scrape up the money to visit the Museum of Modern Art, although any philistine with twenty bucks in his pocket can see the greatest collection of artwork in the United States or possibly the world. Paradoxical, isn't it? Anyway, success, as I've said, is a highly subjective judgment. How do you define it? Some people believe success just amounts to whether you're happy."

"But Dad isn't happy," I remind her. "That's the problem he's having right now, isn't it?"

I write the word "success." Then I get another idea: *the past.*

"What about Dad's parents? How do they fit into the picture?"

Mom cocks her head. "His parents?"

"What I mean is how he felt when they died. When we couldn't get there in time. Could that be considered a crisis?" Both of Dad's parents, who lived in New York, died when I

was eleven. My grandfather went first, suddenly, of a heart attack in the hardware store parking lot while moving lumber into his van. Then my grandmother had a stroke, and we visited occasionally to help care for her. But she took a turn for the worse and the hospital called. Dad left work, and we jumped into the car and raced toward Long Island. The engine overheated on I-95. When we arrived at the hospital she was gone. Linda and I bawled for hours. Dad never shed a tear, but he traded in that car the day after the funeral.

Soon after that, for my twelfth birthday my father got me a three-speed from a used-bike shop. The bike was about fifty years old, painted black, with a two-tone treatment, black and white, on the seat and the back fender.

Dad threw himself into fixing up the bike. We replaced the cracked tires and the gummy chain, hammered bumps out of the rims, and dripped oil into the hub. We rubbed the rust spots from the chrome with steel wool, then waxed the chrome to prevent it from rusting again.

"What will you name your bike?" Dad had asked. "I named my favorite bike Pavarotti. You could call this one Seabiscuit or Rosinante." We were brightening the cloudy paint with buffing compound and a coat of car wax.

"I think I'll just call it Triumph."

"That's a good call."

The brand name "Triumph" appeared five places on my bike: on the tube below the seat in colored squares like a kid's alphabet blocks, in gold letters on the chain cover, in small white letters on the lower tube, and on two coats of arms on the front stem and back fender. With encouragement from all over my bicycle, how could I not triumph?

Now Mom's eyes water. "I don't know, maybe I'm depressed. I haven't felt like myself, anyway, since . . ." She's remembering not only Dad's parents but her own. "The world is a poorer place for the loss of all of them. That whole World War II generation. So brave. You know what they're called now? The Greatest Generation. 'Never give in, never, never, never, never—in nothing, great or small, large or petty—never give in except to convictions of honour and good sense. Never yield to force; never yield to the apparently overwhelming might of the enemy.' Winston Churchill."

"God, now I'm getting depressed too," Linda says, starting to cry again. "How are we going to help Dad if we can't even keep it together ourselves?"

Tears circle the room, contagious as yawning or nausea,

but I'm determined not to give in. I write down the word "family." "Mom, is this kind of thing hereditary? I mean, was there anyone else in Dad's family who had . . . you know, mental problems, that you know of?"

"I'm not sure. Dr. Gupta asked us that too. Maybe I should talk to Marty about it."

Linda lies on her back, staring at the ceiling. "Hey, isn't Dad's cousin Amy a bit, if you'll pardon the expression, nuts?"

"'Nuts' is not a word that we use in this house."

"We used to."

"Well, we don't anymore."

"Okay, I'll try again. Isn't Cousin Amy a bit flaky or a bit off-kilter? The cats, the newspapers, the empty jars and jar lids, the smell? How many cats were there, anyway?"

"I think the population reached as many as thirty-five or more at the point that they were taken away. Now she seems happy with just the seven."

"Ew," Linda says.

"It is a big house," Mom reminds her.

"Let me write that down. And I think I remember Uncle Marty saying that someone else on Amy's side was a kleptomaniac and spent time in prison."

"One of your father's cousins, you mean?" Mom stares. She may never have heard this story. Marty says he finds me easy to confide in. "Could that have been the one who returned a positive RSVP to our wedding but didn't show up? I always thought he was terribly rude. Well, he missed a good meal."

Mom gets up and cracks the door, motioning for silence. "Your father's up. Resume your normal activities. To be continued."

SHADOW

You can see the highway through the slats in the fence behind our house. A tunnel runs under it, where the workmen used to cross back and forth while the road was being constructed. I was forbidden to go inside, but who could resist? A concrete-lined cylinder, cracked in places, rumored to have rats. By the time I had the courage to run through it, I was too tall to get through without stooping, making it a fast, uncomfortable trip with the sound of traffic close to my head. Every kid from the old regime has been through that tunnel and back once. The new ones probably will never even know it's there.

This is the oldest part of Route 128, north of Boston from Hawthorne to Gloucester, where the highway has only two lanes in either direction. The houses on my street were built all on one floor, and they're all identical, although some are turned this way or that on the winding, hilly road. When I was little, you could walk into any house blindfolded and

be able to find a box of cornflakes, a piece of chalk, or a Nerf ball.

From the driveway (no garage, no carport, two economy cars), you walk in the front door (no hallway, foyer, or vestibule) directly into the living room. Here is a big plate-glass window ideal for leaning on for hours, when you were small, in case a rabbit or anything went by, and leaving your hand and lip prints on the glass like white stage makeup.

A dining room with crank-out windows is behind the living room, and if it's summer you have to decide whether to be cool and hear the highway noise or enjoy a sweaty silence. Next to that is a kitchen that looks into the living room over a partial brick wall topped by metal bars, so your mother could see what you were doing if it got too quiet. At one end of the house are a woody den with built-in spaces for books and your family's one TV, then a small cement-floored room for your tools, sports equipment, winter boots, cleaning supplies, and so on. This room contains your oil tank, your clothes dryer and ironing board, and a pull-down ladder for reaching the attic crawlspace to get toys you've outgrown but like to visit, Halloween costumes, and all your grandparents' things. Also a pink kitchen table with black

legs, where your father keeps an ancient suitcase full of small hardware parts that he never bothers to sort. And which you open sometimes, on your own, to crunch the parts with both hands and hear them clank—like a sea that someone drained the water from, leaving only shells.

At the other end of the house are two junior-size bedrooms and a hall bathroom, and one big bedroom with its own sink and toilet. Outside are a bicycle shed, a garden shed, and a patio made of concrete blocks.

All perfectly adequate, you would think. But then in September, our uphill neighbors built an addition, a second-story bedroom the length of the whole house and a mammoth garage with a separate apartment above it for their son who is not much older than me, and just as the builders were finishing the parents' balcony and the appliance store truck was pulling up with the son's gas grill, our house was eclipsed. Mom stood in the shadow beside her rosebushes, shaking a fist at the neighbors' house (although she knew they weren't home at the time).

"How could they do this to us?" she wailed.

I'm not sure, but I think this shadow could be contributing to our problems.

WORLDPAIN

welt·schmerz \'velt · shmərts\ *n, often cap* [G. fr. *Welt* world
+ *Schmerz* pain, fr. OHG *smerzo*; akin to OHG *smerzan*
to pain—more at SMART] (1875) **1**: mental depression
or apathy caused by comparison of the actual state of
the world with an ideal state

Intellectual, no? It would be just like Dad to go for that
one.

NOCTURNE

Just after one a.m. sounds begin in the hall. Two voices so familiar they could originate in my own chest. The rubbing swing of the door over carpet, and the swoosh of two sets of slippered feet. My curtains are partly open, and street-lights are reflected in our first snow. A column of light falls over my bed, illuminating me, Triumph's front fender, and a thumbtacked Escher print of flying fish in formation, like torpedoes.

The people switch lights on as they move through the house. These new lights seep under my door. The other lights cause my window to darken and my column of light to fade.

In the kitchen, the woman talks more than the man. She speaks mostly in whispers. The man isn't a good whisperer. When he thinks he's whispering, he's just talking but adding breath sounds to it.

The refrigerator door opens and closes. A pan rattles

on the stove. Liquid is poured. The fridge door opens and closes again. The burner clicks several times as it heats up. One person stirs the pot while the other pads across the kitchen floor. A cabinet door opens. Dishes click. Liquid is poured from the pot. The kitchen light goes out. Other lights go out. My window gets brighter. My column gets bigger. They stop just outside my door.

"Billy's asleep," Mom whispers.

"Good," says Dad. "Billy's asleep."

MACARONI

I'm resting my head over a plate of macaroni and cheese when someone knocks my elbow.

"Hey!"

Mitchell Zane and Andy Bock sit down with their trays. Mitchell slides the wrapper to one end of his straw, where it crumples into a miniature Japanese lantern.

"You fell asleep in chemistry," he says.

"Did anyone notice?"

"Other than me, you mean?" He nods ominously.

"Zwicker?"

"No, not Zwicker. Just a couple of kids." He dips the straw carefully into one corner of his milk carton.

"Maybe I wasn't asleep. Maybe I was just thinking."

Still, I could take or leave the sciences. The sciences have two flaws. One, they build from week to week, so if you space out for a few weeks, the train leaves the station and there's no hope of catching up. Two, they rely too much on

received wisdom. The reason I haven't done well—and I'm not trying to excuse myself here—is that we were plunked down and expected to memorize the periodic table and all these formulas, and my true question just never got answered. Which is: How do we know all this? How do we know, for instance, that an electron circles around a proton (or whatever), or that carbon consists of five electrons and two protons (or whatever)? Has someone actually seen this with their own eyes? How do we know it isn't all a scam? Had this been answered at the beginning, I may have invested more energy in keeping up.

Now the arts—those are the subjects for me. No building from week to week. You can zone out for days, but as long as you jump back in before the deadline, read the book or look at the painting or listen to the music before that test or discussion, you will get it: the right insight, sometimes a brilliant one, all in a flash. And you don't have to rely on received ideas. You can come up with your own. You can disagree: "No, Ms. Thatcher, I don't think that's what Zora Neale Hurston meant to say." Try pulling that in chemistry!

In the arts, you have a shot at coming up with something new too. While the chances of my discovering or

synthesizing a new chemical element are about nil (Billonium? Morrisonium?), my chances of creating a mind-blowing original work are not bad. Even Dad, having dropped out of art school without getting his degree, could pick up his paints one day and do the painting of his career.

I know myself. I will never be well rounded. I will never respond appropriately to meetings in which my guidance counselor tells me I'm not working up to my potential. I will never catch up in chemistry or biology. Instead, I'll focus on music, and a flash of genius will save me. I'll win a songwriting competition sponsored by some organization like ASCAP and find work as a songwriter in Memphis, Austin, or Nashville.

But it's good of Mitchell to watch out for me. We were born on the same day, although he looks sort of middle-aged. He's rotund, and he holds his pants up with suspenders that make him look even rounder. You can't help thinking that although the suspenders were straight when he clipped them on, now they look like the seventy-fifth and hundred fiftieth meridians on a globe.

In English last year, he would signal to me when he thought a poem we were studying contained a coded

reference to masturbation. He sat ahead of me and would tilt his head at the appropriate time when one of our classmates read aloud. Andy tried to participate but was never good at it. He picked things that were either too obvious or off the topic, having to do just generally with sex. When we studied Robert Frost, Andy tilted his head at the book title, *You Come Too*.

"How come you guys didn't laugh?" he asked after class.

"Too easy," Mitchell said.

"But what about his horse being queer?"

"That has nothing to do with anything, Andy. The fact that a line makes everyone else in the class laugh doesn't mean it gets a laugh out of me."

The killer came when we were reading "Desiderata" by Max Ehrmann. When Sandi Buscaglia read the last line, "Strive to be happy," I saw the back of Mitch's head tilt very slightly, about five degrees, and I nearly had to leave the room.

Now Gordy drops his lunch bag on the table.

"You know, you were asleep in chemistry class."

"I know."

Mitchell drains his milk and opens a second carton.

"Fortunately," he says, "I took tremendous notes. I can come by with them after school."

The cafeteria noise swells in my ears like a jet engine. I bite into a hard, whitish tomato slice that came with the macaroni. Mitchell waits for me to answer, and I look at Gordy but he doesn't give anything away. I don't want Mitchell at the house right now.

"I notice you haven't invited me over for a while. Are you secretly developing some kind of explosive in your room? Perhaps your ignorance of the difference between hydrogen and helium was just a smokescreen."

"Ha!" Andy says. "That's right, he's developing a bomb."

"Um, no."

"You're writing something, is that it? You spend all your time with the headphones on, opening the door only to accept a tray of food and water."

"Anybody, grapes?" Gordy takes a big bunch from his lunch bag.

Mitchell looks at Gordy. "Our mute friend here tells me you're into New Orleans jazz."

"What I'm really looking into is funeral jazz."

"Okay." Mitchell picks up bits of paper trash and piles

them in one corner of his tray. Normally he can find a way to make anything seem funny or stupid. But even he finds it hard to joke about this. The thing that everyone knows about Gordy, even if they've never spoken to him, is that his mother died right after they moved into town. "Well, could you recommend a couple of titles?"

"Yeah," Andy says. "I'd enjoy listening to some of it." He's doing his earnest Boy Scout thing that Mitchell calls his talking-to-adults voice. Gordy is worse off than I thought. His semi-orphaned state is making him not one of us.

"There's one by the Magnificent Seventh that gives you a good introduction," Gordy says.

"And this is all music that gets played at people's funerals?" Mitchell asks.

"Uh-huh."

Gordy grows even more in my estimation. He's taking the weirdness hit so I don't have to.

The pills Dr. Gupta gave Dad have given him what she calls an "atypical dermatological reaction." This sounds much nicer than it looks.

When the rash started out on Dad's abdomen, no one paid much attention. We had gathered around him to wait for improvements, the way a family might pull chairs up to the TV when their favorite show is about to start. Dr. Gupta said not to be too impatient, because the medicine might not completely kick in for weeks. Dad stopped pacing and whistling for a day or two, and it seemed like he might be ready to go back to work.

But then the sores spread to his arms and face, and Linda and I made sickened expressions behind his back. Mom even told him to stop looking in the mirror.

I felt bad that I couldn't deal with the rash.

But one thing I've always liked about myself is that I know my limitations.

SENSITIVITY

The doorbell rings and it's June. Not the month of June, but June from Dad's office.

"Who is it?" Dad calls from his bedroom.

"It's June!" Mom and June sing simultaneously. Then they giggle and hug one another. June rubs Mom's back. "Aw, honey," she says. "How are *you* doing?"

"It's tough," Mom whispers. "He's having trouble with the medication."

"It takes time," June responds, squeezing Mom's hand. "I've heard that sometimes you have to try two or three before you get the right one."

June is a type of woman that usually disturbs Mom. "She treats herself well, doesn't she?" Mom sometimes says, hinting that this may not be a good thing. But she makes an exception when it comes to June. June is wearing a warm-up suit that makes me think of creamy, shampooed sheep. The style of her white-blond hair is practically TV quality.

Dad comes into the living room. June lays a paper cone of carnations and a stack of magazines on the coffee table.

"Ah, *Newsweek*," Dad says.

"I know you like to keep up with the news, Bill," June says.

Dad sits on the couch. I help him roll down his sleeves, careful not to break any of the blisters. "I'm depressed, June," he says. He stares at the floor.

June pats him on the knee. "I hear ya," she says.

Mom, June, and I sit with Dad in the conversation area. Linda is out with her obnoxious friend Jodie. At first June doesn't seem to register that Dad is covered with pink bumps that have grown together to form crests, with rivers of yellow pus running in the valleys. She begins a series of funny stories. One about the people in their office, where she is the bookkeeper. One about the company tennis tournament that Dad sometimes plays in. A couple about her husband, Ben, whom she once considered divorcing but now won't, and about her daughter's bat mitzvah eight months from now, which we are all invited to. Mom goes into the kitchen and gets a tray of chips, salsa, and ginger ale.

"So what's this rash about, Bill?" June asks, leaning across the coffee table. I can't believe she treats Dad's

condition so casually. Just an annoyance, like the caterer who wants to serve mini-crepes instead of make-your-own tacos at Lisa's bat mitzvah.

Dad opens his collar, showing June a set of pustules that form, if you look at them from the side, the letter *D*. June bends over the coffee table to inspect, and I can smell her scent of expensive lotions. I, too, have always liked June, or as I call her, Mrs. Melman. I seem to run into her all over town, with no bad repercussions. Once she came into a magazine store and found Mitchell and me looking at what he called "the naked magazines." Mitchell, in fact, was trying to stash a rolled-up one under his sweater. When Mrs. Melman saw us, she said, "There are many good books on that subject at the library," and I never heard anything from Mom about it, which means Mrs. Melman never told.

"They make him look young again, don't they, Adele?" June says to Mom. "Like an oily-faced teenager. Remember acne? Lisa's starting to break out now. She thinks it's the end of the world, but it's not, is it? I told her to think of it as a signal that she's growing up. She thinks she's the center of the universe, you know. I had to tell her, 'You're a lovely girl, honey, and Daddy and I think you're the most

beautiful thing on earth, but you have to realize that at this age not everyone is thinking about you all the time like you're thinking about yourself. They're all thinking about themselves.' Right, Billy? Anyway, Bill, I could stop by again with some more magazines and a few of the tubes of little creams Dr. Favola gave Lisa, and you could have fun with them, try them all out. I don't know if they'd have much effect, but we have so many left over because Lisa wants to try them all. She and her friends. I tell her, 'Stop worrying about it, Lisa. You're a beautiful girl, and when you get to be my age you'll be grateful that you had a little extra oil on your skin.' Right, Adele? Is Linda getting to be like that too?"

"Oh, June," Mom sighs. "I wish Linda were a little *less* sure of herself. She hasn't found a thing wrong—not yet, anyway. She keeps staring at herself in the mirror, and she's even given herself a new nickname: Lucky Linda."

"I certainly didn't think of myself as lucky at that age," June answers. "Did you, Adele?"

"Not lucky. Yucky." They both laugh and sip ginger ale.

"Well," June sighs, "most of us are somewhere between lucky and yucky. And I think that's a fine place to be." Mrs. Melman is downplaying her own fantastic beauty. I grab a

handful of tortilla chips so I can get the delicate fragrance of her lotions out of my nose.

"I hadn't seen the house next door for a while," June says. "Big, isn't it?"

"Isn't it tacky? People were snickering about it in the supermarket."

June takes a large envelope from her purse and hands it to Dad.

Inside is a card that says, "We heard you were a little under the weather." It shows ten people huddled under a tiny umbrella in driving rain. When Dad opens it to read the signatures, two twenty-dollar bills fall out.

"I tried to stop people from putting money in. I told them it wasn't necessary, but they insisted. Pick up something you really like to eat, or anything that will make you feel more comfortable. I'm sure a number of people would have liked to come in person."

Getting up from the couch, June tugs on the jacket of her warm-up suit. "Thank you for the snacks, sweetie," she says to Mom. She bends down to pat the top of Dad's head, where there are no sores, pecks me on the cheek, and gives Mom a squeeze when Mom opens the door for her. It sounds clichéd, but each of us feels a little special.

Before leaving she looks back at Dad. "Any messages for the poor working stiffs back at the office? Anything you'd like me to report to your fans?"

"Thank them for me, will you, June?" Dad says. He puts a hand up to his neck where his rash is hurting. "Tell them I'll be back soon."

SHRINKAGE

Powerful urges beyond your control. Hospitals, barred windows, white uniforms. Mysterious personality tests that show you black splotches in a butterfly shape. I don't know much about this mental business, but I have to go along for a family visit with Dad's psychotherapist.

I had expected a scientific type in a suit and tie. But when Dr. Fritz stands up to shake hands, saying what a pleasure it is to meet us, he looks like a lumberjack, in a heavy plaid shirt, wool pants, and yellow work boots.

Dr. Fritz leans back in his chair. He looks at each of us for a long time before settling on Dad.

"How are you feeling, Bill?"

Dad doesn't speak right away. Lately he takes a long time choosing his words, as if he has to turn them over first to make sure they're true. He doesn't just throw something out and fix it later, the way healthy people do. And he has plenty to complain about: insomnia and chronic tiredness, loss of appetite and a drop in his weight, seemingly constant

worrying, and most of all, not having an interest in the things that used to make life worth living. Even the pacing, hand-rubbing, and whistling, which let up a bit under the blistery meds, have come back. I decide to answer for him.

"Well, he's still not sleeping, if that means anything."

Fritz raises one hand.

"Thanks very much, Billy. I appreciate your trying to help by giving me that information. But right now it's important for me to hear it directly from your dad."

I feel my face burn, at being caught speaking out of turn and also at Fritz's talking-down tone. Fritz is acting like he may have hurt my feelings, so naturally, after a rush of rage and embarrassment, I don't let on that I'm hurt. But still. I thought the point of his occupation was to get you to speak up, not shut up.

"Ha, ha, Billy, you got busted," Linda says.

When Fritz glances at her she covers her mouth.

"Linda, how do you feel about being here, visiting me with your dad?"

"It's no big deal," she says. Her face reddens, and she looks like she's going to pitch a laughing fit. This always happened when we sat next to each other in church. That was the first reason I stopped going.

Don't look at her, I tell myself. *Don't even look at her part of the room.*

"Linda, Billy, if you feel uncomfortable or nervous about being here at first, that's perfectly normal. Over time you'll grow more relaxed when you visit me. The most important thing is that it means a lot to your dad that you're here to support him. I'd like to speak with you more in just a minute, once I've finished checking in with Bill Senior. How are you feeling this week, Bill? No rush. Take as much time as you need to pull your thoughts together."

Mom wants to say something but stops herself. I can tell what she's thinking. That there's so much to say, and our forty-five measly minutes with a qualified individual is slipping away.

"I hated those spots," Dad says finally. "They itched."

Fritz waits for Dad to say more. What a waste of time. After a week and a half with no meds, Dad's rash has flattened out, leaving faded pink lines like capillaries or coral. Looks to me like it's time for a new cure.

"He—," Mom says, and stops there.

Fritz scratches his beard, a full one, not a little beard thing like Dad's.

"Bill, do you think you're ready to try a new medication?"

Good call.

During a long wait, Linda's shoulders begin to shake again. Instead of looking at her, I review all the words I know that begin with *si* and respell them with *psy*— *psygnpost, psyphon, psylo.*

Mom does a dance of annoyance, wiggling her shoulders and head. She taps her necklace (copper discs). Dad told her yesterday that he felt ready to try a new medication, but she isn't about to speak up now. Fritz will have to muddle through without that information. *Psylent treatment.*

"Yeah," Dad says finally. "I'll try it."

"You'll try it?" Fritz repeats.

"I'll give the new medication a shot."

A photo on the wall shows Fritz in a sailboat with a small child. The boat has tilted up and Fritz is leaning out over the water, working the tiller with a huge, avid smile.

Linda stiffens. Fritz has aimed his attention at her. He's staring at her, the same way he stared at Dad.

"How are you holding up during your father's illness, Linda? It must be affecting you a great deal."

Linda is stunned. Not only is Fritz staring at her, Dad is too. *Psyamese. Psymultaneous.* Her face reddens and I think she's going to lose it. Look away, look away.

Everyone waits to hear what Linda has to say.

When I glance back at Linda, she looks somber, like she's being interviewed for the network news.

"Well, of course it bothers me that Dad's sick and everything, but I just try to be there for him. That's what a family's for, isn't it? To take care of each other?"

What a laugh! Linda couldn't take care of a goldfish. All she cares about is doing arts and crafts projects and huddling with her little friend Jodie.

"That's absolutely true," Fritz says. "I like the way you put that, Linda—to take care of each other." He nods five or six times. "And how's Bill Junior doing during this difficult time for the family?"

Oh ho! So *now* he wants me to talk. When it's my turn. When I'm next in line. When my number is called.

"How's school going, for instance?"

"Well . . ." Nobody has asked me this for a while. "It's a little difficult to concentrate, to be honest."

"Mm-hmm, it is difficult to concentrate. But I want to remind you how important it is, especially if this illness goes on for a while, to take care of your life and make sure you can fulfill your own responsibilities. I have a feeling that you are someone who will make a real contribution to the world."

Fritz continues staring while Linda makes a face at me across the room. A professional psychologist thinks I have potential and not Linda! I will lord this over her afterward. Although it would mean a lot more coming from someone who actually knew me.

I can't get over feeling that Fritz doesn't know it's rude to stare at people, and someone should clue him in. I read once that in many cultures, if someone stares at you it means they're either going to kill you or have sex with you, and either way my parents would be deeply annoyed. I have a flash-image of my father leaping over the desk and menacing Fritz with a paperweight, instantly charged into health by the deep instinctive need to protect me.

Fritz then "checks in" with Mom, who repeats a fancier version of Linda's winning formula about the family taking care of each other. It's unusual for her to try this hard to impress someone.

Fritz makes some notations and closes our folder. "In the course of our work together, we may eventually explore some deep emotional issues that will require a great deal of dedication from you, because they will summon painful and difficult feelings. But we're not at that point yet, and I don't see any need to rush. For today we're going to

practice some new cognitive strategies, or thought strategies. These strategies are quick and—I don't want to say superficial, but superficial is not such a bad description. The main thing is that they are easy to learn and you can start using them right away. Now slide your chairs closer, right up to my desk, that's it."

We've already improved at staring back at Fritz. The four of us are aligned opposite his desk, achieving a four-on-one group counterstare. I should have mentioned earlier that Fritz is not what you would call handsome. In fact, he resembles a Pekingese dog in a landslide. He has a high forehead and Pekingese-like features that occupy only the lower half of his face and nestle into his beard. The beard blends into his chest and neck hair. Everything on the front of him seems to have slipped down one place. But we're seriously concentrating, not only drinking in but also wringing out every word. When he tilts his face to review a pamphlet on his desk, we tilt our faces too, like four gyroscopes.

He pushes his chair back and shrugs his shoulders to loosen them.

"Okay, everyone, deep breath, in and out. *Mmmmmph-pheeww.*"

Mmmmmph-pheeww.

"Loosen clothing if necessary. Get as comfortable as possible."

We shake out our arms and legs like sprinters preparing for a race, plant our feet flat on the floor.

Fritz links his fingers over his belly. "All of us are plagued by negative self-talk that can create anxiety. This can consist of criticisms, negative fantasies, or recurring thoughts of things we should not have said or done, or painful reminders of things we should have said or done but for some reason did not. Does anyone recognize this tendency in himself or herself? An example, anybody?"

"Hooo," Mom whispers, crossing her legs again. I think she means: so many of them, where to even start?

"Bill Senior?"

Dad moistens his lips but says nothing.

Fritz unclasps his hands and looks receptive.

"Sometimes I'm convinced that I won't be able to go back to work," Dad says softly.

"And what would happen then?"

"Well . . . my family would become indigent."

"That means we would be broke," I explain to Linda.

Fritz ignores me this time. "Very good example, Bill." He nods, a rolling, whole-body nod. "Very good example.

Now when you say this to yourself about not working, you know it's negative self-talk because it makes you feel bad."

We nod.

"And the second part of that thought, the part about being indigent, is going to make you feel even worse. So your goal with this technique is to stop the thought as soon as it starts, before you even get to the second part. And you're going to do that by saying these words to that inner voice in your head: 'Cancel, cancel!'"

Murmuring: "Cancel, cancel." We're still nodding.

"And there's a picture, a visual, you can add to it too. While you're saying 'Cancel, cancel,' you can picture yourself drawing an X through the thought, or stamping it out with one of those red circles with the diagonal through it."

"Like the No Smoking symbol."

"Exactly, Linda. Or conjure up your own picture. Whatever works best for you."

"You know, that's very good," Mom says. And she mouths the words to herself: *Cancel, cancel.*

Fritz rests his elbows on the desk. "Challenge yourself to say 'Cancel, cancel' as quickly as possible. Right on the heels of the negative thought. Make a game of it. Because the less time the thought spends in your mind, the less it

will affect your mood and contribute to a downward spiral. Ready to try it?"

Dad seems pretty caught up in this, more involved than he's been in a while.

"Here we go. I'm going to lose my job and—"

"Cancel, cancel," we blurt out.

"I'm going to—"

"Cancelcancel." Three of us are speed-talking, with Dad trailing behind.

"I'm—"

"Cancelcancel."

"Okay." Fritz raises both hands over his head. "Ho!" He laughs in booming, individual cannonball shots. "I'm a negative thought, and I just gave up. You can't get much faster than that. Very good work. Let's relax and breathe for a moment."

Mmmmmph-pheeww.

"Who's ready for another one? You all are. Since you're doing so well, I'm going to give you an opposite, or complementary, strategy to the one you just learned. This one is to reinforce any *positive* self-talk that runs through your mind. Say I observe to myself, 'I've had a terrific day.' I want that thought to hang around for a while. So, to encourage it to stick around, I say, 'Welcome!' To confirm and validate that

positive thought: 'Welcome!' And you can add a mental image of this gesture."

Fritz has struck an openhanded pose, like someone catching rain after a drought.

"Welcome!" we mutter, practicing the gesture.

"I am a useful and worthwhile person," Fritz says.

"Welcome!"

Fritz checks the clock on the wall. "We're done for today. I know you've all worked really hard in this session, especially you, Bill. And I have to compliment you. You and Adele have a lovely family."

"Thank you," Mom says, walking to the door.

"Welcome!"

"How did you like your first session, kids?" Mom asks while she unlocks the car.

"Well, I learned something. We're all supposed to take care of each other!"

"Cut it out," Linda says.

"Don't make fun of the doctor, Billy," Mom says. "Your father feels comfortable with him."

"I'm not making fun of the doctor. I'm making fun of you!"

"That's enough, Billy," Dad says.

It's hard to argue with him right now.

ON THE MALL ROAD

A group of men in heavy parkas cluster by a bench on our main street.

"I like your light!" one calls in accented English. The others guffaw. Well, you can't pay much attention to stupid comments. A headlight is practical when you do a lot of night riding. If they find me foolish, so be it. Some of the immigrants in town ride bikes too, but I get the impression it's because they can't afford cars yet, and as soon as they can buy a nice pickup it will be *adios, bicicleta*.

Everyone's in a rush to get a driver's license, but I'm in no hurry to get a car. You know those old movies, British mysteries or French classics, where you see a guy riding a bike in a tweed jacket and tie? That's very classy. Except that in the U.S. you would have to wear a helmet, which ruins the look.

Why hasn't anyone done a movie about a group of bicyclists? It would open with kind of a skittery theme

on an electric fiddle, which gets louder as a dozen classic bikes appear, another dozen, forty in all. They burst into stunts: ramp jumps and wheelies. The scene looks like pandemonium but has been drilled to clockwork precision. It could be the story of outlaw bikers taking midnight rides on hacked bikes that defy safety laws, or musicians who work as bike messengers by day. Or an action movie about rival gangs, loaded with street-fighting scenes. I can picture the movie poster: "Spokes. What goes around comes around." A closeup of a guy's face through the wheel he's repairing. His eye is circled with a gang tattoo.

Maybe if Dad rode a bike again, like he did as a kid, he could get his old energy back. It could be that easy: tire himself during the day, sleep better at night, and we all go back to normal. Maybe, maybe, maybe. I try not to think about it too much. But Mom and the doctors have to keep trying. If they weren't saying maybe, maybe, maybe they would just sit around asking why, why, why. As in a traditional blues song. Something like:

Why does a man feel tired
Why does a man feel dead

When something something something
And the something in his head

It's a world of trouble, baby
Oh Mister Trouble, let me go
Get your something from my something
And leave me to my—

Studio? Radio?

I should be able to plug in that rhyme. I don't want to use a rhyming dictionary unless I'm absolutely, definitely stuck.

"Hey, Bicycle Boy!"

At the red light I feel something wet across my eyes and cheeks. Not blood? A Ford Explorer screeches forward, bolting from me as soon as the light turns green. Guys in the car are laughing, and one turns back to taunt me, holding a bottle out the window.

I pull the bike over to the curb and press my hand against my face. My heart is slamming. No, not blood. Something cool and clear. I sniff. Probably just water. He squirted me with a bottle of water. Could be worse. Could be bleach. Or urine.

Who would do a thing like that?

Probably frat boys from Hawthorne State, looking for a cheap laugh. If so, is there something about me that provoked this? Were they cruising for victims, or did my appearance make them want to humiliate me? Are they threatened by my challenge to automotive dominance?

Christ, I wish I had had something to throw into their car. Or at least that I recovered in time to say something back. "Bicycle Boy." Really clever. Really humiliating. That put me in my place, all right. Oh my gosh, you're right, I am riding a bike! Thanks for pointing that out, I hadn't realized it! And now I realize how socially unacceptable that is! Idiot me! It's four wheels from now on!

Or was the "boy" part the big insult? Crap, I'm only fifteen! That makes me unfit to live! If only I could be a college guy like you, with nothing to do but drive around soaking people!

Now, what was I just thinking about?

Still, it could be worse. Awful things. Like bleach, right in the eyes. Or, I heard of somebody riding along when a car passenger smashed a glass bottle in front of him, probably hoping that broken glass would fly up into the cyclist's face. Or girls getting their rear ends grabbed. You could

fall right into traffic after something like that. Why can't people just get along?

What could you say to those guys? "Bicycle Boy." Why is that so clever? Is it the repetition of the *b* at the beginning of both words (i.e., alliteration) that they think is devastating? If so, would they be devastated if I alliterated them back? College Clowns? Water-Wielding Wusses?

Explorer . . . Excrementheads? But that's the thing about these incidents. You dwell on them too long, and you never do recoup. You think you'll get your own back, but you can't. It eats away at you. They've got you either way.

Okay, now I've completely lost my train of thought.

TREATMENT REPORT: DAY 27

Dad has started a new med. Now, in addition to being worried, tired, malnourished, and sleep-deprived, his fear level seems to be rising. He looks like he would jump at the sight of a Fauvist painting. And once I saw his hand shake when he drank a glass of water.

I don't know if the pills are causing this or if Dad is simply getting worse, but I suspect the pills are at fault. If so, maybe Dr. Gupta attended the medical school at Paradox College, where in addition to learning things like (1) You have to be cruel to be kind, and (2) If you love something, let it go, she also learned (3) To calm someone down, scare them.

Of course, I don't know anything. Most likely Dad is 100 percent on track for where he needs to be.

At six p.m., it's already been dark for two hours. A thin layer of mixed rain and snow has come down, leaving the road tacky and hissing. After dinner we settle into the conversation area with Dad's brother Marty and watch the tree blink. Marty brought his camcorder so he can film us opening our gifts. He shoots Mom placing a turkey leg on a plate beside Dad's chair.

"He might want to pick at that," she says.

Marty pans across the cards strung on ribbons above the fireplace, a combination of Merry Christmas and Get Well. Dad's office has sent a fruit basket wrapped in gold cellophane, with a note saying "An apple a day keeps the doctor away!"

"Gee, that's easy," Linda said when she accepted the basket from the deliveryman. "Do they think he's suffering from irregularity?"

Marty sits beside Dad and rests his arm along the

back of the couch. He was recently separated from Aunt Stephanie, who was, as Mom and Dad always said, a keeper. She traveled all over the world setting up computer systems for a big hotel chain. When she left Uncle Marty and took Marty Junior, the new baby cousin we never met, we couldn't help feeling, as a family, that she was just too good for us.

Now Marty always dresses as if he's out on a date. Pressed jeans, smooth mustache, styled hair. But he's getting that defeated look some divorced fathers have. The look that says they used to be part of something.

The phone rings in the kitchen. "That must be Sally and Adam," Mom says, jumping up. There's no telling when she'll be back once she starts yakking with her sister.

"Go sit under the tree, Linda," Marty says, hoisting the camera onto his shoulder. Linda poses like a little kid waiting for Santa. She's wearing a long pioneer skirt and a snowman sweater of Grandma Pearl's that she found in the attic.

It's odd having Christmas Eve without music. Normally Mom would be playing a Nat King Cole Christmas CD that someone copied for her, but out of respect for Dad, we're chestnut free. Marty begins to hum.

"Well? Can you make it?" Mom asks on the phone. "Why not? Well, what other plans? I thought you were coming *here*. I never told you we didn't feel up to company. We do feel up to company, very much so. We would have loved more company this year. I made cookies and eggnog and everything. Marty's here. No, just Marty. Well, do you want to drop the kids off here and I'll bring them back later? *Sally* . . ." Mom's voice sounds like it's wearing off. She takes a deep breath, the way the therapist told us to.

"Adele? Is everything okay?" Dad asks.

"Yes, fine." Mom puts her hand over the phone and steps into the living room. "They're not coming."

"Yes," she says into the phone, "Bill received a box from you. He hasn't opened it yet. But he looks very pleased. Actually, to be honest, he doesn't look pleased, but if he were feeling better, I know he'd be extremely gratified to get the package. Call me tomorrow? What time? Okay. Merry Christmas. Yes, you too, 'bye."

"Excuse me a minute." Mom goes from the kitchen into the hall. She's rushing, almost like she has to go to the bathroom. She disappears for a while.

"Do you want to see what I got you?" Marty asks.

"We better wait for Mom to come back," Linda says. She sorts the skimpy stash of presents, reading the name labels and tossing them into piles under the tree. She bumps a branch that holds an ornament with small sleigh bells. The bells jingle, and Dad winces.

"Sorry," she says without looking at him.

Marty fiddles with the camera and hums to himself. Before the illness, Dad spent hours consoling Marty and giving him advice about the separation. Now it seems like Marty's trying to put a holiday face on and not mention his heartbreak.

"Well," Linda says, "this is shaping up to be a Christmas for the record books, isn't it? At least Aunt Stephanie used to bring us decent presents."

I crawl across the floor and drape tinsel on her head. "Cancel, cancel, Linda!"

"That's perfect, kids," Marty says. "Do that again."

Mom comes back, wiping her eyes and looking furious. "Who wants a cookie?" she commands, passing a plastic tray in the shape of a bell. Marty and I each take a couple of cookies. Dad takes one and promptly forgets about it, leaving it on the arm of his chair like a business card or other inedible.

Linda places an oversize box on Dad's lap. "Here's your present from Sally and Adam. Watch out, it's a heavy one."

Marty sets up a shot over Dad's shoulder. "Three, two, one, action!"

"I might need help opening this," says Dad. "It's taped up pretty tight."

I crawl to the couch, feeling like a kid again, and sit next to Dad. I cut the brown paper flaps with my pocket knife. Inside is a corrugated cardboard box.

"Smile again, Billy," says Uncle Marty. "You're helping your dad, huh?"

"Yep."

"I hope they didn't get you anything too expensive," Mom says. "I told them we were keeping it simple this year. I wasn't even expecting to exchange with them."

"It's a fisherman's trophy of some kind," Dad says. "A bass. Why would they send me this?"

"Isn't that handsome?" says Marty from behind the camera.

A large stuffed fish is attached to a wooden plaque. Pulling away the last piece of tissue, I see a switch on the plaque and turn it on. The fish twists its head and tail and begins to sing.

Here's a little song I wrote
You might want to sing it note for note
Don't worry, be happy
In every life we have some trouble
When you worry you make it double
Don't worry, be happy

Dad covers his face with the box lid. "How horrible! Turn it off, Billy, turn it off!"

"It's just a toy, Dad. See?"

Marty drops his camera. "Are you all right, bro? It's okay. It's okay. It's over."

"I can't believe it!" Mom says. "I can't believe they would send a grotesque gift like that instead of showing up. It's so insensitive. Good God, Sally."

"I like it," Linda says. "Can I have it? I'll play it in my room, very quietly."

"Here," Dad says, "you keep it." His hands are shaking.

Linda takes the present to her room, laughing at me over her shoulder as if we had been competing for this piece of musical taxidermy. Sometimes I wonder if Linda would even know what she wanted if I weren't around.

"I can't believe Sally couldn't make it," Mom says, biting into a cookie. "Or didn't want to make it. Do you know this is our first Christmas apart?"

"Shhh, Adele," Dad says. "Don't even think about it."

"Okay, now," Marty says. "Ready for your close-ups. One at a time."

"You're going to leave the camera on, Uncle Marty?" Linda asks when she comes back. "What if Dad gets something else that's freakish?"

"It's fine, Linda," Mom says. "Have fun with it, Marty."

Mom had announced that we should keep our gift buying fairly simple this Christmas. Now we go around the room opening one present apiece, expressing more fake delight than usual. It's hard to know whose benefit this is for—Dad's, Mom's, Marty's, or the camera's. Dad is the only person who isn't playacting, although he tries to say something appreciative each time. It must be good for him to keep busy—even with the bass incident, he hasn't had to get up and pace. Marty has given Linda a handheld video game console, Mom a personal digital assistant, and me a fancy electronic odometer I'll never use.

"Cool!" Linda shouts, winding her face into a grimace

that she'll be embarrassed about five years from now.

"I haven't got your gift yet, Bill," Marty tells Dad. "I need a little more time. I wanted it to be really, really special."

Linda made friendship bracelets for everyone—plain ones for the men and a daisy-patterned one for Mom. I bought a small box of oil paints for Dad, soap for Mom, and socks for Linda. Nothing for Marty because I didn't know he was going to be here. "Don't give it another thought, buddy," Marty says. "You're good to me all year round, right?" Mom gives each person thermal underwear and a box of hard candy.

"Now it's time for your father's presents," Mom says.

"You had time to shop, Dad?" Linda asks. "You didn't have to get us anything."

"Not exactly," Mom says. She takes a handful of small envelopes from the top of the brick room divider and gives one to Marty, Linda, and me, and takes one for herself. "Let's open them all at once," she says.

Inside the envelopes are note cards saying

WHEN I AM WELL

I WILL TAKE YOU

Mine says "to the Museum of Fine Arts." Linda's says "on the Swan Boats." Mom's says "to the North End." Marty's says "to Fenway Park."

"Fun!" Linda shouts.

"God, bro, that's so nice. I can't wait."

"Adele helped me with them."

Marty's chin begins to shake. "It's been such a tough year, with the separation and everything. You've been amazing. Everyone else got sick of hearing about it."

"There goes another one," Linda says.

"Excuse me," Marty says. He goes to the hall bathroom, flushing the toilet as soon as he gets inside.

"I guess that's it, then," Mom says, taking the big tray of cookies back to the kitchen.

Linda and I collect the wrapping paper and stuff it into bags. When Marty comes back, he takes Dad by the elbow.

"Let's go for a walk, bro," he says, walking him to the coat closet. "We'll stroll up and down the street and see everybody's decorations. Let's get you good and bundled up."

Once they leave, Mom retrieves the turkey leg from beside the armchair and wraps it in foil. She turns off the room lights. Only the tree is still glowing.

"That wasn't such a bad Christmas," she says.

FRITZ SAYS

Fritz says:

"It's important for you to feel as functional and normal as possible while this is going on. So shower each day. Get dressed right away, as soon as you get out of bed—don't sit around in your pajamas. Get some exercise daily, even a twenty-minute walk or some calisthenics, sit-ups, and mild push-ups in the living room. Be sure to eat something, especially protein. Even if it doesn't taste good, just get it down. Okay?"

Fritz says:

"I realize that you're just trying to help, and I appreciate that. You're very good people, and I value your thoughts and ideas. But it's important not to interrupt. Although I really am treating you as a family to some extent, I'd like to keep your husband and father as the focus. So I'd like you to try, even though I know it feels

difficult, to hold back a little bit . . . in fact, quite a bit. Thank you. Let's try that again, okay?"

Fritz says:

"Let's see if we can work out some really effective techniques for helping Bill be able to answer the questions in his own way, in his own time. Now, let me model for you how I ask Bill a question and wait for his answer. I ask my question; then I keep looking right into his eyes—see the direct line from my eyes to his—and I wait calmly and patiently while he formulates his answer. I might even be willing to wait five minutes if I have to. Why not? What's to lose if I do? What I really don't want to do is to squelch his answer in any way. He tends to speak very quietly right now, so I don't want the relative loudness of my own voice to drown out his answer. He's also speaking rather slowly, so I wouldn't want the relative quickness of my voice to beat him to the punch and perhaps drive his own answer right out of his head. Once he does begin to speak, I'll listen receptively until I'm sure he's finished. So could all of us take turns trying that?"

HOWL

Someone in the house is shouting.

It's Dad who's shouting. An intruder has broken into our house. An intruder is trying to kill Dad.

I sit up in bed. My body runs alongside my heart, trying to jump on.

I feel for my bike frame and grab the tire pump. It's light but would deliver a solid blow.

The lights are on in Mom and Dad's room. Dad's eyes are shut. Every time he shouts, his head rises off the pillow. Mom kneels on the floor beside him, shaking his arm.

"Wake up, Bill! Wake up! Bill! Stop it!"

"What's wrong with him?"

Linda runs in from the hall, wearing sweatpants and a T-shirt.

Dad shouts again.

Linda shouts back, sounding just like Dad. They're not

shouting words. It's a preword and I don't know where they learned it.

"Linda! Stop it!" Mom says.

"Mom! Why is he doing this?"

"I don't know, Billy. He just is. He just started shouting like this."

"Why don't you make him stop it?"

"I can't!"

Linda looks into the hall, hopping up and down. "Where's Dad? He'll know what to do! I'm going to go get Dad!"

Mom grabs her by the shoulders. "Linda! *Linda!* What are you talking about? This is Dad. He's already here. He's the one who's yelling."

"Oh! He's already here. I forgot." She starts to cry and leans on Mom.

"Linda, you have to calm down. You have to help me."

"But I'm afraid!"

"I can't wake him up. Somebody try something!"

"Come on, Dad," I urge. My voice leaves my throat in shreds like splinters. "You can do it. You can wake up."

I really don't know if he can. What if he can't?

I drop the pump and climb across the bed to shake him. How long has it been since I've crawled into my parents'

bed—ten years? Back then it was a tract, a room to itself.

"Come on, wake up. It's not real. If you wake up, you won't be scared anymore."

"In another minute," Mom says, "I'm calling an ambulance."

"Dad, stop," Linda says. "Please stop, okay? Please wake up. You're scaring me. Okay. Okay." She breathes deep the way the doctor told us to, but each breath has a rattle in it like she's swallowed cellophane. "I know. Let's pry his eyes open."

Bending over him with one fingertip, she slides up his eyelids. He's still shouting without looking at us, in a separate world that we can't get to.

Then Dad's irises contract.

"He's awake," Linda says.

I press Dad's arm. His pajama shirt is soaked. "Dad, it was just a nightmare. Come on. Sit up. Sit up."

"He's awake, Mom. Dad, it's okay," Linda says. "You're home in bed."

"All right."

"You're home. You were having a nightmare."

"Was I? My God." Dad's voice is rough, like that night in the kitchen.

Linda and I surround Dad, but Mom stays back. Dad's nightmare must have scared her. She looks like someone who walks along the edge of a pool not knowing what they'll find. A koi, a piranha, a dead body, their own reflection.

"Are you going to be all right, Bill? I was just about to call an ambulance."

"Maybe he should keep sitting up, Mom. Keep sitting up. You'd better stay awake for a while, until you're sure it's gone away."

"I'm awake. I'm awake."

Linda tugs the corner of his pillow. "I'm the one who woke you up, Dad."

"Thank you, honey." He feels for her hand, squeezes it.

"When you saw me, you were all right."

"What was this nightmare?" I ask. "It must have been a whopper."

"What was it, Dad?" Linda echoes. "Was it pretty scary?"

"I was alone. . . ."

Crawling back to Mom's side of the bed, I settle against the headboard. "So, you were alone?"

"That's right. I was sealed up in a metal box . . . with a window in it."

"Mom," Linda asks, "can I turn on all the lights so we feel less nervous?"

"If it will make you feel better."

"Don't say anything important till I get back."

Lights come on in rooms, shaping our box of life beside the highway. The drivers on 128 may notice a lit-up house, but they know nothing about Dad's nightmare. Probably no other family is awake in this section of Hawthorne.

"What do you think the metal box was?" The obvious thought is a coffin, but I hope he'll say "phone booth" and break this mood.

"It was like a submarine, because I was dropped into the ocean. But nobody knew that I was inside. First it was bobbing on the surface. Then it started to sink. I could see the water through the window."

Dad links his phrases slowly, but we listen without interrupting, as the doctor said we should. I try to picture the dream, picture myself in it. I feel that if I get it right, just the way Dad dreamed it, the spell will break and it won't bother him again.

"I wanted to get out, and I knew it had a door in it when I first went inside, but when the box began to sink the door had disappeared."

"Why were you inside it in the first place?" Linda asks.

"Does that really make any difference, Linda?" Mom asks.

"I'm trying to figure out what it means."

"It doesn't mean anything. Don't you see what the problem is? It's those pills they've got him on."

"That's what it must be," Dad says. "Those pills."

Of course. "Well, that's good then, isn't it?" I comment.

"How is it good?"

It's good because Dad is not really in a metal box that's sinking.

Mom finds a clean pajama top in a pile of folded laundry on the dresser. She holds it out to Dad while he takes off the soaked one. "I could kick myself. How could I let you take anything without looking into it more closely?"

"Dad," Linda asks, "do you think that if you had stayed asleep, you eventually would have found a way out of the box?"

"I don't think we need to know any more about this," Mom answers without looking at Linda. "It doesn't matter what the nightmare means, it's just bad enough that it happened. Try to get it out of your mind, Bill. Do you want to read something?"

"Maybe we should have made the decision together," Dad says, buttoning the new shirt.

"Together? Bill—" It seems like Mom wants to say that Dad hasn't been able to decide anything for at least a month now. But how can she tell him this? No one ever actually says to him that he's anything less than normal. "Well, do you mean you didn't want the pills? If we had decided together, would you have not gone ahead with it? Do you want to go off them?"

"I didn't want them. I knew they wouldn't help." Dad suddenly seems more wise instead of less, like his dream packed him something to carry back to the rest of us. His calmness spooks me, and I wish there were more lights for Linda to turn on.

"Why didn't you say something at the time?" Mom asks. "Why didn't you refuse to take them?"

"Because you seemed so happy."

"You were making me happy?" Mom is still holding the sweaty pajama top. "You took them to make me happy? But I did think it was going to help. Something had to."

"Are you all right, then, Dad?" I ask. "Can we go back to bed now?" I was thinking of getting up extra early. I have an oral report to give tomorrow, and I haven't even

started it yet. I feel like my blood has slowed down finally. A section of my face, right between my eyebrows, had actually been jumping.

"I don't feel like sleeping," Linda says. "Dad, do you want to sit up for the rest of the night with the lights on and watch TV? There might be an old movie on. Then when the movie's over, I'll make pancakes."

"That's all right, honey. Your mother and I will sit up for a few minutes and talk. Oh, God."

"I'm going to bed. Maybe you should move into a different room," I suggest. "To just, you know, forget things. Remove the reminders or whatever. Maybe you should sleep on the couch tonight."

"He'll be all right," Mom says. "But I vote with Linda. Anyone who wants to can leave their lights on."

DAD, HOW CAN YOU GO TO CALIFORNIA?

That same night I have my own dream, that an airline introduced a special reduced airfare from Boston to California. In my dream, the fare was extremely cheap—$142 round-trip—because of the volume of passengers that could be conveyed on a single plane. Each passenger's head, you see, was separated from the body and sealed in a plastic bag. The body was maintained at home with intravenous feeding until the "extra-value passenger" (the head) returned.

Dad's head went to California in a plastic bag, stacked as palletized cargo in a freight compartment with the heads of other budget travelers, most of whom were traveling for business. They would be able to do all the necessary negotiating and communicating in this compact state. Who needed a body to attend a meeting?

But after Dad's head had been away for several days, it struck me that he might be in jeopardy. I rushed into

his room to find his body seated upright in a special chair, wearing white hospital pajamas. His systems were hooked up, his blood was pumping, his chest moved in and out. The only bad sign was that his skin looked shiny and goldish. *But how,* I shouted in my sleep, *could we have let him go to California?* If his head were somehow diverted, like a piece of lost luggage, we would never be able to put him together again.

In the dream I stayed for a week beside his body, always awake, watching every rise and fall of his chest, waiting for his head to come back—across the country, through the dollies, trolleys, hand trucks, and conveyors of Logan Airport, back home to us.

A NOTE TO THE READER

Oh, I know you can never walk a mile in my worn-out bedroom slippers.

But can you see how important all this is?

I want you to see it.

So you will know what was lost.

So you'll never think, while reading this, that I tried to do too much.

BULWARK

"Dr. Fritz, please. Adele Morrison. No, I can't wait. No, I can't hold. I don't care, I need to talk to him *right now*. How long? Tell me specifically how long I have to wait. How many minutes? All right, but no longer."

Mom holds on to the phone, watching Dad. Dad's at the table in his pajamas, breaking a Pop-Tart into small pieces. I finish my cereal and put my breakfast dishes in the sink before Mom starts to speak again.

"Dr. Fritz, the medication you've started us on . . . No, it's not a good morning. No, I'm not going to tell you how I am, and I'm not going to ask how you are. The medication you and Dr. Gupta prescribed for my husband is completely unacceptable. He began shouting in his sleep last night and frightened our children. My daughter was completely terrified, and I almost called an ambulance. . . . Yes, he was shouting. He was having nightmares. Extremely bad ones, apparently, from the sound of it. I had difficulty waking

him. All of us are rattled by the experience. . . . Well, your questions are certainly very impressive-sounding, but to return to my original point without getting bogged down in specifics: This medication is unacceptable. . . . Oh, this nightmare thing is uncommon? Well, that changes the situation, doesn't it? What do we care how uncommon it is if it happens to us?

"No, I'm not willing to 'wait it out.' . . . I don't think we can afford to wait another two weeks for him to adjust. If this is what it's like, we're not going to wait two days, or even two minutes. Here are your choices: You and Dr. Gupta can switch him to something different *today*, and it has to be more effective than what you've given him so far, or you can try to cure him without medication. Which is it?"

Mom listens to Fritz while watching Dad put an edge of Pop-Tart crust in his mouth. Her cheeks are full of air, like she's saying a word that starts with *B*. She puts the receiver back on the wall without saying good-bye to Fritz.

Mom leans against the kitchen counter, her eyes avoiding Dad's chair. "He says he'll discuss it with me at the next appointment."

Mom says the medical establishment has let her down again. She's entirely disillusioned with Fritz. He's fallen off his pedestal. Mom says that Fritz never really cared about helping Dad. He only took the case to help pay for his sailboat.

TREATMENT REPORT: DAY 41

Mom and Dad stay home at the time of the next scheduled appointment with Fritz.

The phone rings and rings.

part two

COMPOSED IN A CHEMISTRY NOTEBOOK

"The Happy Pills"
(Sung by a chorus of doctors)

> *The white one just might help you,*
> *Though it makes your heart beat fast*
> *And it makes your tongue feel sandy*
> *And your eyes feel hard as glass.*
> *So there's clanging in your left ear*
> *And a buzzing in your right—*
> *If you overlook the symptoms*
> *It will help you sleep all night.*
> *Tra-la!*
>
> *Or you could try the blue one,*
> *If you don't care how you look,*
> *If you don't mind tiny blisters*
> *Filled with icky greenish gook*

That will start out on your stomach
And then overrun your skin.
Anyway, you don't get out much—
So you won't mind staying in.
Tra-la!

This new one's just the ticket.
Just ignore the gloomy press.
Those stories are all nonsense
Placed by nuts seeking redress.
Yes, one patient shot his family,
But that doesn't happen much—
We know other patients like it,
And that's good enough for us.
Tra-la!

This red one is a killer.
You'll feel like a brand-new man,
If you don't mind weird sensations
In your procreative gland.
Call my cell phone if it stiffens
And you can't get it to bend—
You'll be rushed back with a siren

And you'll never shtup *again.*
Tra-la!

Tra-la, la, la, la!
That will be one hundred twenty-five dollars, please.

"Oh, that's funny, Billy," Mom says.

"Your father and I have just finished discussing his options," Mom says. "We feel fortunate to have skirted what was obviously a medical disaster in the making."

Uncle Marty talked Dad into watching a college basketball game with him in the den. From the other end of the house we can hear Marty shouting. He has a bundle of money on the game.

"At this point we're going to change our strategy. We're going to do what I initially thought we should have done, and that is to care for him on our own. From this point your father is going medication free, and his symptoms, including the bizarre sleep disturbance, will have a chance to subside.

"Our home routines will be different for a while. I spoke to Dad's office and they're extending his medical leave. We expect it won't be a long one once he recovers from the medications. I'm going to change my work schedule"—

Mom's voice breaks, and she stares at Triumph until she's calm again—"to half-time, from two thirty in the afternoon until six. That will allow us to provide Dad with continuous care throughout the day. Billy, you will come home directly after school so that you can take over from me at two fifteen. It would be best if you and I can overlap for a few minutes before I leave, in case there's anything we need to go over.

"I know how scary it's been for both of you to see him this way. He told me he hates to have you see him like this. He never wanted to be someone you felt sorry for. He wanted to be someone you looked up to. He wouldn't even want me to have this conversation with you. He wouldn't even want me to tell you what I just said. But I did, so there it is.

"Your father and I are going to need all your help to get through this time. Once it's over . . . we'll turn the page on this chapter and never look back again. What do you think about that?"

Linda is flopped on my bed. "Of course, Mom," she says. "We'll do whatever it takes to get Dad well again."

Mom raises her eyebrows at me.

I raise my eyebrows back.

"You can go, Linda."

"Okay, Mom." She kisses Mom on the way out.

Mom stays in my desk chair. I'm down low this time in the beanbag.

"What?" she asks, looking down at me.

"I know you need me and everything."

"Yes."

"But—I'm coming home right after school?"

"Yes."

"And staying here until six o'clock? Monday through Friday?"

"That's right."

"What about Linda?"

"What about her?"

"Shouldn't she come right home too?"

Mom has a few ways of looking at people that make them shut up. One is to remove her reading glasses and place them on top of her head. She kind of combs the arm of the glasses slowly through her hair first in a way that can be scary. But this time it doesn't work.

"Shouldn't she?"

Mom shrugs.

"You're not going to answer me?"

"You know she wants to help. But she can't, really. She's just too young. This is not the time to complain."

"Shouldn't she get a chance to try? Maybe she'd turn out to be good at it. Better than me, even."

"Billy."

"Maybe she has a knack, or a special gift."

"Will you keep your voice down, please?"

"Hey, I know."

"What?"

"You could get her a little nurse's uniform. Wouldn't she look adorable in it?"

"What is the matter with you? This isn't the time."

What is the precisely calibrated bored look that says Mom's judgment is so obviously wrong that everyone realizes it except her?

"What if I want to do something after school?"

"You have important plans?"

"That's neither here nor there. What if I did have them?"

"This isn't forever. It's just for a few weeks. Until he's over it."

"What if I say no?"

"I'm not giving you a choice."

"All right, then, I guess I won't say no."

"It's only for a few weeks."

"A few weeks. All right."

After Mom leaves, I take her spot at the desk. Inside the desk is a Hohner Special 20 harmonica Grandma Pearl got me. I had asked for it, in fact, but it's still sealed in the package with the instruction book. Had I ever learned to play it, I would create an ugly sound at a special decibel level only Mom could hear, letting her know I will never be her orderly.

BATTLESHIP

I've been playing Battleship with Dad. Somehow, he always ends up looking for my Destroyer last.

The Destroyer is the very smallest of five boats—it occupies only two spaces on the game board—and so it can be hidden anywhere. Dad seems to have guessed a hundred times, systematically, all over the board. In fact, he seems to be creating a scientific net of guesses to throw over the grid and ensnare my Destroyer. I can see his web of guesses spreading over the grid, from A1 way up in the lefthand corner, seeping downward and outward over the transparent green plastic of my ocean and covering the four boats of mine that he has already sunk.

Yet somehow he's missed D9.

In the meantime I'm just as systematically trying to avoid sinking his last boat, the massive, five-space Aircraft Carrier. I'm doing a kind of hot-coals dance around the perimeter of the only five spaces where his Aircraft Carrier

can possibly be. I waste guesses. I guess some spaces twice, although Dad doesn't seem to notice. But what I'm most occupied with is telepathic bulletins. As his guesses get quieter, more discouraged, and further apart, I stare down at the dinky little Destroyer stationed on D9 and 10 and I chant to myself, *D9, D9.*

And Dad looks up and says, "C7?"

Earlier we played Thousand Rummy. And just as on the previous days, Dad was the one to draw the ace of spades. If it was Gin, Thousand Rummy, or even Concentration, Dad would sit there in his pajamas (he sometimes wears his pajamas all day now), press his lips together decisively, and flip over a card . . . and there it would be.

The ace of spades, the Death Card.

How can this keep happening? It's getting so that we wait for the ace of spades. It seems to look for Dad. Since we stopped seeing Fritz and ended the medicines, a sense of doom sits over Dad like a mist.

So there it is, Dad seems to say. He looks at the card like he's been expecting it. He drops his head into his hands like a condemned man. The writing on the card, which seemed innocent before he got sick, seems to have turned into an ominous message.

DEBONNAIRE, OLEET PLAYING CARD CO.,
MOUNT VERNON, N.Y. "SUPERKOTED" ™

What does this mean to Dad?

The ace of spades stands on its unipod and stares my father down. It's a heart upside down. It's the opposite of a heart.

Mom and I return to the house after a Saturday afternoon in the library.

"Whatcha got there?" Marty asks. Dad trails him into the dining room.

Each of us dumps a double armload of reading material on the table. I have nine books, including *Affirmations in the Key of Health* by Lillian Drakava; *Make Up Your Mind: Self-Empowerment Through Mood Selection* by R. Candelbaum, MD; *Go for the Joy* by Sybil Lucien-Simple, MSW; and a thinner one called *Darkness Manifest* by an award-winning novelist, as well as a stack of journal and magazine articles, some photocopied and some printed off the computer.

On the way there, Mom said she was lucky, in this difficult time, to have a teenage son with my capacity for understanding human nature. I have to admit that it was strangely fun finding books that described what Dad was

going through. There were almost too many matches to choose. When I asked the librarian how I could tell if a book was any good, he told me to look for letters after the person's name. A shelf full of credentials—PhD, EdD, LICSW, and DDiv—cleared its throat at me, but I chose some authors with no letters, like the novelist (ultrasad eyes, extra neck skin), just because I liked their pictures.

"You can tell a lot from their pictures," Linda agrees, picking up books and flipping them over.

The books in Mom's stack include *Feed Your Brain* by Wilbert and Orralie Curtis, *The Feel Good Vitamin Bible* from the publishers of *Feel Good* magazine, and *Peace Without Pills: How Eating Right Can Replace Costly and Potentially Harmful Psychotropic Medications* by Evgenia Sutter, CNC. Behind the crinkly, scuffed plastic library covers, the smiling Curtises wear matching red-and-white checked shirts and hold out palmfuls of unprocessed grain. Evgenia Sutter has long brown hair and wears a white lab jacket with eyeglasses in the pocket.

Some faces are like a hard pill. Others are more of a loose powder. One of them will be the cure for what ails Dad.

AUTODIDACT

Mom stays up late cramming information from her library books and articles. She reads paragraphs aloud, as if putting words in the air will pollinate Dad with a cure.

Like most Americans, she says, she has always known the basics about proper nutrition without bothering to follow them. But now, like the cop or soldier in the movies whose buddy is killed, she announces, "This time, it's personal." She memorizes the foods and supplements that provide B vitamins 1 (thiamine), 2 (riboflavin), 3 (niacin), 6 (pyridoxine), and 12 (cyanocobalamin), as well as folic acid, inositol, vitamins C and E; crucial minerals such as calcium, chromium, magnesium, selenium, iron, iodine, and zinc; and the amino acids gamma-aminobutyric acid (GABA), S-adenosyl L-methionine (SAMe), serotonin, melatonin, L-tryptophan, 5-hydroxytryptophan (5-HTP), DL-phenylalanine (DLPA), trimethylglycine (TMG), omega-3 fatty acids, and tyrosine.

These substances, Mom learns, improve brain function, restoring the moistness and flexibility of certain membranes and helping brain cells to manufacture the chemicals they need to keep the neurotransmitters signaling. But so many expert opinions, she tells us, are difficult to sort out. One book says that serotonin and melatonin are chemicals that the brain will produce after a body consumes the right combination of foods. In another book, melatonin and seratonin are capsules you can buy in the health food store. If both are true, where did the chemicals for the capsules come from? Mom shudders. Maybe she's getting morbid because it's so late (Dad is already in bed and listening to a talk show on the radio), but as I pass by her chair, she tells me her thoughts are taking a ghoulish turn. You hear about gravediggers and organ thieves. Is someone stealing brains and selling the chemicals from them?

The experts in Mom's books agree that someone with Dad's symptoms should avoid coffee and cola, alcohol, sugar, and dairy products. But a major source of two crucial substances, calcium (helps to maintain a healthy central nervous system) and tyrosine (stimulates the brain's production of norepinephrine), is cheese. Mom wonders aloud if she should give him cheese or not. Should she look

for a special, nondairy cheese? Kosher cheese? And where would she find extract of *Griffonia simplicifolia*, an African plant (and source of 5-hydroxytryptophan)?

And, Mom wants to know, what about Evgenia Sutter's habit of saying "widely celebrated in Europe," "available inexpensively in Europe," and "exhaustively tested throughout Europe"? Have these chemicals been tested in America? Are they known by the same names here? Do they maybe have a "street name"?

Mom tells me she fell asleep earlier this evening and had a nightmare that she was arrested for trying to procure *Griffonia simplicifolia* in a back alley. She describes the dream: A bus ride back to New York, the city she thought she had left for good. Returning just once more, for Dad's sake. Walking late at night from playground to decrepit coffee shop to back alley. Looking over her shoulder whenever she hears a sound. She can't find the right address, the city makes no sense. The layout of the city resembles Granada, Spain. Has New York really changed so much since she left? When she finds the place where the deal will go down, it's an alley behind a deserted high-rise. A gaunt, shivering figure approaches and asks for the password.

"Ignorance."

"No."

"Impotence."

"No."

"Hegemony?"

"No."

"Fluoridization?"

"Okay."

"How much?" she asks.

"Two thousand," he says. "Cash." Mom has only twelve dollars. In the dream, she forgets that she can go to an ATM. She finds a knife in her pocket, Grandpa Eddie's old fishing knife. The knife flashes under the streetlight, and a siren begins to wail.

Hours later Mom's reading lamp is still on.

"Mom, go to bed. It's the middle of the night. You're asleep again."

"I never meant to cause any harm," she says out loud.

"It all seemed so simple," she says.

"Mom, you need to stop reading."

I shake her awake. The tip of her index finger is white where she has used it as a bookmark.

LIGHT

The four of us are playing Monopoly in the dining room when Uncle Marty struggles into the house with his arms around a box, walking it in on top of one shoe.

"Good grief," says Mom. Mom, Linda, and Dad crowd around him while I stabilize the game. Mom was winning.

"You thought Christmas was over," he tells the family, "but it's not. A late Christmas gift for the lord of the manor—my big brother, Bill."

Even Dad is impressed. When Marty lays the mammoth gift in the center of the living room, Dad crouches over it to peel away the Christmas paper. Large block letters on the side of the box say VITA-LITE.

"I can't get the flaps open," Dad says over his shoulder.

"I've got it, bro, no problem." Marty borrows my pocket knife and pries off the heavy-duty staples.

Dad removes several sheets of crumpled newsprint and slides out the light box. It's about the size and depth of a small

kitchen table. Marty pulls out the rear leg to stand it upright.

"Thank you, Marty," Dad says.

"Don't thank me yet. Wait till you see this."

Marty crawls under the Christmas tree, reaches for the outlet, and unplugs the holiday lights.

"Oh, no!" Mom complains.

"Mom," Linda says, "it's January eighteenth. It had to happen sooner or later."

"But it was so cheerful." She drops into a seat in the conversation area.

"Sorry, Adele," Marty says. "But this thing uses a good flow of juice. I wouldn't want you to short anything out."

Half the lights in the house pulse, then flicker. The part of the living room where Dad is gets flooded with white light, like a prison courtyard during an attempted break.

"Aack," Linda says, lifting an arm to shield her face.

"I think it's too strong," Mom agrees.

"But this could be just the thing for Bill," Marty argues. "Don't close your eyes, bro—open them. You have to have them open so it can act on your retinas."

"It's going to blind him."

"No, it has to be strong in order to work. Look at him—I think he looks better already!"

"That's because he's getting a tan," says Linda.

"Such a costly gift, Marty," Mom says. "You must have spent several hundred dollars." Normally Dad would have said something like this too. He was always warning Marty that his credit card balances were too high.

"It's just a way of saying thank you, Bill, for all the support you've given me this year, with everything I've gone through. I can honestly say that this has been the worst year of my life. Without you to talk to, I don't think I would have made it." He presses one eye with the back of his knuckles.

Then he takes Dad by the elbow. "Sit down, bro, and I'll tell you more about how it works. This unit runs at twenty thousand lux—that's up to forty times the brightness of normal indoor light!"

"What good does that do?" Linda asks.

"You just sit in front of the light each morning—"

"For how long?" Mom asks.

"Up to about an hour—and the light travels up your optic nerve and basically tricks your brain into thinking it's summer. The light tinkers with the chemicals in your brain, and you, you know, just stop being depressed. Everyone is happier in the summer and sadder in the winter. Haven't you ever felt that way? Doesn't it make sense?"

"The theory sounds plausible," Mom says. "But the execution is so *extreme*."

"It only seems that way, Adele. You find yourself getting used to it. Come on, bro, we'll sit in front of it together and test it out. You don't have to look right into it, you just glance at it from time to time. The instructions say you can read if you want to, or knit. Come on, buddy."

"Dad knits?" Linda asks.

"It's so big—," Marty begins.

"I hadn't noticed," Mom says.

"It's so big that I suggest you decide on a permanent spot for it," Marty continues. "So it won't be in the way."

"Why don't you put it against the north wall there," I tell him, referring to the divider between the living room and the kitchen. "That way Dad can get light from this in the early morning, and then natural sunlight from the picture window in the afternoon."

"Marty," says Mom, "all kidding aside, I just have to question whether this is really safe."

Marty drops into the loveseat opposite Mom. "I thought you'd all be pleased, Adele. This technique is medically approved. By the American Medical Association and the National Institutes of Mental Health."

"And the electrical utilities, no doubt," Mom says. "I'm sorry, Marty. I shouldn't joke. I do appreciate that you're only trying to help."

At last I join the family in the living room. "Well, I think it makes a lot of sense," I say, as if I just decided.

"Good boy," Marty says, and winks at me.

The others have no idea that this was all my suggestion. I read about it, I researched it on the Internet before Christmas, and I got Marty to pay $729 for it. Soon, I know, Dad will be well, and the expense will have been worth it.

"It's so *bright*, though, Billy," Mom says. "Just look at it. I'd be afraid of it burning a hole in my retina or something. Marty, isn't it dangerous to look directly into the sun?"

"Mom, this isn't anything like the sun. The sun is—I don't know—probably a million lux, probably. A lot more than this, anyway. And remember: It's only for a few weeks."

"Well," Mom says, "I speak on behalf of my husband when I say that it's very impressive, dangerous or not." Mom all at once looks younger—but just a couple of months younger, like the way she looked when we started going to Fritz.

"Why don't we try an experiment?" Marty suggests.

"Everyone, make note of your mood right now. Then we'll try it for ten minutes and see if anyone feels better."

"Okay," Linda says, "name your mood. Amused. Next?"

"I didn't mean name your mood like name that tune, hon. I just meant make a mental note of it to yourself."

Mom, Dad, and Marty line up on the couch facing the north wall, while Linda and I sit on the floor in front of them.

Actually, once I experience the light I almost think Mom has a point. Its intensity is hard to get used to, like it might burn away even the memory of color. But Dad seems calm. So we keep doing it.

The books contain so many valuable suggestions that it's hard to know what to choose. But after deliberating, I choose three areas: affirmations, occupational rehabilitation, and light therapy. Mom feels that diet and exercise are surefire winners. Linda wants to work on aromatherapy.

So Mom presents a plan for the three of us, the treatment team. Already, Linda has begun wafting Kleenexes saturated with lemon oil under Dad's nose. Every time she does this, his eyebrows shoot up. The lemon oil has a piercingly clean smell, like furniture cleaner or dishwashing liquid. Mom has determined a nutritional baseline for Dad. Each day he will eat a bowl of hot bran cereal, an ounce of aged natural cheese, a slice of health bread with natural peanut butter, a serving of seafood, a cooked salad of kale and onions, a mound of navy beans sprinkled with brewer's yeast, and twenty pomegranate seeds. The Curtises call these the Seven Brain Foods. Mom likes the idea of brain foods, because in

addition to making Dad less happy and less confident, the depression has also made him less smart.

As for the remaining approaches, first thing in the morning Dad will be expected to switch on his light box and sit in front of it while Mom reads him the most uplifting highlights from the morning newspaper. When I take over after school, I'll work with Dad for fifteen minutes on repeating powerful phrases: "I am well." "I am happy." "The universe is moving toward perfection." Afterward, we'll spend an hour or two on cards, board games, and educational television—as long as Dad can stay still. No junk TV, like reality shows or cop shows—only things that are soothing and that elevate the mind. After Mom gets home and we have dinner, Mom will lead him through a program of calisthenics demanding enough to tire him out but not so stimulating that they would wake him up at night. I'll keep periodic records showing changes in sleep, appetite, concentration, and mood.

A MULTIPRONGED PLAN

"I call that a plan," Linda says.

"Okay, but . . ."

"You have an objection?" Mom asks.

Although I hate to be a wellness wet blanket, I have to ask how, if we try so many different treatments at once, we will be able to tell which ones are working.

"What about the whole idea of the scientific method? Controls and variables. You maintain the same conditions for a set period of time and change just one factor."

"You don't have to tell me about the scientific method," Mom says. She seems miffed that I haven't swooned over her program.

"Well, what if one of these treatments works and the others don't? How will we know to keep doing the right thing? Or what if one of them causes him to backslide, and they cancel each other out?"

"Well." Mom places her glasses on top of her head. "I

appreciate what you're saying, Billy, but I think, given the fact that your father has already been ill for a couple of months, we should try everything we can in order to save time, even if that means employing many treatments at once and not developing the kind of complete data set you think would be so edifying."

"I totally agree with Mom," Linda adds. "You're going off on a tangent as usual. Don't you even care whether Dad gets back to normal?"

"Of course I do. Don't you care about anything other than agreeing with Mom? Mom, say Dad suddenly starts to get better—"

"Then he gets better, right? And that's what we want. End of story."

TREATMENT REPORT: DAY 61

The treatment team has rolled out Dad's complete new wellness program, and we are off to an excellent start. We started slow on the light box (phototherapy), with just twenty minutes, per orders of Mom, who is still skeptical. Then did twenty of each affirmation. Dad ate at least a bit of all his brain foods, plus two handfuls of nuts. When Mom came home he moved gamely through his calisthenics. Linda did two sessions of wafts.

TREATMENT REPORT: DAY 62

Today Dad had trouble focusing on Monopoly and staying in his chair. I had to explain his old strategy back to him, of buying every possible property even if it meant mortgaging something until he passed Go. Discouraging. But Linda came home with nachos and Dad wanted some, even though junk food is against the program. Mom said it was good that he had an appetite, so he ate a few pieces, but from now on when Linda and I are at home we will have to eat what Dad's eating. We agree that calisthenics are helping him sleep. He is learning the affirmations well and could probably do them alone.

A NIGHT OUT: PART I

On Thursday afternoon the phone rings. Linda is making bead jewelry in her room with her little friend Jodie. Dad is trying to nap on the couch, so after the first ring I answer the phone in my parents' bedroom instead of the kitchen.

"You'd better sit down," Gordon says.

"Why?"

"Are you sitting down?"

"Yes." I sit on the edge of my parents' bed.

"I have tickets to Buddy Guy tomorrow night. In Boston."

"What?"

"Buddy Guy. At Berklee College. My dad got the tickets as a surprise, and we were going to go together, but he has a business thing and he can't go. It's a miracle, Bilbo—Buddy Guy. My dad said we could take the train in *by ourselves*. The concert starts at eight fifteen. We pick you up at seven o'clock. He gave us money to go out to eat afterward—"

"Whoa. I just have to make sure I can go."

"Whoa back. You would consider missing a Buddy Guy concert? It's free. We have great seats. You don't have to pay a cent."

"I know. But sometimes I have to babysit," I whisper.

"For your sister?"

"No, for, you know, my dad. I didn't mean to say babysit. I meant to say watch, or just sit with. My mother works, and my sister is too young. You know, he's sick. He doesn't stay home by himself."

"That's right." In the silence that follows looms the thing I haven't been mentioning. Gordy is here again, in our living room, while Dad walks back and forth without talking to him. How could he understand this? I barely understand it myself.

"I'm sorry," Gordy continues. "I shouldn't put the pressure on. It's just—"

"Just what?"

"Well, when my mom was really sick, my dad hired a nurse. Two nurses actually. Around the clock. He had to work a lot, that's why. But I get it, I completely understand. So . . ."

Suddenly going to a concert by Buddy Guy, legendary

Chicago bluesman, is what I want more than anything in the world. Sitting on a commuter train that's nearly empty because everyone's going in the opposite direction. We each have our own bench, so we talk to one another across the aisle. Gordy drums the metal part of the seat in front of him while we hum "Ninety-Nine and One Half" and "What Kind of Woman Is This?" We eat Chinese food or pizza in a restaurant where the customers are all city kids. Just us, in the city at night. No adults telling us what to do.

"How would we get home, anyway?"

"We take the train home, too. My dad's going to pick us up at the station. We have it all worked out, Bilbo. The whole situation is ready, it's just waiting for you to step into it. I could ask somebody else, but I thought you were the one who would really appreciate it. Anyway . . ."

"I think I can. I'll ask. Assume that I'll go, okay? Assume that I'm going, unless you hear otherwise. No, wait—I really have to think about this."

"If you can't go, I'll see if Mitchell wants to. Or Andy. Are you a definite yes? Do you want to give me their phone numbers just in case? Or should I wait to hear back from you first?"

"No, I'm almost definitely a yes. Assume I'll go."

"That was confusing. But I completely understand."

"I have to go," I whisper. My voice got loud there for a minute when I pictured tomorrow night in Boston. It was almost like I was there, even.

When I hang up the phone and walk down the hall, Dad is waiting on the living-room couch.

"Is something wrong, Billy? Did someone get hurt?"

"No, no one is hurt."

"From the tone of your voice, I thought something was wrong."

"It's okay, Dad. It was just Gordon."

"Should we watch TV, then?"

"Yes. Let's watch TV."

A NIGHT OUT: PART 2

When Mom gets home from work, she brushes the snow off her coat and drops a pile of museum papers and American history journals on the coffee table.

"God, I hate dealing with the public. You wouldn't believe how many of these local types think just because you're a museum you want to hear about every generation of the family that ever touched a piece of leather. And the pictures. And the diaries. And the letters. And would we *pay* for the letters."

"I thought you liked all that stuff, Mom."

"I couldn't get them to leave!"

I follow her around until she seems settled. I've decided to use the announcement method.

"I'm going out tomorrow night."

"Where are you going?"

"Gordy has tickets for a concert."

"Who's playing?"

"Buddy Guy."

"Ah, Buddy Guy! Bill?"

"Yes?" My father appears in the hall, already wearing pajamas.

"Billy's going to a Buddy Guy concert."

"Okay. . . . Enjoy yourself."

"It's not till tomorrow, Dad."

Dad doesn't seem too interested. Ordinarily, he would try to impersonate an old bluesman, the way John Belushi did.

"The tickets are free. We're going to take the train into Boston and go out to eat afterward."

"Sounds like a great time." Mom opens the dishwasher and stacks some clean plates.

"Let me do that, Mom."

I've never gone to Boston by myself, but it seems that, rather than our bad situation causing Mom to clamp down on me more than normal, it's distracted her enough that she doesn't question what I'm doing. This is an unexpected side benefit, a victory. I'm about to go into Boston at night, alone, with Gordy.

More and more, the concert sounds like a great opportunity. Right before Mom's arrival, while watching TV with Dad, I imagined eating in some hole-in-the-wall near

the auditorium and seeing a couple of Buddy Guy's musicians come in for a drink or a late supper after the show.
They'd be wearing sharp suits with the necktie undone and
possibly carrying an instrument case. Although that might
be ridiculous, now that I think of it—they must have road-
ies to carry the instruments. "Bravo!" Gordy and I might
shout as they walked in the door. We'd jump to our feet for
a standing ovation that would make the rest of the diners
stare. *You boys like the old music?* one would ask, throw-
ing a bill to the bartender and bringing his scotch to our
table. Although Gordy would hold up most of our end,
the musicians would be incredulous meeting two kids who
could talk to them about their work. When it was time
for our train to leave, the musicians would clasp us on the
shoulder and we'd all agree to keep in touch. *Best of luck,
kids. Don't ever change.*

"Okay, they're picking me up at seven."

"That's not going to work."

"What?"

"I have to stay a little late tomorrow. A group of researchers
are coming all the way from Pennsylvania to spend the day in
our archives, and I have to keep the library open for them."

"Can't Pudge do it?"

"Pudge. Pudge has some kind of fund-raiser he has to go to. You know, like a dress-up thing. He's not going to stay late at the Brooksbie."

"What about Mrs. Arabian? She's a volunteer. Won't she do whatever you tell her to?"

"Billy, I don't want to push it. I've already asked for enough special treatment. I just want to do the Pennsylvanian thing and make myself useful."

"Could you even ask Mrs. Arabian?"

"Billy. Do you have any idea how many people in the entire United States have a job that allows them to work from two thirty to six? Me. Just me. I'm the only one."

"So I have to stay home while you're at work?"

"That's what I expect. If I came home and found you gone, I'd be upset."

"What about Linda?" I ask.

"What about her?"

"She can't watch Dad?"

"Come on, Billy. You know she's too young."

"You won't ask Mrs. Arabian?"

"Will you stop it, please? You're getting on my nerves."

"I'll have to call Gordy, then. I'll have to tell him I can't go."

Now Gordy will ride the train with Mitchell, or worse, Andy, who would make inappropriate comments, act immature, and call his parents every half hour to let them know he was okay. It would all be wasted on him.

"I have an idea," Mom says. She's poking the pot of navy beans that were soaked all day, to see whether they're tender enough. "How about getting Marty to cover for you?"

"Marty?"

"Why not? He could come over and sit with Dad between when you leave and when I get home."

"That's a great idea."

"But I don't want you going anywhere until Marty arrives. Got that?"

"Sure."

"Hey. Got that?"

"Yep."

A NIGHT OUT: PART 3

I call Marty from the bedroom so I won't be in Mom's way in the kitchen. His cell phone rings five times.

"Bro?"

"Marty, it's Billy."

"Who is it? Sorry, it's noisy here."

"It's Billy, Marty."

"Billy! Good to hear from you. Is everything okay at home?"

"Yeah, it's fine. I need to ask for your help. Could you come and sit with Dad for an hour tomorrow night?"

"Sure! I'd love to. No problem."

"Thanks. Mom's working late and I need to leave to go to a concert. Buddy Guy. In Boston."

"That's great, Billy, just great. Now, what time would you want me there?"

"By seven o'clock."

"Seven o'clock. Just a minute. Hold on and I'll be right back to you."

Marty is part owner of a bar and restaurant in the next town. I hear him ask a question of someone else in the bar, probably his partner. The sounds of the business—clinking glasses, a cash register drawer, a cart full of dishes—unpause my mental movie about tomorrow night. The musicians are leaving. They clasp us on the shoulder, shake our hands. *Best of luck, kids. Keep in touch. And if you ever need a favor . . .*

"You're in luck. I can be there by seven thirty," Marty is saying.

"Seven thirty, not seven?"

"Seven thirty. Best I can do. Although I'm glad to do it. I want to talk to Bill anyway. I have some investment ideas I'd like to run by him."

"Seven thirty won't work. Is there any way you could be here earlier?"

"No, I can't. I wish I could, though."

Now Andy will sit with Gordy in the restaurant. The musicians will come by with their glasses of scotch and start talking to Andy, not to me. Andy will get to stand outside with them while they smoke. Andy will insult them by letting his eyes drift over the shoulder of Orlando Wright, Buddy's bass player, to the TV over the bar, and becoming

rapt in a game show on which a supermodel is being forced to eat a bucket of slugs.

"I can't go to the concert, then."

"Gee, I'm sorry. I really wish I could help you out, Billy. I'm awful sorry."

"Thanks, anyway. I know how it must be, having your own business. You always have to be there, right?"

"That's right. Look, is there anybody else you could ask?"

"Not really. There are people. But nobody who really knows how to take care of Dad."

"Well, Billy, if things change and seven thirty would work out, will you call me right back?"

"I will. I'll call you right back."

My only chance now is to find a way of getting there without taking the train. Someone will have to drive us all the way to Boston, all the way to Berklee Performance Center. It can't be Gordy's father, he already has something to do. It can't be Mom—she'll be at work. It can't be Marty—he'll be here. It can't be Dad, either. Whoever it is, we would have to leave the house at exactly seven thirty, no later. The driver will speed. We will fly down Route 1 to the auditorium, assuming there is no traffic. We will not look for parking spaces. We will be ejected, thrown, rolled, whatever, out of the car right at the entrance, and the driver will take off. We will run, panting, into the building with our tickets out, past the ushers, into a darkened auditorium, the last people to take their seats, provided the show hasn't already started, in which case we might be asked to wait, during the opening number, right inside the door. Who can I find? Who will help me?

What, you kids are planning on taking the train?
Nobody should take a train on a night like this. Here, take
the limo.

Who can I find?

I can't find anyone.

A NIGHT OUT: PART 5

Okay. I can do this. I can call Gordy and tell him I can't make it to the concert tomorrow. He can invite someone else. I can call Gordy and tell him to take Mitchell or Andy, although Andy will laugh at the wrong times. Andy will also sing along loudly with any song he's heard before, drowning out Buddy Guy's one-time interpretation, unrecorded and unique to this Berklee College concert, ruining it for those immediately around him.

I can do this. I'm lifting the phone. I'm dialing.

A NIGHT OUT: PART 6

It's funny what's happening right now. I had meant to call Gordy yesterday and tell him I couldn't go. I dialed and everything with the best of intentions. But instead I called Marty and told him to come at seven thirty. It's not that I feel angry or rebellious or anything. I'm just sort of watching myself from the outside—watching myself settle Dad in front of the TV and tell him to sit tight for a few minutes until Marty arrives, watching the car pull up, and watching myself go.

I go.

GOING

On the train, knowing I'm where I shouldn't be sharpens my senses. The world is shouting at me: SCHRAFFT'S in pink neon from a clock tower like a cathedral, H. P. HOOD on the big dairy office building. The graffiti on the empty freight cars are strangers shouting "I was here." On the Boston Sand and Gravel plant, a big sign cautions ACCIDENTS HAVE NO HOLIDAYS.

With no cell phone, I can't get pulled back. No one knows my location for sure, though they could hazard a guess. Watching father-son dyads board in matching Bruins jackets, I try not to think about Dad alone. Looking to the right as the train crosses the Charles River, I try not to think about Dad's dream of sinking in the metal box. When we see the suspension bridge topped with two Washington Monuments and lit in blue lights, the father-son dyads are already standing, so we elbow around them, through the station, and between the ticket scalpers out-

side. This is Boston. Streetlamps shining through maple trees with polluted-looking branches. Double-parked cars, brick buildings with garbage bags growing like mushrooms at the foot.

We take the Green Line to the Hynes/ICA stop. Crossing Boylston, we do a curb dance as an unmarked car and two cruisers careen around the corner, sirens barking. Drunks ask us croakily for a cigarette, and a woman asks for money to buy formula for her grandbaby. See? None of this would be happening in Hawthorne.

The theater is big, a thousand seats, though not anywhere near as big as the arena at North Station. It feels right to be here instead of home. The theater is already dark and Buddy's band is already performing when we scuttle to our seats in the front row.

THOUGHTS THAT INTRUDE
ON MY ENJOYMENT,
ALTHOUGH THEY DON'T ACTUALLY
RUIN THE CONCERT FOR ME

a. This should be fun.

b. This is going to be fun.

c. This should really be a lot of fun.

d. Obviously, there's been a serious lack of music in my life lately. Unless you count the school assembly that featured a performance by the Hawtones, our high school a cappella group. They are known in a cappella circles for their unique medley of classic songs about New England ("Massachusetts," "Old Cape Cod," "Charlie on the MTA"). I'm sure it plays better on the road than it does back home in Hawthorne, in the heart of the region they are singing about.

e. I met someone my age once who had a subscription to the Boston Symphony Orchestra and sat in the same seat every year, at the edge of the right balcony, overhanging the musicians. He impressed me as quite the egghead until he said the main reason he liked going was

to feel the vibrations against his skin. That's something you miss when you listen to music on headphones.

f. Gordy just gave me the quick-glance-nod-and-smile-with-eyebrows-raised. He's obviously having fun. Good for him.

g. I wonder what we're going to eat later.

h. For a while Dad was getting me to sing his favorite tenor/baritone opera duets with him, with the volume of the CD turned way up. Especially a duet from *The Pearl Fishers*, in which a pair of best friends are in love with the same woman. "It's her! It's that goddess!" he would sing in French. "She threads her way through the crowd." And if Mom walked into the room at that moment, he would really play it up. Toward the conclusion of the song, some falsely tense music signals the strife in the friends' relationship. It always reminded me of the soundtrack to an action movie with planes colliding or planets exploding. It's like someone went in with a Roto-Rooter and churned up the orchestra, and you could tell the story would come to a bad end. But the two friends sing, "Nothing must separate us! Let's pledge to always remain friends!" Slashes from the strings, and a big crescendo: "Let's stay united UNTI-I-I-IL death!" And

the orchestra does a bunch of big chords, like the words THE END rolling across a movie screen not once but four times.

He asked me to sing that with him a few weeks before the Gordy incident, but I was just leaving for Mitchell's to watch a movie. I see now that that happened right when Dad was first getting sick. Maybe I wish I had gone along with it?

i. Now Buddy Guy has stepped off the stage and is traveling up the aisle with his guitar. (One of the sound men follows him with an extension cord coiled around his shoulder.) I don't think the restaurant-networking thing is going to happen, but I do think he just nodded at me.

TREATMENT REPORT: DAY 66

Although there was no one to see what was happening during the half hour that Dad was left alone, it seems to have been pretty bad. Dad didn't know what had happened to me, he invented all kinds of things in his mind, and he ended up calling the police. Marty sent the police away as soon as he got here.

"I didn't want to rat you out to your mother, Billy," he told me in the kitchen when I got home. "Believe me, it totally killed me, and I completely remember what it was like to be a kid. But I was so concerned for your dad that I had to say something. You forgive me, don't you, buddy?"

Mom had stayed at the Brooksbie until ten thirty with the Pennsylvanians, so she had only been home for an hour when I got back. Marty had everything under control by then. After Marty spoke to me Mom took me to the utility room, where Dad, Marty, and even Linda couldn't see or hear us.

"We worked so hard to set up a complete, elaborate, minute-by-minute plan for caring for your father," she said, "and you have selfishly bungled it.

"Did you see how your father looked tonight?" she continued, whispering. "How white and shaky? What do you think he looked like at seven thirty when Marty got here? He doesn't even know if he can trust us anymore. He doesn't even know if at any minute he'll be left by himself to do who knows what."

Mom was so upset that she didn't even say the one thing I was counting on: "I hope you enjoyed yourself," after which I had planned to say, "I sure did!" Then I would tell her that I really had wanted to go to the concert and I didn't think she had lifted a finger to make it happen. But instead I started saying, "I'm sorry. I'm sorry. I'll make it up to you. I promise." Something about Dad looking so white and weird, and the house being so quiet when I came in, and all four of them looking at me with an accusation (except Dad, really, because he doesn't have that much expression).

Around midnight Mom came to my room. I was lying there watching my Escher drawing shift in a square of street light, foreground, background, foreground, background,

anything but solid ground. Mom said she understood a little bit of what I was going through, and maybe she should have tried harder to let me go to the concert. Then she said that in fairness to me, Linda was going to have to come home right after school too.

And that was today's change to the treatment plan.

AN AERIAL VIEW OF MOM AND DAD

Some nights my mind is a night watchman. It leaves my body and roams the house checking on everyone. My mental bedroom slippers are becoming as worn as the carpet Dad makes his circuit on. I don't think this is a bad thing. If I can be sure everyone is sleeping, then I can sleep too.

Here is the front door with both a doorbell and a knocker. Here are some shoes and boots, once wet or sandy, on a hard plastic mat inside the door. Here is the plate-glass window with floor-length draperies. Here is the conversation area, littered with schoolbooks, Brooksbie papers, and old *Newsweek*s. Here are throw pillows with sayings on them: "I Don't Do Perky," "Welcome to Our Piece of Paradise," "Mothers Nurture the Flowers in the Garden of Life," "Your Point Is?" One pillow has fallen under the big square coffee table. I'll pull it out and put it on the couch. There.

I mustn't trip over the boxes on the floor. Fragile items

are contained in them. Linda got exasperated and started taking the decorations off the Christmas tree. I know what I'll do. I won't walk anymore. I'll float.

Here is the dining room. The curtains are open and the backyard is dark. Bars of light appear between the slats of the back fence when a car passes on the highway, like the moving pattern on the top of a jukebox. Here is the kitchen. An oil painting of a chicken, done by one of Mom's friends at Brooksbie, looks friendly in the daytime but evil now. Its hard chicken eyes are the brightest spot in the room. They're the kind of eyes that follow you. Bad chicken! Why does it have to look so real?

I float along the hallway with its wall-to-wall carpet. It was a good idea, putting carpet here, so if you were walking, and someone else were sleeping, you wouldn't wake them up. Linda's room. Linda is sleeping, of course. She sleeps under a Garfield comforter, holding a plush Garfield, and beneath a photo collage of all the mad times she's had with her shadow, Jodie. Garfield is her night watchman.

The big bathroom has a shower curtain with a graphic design of black-and-white blocks. No one has cleaned the tub for a while. Who can be bothered? Someone should step up for that. Not me. People always end up doing the

things that are most important. If it were important, some-one would surely do it. Ergo, it is not important. Here is the laundry hamper. It's full. We've gotten accustomed to seeing one another in a lot of the same clothes over and over again. I don't even remember what I have in there. It will be exciting to find out, when that day comes. It will be like getting new clothes.

Now I'm at the door to my parents' room. The door is open a bit, not latched. I won't make a sound. Should I go in, or leave them to their privacy? I'll go in, just to check. I push against the door with all the purchase I can get in my floating state. My back rubs against the ceiling. There is their bed, with piles of clothes on the floor on either side. There is their bathroom, the sink piled up with laxatives and other things I don't want to know about. And there they are: two parents, joined at the hand.

Their hands meet with the palms crossed, the elbows bent, so the two arms form one W. Mom's arm is bare—she's wearing a sleeveless nightgown. Dad's arm is in a pajama sleeve with a frayed cuff. Their faces are sixteen inches apart.

Dad's age has seemed to change while he's been sick. Sometimes he seems old. Other times he seems young.

Right now he's young, listening to Mom. (It's so serious in here!) His profile doesn't look adult. His nose is short, and his upper lip rises in an expectant way. He reminds me of someone, but I don't know who. A light from the bedside table on the right, an old porcelain one of Grandma's with a rose painted on it, is reflected in Dad's forehead. Now I know who it is—*me*. He looks just like me when I had my silhouette done out of black paper when I was ten. When did he start to look like me, instead of me looking like him?

On the left is a clock radio. When each minute goes by, two flaps that make up the numerals break apart and recombine to make up a new number. Right now it says 12:21. Between 12:21 and 12:22, eight cars go by on the highway behind the house.

Mom and Dad stare into one another's eyes. Three times the minute changes. Twenty-six cars go by on the highway. Mom's lips move. At first, her having spoken is so unexpected that it's difficult to realize what she's said: "Magnolia."

Dad moistens his lips. He swallows, and his forehead tightens for a second, which makes the shiny spot jump almost to his hairline, then back down again. A car door

slams in a driveway a few houses down the hill. The lamp goes "tink" for no reason, in that way electrical appliances sometimes do.

"Marigold." Where did that come from? From Dad. His lips are still moving. He squeezes Mom's hand, like a twitch, and then relaxes. He swallows again.

Mom stares. It seems to be a new stare, more forceful, lower and more insistent, even though she hasn't moved. Maybe the depth and hypnotic quality of her eyes changed.

"Narcissus," Mom has said. Mom's voice is a city voice. She's having him name a flower for every letter of the alphabet. I didn't know they played this game. I didn't know Mom had games of her own, apart from the ones I play with Dad. I thought I knew everything about these people.

The numbers on the clock turn over again. Why hasn't Dad answered? Nasturtium would be a good answer. A pattern of lilies, in the sheets, surrounds their heads. Lines of dust gather in the creases of the folding closet door. I would definitely go with nasturtium.

A motorcycle spits by on the highway, and the corners of Dad's mouth jump. He can't help it. The clock says 12:32. Mom stares.

Why hasn't he said nasturtium? I want to get between them and shake things up.

"Narcissus," he says.

Mom doesn't take her eyes from his. A tendon stands out on the side of her wrist.

"I already said narcissus," she says.

Dad moistens his lips again. "Okay," he says. He waits. Mom waits. Oh, no. I think I fell asleep for a fractosecond. I am literally falling down on the job here. Which one had Mom said, nasturtium or narcissus? Well, whichever one it was, why doesn't Dad say the other one?

Mom's hand slowly releases its grip on Dad's. Their hands make a sucking sound as they pull apart.

Mom rolls over. She's facing the ceiling. She's facing *me*. She closes her eyes, hiding the tiredness that Dad isn't meant to see.

I'm falling again. It's 12:47. For this minute at least, everyone in the house is asleep.

Occupational therapy keeps both Dad and me busy after school, but I can't help feeling discouraged. When we watch *Painting with the Light-Teacher* at four p.m., Dad keeps saying, "How does he do that?" I selected the show because it is wholesome, educational, nonviolent, etc., but it is *way* below Dad's level as an artist. In fact, he always laughed at the show before, calling the Light-Teacher a gimmicky charlatan.

I see now that by taking my trip to Boston, I shot myself in the foot. Because now that Linda has to stay home out of fairness to me, Jodie is always here, the three of us plus Dad, and I am in charge of the household, the prisoner of my night of freedom.

BARRETTE

"I'm tired of the food you serve here, Billy," Jodie says. She is helping Linda pick the seeds out of a pomegranate.

"We don't 'serve' anything here. This isn't a restaurant."

"Do you like pizza, Mr. Morrison?" she calls into the next room.

"Yes."

"Why don't you get him a pizza?"

"Because he can't eat pizza right now, and he isn't hungry, anyway."

"Well, all right," Dad says.

"Dad, since when have you felt hungry? Jodie, didn't Linda tell you he's on a restricted diet?"

"Why?" Jodie asks. "He already looks awfully skinny to me."

"I can't explain the whole thing to you. It's very complex, and it involves enzymes and things like that. My mother can tell you."

"It's almost time for your wafts, Dad," Linda says. She puts the bowl containing the pomegranate and its seeds aside. She takes a lemon half out of the refrigerator and peels off the plastic wrap.

"What's a waft?" Jodie asks.

"It's a special technique I use, where I squeeze a lemon under his nose and the oil from the lemon's skin perks up his olfactory bulb."

"Where is the bulb? Right there in his nose?"

"No, in his brain. So it makes his brain work better."

"Do you really think it helps?" Jodie asks, as they both hover over Dad in the living room.

"See? Squeeze, stimulate. And that makes his brain better."

"I can't believe something like that could really work."

"Maybe I'll let you try it sometime after I show you the proper technique."

"I don't know if I want to."

I'm waiting next to Dad with the newspaper that was just delivered, so we can start the crossword puzzle.

"Why are you here again, Jodie?" I ask.

"What do you mean?" A piece of hair with a purple barrette falls in front of Jodie's eyes, and she bats it back against her freckles.

"You were here yesterday, too. Don't you have anywhere else to go?"

"I wanted to come over and help Linda."

"Help her with what? She doesn't even do anything other than juice a lemon once in a while. I'm the one with all the responsibility here."

"You don't seem to me like you're doing all that much."

"I am. I have a very ambitious program going on here."

"I didn't mean to upset you, Billy."

"I'm not upset. We just have stuff to do right now. Just keep your opinions to yourself, okay?"

CITRUS CITY

Linda has gotten the idea that Dad would benefit more from constant stimulation of his olfactory bulb than from separate wafts of lemon oil or fresh lemon, so she comes home with a small lemon candle from the Dollar Store, which she and Jodie light in the living room near where Dad and I are playing cards.

"No you don't," I say.

"No I don't what?"

"Somebody's going to knock that over and cause a fire. Candles are for two things, Linda: churches and birthdays. Do you see either of those in this living room?"

"Stop trying to be such a big boss."

"Why do you think I have to be home day in, day out? Because I'm the only one with any sense around here. So put the candle out." I look at Dad's hand. He has three threes, and if he gets a fourth one he might be able to win. I try to remember how long ago one of us turned over a three.

"It won't fall over. It's in a votive glass. And what about Dad? He has lots of sense."

"That's not what I meant, and you know it. Now put the candle out, and don't start me arguing in front of Dad. It just upsets him."

"Dad's doing better. He slept for two hours last night. That's because of my upping the lemons." She balls up the wrapper from the candle and puts it in the pocket of Grandpa's overalls.

"Why do you two always fight so much?" Jodie asks.

Dad gets up and starts pacing again. "That's a good question," he says.

"Always?" I say. "Oh, I thought you were saying your own name, Always. Because you're Always Here!"

"Why are you getting so angry again?"

"Look, Jodie, we're under a lot of stress in this house. I don't think you realize that we have some very serious problems going on with my father's health. I don't know if I need to talk to your mother or what I need to do, but we have to arrange for you to not be here so often."

"I like having her here," Linda says. "She makes me feel better."

I put away the cards and go into the den to see what's

on TV. Dad stops pacing when he sees Michelle Kwan in a figure-skating competition. So the four of us watch that with the sound off. Jodie says Michelle is like a soul dancing. I like Michelle's triumphant yet humble openmouthed smile.

TREATMENT REPORT: DAY 69

Mom has been using jumbo shrimp as the seafood choice, and Dad is happy that something he likes, something he used to order when we went to a restaurant, is on the program. Mom has been cooking the shrimp with extra garlic, per E. Sutter, and we all eat the shells and the tails, too.

Last night Dad had an unbelievable sleep performance of four hours. This means he is finally getting better. I spent all day in school wondering what's causing this improvement, so we can build on it. Could it be Michelle? The shrimp? The calisthenics? Could the candle really be doing something? I've noticed that Dad may be getting bored by the affirmations, so maybe I should pick a single really good one. "We are one"?

After weeks of feeling sleepy in school, I'm beginning to feel more alert. Linda and I both believe that the special foods are improving our brain function.

We did it. We've turned it around.

Dad has stopped eating shrimp because he says they remind him of curled-up babies. Mom offered him sardines instead, but he says they look like corpses stacked up in a concentration camp. The past couple of days he has eaten only a forkful or two of four of the brain foods, so he also has to take vitamins and supplements in pill form. But then, once in a while, he gets a craving for nuts.

Linda is gloating. Yesterday she ramped up the aromatherapy by going from one candle to two, each the size of a drinking glass. Then a girl at school who normally doesn't talk to me asked, "Bob, why are you wearing insect repellent in the winter?" When I asked Mom if we could stop using the candles some of the time, she said no. But are they doing any good? Is Mom backing Linda up only to make Linda feel she's contributing something?

Dad was awake the past two nights and very agitated. Mom stays up as long as she can but sometimes asks me

to take over at two or three a.m. so she can nap. I walk Dad around the house, sometimes saying affirmations at the same time. I no longer can be sure if anything's helping, but I don't know if I should say anything to Mom. Maybe it would make more sense to continue as we are for a few more days, just in case the situation breaks. When Dad started on meds, the doctor said the chemicals had to build up in his system. Maybe it's the same with the food, the light, and the other cures.

"What's all this?"

"We're mashing up leaves."

"Why."

"We're going to make paper."

So this is Linda's revenge. Shredded brown stuff, pulpy and stemmy, lies in a puddle of tea-colored water in the bathtub. Linda is using the potato masher, and Jodie has the wooden thing you use to pound meat—a mallet, I guess it's called.

"Get this mess out of here. I'm not running a day-care service, you know."

"This isn't a mess," Linda says. "It's a worthwhile endeavor."

"You never have any fun," Jodie says. "Is that why you're mad?"

"No, it's because every time I open a door, you're behind it."

"Do you want to make paper with us?"

Mom had to go in for a special meeting at her office yesterday morning. Pudge was pressuring her to name a date when "all this" would be over and things at Brooksbie would get back to normal. I had to wait for Marty to show up at the house before I could leave for school. Then Mom was enraged at my allowing Dad to sit in front of the light box, between my watch and Marty's watch, a total of two hours. She said he will have to skip the light box for a few days because she thinks it's dangerous. I said I thought that was a mistake, even though deep down I'm not sure it's doing any good. And of course we had to pretend everything was okay, because we were talking in front of Dad.

When I managed to get Mom out of the room, I told her that I couldn't meet my family obligations if Jodie was going to be over all the time, that I would have to be paid for babysitting. "I'll take care of Dad," I said. "I'll even take care of Linda. But I won't take care of Jodie."

Dad went back on the light box today, starting small with ten minutes. I could have pushed to do more, but oh, well. He skipped it entirely for a few days because Mom thought he had had a light box overdose. He seems tired, so we're scaling back on both the affirmations and the calisthenics.

Most days he has been eating just a few forkfuls of the brain foods and maybe some nuts and a yogurt. But Mom thinks it's important for him to get his seafood component so his brain functioning will improve. She offered him either tuna salad or crabmeat salad, but he wouldn't eat it. Then she asked if he would eat lobster if she bought it, but he said no, so she isn't spending the money. He lost a lot of weight last week. Would it be better for him to eat just anything to keep his strength up (as Jodie originally said)?

I told Linda I couldn't stand the candles anymore and demanded that she remove them. Complained about it to Mom, who sided with L.

POISSON/POISON

At dinner Linda and I are sitting at the table, eating our cooked salad. Dad has eaten only a small bowl of strawberries and is standing behind his chair. Jodie is miraculously absent.

"That's not enough," Mom tells him. "Remember? You have to have some seafood every day."

"I can't eat any more," Dad says. "I'm full."

She already told him yesterday that if he doesn't eat seafood he will have to take a drink of fish oil. She rustles a paper bag on the counter and comes back with a small cocktail glass.

"You have to drink this," Mom says.

"Does it taste bad?" Dad asks.

"No," Mom says, and she takes a sip from it. "Look, I'm doing it." Then she starts to cry.

"Are you lying to me, Adele?" Dad asks her.

"No," she says, and she starts crying again.

Then she leaves the glass on the table and goes to her room to get ready for bed. I pick up the glass. Linda and I both sniff it. It smells terrible. Mom stays in her room with the door closed, Dad is agitated, and I walk him around all night.

A DISTANT SHORE

A mouthful of steak-and-cheese challenges my jaw. The cheese forms a white glaze over knots of shaved meat. Bubbles of fat pop against the roof of my mouth. My mandibles ache. This is not a dream.

I whisk inadequate napkins one after the other from a dispenser to absorb the grease. "Another one?" Gordy asks.

I say no, still chewing, and chase the meat with black cherry soda that rinses clean and dry, almost salty.

Gordy finishes his soda, and the door of the sandwich shop pulls closed behind us on a spring. Sand washes across the threshold and rubs the soles of my sneakers.

"I'll pay you back sometime."

Gordy shrugs. "Forget it."

We walk down the road to a beach. A recent sleetstorm has left pockmarks in the sand, and the tide has gone out, leaving patterns like dragged hands in the wet areas, Vs within Vs within Vs. Our shadows walk with us dully.

Everything on this beach seems humanish to me. The moon, already visible at four p.m., resembles a fingernail clipping, and the fallen shreds of curly brown and black seaweed are snips from a giant's beard.

"What a great place." The beach is right near Gordy's house. It might even be a private beach. Once again it strikes me that everything about Gordy seems excellent. He's one of those preppy, well-rounded types and will probably be way more successful than me.

"Do your parents have a boat?" I ask.

"My dad has a modified lobster boat. It's in the marina for the winter."

Crap. I said "your parents" instead of "your father."

"We go out fishing for the weekend once in a while. Maybe you'd like to go with us sometime?"

On the spectrum of moronic things to say, asking about someone's dead parent as if they are still living is probably at the far end. How could I do this? Gordy's mother died shortly after they moved to town, of cystic fibrosis. People were talking about him when they first got here, because when his mother brought him in to register for school, she kept spitting blood into a handkerchief, right in the administrative office.

"Sorry. I forgot about your mom. Stupid."

"That's okay. It's not as bad anymore. She spent the whole last year talking to me about what to expect. That part was harder than it is now."

Then he surprises me by tossing an imaginary Frisbee. I catch the Frisbee and set the figures in my mind on it—the mother and father, little kitchen figures, diorama-like. I set them on it and whirl them out to sea, on their problem-plate, their Thought-Frisbee.

I walked out again! I walked out and left Linda in charge! Linda and Jodie are in charge of Dad. If Lucky Linda knows so much about what he needs, and Jodie is so indispensable, they will do a fine job taking care of him. I don't know whether Linda will tell Mom or not.

A barge heading into the harbor makes an engining thrum that carries. Gordy and I race to the end of the beach, where a copper-colored granite shelf is ideal for sitting but sends cold through the seat of my pants. At our backs is a stone wall. Above it, trees have twisted into tough survivalist shapes.

Gordy pulls a knit cap from his coat pocket. "Can you picture me out here this summer, maybe on the Fourth of July, with Brenda Mason or some other girl? I would have

a blanket all spread out, maybe a portable grill. We'd be watching the fireworks over the harbor. You could come out too. Maybe it could be a double date. Who would you bring?"

Out on the water, the barge has cut its motor and a tugboat aligns itself behind it.

Is there anyone I can want? The prettiest girl I know is Lisa Melman, but she's in Linda's grade, and anyway, she's not as nice as her mother.

"I'm trying not to think too much about that stuff now. I'm trying to stay—I can't think of a better word—pure."

"Pure with girls?" Gordy asks.

"No, pure with thinking about only one thing at a time."

The tugboat, pushing, and the barge, gliding, are little and big, like the two-space and the five-space boats in the Battleship game. Concrete thoughts of chores to be done at home soften and rise. Mists, wishes, smoke signals. *I'm not there. I'm here now.* I got away.

"How is your dad, by the way?"

What to say? I brush the powdery sand into arcs with one hand.

"He's much better."

"That's great."

"What was wrong with him, anyway?"

"He was depressed."

"That must have been rough. He seems like a great guy."

"He really is."

"Glad to know he's better, then."

I rub my palms together slowly and watch the grains fall. "It takes a while to get better in a really obvious way that you would see by looking at him or talking to him, but things are getting better . . . underneath. It's more like an improvement in a different layer. An unconscious or subconscious layer."

"The human mind is fascinating, isn't it?" Gordy says. "I've always wondered about stuff like that."

"He'll probably be fully recovered soon. Maybe you can come by the house again."

"That would be great."

We're both lying back now, watching scuds of clouds move in to smother the moon.

"Do you want to get an ice cream or anything?"

"No, thanks. The sandwiches were enough. I should go home soon. I left without charging my headlight."

An arm of land reaches around the harbor. Across the water from us is a castle built by an eccentric inventor. It

contains all kinds of things he lifted from humble little towns in Europe. A pipe organ, a reflecting pool of blue tile, even the coffin of a young girl. At the edge of the horizon, lights fall slowly from the sky—not shooting stars, but airplanes making their descent into Logan.

"Right after my mom died," Gordy says, "I would sit and look out here. Not toward Boston, but past it, where you could just keep going. I would try to convince myself that if I went far enough there was a place where we could all still be together."

"I know."

The sky darkens, but we lie on the rock like sacrifices. Then rain comes, hitting our faces like a metaphor.

TREATMENT REPORT: DAY 77

Dad refused to take his vitamins and supplements because he thought they might be unsafe. Mom was upset that he didn't trust her, and she is still getting over the fish oil incident. She bought some nutrient milkshakes in small cans, and Dad agreed to drink one.

A THREAT

Mom is at the supermarket. I tell Linda that the lemon candles are driving me berserk and that if she does not remove them I will tear a hole in her plush Garfield and stuff the candles inside. We're in her room, and I'm holding the Garfield and a pair of scissors. She leaps. We scuffle (quietly). We stop scuffling as Dad shuffles by.

Linda looks in a book Mom bought and calls Jodie, who comes over with two new lavender candles from the drugstore, each the size of a coffee can. Linda explains to Jodie the healing properties of the new candle scent.

I tell her the new candles are perfumey, cloying, and sickly sweet and I am sure Dad would feel the same, but she says too bad. She threatened two days ago to tell Mom about my leaving the house but has not done so yet. Jodie says I am a bad brother. It's obvious from Mom's expression when she gets home that she's noticed the new candles, but she doesn't say anything.

TREATMENT REPORT: DAY 81

Yesterday Dad ate nothing but two nutrient shakes and his pomegranate seeds. He slept well for a couple of hours, though.

Then tonight, Dad got a craving for vanilla ice cream, possibly stimulated by his recent experience with fake milkshakes.

"You really want ice cream?" Mom said. "I guess it's all right, but I want you to have fruit and nuts with it." She looked happy.

Linda and Jodie walked down to the nearby ice-cream place and brought back a quart of vanilla and some bananas and walnuts. Dad ate one and a half bowls, and Jodie commented that we looked just like a normal family. Dad actually smiled at Jodie. Mom smiled a lot then and danced Dad around the living room during calisthenics. Then Linda installed a third lavender candle in the bathroom, and no amount of towel-rubbing can get the stench off my body.

Why did Dad sleep for two hours last night? No one knows.

Why did he smile and eat ice cream? No one knows.

Do you hear that sound? It's the treatment team whistling in the dark.

A SYMBIOTIC RELATIONSHIP

Linda and Jodie have taken up calligraphy and are leaving ink everywhere. They are trying to get Dad to join them, even though occupational therapy is my treatment area.

"Linda," I tell her right in front of her friend, "Jodie has a home. It would be okay to leave her there sometimes."

The three of us were supposed to be the treatment team, Mom said. We were going to take care of Dad as a family. So why *is* she always here? Jodie seems to have no existence outside of being my sister's friend. It's like Linda is a slide projector and Jodie is a slide. If Linda were to die suddenly, Jodie would die at the same instant, of the same illness. Even if they were on opposite sides of the world.

Yesterday Dad had one nutrient shake and a dish of ice cream, and M. told him no more ice cream until he ate some of his brain foods, but then she let him have another bowl because he looked so skinny.

Then he had another bad night, so we took turns staying up with him. Linda did a couple of hours, and I'm sure Jodie would have too if she'd been allowed to stay. Mom kept asking him questions. Wasn't he feeling good the day before? What went wrong? Of course he can't answer this. What's he going to say?

BREWING

Dad has had another bad night and day. At suppertime, Mom starts fixing the cooked salad and navy beans while Dad paces the other end of the house.

"Is Jodie gone? Is Linda ready for dinner?" she asks.

"I don't know." Reading some additional library info in the living room, I rattle the photocopies loudly so she'll know she's interrupted me.

"Well, could you call her?"

"I'll call her in a few minutes. I just want to finish this article."

"Oh, you're no help," she says over the room divider.

I put my article down and go into the kitchen. "I'm no help?" I repeat.

"Go on. Go back to what you were doing. I'll call her myself." She waves a pot holder dismissively.

"Linda!" I shout without leaving the kitchen. "Supper!"

"Billy."

I put my hands in my pockets and raise my shoulders. "You just said I was no help. What exactly did you mean by that?"

"I didn't mean anything. I'm tired, okay?"

"No help with Dad? I'm no help with Dad?"

"Just forget it." Mom turns down the heat under the bean pot, then removes the jar of brewer's yeast from the cabinet and checks the label.

"What other help do you have? I'm it. I'm the help."

"I'm going to have to try something else," she says in a low voice. "I'll look in my books again after supper. I don't understand why he has good days and bad days, but overall—so far, anyway—he's not getting any better."

Linda comes into the kitchen and opens the silverware drawer to start setting the table. "Have you thought about starting Dad on yoga, Mom? Jodie's mother says it's very centering."

"That sounds worthwhile, Linda. Can you find out a little more about it?"

"Of course he's not any better!" I snap. "He's not getting better because we keep changing the treatments!"

My voice fills our small house. Dad comes in from his bedroom.

"Son . . . ," he begins, laying his hand on my arm.

"We can't start him on yoga now! There are already too many variables! How are we going to know what's working?"

"Too many variables?" Mom repeats.

"Variables! They're the things that change! Constants are the things that stay the same! You keep the constants the same and then you test the variables! You don't start five or six treatments at once and have them all over-lapping! You use the scientific method! You only test one variable at a time! You pick one and you test it!"

"You don't have to explain the scientific method. I know what variables are. You don't have to explain anything to me." Mom clutches the yeast jar with both hands, like a little kid. "I thought we decided it would be best to try everything we could."

"Please don't argue," Dad says, looking at his hands, flexing them.

"Well, obviously it's not best! We're not accomplishing anything! We have to start over, and this time use the sci-entific method! Just start all over, from scratch, and try the treatments one at a time."

Linda dumps the utensils in a tangle on the table. "Can't

you keep your voice down, Billy? Look how upset Dad is getting."

"But we will have lost all these weeks," Mom says.

"You can't look at it that way. If you really cared about Dad you would take what I'm saying seriously."

"Take it seriously!" Mom snaps. "I'm not taking this seriously?"

"Things were getting better, Billy," Linda says. "They were. We just have to figure out why. We just have to figure out what to do next. Why don't you lighten up on Mom—she's really stressed."

Dad goes to the stove and puts one arm around Mom.

"Son," he orders faintly, "apologize to your mother." He's trying to be the old peacemaker Dad, but it comes off like an echo of an echo. A photocopy of a photocopy.

"But I'm right, Dad," I plead. "You know I'm right."

Mom's face looks soft and somehow dented.

"Apologize to your mother, Billy."

"I'm sorry."

"You don't sound very sorry."

"Say it like you mean it," Mom says.

"No."

"I'm sorry to you, Dad." I touch his arm briefly, the

red hairs there that I also have. "I'm just not that sorry to Mom."

"I can't take this," says Dad. He leaves the kitchen to pace and rub his arms.

I go to my room and throw on my coat and shoes. I wheel Triumph across the living-room carpet. I leave a nice thick line of soil and sand.

"Can I come in?"

"Sure. *Mi casa* . . . Wow. You don't look good," Gordy says.

He doesn't look good either. He's wearing sweats and white socks, and his face seems puffy and strange. Through the doorway comes the music of a brass band, turned up to a high volume.

"I'm sorry. Is this a bad time to stop by?"

"No, it's okay. I'd just as soon not sit around by myself." He steps aside and turns down the stereo until it is merely loud. I drop onto the couch with my coat on. Inside my chest, something thin and gray and hollow as a used light-bulb is finally breaking.

"I hate to repeat myself, but you really don't look good," Gordy repeats. "When was the last time you got any sleep?"

"He's not getting any better."

"He's not? But you thought he was, didn't you?"

"Well, he's not." I press both sets of fingertips into my closed eyes.

"You don't look right. Do you need something to eat?"

"No. In fact, I might prefer to throw up."

Gordy goes into the kitchen and comes back with a bottle of blue Gatorade and two of the largest-size beef jerky sticks.

"Here." He opens my left hand and slaps a sausage stick into it. "Bathroom's down there." He points along a hall.

I let the hand drop into my lap. Gordy peels the wrapper halfway and slaps it into my palm again. "Take at least a few bites. When you're done eating, you can stretch out and take a nap on the couch."

"Where's your dad?"

"He's working. He usually is. Don't worry, you're not disturbing anything."

"I can't sleep now," I tell him. "I shouldn't even stay."

"Do your parents know where you are? Do you want me to call them?"

"No, don't do that. Let them wonder. Let them wonder where I am." I picture Mom, that tiny faraway holographic Mom, getting along without me. We could abandon one another.

"I'll tell them you're staying here for a few hours."

"No, I won't stay." I tear off a bit of the leathery jerky. "I just needed to get out for a while."

Gordy opens a bottle of blue Gatorade for himself. "So your dad isn't any better?"

"No."

"Is he worse?"

"He might be."

"Is there anything I can do?"

"I don't know what the next step should be. If I knew, I would do it myself."

Once I've finished both jerky sticks and drunk some of the Gatorade, Gordy brings me a pillow and a New England Patriots blanket. I push my sneakers off toe to heel. The room is painted dark green, with a grandfather clock and glass-front cases filled with old books. On the stereo, a solitary drum taps like a heartbeat. After a signal from the cornet, the band begins "Just a Closer Walk with Thee." But the sound is slow, screeching, and loopy, not like church music, from any church I've been to at least. It sounds drunk and dizzy, like the soundtrack of an ancient cartoon. The musicians veer off in different directions with no unison in pitch or timing. Like some grief has set them loose and cursed them to wander.

When I close my eyes, pictures are there, of a brass band in black suits, a hole in the ground with my mother and Linda standing beside it. Where am I? I'm playing in the band. But I won't cry. I won't cry yet.

When I open my eyes again, the sad music is over. I sit up and push the blankets aside. The band is playing "Oh, Lady, Be Good," swingy and brash with curlicues of improvisation. Gordy is waiting in the doorway, having changed into khakis and a sweater.

"How long did I sleep?" I ask him.

"About an hour. Let's go do something."

"I should get home."

"Have you done anything remotely fun since Boston?"

"Fun? *No comprende* 'fun.'" I dig under the blanket for my coat. "I need to get home. Thanks for the break."

"Let's go to the arcade for an hour." He hands me the cell phone. "You can call your parents and tell them where you're going."

"Nope. Thanks."

"Too bad—I'm kidnapping you," Gordy says, getting his parka from the hall closet. "Call the cops if you want to. We're going."

We walk half a mile along the shoreline. The low tide

smells like the fish oil Mom tried to give Dad. The sky hangs cold and black, fingered with gray where clouds have been.

The arcade is a creaky wooden building that once had a carousel, nickelodeons, and other little-kid amusements. My parents had brought me here to play Skee-Ball, watch cartoons in a machine for a nickel, or pay a puppet fortune-teller a dime to wave her arms over a crystal ball and spit out my fortune. After a while someone caught on that the whole operation was too cheap. They sold the old amusements and put in carpeting and overhead TVs and much newer games that cost fifty cents or a dollar. I begged and begged my parents to take me to the place they now called A Big Waste of Money.

Gordy slides ten dollars into a change machine. He dips his hand twice into the mouthful of quarters and hands me some. The air is thick with electronic shooting sounds— *voot, voot*—and the voices of synthetic race announcers. Bells mark a hundred microsuccesses, important in the moment but quickly forgotten.

Gordy stacks quarters on the counter to reserve a turn on the Dethbord, a skateboard simulator that has a safety bar on four sides and orange warnings all over it. We watch the

current player, a boy younger than us, nearly fall over as the board approaches, at high speed, a pit of flames. He seems surprised when the skateboard on the video screen starts to fall away from his feet, first skidding forward without him, then twirling downward like something running down a drain, getting smaller and smaller. He collapses against the handrail. Heartbreaking.

"Hunker down!" Gordy shouts to him. "Reach for the board!"

I drop two quarters into a game that involves tossing small plush animals—possibly prizes left over from the old arcade—into the gullet of an animatronic figure that looks sort of like a man but is covered with hair and has scary green eyes. The monster breaks through a gate toward me, bellowing, as soon as my second quarter lands in the coin-box. I toss a buck-toothed beaver in a construction hat, then a brown teddy bear with a patchwork heart, and then a yellow kitten in a square-dancing dress. The animation is so lifelike that you can see muscles moving under the monster's skin, and each time a cute little animal goes down the monster's throat, the bellows are interspersed with a high-pitched scream like a baby falling out a window, and the panicky shouts of helpless townspeople.

By the third round of the game I feel jumpy and robotic. The hundred points per cute stuffed animal makes me feel guilty, but I don't want the monster to bellow all the way down his platform to me. So I lob and lob, reacting only to the advancing monster and the beeps of the electronic scoreboard, blocking out the pathetic cries of the little prizes: 6100, 6200—*Eeee! Eeee!* Then I hear Gordy hollering. I wonder, is he in trouble too? I lob a pink snail with a rainbow-striped shell and big sunglasses, then glance over my shoulder until I see him, attracting a crowd around his stint on the skateboard. Turning back to my game, I see Mitchell at the pinball machines, with Andy.

Mitchell has been lobbying to come over, or to have me to his house, for the past two and a half months. "I don't know what you did to get grounded on this scale," he said a few days ago, "but I hope it was fun." That was his parting shot, I guess, since he has stopped asking.

Now Andy notices me, but Mitchell hasn't. I reach into the bin of small plush animals while watching Mitchell over my shoulder, and the bin feels empty. I see that the monster is only two feet away; if I don't weave or duck he could graze me with the horrible black nails on his subhuman, flailing hands. Having missed the last few throws, I've been

punished with an empty bin. My score disappears and an electronic display flashes: WHAT WILL YOU DO NOW?

I leave my game to go and yank on Gordy's jacket. He has begun another round on the skateboard, several feet above a cheering crowd of girls, kiddies, and moms.

"We have to go!" I tell him. "It's late!"

Gordy turns his head for a second. "Not now! I'm in the Seventh Circle!"

Across the room, Andy is telling Mitchell something and pointing toward the plush-animal game. Mitchell starts looking around.

"I'm going now, with or without you."

Gordy hops down. He picks one little kid from the crowd.

"You, little fella. You can finish this game," he tells the boy.

"You mean it?"

"I'm going!" I tell Gordy. I break into a run.

We're almost out of the arcade, but Gordy looks back at the last moment. "Hey. Did you see who's here?"

"Wait a minute, you guys," Andy calls out.

They catch up to us between the customer service stand and the lost children booth.

"Oh, hey, Gordy, Morrison," Mitchell says. "Morrison, I thought you weren't allowed out except to go to school. I thought you were grounded or something."

"Hi, Mitchell. How was your score?"

"The hell with that, okay? You said you weren't allowed out. I've known you since birth, practically. You could just tell me if you didn't feel like getting together."

"I'm having some problems, okay? Some personal problems. I can't really talk about it right now."

"Then why are you here?"

"I made him come with me," Gordy says. "I kidnapped him. Really."

"Why can't you leave the house?"

"All I can tell you is, any time I'm not at home, I feel sort of sick and lousy."

"That doesn't sound good," Andy says. "Are you getting that disease where people are afraid to leave their houses? I think it's called acrophobia."

"Agoraphobia," Mitchell corrects him, keeping his eyes on me. "Well, don't expect me to ask you to do anything again. Don't hold your breath about hearing from me, period."

"It's my fault," Gordy says as we walk past the beach

again. "I shouldn't have pushed you into it. I thought you might feel better if you had a change of location. When my mom was sick, I always got an energy boost if I went out once in a while."

Back at Gordy's, I retrieve Triumph from a stone archway leading to the front steps. It's one of the few times I've left the bike without the Kryptonite lock, and I have to make sure I don't do this again. Starting out, my headlamp is weak too—the battery could get permanently drained. I can't let this happen again, that I stop thinking and just let things go. If I can't manage myself, how can I help anyone else?

Must get home, must get home, I chant. I burst into a sprint at the bottom of our hill. The sound of my wheels brings Mom and Dad to the picture window. They're already in their bathrobes. Their silhouettes are dark against the bright glass, like two lighthouses in negative, and I open the door.

Mom tried to reprimand me for running out like that, but since she had been home at the moment and I had no specific responsibilities at the time, her complaint slid through my head without gaining traction.

"But you really upset your father," she said. She said it's disturbing for Dad to hear us fighting with one another, and we all have to be really careful not to argue in front of him.

A FRIENDLY VISIT

The doorbell rings and it's June. Not the month of June, but June from Dad's office.

"Hi, sweetie!" June says when Mom opens the door. "How are things?"

Mom looks like someone has squeezed three drops of water inside the back of her collar with an eyedropper. June begins to reach toward Mom for a hug, then, thinking better of it, puts one hand back on the doorknob. She's carrying a paper cone of white carnations.

"I'm sorry, June," Mom says, "but this isn't a good time. I was just doing the dishes."

"Oh, do you want some help?" June asks. "I'll do anything you haven't had time to do, including wiping out unidentifiable green liquefied substances that may have congealed on your refrigerator shelves. Just toss me a pair of rubber gloves and put me to work."

"Hello, Mrs. Melman." June is wearing a sweater and

pants in the palest shade of pink, the color of rose petals.

"Billy, honey, are you doing all right?"

"Not too bad. I guess we're all a little tired and worn out." I feel like collapsing against her and breathing in those roses.

"Who is it?" Dad asks from the bedroom.

"It's June!" June sings over Mom's head, at the very moment that Mom mutters, "It's June" at the lowest end of her register, so the two of them sound like a woman and a man performing a duet.

Dad comes into the living room.

"Hi, Bill," June says softly. She intertwines her free hand in Dad's and hangs there with him for a minute, standing with her head down the same way he does. "Everyone says hello. They are counting the days until your return. We don't have anyone to play 'Guess That Opera' with us anymore. It's a very quiet place these days."

She turns to Mom. "May I put these in water, Adele?"

"I'll do it." Mom walks briskly to June and removes the carnations from her hand.

"Let's sit down for a minute, Bill, and I'll bore you with all the current office problems. The whole sorry state of things. You know, Adele, I'd be glad to cover for a while if

you need a break. Why don't you take a rest, go out and see a movie or something, and I'll stay here? Lisa's at a friend's house, but I can have her get dropped off here when she's done. Is Linda home? The bunch of us will order Chinese or something."

Despite my reluctance to leave Mrs. Melman, I go into the kitchen to see what Mom wants to do. Filling a vase with water, Mom stares stonily out the kitchen window at the darkened backyard. "Typical, typical June," she says to me in a low voice. "No sense of the situation. I can't believe she didn't call first." Another drop rolls down Mom's spine.

Mom returns to the living room with the vase. Her back is rigid.

"June," she says finally. "Have you noticed that Bill is not quite himself? Don't you see that he's not behaving as usual? Do you even notice that you're talking to him and he's not answering you?"

"I'm sorry, June," Dad says, not meeting her eyes but ruffling the tips of the white carnations in the vase, until the petals are bent and brownish. "That's right. I'm not feeling well."

"That's all right, Bill," June says, still sitting on the

couch beside Dad. "I know you're not well. That's why I'm here. Adele, I didn't stop by expecting anyone to entertain me. I didn't expect a big cocktail party when I showed up unannounced. I didn't expect a lot of laughs. Just a short, pleasant visit, to check up on you and see if you need anything, to say everyone at Liberty Fixtures is thinking of you two. Today I entertain you; another day, when I need entertaining, you'll entertain me, right? That's how it goes. That's a corny old practice that some call friendship."

"June—Mrs. Melman," I interrupt. I'm standing in the living room near Dad. Mom and I thought we sent a clear signal by not sitting down. "I'm sure Dad appreciates your visit, but we haven't been in that type of situation for a while. We don't want anyone to entertain us."

"We're just trying to get through the day here," Mom adds. "Doing the bare minimum that needs to be done. Getting up in the morning and trying to eat a meal. Putting one foot in front of the other. Trying to make it from Monday to Tuesday to Wednesday."

June stands, smoothing her sweater and slacks. "Are you saying you don't want me to come back? Should I tell everyone at Liberty not to come?"

Mom shrugs—let June draw her own conclusions.

"There's a lot of suffering in this house," she says, so low you can barely hear.

"Why suffer alone?" June says. "Why not share it? I just came from tennis—my brain is flooded with endorphins. I was singing in the car on the way over here. I can stand a little of someone else's suffering."

"Thanks for these, June," Dad whispers, pointing to the flowers.

"Do you want me to phone, is that it? May I visit again if I phone first?"

"We'll see you at the bat mitzvah when the time comes," Mom says to her.

"Adele . . ." June widens her eyes and shakes her head, as if this will help her understand better. "Do you need anything from the supermarket?"

Mom swings her head—no.

"All right, Bill," June says. "I'll see you back at work . . . soon, I hope." Dad is sitting on the couch, nervously ruffling the flowers. June squeezes his shoulder, winks and smiles at me. Then, at the door, she hugs Mom more tightly and for longer than anyone expects.

IN PRIVATE

A man and a woman kneel beside their bed. He wears a tired pair of geometrically printed pajamas, and she wears a white kimono with gray at the edge of the sleeves. Their heads are bowed, their hands folded. She speaks for both of them, in a low, unassuming voice.

Dad has always called himself an agnostic, saying he does not know whether there's a God, and cannot know, but that if there is a God, then that God is most likely an all-knowing, understanding God who will understand why Dad might not believe in Him. That Dad's older child has attempted to cover his bases in the same manner is disappointing to Dad. Because Dad seems to think, or did once think, that the larger the number of believers in the family, the greater the chance that the entire family would be saved. Or if "saved" is too strong a word, the greater the chance that the entire family would be entitled to whatever Treats are in store when this candy store is closed for business—

eternal life being the ultimate, of course, and forgiveness being nothing to sneeze at either. Dad has also hoped that one believer, one very strong believer—Mom—will produce enough salvational energy to carry him to Heaven on her coattails if necessary, so he won't miss anything.

But for now, these philosophical questions must be put aside. For now, Mom must speak for both of them, because over the past two weeks Dad has gradually stopped speaking. He sits with us at mealtimes, still getting up to pace, he watches the painting show with a slight smile on his face, and it's hard to know whether he thinks the show is pleasant or whether he is sneering at the whole endeavor of painting. He might say a few words—"yes," "no," "it's on the nightstand"—but he no longer initiates communication, and he shares nearly nothing about his inner state. He seems to have put himself away, placed himself in another room for safety, while the him we see walks among us, acting convincing enough to distract us from the body in the closet.

Mom stops murmuring and shifts her position, and it looks like she's going to get up. But instead she positions herself behind Dad's shoulder and wraps her arms around him from the back. She clasps her hands around

Dad's hands like a parent helping a child to hold a pencil. She murmurs again with her cheek pressed to the cloth on Dad's back. Either she's showing him how to pray, or she's doing Dad's praying for him, transmitting from another station, faking God into thinking that the prayers are coming from him.

TREATMENT REPORT: DAY 89

Having stayed up with Dad for three nights, Mom doesn't have the energy for leading calisthenics or cooking special meals. Linda has her own interests. Investment in the multi-pronged treatment plan is at an all-time low. With my long-term doubts, I won't push to continue it.

Under the treatment plan we disagreed, but we worked as a team. Now our minds have chosen separate corners, like four strangers dividing the space in an elevator.

What is it that Dad finds when he hides in *his* inner room? That's what I want to know. Maybe it's some sadness that's stuck in there and isn't coming out, like the opposite of music.

THE VOICE

I remember an article I printed out at the library when Mom and I were doing our research. It's by Robert W. Firestone, from a 1986 issue of *Psychotherapy*.

The voice refers to a system of negative thoughts about self and others that is antithetical to self. Our operational definition excludes those thought processes that are concerned with constructive planning, creative thinking, self-appraisal, fantasy, value judgments, and moral considerations. The voice is not an actual hallucination but an identifiable system of thoughts experienced much as an actual voice. The author feels that suicide is the ultimate conclusion of acting upon this negative thought process.

The voice refers to a generalized hostile attitude toward self and as such is the language of an overall self-destructive process. It is an overlay of the

personality that is not natural, but learned or imposed from without. Although the voice may at times be related to one's value system or moral considerations, its statements against the self usually occur after the fact and tend to increase one's self-hatred rather than motivating one to alter behavior in a constructive fashion.

The voice becomes the core of a negative concept of self when it goes unchallenged. The process of "listening" to the voice predisposes an individual toward self-limiting behavior and negative consequences. In other words, people make their behavior correspond to the distorted negative perceptions they have of themselves. . . .

The voice operates along a continuum ranging from mild self-criticisms—thoughts that promote self-denying and self-limiting behavior—to vicious abuse or self-recriminations that are accompanied by intense rage and injunctions to injure oneself. . . .

Our clinical material indicated that a process of actual self-denial on a behavioral level parallels the voice attacks, and that this self-denial can lead to a cycle of serious pathology. As a person gradually

retreats from seeking gratification of self in the real world of object relations, he or she becomes progressively indifferent to life. He or she tends to give up more and more areas of experience that were once found pleasurable and worthwhile. Actual self-harm is much more likely to be acted out after the individual has withdrawn his or her interest and affect from the external world and from an active pursuit of personal goals, a form of "social suicide."

THE CASE OF MIRIAM H.

This sends me back to a chapter from *Mind and Motivation* by Missy Bernard Welton:

> Miriam H. was a vibrant, talkative thirty-five-year-old who was building a successful career in finance. She enjoyed the lifestyle of a single young professional, with a large circle of friends and a variety of regular activities that included cooking classes and swing dancing. Several months before commencing treatment, however, she was passed over for a promotion at work. Shortly afterward, she served as a bridal attendant in the nuptials of a younger sister. These two events caused her to reevaluate her life, mostly in the form of a running internal critique of her own value and abilities. An interview with Miriam showed the progression of her self-critical thoughts:
>
> **Miriam:** I had this speech in my head, like a tape

recording. "You've been deluding yourself all this time. You thought things were okay, and they really weren't...."

It was as if my life were being lived behind a facade or a veil, and someone had lifted the veil off and I could see how ugly everything really was. . . . My happiness was an illusion, and now I was being shown the reality.

MBW: And the reality was . . . ?

Miriam: That I wasn't really valued the way I thought I should be. . . . That I had been kidding myself. People pretended to think a lot of me, but when push came to shove, there were a number of other people that were held up as superior. I was in a lower category, like, a lesser category. Something seemed to tell me that I should try to isolate myself as much as possible, and prepare, because those incidents were just the beginning, and the end was coming soon.

MBW: The end?

Miriam: That the end was coming, and that it would be a relief. That I could hurry it up. I was in control, you know? It was all up to me. And the more I hurried it up, the sooner I would be free.

Could this be why Dad has stopped communicating?

CONVERSATION #1

Me: Do you want anything to eat?

Dad: What?

Me: We're having dinner soon. Mom wants to know if you're hungry. We're having ham and potato salad from the deli. Either? Both?

Dad: No, thanks.

Me: Are you sure?

Dad: Yes.

Jodie: I think he wants to become a vegetarian. Is that it, Mr. Morrison? You want to become a vegetarian?

Me: He said no, Jodie.

Linda: You don't know anything about what Dad wants.

Mom: Please stop arguing.

Me: Hey, Lucky Linda, why don't *you* go eat dinner— animal, vegetable, or mineral? How about rocks? Why don't you try eating a great big rock so you finally shut up?

Dad:	Sssssss.
Linda:	You're upsetting him. See?
Me:	Why don't you just go away?
Me:	Okay, then. You're not hungry. Let me know if you change your mind.
Dad:	All right.
Me:	How about a game?
Dad:	I don't think so. Not right now, anyway.
Me:	Don't you want to do anything?
Dad:	I'll just sit here. Quiet.
Me:	Do you want company?
Dad:	No.
Me:	You like being by yourself?
Dad:	Yes.
Me:	Mind if I stick around?
Dad:	Suit yourself.
Me:	I'll stay, then.
Dad:	All right.
Me:	I wanted to see you. I worried about you during school today.
Dad:	Can you be quiet?
Me:	Sorry. I'll sit here quietly.
Me:	Are you okay? You don't look too good.

Dad: Nothing new. Just the same.

Me: Something seems wrong.

Dad: Can you be quiet?

Me: Yes, I'll be quiet. I'll read.

Me: This is interesting.

Dad: Quiet?

Me: Sorry.

Mom: I'm going to bed. What about you?

Dad: I'll sit for a while.

Mom: Do you want to take a bath?

Linda: I have bubble bath, Dad. Do you want to take a bubble bath?

Dad: No, thanks.

Mom: You'll go as is, then?

Dad: Yes.

Me: I'll sit with you, Dad.

Dad: I'm all right.

Mom: Don't stay up too late.

Dad: Go to bed, son.

Me: I'm not tired. I'll sit quietly, I promise. I'll read.

Me: This is interesting.

Dad: Shhh.

Me: Dad, are you hearing some kind of voice?

Dad: I'm tired, son. Please go away.

Me: Dad, is the voice telling you not to talk to me?

CONVERSATION #3

Me: Dad. Mom's out, and you and I are going to have a little talk.

Dad: (Silence.)

Me: I know what's happening to you, see? I know all about it.

Dad: (Silence.)

Me: I don't know all about it—I didn't mean to say that. But I do know about it. I feel fairly confident.

Dad: (Silence.)

Me: I really don't like that expression on your face. It just isn't you.

Dad: (Silence.)

Me: Look at me, okay? Look toward me. Please.

Dad: (Silence.)

Me: Okay. Now, Dad. I want you to know that the comments you are about to hear are not directed at you. So please don't take any of them personally. They're directed at that voice you're hearing.

~~I repeat: This is not directed at you!~~

Dad: (Silence.)

Me: All right. . . . I'm going to exorcise you, you parasitic bastard!

Dad: (Silence.)

Me: I'm sorry, Dad. Could you possibly forgive me?

Dad: (Silence.)

Me: Look at me, please. Look right into my eyes.

Dad: (Silence.)

Me: Right in the eyes. Right here. Sorry.

Dad: (Silence.)

Me: Bastard! *Vamos!*

Dad: (Silence.)

Me: Don't you get it—you're not wanted! Get the hell out and leave him alone!

Dad: (Silence.)

Jodie: Here we are. My mom bought us all chicken nuggets.

TREATMENT REPORT: DAY 91

Why does Dad refuse to discuss the voice? Is he protecting the voice by not talking to me?

My best hope is to go in, way in, into what you might call enemy territory, and see if I can hear the voice myself.

CONVERSATION #4

Me: Hi, Dad.

Me: How's everything going?

Me: No need to answer me.

Me: I'm just going to sit here quietly and observe you. But don't be self-conscious. Pretend I'm not even here.

Dad: I'm so tired.

Me: I know you are. I heard you walking around last night. Now, I want you to just behave as you ordinarily do. Talk to your voice, or whatever. I think I have a pretty good handle on this, and I'm going to fill in the blanks for myself as best I can. So, begin whenever you're ready.

Dad: Why don't you go away and leave me alone?

Me: Was that addressed to me? I'm not going anywhere. Sorry.

Me: I can wait. I brought something to read.

Dad:	(Silence.)
Me:	As I said, it will be just as if I'm not here.
Me:	(Silence.)
Dad:	(Silence.)
Me:	Proceed.
Dad:	(More silence.)
Me:	(Even more silence.)
Dad:	God, I'm tired.
Voice in Dad's head:	Of course you're tired. And you're not going to get any better. You're only going to get worse.
Me:	(!!!)
Dad:	I don't understand. . . .
Voice:	Speak up! You're so slow all the time! Why don't you just say what you mean.
Dad:	I don't understand how I got to be this way.
Voice:	What way?
Dad:	So tired like this. And unable to do anything. When I used to do so many things.
Voice:	Like what?
Dad:	Like—
Voice:	Go ahead! Name them. So many, right? Go ahead and name even one!

Dad: I can't.

Voice: Why not, big shot?

Dad: Because I'm so tired.

Voice: You know, you think you're really something special, don't you? You think the world revolves around you, the sun rises and sets—

Dad: No, I don't.

Voice: Don't interrupt me when I'm talking! The sun rises and sets on your feeble head, doesn't it?

Dad: No, it doesn't. I never said that. See . . .

Voice: See what, blind man?

Dad: You know, you were wrong before. They do care about me.

Voice: Well, yeah. When you're sitting right in front of them. They're just pretending.

Dad: But if they're pretending in order to make me feel better . . . Doesn't that mean . . . ? Forget it—it's too complicated now.

Voice: How do you think they act when you're not around? If you went out for the day, how do you think they'd talk about you?

Dad: God, I'm tired.

Voice: Have you even thought about that?

Dad: I don't believe you. Enough.

Jodie: Can I play?

Me: We're not playing. Why don't you get out of here?

Linda: You can't tell Jodie what to do. Not anymore. We're all living in peace and harmony.

Jodie: Well, I thought you were playing a guessing game or something.

Me: Hold on there, Dad. It's nothing you two will understand.

LINDA

"You have to tell us," Linda says.

"Yes, tell us, Billy."

"You're not supposed to go off in your own direction and make up your own treatments. We're supposed to be a team, remember?" Linda insists.

I take Linda and Jodie into Linda's room and tell them what I've been working on. When Linda hears that I think Dad might have a voice in his head that could make him hurt himself, she doesn't start to blubber the way she did that first night, when we talked about the suicide movie. Instead, she looks completely calm.

"Okay, well, the most important thing," Linda says, "is that we not tell Mom about it. We have to take care of it ourselves, and not worry Mom with it, because she has too much going on and she couldn't handle it."

"Should we tell my mom?" Jodie asks. "She always knows what to do."

OF MUSIC · 220

"Could she keep it to herself?" I ask.

"Probably not," Linda says.

"Then no."

"Then it's just us," Jodie says in a small voice.

Dad: Maybe I'll be able to get some sleep tonight.

Voice: Ha!

Dad: What?

Voice: How can you think you're going to sleep? You should know better by now.

Dad: There's a chance that I might sleep, isn't there? A little bit of a chance.

Mom: Bill, should we start getting ready for bed?

Dad: I don't think I want to go yet.

Mom: Why not? It's late.

Dad: I don't think I'll be able to sleep.

Mom: Well, you do have trouble sleeping most nights, but that doesn't mean you should stop trying. What about the little sleeping pills, Bill?

Dad: I don't want one.

Mom: Why not?

Dad: I'm afraid I'll get hooked.

Mom: Bill, honey, look at it. See—it's just a tiny, white, store-bought, over-the-counter, nonprescription, not even very powerful, little PILL!

Voice: What do you care? Take the whole bottle.

Dad: I'm not going to take it.

Mom: Honey, it's such a tiny pill. I'm sorry, I know I'm beginning to sound exasperated. *Mmmmmph-pheeww.* We won't let you get addicted, I promise. We'll monitor you. Billy, you'll help me monitor Dad so he doesn't get hooked, right?

Me: Sure. I love to monitor my parents. That way they're less likely to monitor me. Heh, heh. Just kidding, Dad. But seriously, Mom, I don't think Dad should be taking those if he doesn't want to. Isn't there something else he can do?

Dad: Could I only take a little piece of one?

Mom: I don't know if that would do any good.

Voice: Hell, take all of 'em! What do you care?

Dad: Maybe I'll take a little bit of it. A quarter of it.

Mom: All right, then. Take just a quarter if that's what you want to do. If you feel okay with that, maybe you'll want to increase later.

Dad: Okay. I'll take a quarter.

Mom: Billy, cut this into quarters, will you?

Me: This? Cut this into quarters? I'll do it, but I'm going to need an electron microscope. Are you sure we shouldn't just skip it?

Linda: Maybe he should just skip it, Mom. Maybe he should take a bubble bath instead. Do you want some of my bubble bath, Dad? It makes you itchy afterward, but the bubbles are really big. Your entire body disappears under the bubbles. It's very relaxing.

Dad: I don't think so.

Mom: How about a shower?

Dad: No, I guess not.

Mom: So you'll go as is again, huh?

Dad: Yep. Just as is. Just as I am.

Mom: How are you doing with that sleeping pill, Billy?

Me: I'm getting it. I'm using a razor blade. If it would just stay still long enough while I bear down . . . Unnh. That's halves. Wait a minute. Quarters coming up next.

Mom: Try not to cut into the surface of the table. Or your hands, for that matter.

Me: Okay. Here are your quarters. Are you sure you want him to have this if he doesn't want to?

Mom: Get that down. Water. Good.

Dad: Wait . . .

Voice: This could be just the beginning.

Mom: Did it taste all right?

Voice: Just the beginning.

Dad: I wish I hadn't taken it.

Mom: Did I pressure you too much? I didn't mean to pressure you.

Me: I don't think he wanted to take it. Maybe we shouldn't be giving those to him.

Linda: What about trying warm milk again? Isn't milk supposed to be good?

Dad: Cancel . . .

Voice: The beginning of the end.

LINDA'S DREAM

The next afternoon, while Dad's watching TV, Linda tells me that she had a bad dream, just as bad as Dad's with the metal box. In the dream, all of us were dead except for Dad, who was walking around outside. The rest of us had been lying for weeks inside the house with the door and windows sealed up, but Dad couldn't get to us and so there was no one to help him. Linda takes this as a sign that he is about to hurt himself soon, just like I said when describing the article. She says she needs to do something about it, she just doesn't know what. And we both agree not to tell Mom about the dream.

CONVERSATION #6

Mom: What are you two doing over there? I'm hearing an awful lot of quiet.

Me: I'm doing a sort of quiet meditation with Dad. Sort of an hypnosis.

Mom: An hypnosis? Do you mean *a* hypnosis?

Me: Whatever.

Mom: Well, is it working?

Me: I think so. We're concentrating very hard right now.

Voice: He doesn't need you. I'm the one he needs.

Me: That's ridiculous.

Voice: I'll tell you what's ridiculous, or should I say who.

Me: I'm ridiculous?

Voice: You already know that, don't you? You're going to lose him.

Me: No.

Voice: Can you wave good-bye? Wave good-bye, Billy! Wave good-bye to Daddy!

Me: You are a parasitic leech that serves no human purpose whatsoever, and you should be going now.

Voice: No human purpose! I offer him the Biggie.

Me: What's that? What's the Biggie?

Voice: Relief.

Me: I offer that. Mom and Linda and I do.

Voice: Oh yeah, how?

Me: We do all kinds of things.

Voice: I can read your mind, you know. I know you realize you're full of it.

Me: That's it. I'm done with you.

Voice: Wave good-bye, Billy! Don't you know it's rude to leave without saying good-bye?

CONVERSATION #7

Mom: How are you doing with the mail, Billy?

Me: There's an awful lot here. It's really piled up. But I don't see anything urgent.

Mom: What's in the shiny envelope?

Me: Something from Dad's office . . . It's an invitation to the Mardi Gras.

Mom: Oh, no.

Me: It has a handwritten note at the bottom, from June.

Mom: Is she kidding?

Me: She says you both have to go. It's going to be better than ever because she's the chairperson this year.

Mom: Who is she kidding? Doesn't she know we're sick here?

Me: It looks like she really wants you to go.

Mom: We'd have to put costumes together. . . . And see all those people . . .

Me: Breathe, Mom. Breathe.

Mom: You don't want to go, do you, Bill?

Dad:	No.
Me:	It says RSVP.
Mom:	What is she thinking? She and her Mardi Ridiculous Gras.
Me:	*Mmmmmph-pheeww.*
Mom:	*Mmmmmph-pheeww.* It says RSVP? Will you take care of it?
Me:	There's a card and envelope inside. I'll take care of it.
Me:	Do you want to sit quietly together again, Dad?
Dad:	(Silence.)
Me:	(Silence.)
Dad:	All right, I'll go.
Me:	What? You want to go to June's party? You feel well enough to go?
Dad:	I have to go.
Me:	Wow . . . that's great news. I'll tell Mom. Maybe she'll go too.
Voice:	Maybe she'll go too? I don't think so.
Me:	You're not talking about the party, are you?
Voice:	It's a big, big party, Billy.
Me:	Are you going to be all right, then?
Voice:	It's a big, big party, Billy. Like an open house. Everyone who's anyone shows up. Eventually.

CONVERSATION #8

Voice: Why don't you rest for a while, Billy?

Me: Me?

Voice: Yes, close your eyes and contemplate peace.

Me: Okay. What about Dad?

Voice: What about him?

Me: Is he closing his eyes and contemplating peace too?

Voice: He's going to get up in a minute and go to the kitchen.

Me: He's going to have something? Mom will be glad to hear that when she gets home. What's he in the mood for?

Voice: Hmmm. Something sweet?

Me: Yeah. Dad used to love sweets.

Voice: No. Something sour? Mmm, no.

Me: How about salty?

Voice: Salty? No. Something sharp? Yes, something sharp.

Me: Should I go help him?

Voice: No, stay where you are and contemplate peace.

Me: And he'll be all right then? He'll find what he needs?

Voice: Peace.

Me: Peace . . . But I—

Voice: I told you to keep your eyes closed!

Me: Wait! Dad, don't get up!

Dad: Huh?

Me: Linda . . . Linda!

THE INVENTORY

On the afternoon of February 25, I set Dad up to watch TV while Linda, Jodie, and I begin to gather all the dangerous objects in the house—medicines, sharp knives, sharp tools, razors and scissors, drain cleaners and other toxic chemicals, and rope or anything that could be used as rope—and hide them in a metal box that will go in the attic. We start in the utility room with the tools, then add my pocket knife and Grandpa Eddie's fishing knife, and then we move on to the bathroom cabinet. The pills Dr. Gupta prescribed in the fall were flushed long ago, but Jodie does the same with the white placebo sleeping pills. In the kitchen, we disagree about which utensils are dull enough to be kept downstairs for Mom to use in everyday cooking. Linda is standing by the utensil drawer with a carrot peeler and eight serrated table knives, I am testing the cheese slicer, and Jodie is holding the box and padlock. This is the way we look when Mom finds us and decides to go back to the doctor.

TACKING

We file into the office, Mom first, then Dad, then me. Linda and Jodie are home with Jodie's mother. Most of the lights are out in the waiting room, and the receptionist has gone home. We've been squeezed in at the last minute, the last appointment of the day. The sky outside the large windows is dark. A set of headlights illuminates the snowy hedge briefly before swerving out of the lot.

Fritz closes the door behind us. Our folder is right there at his fingertips and he had obviously been reviewing it before we came in. He bites his bottom lip and looks around at each of us.

"How's everyone doing today?"

I evade Fritz's gaze and open my mouth to speak. No sound comes out. Then the room starts to blur and swim, and a repetitive sound, between breathing and speaking, comes from the back of my throat: *Ah. Ah. Ah. Ah.* I force my knuckles into my mouth.

"It's okay, Billy. All sounds are appropriate here. Now take a deep breath. Deep breath, in and out—*mmmmmph-pheeww*—nice and deep, from the abdomen. What's been happening since I last saw you? Anyone?"

"I think I'm about to lose my job," Mom says.

"And why do you think that?"

"I'm not there enough."

"That must be very difficult."

"It is."

"It's been a while, hasn't it?" Fritz continues. Fritz clasps his arms over his woolly shirt and tries to get Dad's attention. He does a funny thing with his eyes, making them gentler, yet more powerful, like a kindly hook that tugs the truth out of you.

"How are you feeling, Bill?"

"He doesn't talk much anymore," I say helpfully, having dried my face with a Kleenex.

"Bill, are you having thoughts of harming yourself?"

Dad stares at his hands. I realize that he hasn't been shaving or trimming his beard. The different lengths of hair on his face make him appear rough, although he doesn't act that way.

Dad nods.

"How often?"

"Every day," Dad rough-whispers.

"Have you made a plan for killing yourself?"

"Yes."

"Bill!" Mom says. She reaches over and puts her hand on his arm.

"It's all right, Adele," Fritz says. "Everything is going to be taken care of. Your husband is going to get the proper care now." He writes something on a pad, then addresses us again. "I wish you had come in sooner," he says. Then he softens his tone a bit. "I'm really glad, very glad, to see you today." He says that in this hour he would like to speak with us individually, beginning with Dad.

Mom and I go out to the waiting room while Dad stays in with Fritz. We don't look at each other, but I sense Mom not wanting to let go of him, as if she could *shoosh* through the solid material of Fritz's door and be in there. She jumps up immediately when Fritz calls her name. Dad paces around the waiting room, and I find myself rubbing my hands too. Then I go last.

"Billy, tell me in your own words what's been going on at home."

He waits while I say nothing.

"For instance, describe what yesterday was like."

"Well, I came home from school. . . . And we watched a show about home remodeling on TV. . . . And I sat with Dad for a while. The voice inside Dad's head was telling him . . . to harm himself. To do away with himself."

"And you spoke to the voice?"

"Yes, to the voice."

"Not to your father?"

"No. They're two separate things, really. Two separate entities."

"Does this voice speak through your father? Can you hear it out loud?"

"No, I figured it out by listening to him. It's in his thoughts. It's trying to take him over and control his thoughts. I can guess what he's thinking."

"Like mind reading?"

"Yes." I'm pleased at how surprised he is.

"You're very close to your father, aren't you?"

"Right now I am."

"And you've worked very hard to take care of him during this time. Your mother has too."

I nodded.

"But I have to be very clear and firm with you, Billy:

You can't ever know for sure what someone else is thinking."

"You can't?"

"No. You can get information from what they tell you, you can look at body language, you can develop hunches that you might later be able to confirm. But you can't actually ever read someone's mind."

He keeps watching me, staring in that strange way, holding me in his gaze, and though what he's saying sounds like he's judging me, his eyes are saying he's seen everything before, everything. That noise starts again: *Ah. Ah.* And I think it's outside me, in the room itself, before I can feel that it's coming from me.

We just sit there for a few minutes, me struggling to control myself, then finding I don't have to, Fritz holding me with that gaze. After a while I stop looking all over the room and gaze back at him, like a staring contest but better. He says he will meet with my parents now to decide what's to be done.

"We're all here," he says when my parents come back. He smiles at Dad, writes very quickly, then smiles at Dad longer. "We need to start doing something for you, Bill, right away."

"Yes," Mom says, "we realize that. We'd like to resume treatment immediately."

"In terms of treatment options that remain, the time we've lost means we're now severely limited."

"I think that at this point . . ." Mom takes a deep breath. "Knowing what we know now, I would be much more amenable to putting Bill back on meds."

Dr. Fritz rests his elbows on Dad's file. Then he rubs the bridge of his nose. "What I mean to say, Adele, is that we don't have time to try another medication. We need something that acts more quickly. I have some calls in for you to look into electroconvulsive therapy."

"Wait a minute," Mom says. "Let's slow down here."

"What is it, Adele?"

"Please don't tell me you're considering shock treatments," Mom says. "Please don't tell me that."

"This may be a difficult decision, Adele. Do you want Billy to be present during this discussion?"

"He can stay here for now." This time Mom isn't saying she wants me here to take notes. I heard her telling Marty that she just doesn't want me to be alone.

"Well, let's not say 'shock,' Adele. It's an ugly word, and it shocks the patients. This sort of treatment isn't really

what you're picturing. It's much gentler than it was years ago."

"Wait. Let's go back as if the last few weeks never happened, and start where we were before. We'll try another medication. Which one were you going to recommend next?" She feels on top of her head for her glasses, as if she's going to be given another prescription slip to read.

"Adele . . ."

Dr. Fritz seems a bit tired of Mom, as if he wouldn't mind never seeing her again. Has she become a medical obstacle? But he tries hard to hide it. "We're running out of time here, so we may need to continue this discussion over the phone. Adele, I'm always pleased when my patients and their families take an interest in their own care. I know you're all trying to be good consumers in trying to find what you think is best for Bill.

"But when we're dealing with a suicidal patient, time is extremely important. Your original psychiatrist, Dr. Gupta, doesn't generally supervise electroconvulsive therapy herself, so we will need you to meet with a different psychiatrist. I'll give you the name of someone with whom I occasionally cooperate. I've worked with him a few times over the years." He opens a drawer at the left side of his

desk, pulls out a business card, and hands it to Mom. Doing so gives him a chance to stand up. He remains on his feet and so, even though nothing has been resolved, we realize it's time to stand up too. A massive tiredness hits me. I wouldn't care if I wasted my life sleeping.

Fritz walks us to the door. "Make an appointment with him right away—for no later than the day after tomorrow. I'll phone him to let him know you're coming. It isn't a hundred percent sure that this will help, but if it does work, it could start to help very quickly. And this time you *must* follow the treatment plan. I'll check in with you. And him. And you again."

Fritz chuckles. He sounds like the old Fritz. The Fritz who said, "Welcome!" to us and made us laugh by the door that day. That good day.

LITTLE GREEN HOUSE

Little green house, half an inch square. I've kept it in a tissue, in the toe of a sock, in my sock drawer. It's hollow. It fits on the end of my pinkie like a cap. Ten houses could dance on the fingers of my hands like finger puppets in a hurricane, but I've only kept one. If I set it on my palm the two long lines in my skin swoop in to make a driveway.

A molded plastic house made in a factory somewhere. It's made of one piece, with the details pressed outward. The chimney is just a button. The front and back of the house are identical, with a door smack in the middle and a window on either side. The two other sides have no features, no windows or doors, just a sharp line that shows you where the roof ends. How simple. How nice. Someone made a plastic house. I cup the house in my two hands, cover it, and blow on it. My breath is warm and it warms the house.

Oh, God of houses and lots. Oh, great monopolizer.

Protect this house. Whoever and wherever You are. Whatever You have the power to do. However You are able to know all our names and our streets' names. Whether You are watching from far away, like heaven, or from somewhere closer, like a low-flying helicopter. Don't turn Your back on us, okay?

People's luck is always changing. You made us that way. But You meant the bad times to be brief, didn't You? So why are our troubles hanging on?

Don't let our four walls collapse. Don't let our floor drop into the center of the earth. Don't let the air poison us. God of houses and lots, watch over this house.

MACARONI AGAIN

It's almost the end of lunch when I sit down with my tray. Gordy is out sick, and I plan to eat alone to avoid unwanted peer contact. I took my time leaving class and visiting my locker and stopped twice, without really needing to, in the bathroom so the food line would be almost closing when I got my plate of mac and cheese. I found a table on the outskirts of the room where I could sit by myself. Actually, there is one other person at my table—a stooping guy with a stubbly jaw, in a white uniform and a cloth cap that resembles a dinner napkin. He's the worker who sets up and removes the food in the steam tables, and he's taking a short break.

"How's the macaroni?" he asks. Despite the hat, his professional interest gives him a kind of dignity.

"Pretty creamy. You should find better tomatoes, though."

"You know how it is," he says. "They go with the cheapest stuff they can find. Every place is like that."

I heard a rumor that this guy, Ray, has an alcohol problem. I wonder if he deliberately went looking for a job in an institution in which most of the people have never had their first drink. Maybe it makes him feel safe. Innocent, even. Like he's one of us, just starting out in life.

I wouldn't go so far as to say that we're two peas in a pod, but our sitting together seems right. Ray and I, Ray and me. Not really innocent, but two guys who've been batted around by life. The drunk tank, the shock treatments, the carnival jobs and the cafeterias, maybe one or two eviction notices, desertion, disappointment, we know it all cold, and what I don't know I can imagine. Bits of a song enter my mind, a blues song, Ray's blues, and I wish I knew him well enough to try it out loud.

They don't like what I'm dishin'

No, not they. *She.*

She don't like what I'm dishin'
She (something something) bad
She only knows she's missin'
What she never should have had.

Well, this is real life, baby,
It's what's cookin' everyplace,
And if you don't like what I'm servin'
Find someone else to feed your face.

I'm not sure that captures Ray, though. I don't think he would turn mean like that at the end. If his wife or girlfriend were dissatisfied with him, he'd be more the type to just live with it, grateful for what he had.

The first bell rings and the shuffling starts—just a few sneakers at first, then hundreds and hundreds of them, an orchestra of feet. Mitchell and Andy walk by in the crowd. Andy spots me and stops, but I shake my head, look down at my plate, and wave him along. For once he does the right thing: He keeps moving.

WAITING

Mom, Dad, and I sit in the waiting room of a highly recommended psychiatrist. Everything in the room is perfect, telling us we are lucky to be here even though we don't want to be. Mom begins to chatter, pointing out that the walls are an intriguing gray or silver color, neither bright nor dull, but rich with layers. Each chair is like its own museum exhibit, with skyscraper lines and aggressively rough cloth, rough brown cloth for a poor monk to rest on, or maybe a rich person who thinks that too much comfort looks cheap.

A metal cube in the middle of the room, like a coffee table for astronauts, holds magazines in neat stacks just out of reach. Mom takes the half step needed to pick up a copy of *Architectural Digest*. I don't know what kind of impression she'll make. She hasn't washed her hair today. But we are only background. All our effort was put into the presentation of Dad.

Dad is shaved and trimmed. Dad has lost seven more pounds and is wearing a pair of my pants because none of his fit. Dad is pacing the space-age room with his hands in his pockets because the doctor is five minutes late for our appointment.

There's no reception desk to welcome us. One door in the waiting room is the one we just came through—it leads to the elevator lobby. The other door is made of dark wood with a stainless-steel handle—thoughtfully, the long, handicapped-accessible type—and it has no markings. No sounds come from behind the door, but we sense that behind this door is where the doctor is hidden. Having paced for seven minutes, Dad tries the door.

"No, not yet!" a voice calls sternly. We glimpse a bald head and a dark suit. Dad closes the door quickly, as if he'd walked in on someone in the toilet. He resumes pacing.

We three glance at each other. I crush my arms over my chest and slide way down on the rough seat, pretending to sleep. Mom tosses her magazine back to the table. It lands on the floor, so she gets up and places it neatly on the top of the stack. Not a sound comes from behind the door.

Another several minutes, and the door opens again. There's the doctor—bald, black suit, one and a half heads

shorter than Dad and me. His office is painted a shade of gray that Mom would call pewter, with shiny black furniture. The wall behind his desk displays some precisely spaced three-inch photographs in yard-high black frames. We're inside now, so we quickly forget about the wait.

Dr. Mieux has an electronic notepad in the center of his desk. He holds the stylus over a screen as thin as a sheet of waxed paper.

"I'm seeing *all* of you?" he says, staring at me.

"Billy's helping me gather information," Mom says. "He has a very good memory for doctor visits."

I hold a pen over my own notebook. I too can document.

"I understand you've been feeling agitated, Bill," the doctor begins. He looks down at the tip of the stylus, then up again. "Bill? Aren't you going to answer my question?"

"I don't think you asked a—," Mom points out.

"Please! Mrs. Morrison! Allow the patient to speak for himself!"

"My father doesn't talk much," I say.

"He has to talk," Dr. Mieux says, watching the screen, "or we won't get anywhere."

Dad peers at Mom and begins rubbing his hands. "What do you need to know?"

"How long have you been feeling this way?"

Dad swallows hard. "About three to four months."

"And you've tried antidepressants? Which ones?"

Sliding and thudding noises have started in the waiting room, and there's a knock at the door.

"Yes?" the doctor calls. He lays down his stylus. He glances at his watch and smiles for the first time.

A man in a brown workman's coverall and cap leans his hand, shoulder, and arm into the doorway. "We've got everything up," he says, gesturing backward with a gloved thumb.

"Superb!" the doctor says. He gestures at the three of us. "You'll have to go back out to the waiting room for a bit. I'm taking delivery on a new set of furniture."

"Go back out?" Mom asks. "Now?"

"It won't take long," the doctor says.

We file back into the waiting room, where two immense packing crates now occupy most of the space. The magazine cube has been pushed into a small corner of the room, and the skyscraper chairs are squeezed around it at odd angles. We sit down in the available chairs, Dad facing the wall and Mom and I with our backs to him. Mom rests one foot on the cube, pushing a stack of magazines onto the floor.

"Oops," she says.

A second workman helps the first slide the largest box into Dr. Mieux's office.

"This isn't going to make it," the first man says.

"Why don't you take the door off the hinges?" suggests Dr. Mieux.

I exhale loudly, letting my head weave from side to side like a balloon running out of air. The second man kneels on the floor with a screwdriver. Dr. Mieux stands between us and the workmen, creating a visual barrier. He blinks at me to let me know I shouldn't be watching. Mom's foot starts bouncing on the table, while Dad continues to face the wall.

The workmen are highly efficient. The first packing crate goes into the office. Ripping, thudding, and sliding sounds follow. The men pass through the waiting room with the crate again, but this time they're walking backward. One of them presses the elevator button. The elevator dings. For a while the waiting room is quiet, except for the sound of drawers opening and closing in Mieux's office.

Soon the elevator dings again, and the two workmen enter, discussing a hockey game. One of them is carrying a bottle of soda. He takes a huge gulp that makes his Adam's

apple seem like it's becoming dislodged. They squeeze through the office doorway with the second crate. This one appears much heavier. Then ripping, thudding, and sliding.

"Is this some kind of joke?" I ask Mom. "It's so unprofessional."

"Be patient, honey," she responds, waggling one foot.

I get up to check Dad. He's completely still, with his eyes closed.

"That's not right," the doctor says. "Let me look at the bill of sale. . . . No, I see, it's all right."

More sliding. Then the sound of padded blankets being heaped together. *Thwop, thwop, thwop.* The workmen walk past us with the second crate. Then they reappear carrying the office door. They attach it to its hinges. One workman tests the motion. Smooth. Mieux closes the door, and we don't hear any more sounds from his office. The workmen leave, the one carrying his soda bottle. Out in the hall, they wrestle the second crate into the elevator.

The situation is now exactly the way it was when we first came in, except that the waiting-room furniture is in disarray and crowded into one section of the room. Dad gets up and opens the door to Mieux's office.

"No! No!" Mieux cries. He has been arranging objects in the desk drawers. He rushes to the door and presses his body weight against it while Dad still has his hand on the handle. "I'll call you when I'm ready for you."

I cross over to Mom's seat and whisper, "Why don't we get out of here?"

"Shhh."

Dad paces around the room while rubbing his hands. He's trying to get interested in some of the art that hangs on the walls, stark black-and-white photos of shadowy mountaintops and of ice floes settling into abstract shapes. Dad walks up to them one by one. He used to do some photography and painting. He went to art school, on a full scholarship.

The door opens.

"I will see you now," the doctor says, nodding as if he's meeting us for the first time.

We take our places opposite Dr. Mieux at his desk. The stylus and screen are ready, but he doesn't use them. Instead, he folds his hands on the desk.

"First of all, we need to establish some ground rules if we're going to work together. You need to know that what just happened in *my* space was none of your business." He

looks at each of us, but most sharply at me. "The boundaries between doctor and patient are absolutely paramount in this office. Is that clear to everyone?"

I respond by making my eyes go defunct, which he can interpret any way he likes: that I'm bored, that I hate him, or that I think he's a fake.

"Yes, of course," Mom mutters. Dad nods.

"Now let's get back to your situation, Bill." The doctor examines a few pages of records sent to him by Dr. Fritz. His black, perhaps ebony, desk and chairs have been replaced by another set. The surface of the wood has parallel waves too beautiful to have been painted by a human hand. If I didn't despise his furniture by association, I would trace one wave with my fingertip. Dad would have loved this.

The doctor sees me looking. "It's bubinga," he says. Then, to Dad, "You've tried a couple of antidepressants, with poor results. And there is suicidality?"

"What?" Dad asks.

"You sometimes think about killing yourself."

"Yes."

Dr. Mieux holds Dad's records between us. "Look, Bill, if you would like me to authorize this treatment you're requesting, I'm going to have to have you in my care round

the clock—in order to monitor your progress and forestall any problems."

"I don't understand," says Dad.

"This type of treatment is generally available on an inpatient basis only. In cases where there is suicidality, it's best to have the support system in place, trained staff, monitoring . . ."

"You mean . . . a hospital?" Dad asks.

"Wait a minute," Mom says. "Why don't we discuss the options? We haven't even decided if we want shock treatments yet."

I plant my feet one at a time as loudly as possible, as if I am a giant with giant feet in giant boots.

Okay. Let's go, Mom. Let's just go. Thank you for your time and everything blah blah blah.

"Billy," Mom says, "would you rather wait outside?"

The doctor narrows his eyes at me and then continues. "Yes, a hospital. Hospitalization. You would be on my floor, getting the best possible care, under my direct attention. People come from all over the world—some very prominent people, members of royal families, although patient confidentiality constrains me from saying exactly who—from all over the world, to be on my floor."

But I'm not hearing this—*inpatient, hospitalization.* I'm hearing *the mental ward.* Restraints, barred windows, icy baths, screams at two a.m., disturbed people surrounded by other disturbed people who frighten one another with their delusions. How would Dad survive there?

And Mom looks like she's thinking, *If I put him in, will I ever get him out again?*

"I'm not sure that would work," Mom says. Her voice wobbles while she twists her necklace of wooden beads. "We haven't decided if we want shock treatments."

"This isn't cosmetic dentistry, Mrs. Morrison. This isn't something you choose or don't choose. You can't dillydally among the treatments, comparing caps and crowns and whether you should bond or whiten. Your husband is at risk of harming himself."

"We can take care of him at home."

The doctor refers back to Dad's record. He speaks to Mom without seeing her. "You've had him at home for— how long is it?"

"Almost four months," says Mom.

"And he hasn't gotten better in all that time. . . ."

"We're taking fine care of him at home." Mom's nervous, and her voice is up and down all over the place.

"You want him to get better, don't you? You don't want to be negligent." Mieux is staring at Mom now. "If the worst happens . . . It's ten past five, Mrs. Morrison. We have only a few minutes to make a decision here."

"I'm not putting him in the hospital," Mom says. "That's all there is to it. I'll see what our choices are. Maybe we'll leave the country and seek treatment elsewhere. Perhaps we'll try Canada, or Mexico. But he's not going into the hospital."

Why don't we just go then, Mom? Why don't we just up and leave?

I rise.

Ignoring me, Mieux writes a few comments with the stylus. He touches up the comments. He frowns.

"Well, I'm willing to try it this once, to supervise your husband as an outpatient. Keep in mind that I'll be paying very close attention to this case, to make sure it's handled correctly."

"I appreciate that, but let's not get ahead of ourselves," Mom says. "We haven't decided on anything. I need to know more. How do these treatments work, if they do work? We have no idea what to expect!"

Mieux sighs. He gets out of the chair and goes to a

cabinet with an empty vase on top. He gives Mom a brochure. *ECT: A Powerful Tool for Change,* by L. F. Mieux.

Mom hands the brochure to me and tells the doctor she'll call back after she's had a chance to review it. I clap my notebook shut with only a few lines filled. Mom and I leave with Dad between us.

In the parking lot, when Mom searches her purse for her car keys, her hand is shaking. I secure Dad gently in front, but once in the backseat, I slam my door loud enough to echo off pewter walls.

"Not now, Billy."

"You know what I'm going to say then, don't you?"

"Nothing, Billy. Not a word until we get home."

"I didn't like him," Dad says.

Back at the house, I escort Dad inside while Mom waits in the driveway. She'll be leaving again to get Linda.

"I'm not closing off my options, Billy," she says when I come back out. "We may want to continue with him. I checked with someone I know at the college. He has a very good reputation."

"You can't put Dad in the hands of a nut job!"

"Don't be such an alarmist. So he's a little eccentric. A

lot of brilliant people are. He probably puts all his effort into keeping up with research and hasn't developed good interpersonal skills. In the academic world, at least, that's fairly typical."

"This isn't the academic world—he's supposed to be a doctor! You hated him yourself. Why are you making excuses for him? What about being a good consumer, like you always told us to be? What about shopping around?"

"Sometimes—" The lady next door is just getting home from work. Mom waves. "Would you keep your voice down, please?"

"You didn't think he was any good. You thought he was full of it. You wanted to turn around and walk out, the same as I did."

"Maybe, but I restrained myself. He has a very good reputation. We have to put our personal preferences aside. It's just something that we have to overlook."

"He treated Dad like he wasn't even a person. Like he was a prisoner or something. Like he had no will. He treated us like we were less than human. People like that should never be given any kind of power."

"It's irrelevant."

"Irrelevant?"

"So he's rude to the patients. So what? Does that really make any difference? It's like saying he can't do a good job because he's bald."

"He *is* bald. And obtuse and—"

Mom reaches for the handle of the car door. "Listen, Billy. When I was in grad school, there was a professor in the biology department that no one could stand to be in the same room with. He smelled bad, he insulted the other professors, and he distributed fliers saying the women's studies department should be cut because it wasn't a real subject. But you know what? He contributed to the discovery of an oncogene. The first step toward a cure for cancer. How many people do you think he helped?"

"But did any of the people with cancer ever have to meet him? I don't think so. This guy is a *psychiatrist*, for Christ's sake. He's supposed to know how to act around people."

"We can find someone else to be nice to us. We can *pay* someone to be nice to us. But we can pay *him* to do what he does."

The curtains move and Dad looks out at us. I hold up my finger to say "one minute."

"You'd better go in," Mom says.

"Well, I'm glad I'm not the one paying the bills. He's not getting one cent of my money."

Mom drops her head and rests both gloves on the car hood, as if she's watching her reflection, except that the car is really dirty. "Maybe I shouldn't have brought you with us," Mom says. "I thought you might be up to taking notes."

Not bring me? If I hadn't been there, who knows what might have happened? Dad might not have come home. He could be watching the world through iron bars right now.

"Now everything is getting too complicated," Mom says as if I'm not there. "I'm the only one who can decide."

"How will you decide? Everything we've tried so far has been a disaster. The other day I was trying to remember what Dad was like before he got sick, and you know what? I can't even remember. I can't remember my own father and he's not even dead, he's living right here in the house and sleeping down the hall."

"Go in. I'll decide. I'll look into it, and I'll decide."

I hold up my notebook. "We got that brochure, right?"

"That's right. Where's the brochure?"

ECT: A POWERFUL TOOL FOR CHANGE

- The wife of a former governor and onetime presidential hopeful calls the results of her regular ECT program "wonderful."
- The chairman of psychiatry at a prestigious medical school says, "Most people today in patient surveys say it's no worse than going to a dentist."

For nearly seventy years, electroconvulsive therapy has been used to restore depressed patients to health. What can ECT do for you?

- *Restore* your zest for life
- *Revive* your appetite and help you maintain a healthy weight
- *Release* you from insomnia so you enjoy a good night's rest
- *Return* your performance level at school or job, honing your "competitive edge"

Are you a candidate for ECT? Ask your doctor, and begin to harness the healing power of electro-convulsive therapy now.

"Oh, for crying out loud," Mom says.

RESERVATION

Now it's Mom who paces the house, trying to decide whether to go ahead with the treatments. She has already told Mieux that she will go forward, and Dad has had all the necessary prep work done. But she has misgivings. She carries the appointment card for Dad's first treatment. She folds and unfolds it so many times that it turns silky.

"Listen to yourself," I tell her. "You obviously have doubts. Why do you have doubts? Because you know he's a quack. He shouldn't be practicing medicine. He wouldn't care if Dad died in his office, as long as it didn't leave a mark on the furniture. You should have told him no in the first place."

Linda agrees. "Too risky," she says. "The things we did before, they didn't work, but at least they were safe."

"It's just a piece of paper," Mom says. "We can cancel at any time. We can just fail to show up, the way we did with Fritz. The situation only *seems* to be out of our control, see? They need to act like they're in charge, but *we're* the ones who are in control. We're the ones they need to show up."

RESOLUTION

Someone approaches the bike rack behind the library as I'm going in the entrance. He hovers near Triumph.

"My bike," I boom in my strongest voice, retracing my steps.

A middle-aged guy stands up. He's a little younger than my father, and he's wearing a peacoat with a plaid muffler.

"Beautiful bike. English, isn't it?"

"Yep." With the hand holding my keys, I point to a plate on the top tube that says MADE IN ENGLAND.

"I always wanted one of these. How does it ride?"

"Three years with no problems. And a lot of decades before that."

"They're a little heavy on the hills, aren't they? Have you considered putting a larger cog in the back?"

"I don't mind working up a sweat on the hills once in a while. I'm trying to keep it as intact as possible. I could use a springier seat, too, with all the potholes, but I just like the looks of this one." I wait for him to step away, but he doesn't go.

"It's in beautiful condition," he says, running his hand over the handlebars. "Have you ever thought of selling?"

"No, I haven't." That sounds ruder than I intended. "Sir, this is my primary mode of transportation."

"Well, I wouldn't want you to lose your transportation. I would give you enough to get another decent bike. How about three hundred dollars?"

"It's not worth that much."

"Then why don't you take the money?"

"It's not worth that to anyone else, I mean."

"How about four hundred, then?"

"Are you crazy? You can find five of them for that much on the Internet."

"Why is this bike so special to you?"

"It's practically my first bike. It feels like that, anyway. I fixed it up myself. . . . My father and I did." A light snow is falling, and I want to be inside.

"Well, it's really just what I'm looking for. And I have been looking on the Internet. Will you take my card, in case you change your mind?"

I wave the card away and go upstairs. Once inside the door I check back to see if the guy has his grubby hands on my frame again, but he's walking to his car. Four hundred

dollars! Out of nowhere. It almost seemed like one of those situations they warn you against, when someone pretends to share your enthusiasms or offers to do you a big favor, and they're really a sexual predator attempting to get somewhere with you. The card and everything. Or perhaps he was the devil incarnate. He did seem to genuinely like the bike, though.

I go inside and find a computer carrel in the corner of the third floor, where I'm least likely to encounter other students from my school. I pass two guys a year older than me—"It's all right," one guy says, "it's just Bob."—who seem to be participating in a chat room. "Say you're a 40DD," one of them whispers to the other.

Four hundred dollars. I don't know whether I should tell Mom and Dad. On the one hand, it's a lot of money that perhaps we could use (I actually know very little about our financial situation), but on the other hand, I have no intention of selling. We do, after all, need my bike. With Dad out of commission, it's our second car. It allows me to do important errands like this. With the saddlebags, I could conceivably do grocery runs as well. Maybe I should offer to do something for the Brooksbie once in a while. Yes, I am sure they would not want me to sell the bike.

Tuning out the guys in the nearby carrel, I do a key-word search on the words "electroconvulsive therapy." The search brings up several websites with pleasant and soothing names like Personal Wellness, Web MD, Family Doctor, and the National Institutes for Health. I print up a page of questions and answers from Family Doctor.

What conditions does electroconvulsive therapy treat?
Electroconvulsive therapy (also called ECT) may help people who have the following conditions:

- Severe depression with insomnia (trouble sleeping), weight change, feelings of hopelessness or guilt, and thoughts of suicide (hurting or killing yourself) or homicide (hurting or killing someone else).
- Severe depression that does not respond to antidepressants (medicines used to treat depression) or counseling.
- Severe depression in patients who can't take antidepressants.
- Severe mania that does not respond to medicines. Symptoms of severe mania may include talking too much, insomnia, weight loss or impulsive behavior.

How does ECT work?

It is believed that ECT works by using an electrical shock to cause a seizure (a short period of irregular brain activity). This seizure releases many chemicals in the brain. These chemicals, called neurotransmitters, deliver messages from one brain cell to another. The release of these chemicals makes the brain cells work better. A person's mood will improve when his or her brain cells and chemical messengers work better.

What steps are taken to prepare a person for ECT treatment?

First, a doctor will do a physical exam to make sure you're physically able to handle the treatment. If you are, you will meet with an anesthesiologist, a doctor who specializes in giving anesthesia. Anesthesia is when medicine is used to put you in a sleeplike state. The anesthesiologist will examine your heart and lungs to see if it is safe for you to have anesthesia. You may need to have some blood tests and an electrocardiogram (a test showing the rhythm of your heart) before your first ECT treatment.

How are the ECT treatments given?

ECT may be given during a hospital stay, or a person can go to a hospital just for the treatment and then go home. ECT is given up to 3 times a week. Usually no more than 12 treatments are needed. Treatment is given by a psychiatrist.

Before each treatment, an intravenous (IV) line will be started so medicine can be put directly into your blood. You will be given an anesthetic (medicine to put you into a sleeplike state) and a medicine to relax your muscles. Your heart rate, blood pressure, and breathing will be watched closely. After you are asleep, an electrical shock will be applied to your head. The shock will last only 1 or 2 seconds and will make your brain have a seizure. This seizure is controlled by medicines so that your body doesn't move when you have the seizure.

You will wake up within 5 to 10 minutes after the treatment and will be taken to a recovery room to be watched. When you are fully awake, you can eat and drink, get dressed, and return to your hospital room or go home.

What are some side effects of ECT?

Side effects may result from the anesthesia, the ECT treatment, or both. Common side effects include temporary short-term memory loss, nausea, muscle aches, and headache. Some people may have longer-lasting problems with memory after ECT. Sometimes a person's blood pressure or heart rhythm changes. If these changes occur, they are carefully watched during the ECT treatments and are immediately treated.

What happens after all of the ECT treatments are done?

After you have finished all of your ECT treatments, you will probably be started on an antidepressant medicine. It is important for you to keep taking this medicine the way your doctor tells you to so that you won't become depressed again.

I ride home standing on the pedals instead of sitting on the seat. I take the route that allows me to coast down long hills. Triumph, it's going to be all right!

At home, Mom is checking the maintenance bills for Brooksbie while Dad allows Linda to give him a cucumber

facial. I drop the printouts on Mom's lap and she reads them quickly, her lips moving at certain key words. I was surprised that the treatments didn't sound that bad. It looks like Mom might be right to go ahead, although I would never tell her so. When she's done, she chucks me on the head and holds up the appointment slip like it's a winning lottery ticket.

VACILLATION

But the night before Dad's first treatment, I bike back to the library on the pretext of returning some books. The computer carrel I used last time is available. After all these months, is our problem really going to be solved so easily? I get on the Internet and search for the phrase "shock treatments."

The results that come up are different this time. In addition to pleasant-sounding organizations like Healthy Place, there are many more with worrisome names such as Antipsychiatry.org and Ban Shock, as well as groups such as the Committee for Truth in Psychiatry and the Foundation for Truth in Reality. I click on an article called "ECT and Brain Damage: Psychiatry's Legacy," posted by a group called Say No to Psychiatry!

The story of electric shock began in 1938, when Italian psychiatrist Ugo Cerletti visited a Rome

slaughterhouse to see what could be learned from the method that was employed to butcher hogs. In Cerletti's own words, "As soon as the hogs were clamped by the [electric] tongs, they fell unconscious, stiffened, then after a few seconds they were shaken by convulsions. . . . During this period of unconsciousness (epileptic coma), the butcher stabbed and bled the animals without difficulty. . . .

"At this point I felt we could venture to experiment on man, and I instructed my assistants to be on the alert for the selection of a suitable subject."

Cerletti's first victim was provided by the local police—a man described by Cerletti as "lucid and well-oriented." After surviving the first blast without losing consciousness, the victim overheard Cerletti discussing a second application with a higher voltage. He begged Cerletti, *"Non una seconda! Mortifiere!"* ("Not another one! It will kill me!")

Ignoring the objections of his assistants, Cerletti increased the voltage and duration and fired again. With the "successful" electrically induced convulsion of his victim, Ugo Cerletti brought about the application of hog-slaughtering skills to humans, creating

one of the most brutal techniques of psychiatry. . . .

Electric shock is also called electroconvulsive "therapy" or treatment (ECT), electroshock therapy or electric shock treatment (EST), electrostimulation, and electrolytic therapy (ELT). All are euphemistic terms for the same process: sending a searing blast of electricity through the brain in order to alter behavior. . . .

ECT is one of the worst and most permanently destructive methods used by psychiatry. Before heavy tranquilizers and muscle relaxers were used to render the patient completely immobile, shock treatments often caused broken vertebrae due to the severity of the force involved with electric shock. There is nothing mild about this "treatment." Slick advertising campaigns and glossy brochures cannot turn this very harmful procedure into a useful and safe one.

If a psychiatrist or mental health "professional" tells you that ECT is safe, ask him or her to let you watch as they themselves receive a "treatment." Their negative response should set your mind straight on the subject. If they do consent, then I suggest getting away from them as quickly as possible—they truly must be crazy as a loon to accept your proposal!

The website quotes Ernest Hemingway and claims that the reason he shot himself was that shock treatments destroyed his mind. "Well, what is the sense of ruining my head and erasing my memory, which is my capital, and putting me out of business? It was a brilliant cure but we lost the patient."

Antipsychiatry.org has a page called "Psychiatry's Electroconvulsive Shock Treatment: A Crime Against Humanity." At the top of the page is a photograph of a woman in a hospital gown, strapped down to a table, with some kind of bit in her mouth. Wires on either side of her head lead to a box with switches and dials, where two hands wait, seemingly about to throw the switch. Because the woman's mouth is forced open by the bit, you can't tell if she's trying to shout for help. She might be.

Some psychiatrists falsely claim that ECT consists of a very small amount of electricity being passed through the brain. In fact, the 70 to 400 volts and 200 to 1600 milliamperes used in ECT is quite powerful. The power applied in ECT is typically as great as that found in the wall sockets in your home. It could kill the "patient" if the current were not limited to

the head. The electricity in ECT is so powerful it can burn the skin on the head where the electrodes are placed. Because of this, psychiatrists use electrode jelly, also called conductive gel, to prevent skin burns from the electricity. The electricity going through the brain causes seizures so powerful the so-called patients receiving this so-called therapy have broken their own bones during the seizures. To prevent this, a muscle-paralyzing drug is administered immediately before the so-called treatment. Of course, the worst part of ECT is brain damage, not broken bones. . . .

Defenders of ECT say that because of the addition of anesthesia to make the procedure painless, the horribleness of ECT is entirely a thing of the past. This argument misses the point. It is the mental disorientation, the memory loss, the lost mental ability, the realization after awaking from the "therapy" that the essence of one's very *self* is being destroyed by the "treatment" that induces the terror—not only or even primarily physical suffering. ECT, or electroshock, strikes to the core personality and is terrifying for this reason. . . .

Since the "patient's" fear of ECT is one of the

things that makes ECT "work," psychiatrists often get results by merely *threatening* people with ECT.

I print out my findings. I take them into the men's room so I can read them in their entirety. I could throw them away, right in this wastebasket under the paper towels, before I leave the library. I could keep quiet about what I know and just watch Dad for signs, hover above Dad's situation like a guardian angel. What would be the point of showing Mom, anyway? We have no other options on the table. We have Plan A but no Plan B.

When I get home, Dad has gone to bed to prepare for an early start in the morning. Mom is drinking tea and staring out the window over the sink. I doubt she can see anything out there, with lights on inside the house. I hand her the printouts. They're crumpled, damp, and probably unsanitary. Mom puts down her mug and begins to read them, with one hand at her throat. For a long time she doesn't react.

"Not Hemingway!" she eventually gasps. I knew that would get to her—Mom's master's was in American studies.

She shakes her head and leans against the counter. She touches the necklace my father gave her when they were poor. We could be poor again.

"You may not show any of this to your father or your sister."

"You have to cancel the appointment, Mom."

She rinses the mug and puts it in the dishwasher without saying anything.

"Right? Mom? You have to cancel the appointment, or they'll turn Dad into a zombie."

"I'm not going to cancel it."

"But look what happened to Hemingway—and all those other, ordinary people. Their minds got wiped out. Anything that was special about them—pfft. And even anything that wasn't special."

"Billy—"

"Come on, Mom! *Where's that phone number?*"

"Shush." She lays her hand on my arm, but I knock it away.

"Don't shush me! I won't be shushed anymore!"

"If you yell and act agitated, you'll just make things worse. Don't you want your father to get some rest before his first appointment?"

"So you're going, then? You're doing this to Dad? You don't even want my opinion."

"I want your opinion, only in a lower register."

"I won't let you do it."

"Oh, really? How will you stop me?" Mom steps backward. A bag of recycled Brooksbie papers blocks her path, and I don't even warn her. She doesn't fall, though.

Mom has no idea that in the last five minutes of my bike ride I developed a secret plan. If she decides to go ahead with this, I'll take Dad away. The nights are getting warmer—we could live in a tent on Plum Island. Any court in the United States would see it my way.

"Billy," Mom asks me after a while, "what percentage of your father would you say is still there?"

"Maybe thirty," I answer. "But at least it's something."

"That's exactly the figure I was going to give."

DAWN

My social studies teacher, Mr. Misuraca, distributes a test up the aisle. He moves like a trained bear, and every test, no matter what the alleged subject, ends up being about the nineteen sixties.

Brenda Mason strokes the shoulder of her sweater as she writes her name on the test, almost as if she's patting herself on the back.

I write my name but nothing after that.

They leave the house at dawn.

They stop for coffee at Dunkin' Donuts, but Dad isn't allowed to have anything. Mom puts two honey-dipped Munchkins in a wax bag for later, should Dad choose to accept them.

Uncle Marty drives because Mom and Dad were up most of the night, and Mom's too tired to drive. In the passenger seat, Mom navigates with the map.

The landmarks of Route 1 pass their windows. A

lighthouse, a ship, and the tower of Pisa, all of which are really restaurants. An orange Tyrannosaurus rex that guards a miniature golf course. They've seen it a hundred times, but this time it startles them, and they wonder whatever possessed someone to put it there. Questioning, questioning.

The traffic doubles and redoubles. The Boston skyline ascends, gathering memories of family trips around it like a broad gray skirt.

Coolidge Hospital is the size of a town. Marty follows signs for Building G. He drops Mom and Dad in front, then goes to park the car.

They sign in at the front desk.

They take the elevator down to the basement.

The basement is a plain, concrete-walled clinic.

Dad is wearing his snappy first-day-of-school clothes.

The other patients are all in pajamas and bathrobes, because they're living here.

A nurse calls "Bill Morrison," and Dad looks up.

He and Mom are shown into a second room.

In the second room is a new doctor they've never met before.

He and a nurse take Dad into a third room.

Dad lies down on one of three beds.

The nurse straps him in and gives him an injection.

His body relaxes and his eyes close.

The nurse smears something on Dad's head.

She places an oxygen mask over Dad's mouth and nose.

The doctor presses onto Dad's head two circles attached to a wire.

He seems to be asleep now.

The doctor throws a switch.

May God forgive me.

That I would do nothing while a doctor sent fire through my father's body.

A current passed through Dad's brain, producing a seizure that lasted thirty seconds. His arms and legs never moved, but his fists clenched involuntarily and his toes twitched.

Inside Dad's brain, neurons resembling tall, thin trees stood in groves. Their spidery branches were intertwined, almost touching. Lightning shot from tree to tree and from branch to branch, making the bare wood rattle and hiss. This lightning had the power to revive or destroy whatever buds of thought or nests of memory ever lived there. Dad's soul walked at the base of the trees, fearful and wondering. Some branches were cut and fell to the ground like dry kindling. Others crackled, swayed, and absorbed the shock, eventually becoming still.

THIS —

Is this my inheritance? Red hair, blue eyes, and a dark place in the mind that will call me when my time comes, and I will have to go there?

Like a church bell, a factory bell, or a funeral bell?

I am (after all) Bill Junior.

part three

TREATMENT REPORT: DAY 109

Dad has completed three sessions of electroconvulsive therapy, each of which has obliterated his memory of the past twenty-four hours and taken with it some of his other mental abilities, too. In other words, he is even more less-smart than he was from not sleeping, although we hope that one day he will become more smart again.

THE DARK SPACES

"Sixteen across: patella."

Dad and I are doing the newspaper crossword on a Saturday afternoon while Mom reads a magazine in her chair in the corner. When he was well, we would time ourselves on the crossword puzzle—usually thirty minutes, once as low as twenty-six minutes, thirteen seconds—but now we're taking all the time we need, not looking at the clock.

I give him a head start before I make my suggestion. "Okay, how about 'kneecap'?"

Dad begins writing in the squares. N-E-E.

"Wait! There's a *k* in 'kneecap.'"

"Where?"

"At the beginning."

He erases what he's done and starts again. The word fits.

"Does 'needle' also have a *k*?" he asks, trying to find the pattern.

"No, it doesn't. But 'knead' does, like when you knead dough to make bread. And remember, 'know' does, as in 'I know you.'"

He nods. "I'm pretty sure I have that one."

None of the articles mentioned that the treatments would cause Dad to lose—temporarily, we hope—his ability to spell. But I see it each time we do the crossword puzzle. The first time I noticed it, I felt embarrassed for Dad. Maybe I even pitied him. But now my reaction has changed. For the most part, I feel curious and just basically interested. Because the articles I've read say nothing about this problem, I feel like I've discovered something. I strangely enjoy watching him and looking for trends in what he does and doesn't remember. Still, it seems a little cold. I excuse myself by deciding it's the kind of thing he himself would find interesting, if it weren't happening to him.

A car goes by the picture window, up our hill. Mom lays down her magazine and waves. "The man who stopped in yesterday just went by," Mom says.

To help Dad with his memory loss, I've developed a technique I call "backgrounding," and Mom helps me implement it. With this technique, we assume that he

remembers nothing, and we fill in for him as much as we can. Normally, Mom might have said just, "There he is again!" about the passing driver. But with my background-ing program, she beefs up her comment with a short reference to yesterday's meeting.

"Someone stopped in yesterday?" Dad asks.

"Yes," she answers. "We were just getting out of the car, and he pulled in the driveway. He was thinking of buying the house at the top of the street, and he wanted to know how long we had lived here and what we thought of the highway noise. You were very honest with him and said it bothered you, but we explained that you were a light sleeper and I'm a heavy sleeper."

"Uh-huh," Dad says, waiting to see if the information resurfaces in memory. Sometimes it does, and sometimes it doesn't. But in giving Dad that information, Mom is treat-ing him as if he can step back into the conversation once he has the background. He can still participate. I call that technique "normalizing."

"He must be serious about buying if he's back again today," Dad says. "Did he say whether he was a light sleeper?"

"No, he didn't," Mom says. "He mostly listened to us."

"He's probably not light then," Dad continues. "Or he would have mentioned it. Maybe he's in-between."

If only Hemingway had had someone to background his short-term memory. Would things have turned out differently for the American novel?

AN AMBIGUOUS STATEMENT

Dad stands at the living room window with his back to me. It's 5:20 p.m. on March 16.

"The days are getting longer," he says.

I'm rereading an old *Newsweek* in the easy chair. "Dad, is that longer-good, as in more natural light/more time to enjoy activities, or longer-bad, as in you can't wait for the day to end?"

Dad looks at me, then turns back to the window.

"The days are getting longer," he repeats.

The house is quieter now after school. Linda and Jodie have disappeared from the afternoons and are now meeting at Jodie's house. They left behind clumps of brown paper wadded with ink, and some burnt ceramic scat that may have been beads that stuck to the oven when I wasn't paying attention. I didn't have to clean up because Mom said I should take it easy for a while.

But beyond that, there is a sense of peace in the house,

though I can't put my finger on it exactly. Dad's right—the days *are* getting longer. Could that have been what went wrong with Dad, that the days were getting too short? Might the light box really have worked, if we hadn't been so quick to discontinue it?

But thinking this way doesn't do any good. We had another follow-up visit with Dr. Fritz, and he said that although, again, he wished we had come back in sooner, we shouldn't be kicking ourselves, because to a certain extent we were just doing the best we could with the tools and resources we had at the time. But it seemed to take a lot of effort for him to say this, and while he said it he looked at our file and not at us, not staring at us at all, as if he didn't like us anymore, and this made us feel worse.

For Saturday lunch the day after his sixth treatment, Dad ate a ham sandwich, a hard-boiled egg, a quarter of a melon, and a piece of chocolate cake. Mom and I eyed one another and kept bringing out more food.

SOLILOQUY

Reading in bed that night, I find this section in Walter Merig's *The Progression of Major Depressive Disorders*.

It is perhaps ironic, therefore, that the greatest rates of morbidity occur when the patient appears to be getting better. This seemingly paradoxical phenomenon can be traced to two developments: first, that the patient may have wished to self-terminate much earlier and did not have the physical strength, powers of resolution, and planning resources to do so, resources which are now, with some improvement, more easily at his command; and second, that the recovering patient, now viewing the illness from "the other side of the hurdle" as it were (Femmigant, 1998), regards the recently concluded illness with his improved perceptive powers as a torturous ordeal, the recurrence of which must be avoided at all costs.

I sit up and reread this a few more times, allowing its meaning to unwind in my tired brain. We were happy to see Dad getting better. We high-fived each other over him finishing a ham sandwich. But now he's in more danger than he's been in the past four months? Still . . .

I get out of bed and pace across my room. What do we do now? Do we try to keep him at this level? Do we try to prevent him from getting any better? Do we hope that he stays just sick enough that he never sees the big picture? That he concentrates on surviving day to day and never looks back to realize how terrible it was?

It's a philosophical problem, isn't it? If the risk of suicide is greater as you recover, would it be better to stay at least a little sick—let's say an easily controlled low-grade melancholy—and live longer but not as well? Or would it be worth it to end it all on the up cycle, savoring the taste of hot French toast with maple syrup? The brightness of a tube of aquamarine? The feel of salt spray? I imagine Dad as a ski jumper. He sees the mountain slide away beneath his feet, then fade into the distance. He decides never to come back down.

When did I pick up Dad's habit of pacing? I have to calm down and get back in bed. I have to stop being theoretical.

I have to remember that I'm not a philosopher or a psychologist, I'm a son. This is Dad I'm talking about, not some experiment, not some patient in a book. Of course he has to keep getting better.

And even though I'll say, "Whoa! What's your hurry?" when in the next few days he talks about getting out his paints or stopping by the office to say hello, I can't get in the way of his recovery.

ANATHEMA

Except that Dad hates the treatments.

Hates the way the other patients look, wan and stick-like in their bathrobes. Hates the wheelchair he rides from the treatment room to the car. And especially, hates the moment when he lies down, waiting to be knocked out so his mind can be taken out of his control and . . . not wiped clean, but smudged around the edges, the way your sweater sleeve smudges words off a chalkboard.

INTROSPECTION

Every once in a while I come across Mom standing in the kitchen and twisting her necklace. She might be steeping a teabag or sorting through the mail. She doesn't show much on the surface, but I can tell by the way her eyes aren't seeing what she's looking at that she's pitching a silent, internal horror fit over the fact that we almost lost Dad. I wonder exactly what she tells herself at those times. I could break into her thoughts at one of those moments, engage her in conversation, but to be perfectly honest, I would rather not know.

SWEETS

The cute girl in our bakery hands me the price list. Mom has given me "carte blanche" to buy whatever we need for the celebration of Dad's eighth and last treatment—whatever looks good, she says. A fancy cake two or three times as much as we can eat, maybe some cookies or Italian pastries on the side. Linda has already bought the party decorations and hidden them in her room. Uncle Marty and Jodie have been invited.

Cannoli are always good, and chocolate-chip cannoli are even better, although both get soggy if you don't eat them the same day. I crouch in front of the case to get a better look at the cakes waiting for other customers, and I see, along with my own reflection, a boy's birthday cake with sky blue frosting and *Star Wars* figures—Darth Vader and Luke Skywalker facing off with their lightsabers. Too theatrical to be appetizing. I like the golf-themed cake better. It's covered with green-tinted shredded coconut that resembles

grass and dotted with mini-marshmallows for golf balls. Beside it is a dignified white-frosted cake that says "Best of Luck Stan" in a circle around a small plastic adding machine, possibly for someone who is an accountant.

Needless to say, there's no precedent for our specific occasion. I look at the price list again. Color photos of sample decoration styles, with a variety of messages, are ranged along the top. Are we a "Good Luck"? A "Congratulations"? A "You Did It"? "Happy Last Treatment" would be too specific, and "It's Over" is too vague.

While I'm making up my mind, the loud and distorted electronic doorbell over the bakery door rings: *bwing-bwong!* A woman enters the store and speaks to the girl and her father, the baker. It's June. Not the month of June, but June from Dad's office. The scent of her perfume mingles with the bread-and-sugar air in the bakery. I curl into a cannonball position in front of the case, hoping she won't recognize me.

"Billy!" She stoops toward me and I straighten up.

"Hello, Mrs. Melman."

"How's your dad doing?"

"A little better, actually."

"Fantastic. Will he be coming back to work soon? We

have a temp working at his desk. A nice kid, but he seems to have accidentally deleted half the files on Bill's computer. Maybe he thinks that will make us keep him on longer. But tell Bill that as soon as he gives the word, we'll clear things out and give the temp his marching orders."

"Well, I don't know how soon it will be. You better wait to hear from him. See . . ."

"Yes?"

"See, we've sort of had a routine."

June searches my face. "You had a routine. Routines can be good."

"Yes."

People on the outside don't realize how tricky a situation like this can be. You don't want to rush things. You don't want to upset the delicate balance that causes a sick person to get better. It's not like you just decide that someone will improve and they do. Mom was right when she called her "easy-breezy June."

June pays for the Stan cake and gives the girl a two-dollar tip, even though there's no tip cup. She turns back to wave to me on the way out the door and catches the baker studying her rear view. She smiles and waves to him, too.

I pick out both a golden raspberry-filled cake with

buttercream frosting for twelve and a Boston cream pie. The bakery can stack the two cakes in a corrugated crate for me to carry home. I watch the girl's father move my raspberry cake to a work counter. Then he adorns it to my specs: "Congrats Dad" plus balloons and ribbons drawn in every frosting color they have, exuberating around his name and cascading into heaps on the cardboard plate.

SHRINKING

The night before Dad's eighth treatment, I walk him around at midnight while Mom takes a rest. Dad *really hates* the treatments.

"I can't get back on that table," he says.

"You have to. It's all planned. They're expecting us."

"Why don't you call them, early in the morning, and let them know we're not coming."

"We can't, Dad. You have to go. Just one more. Then never again. Then you can relax. I promise."

I'm as tall as Dad, and my arm feels good where it rests along his bony shoulders. My outside hand holds his wrist so I can suppress any rubbing compulsion. We look like a couple about to begin a square-dance maneuver.

I feel alert and happy tonight. Although it seems strange, I'm realizing that these have been good times. I've felt occupied and useful, and I've never spent so many hours with my father. But now our togetherness may have

peaked—he's been talking about going back to work again.

No one can deny that Bill Junior has been there when needed, like Mom's uncle Jack, who fell into the tight squeeze in Normandy in World War II by standing under a blanket filled with air.

Will life be cutting me down to size now? I feel my regular life, boring, disappointing, and mediocre, tugging me back with a hundred strings. It wants to turn me into a two-inch-high toy parachute man who will sit in a drawer until someone takes him out again. Folded, rubber-banded, put aside, waiting.

SYNONYMS

Saturday morning we sit outside Dr. Stone's office at Coolidge Hospital, waiting for Dad's last treatment. Mom and Uncle Marty know the place well, but Linda and I have never been here before. Our family, including Dad, are the only people in street clothes. The rest are bathrobed inpatients. Dad keeps to himself, while Mom and Marty exchange a few words with the patients around them. The cast of characters changes a bit every time, Mom explains. Two patients that she used to talk to regularly, Mike and Irene, have finished before Dad and gone from the hospital. She wishes she could find out how they're doing.

This time, when the assistant calls Dad's name, Dad makes a brief announcement to the other patients. "I won't be seeing you again after today. So, good luck to you all." He waves over his shoulder to them and to us as the double door to the treatment room swings closed behind him.

Twenty minutes later we are waiting for him to wake up when Dr. Stone calls Mom and Uncle Marty into his personal office.

"Should we stay out here and wait for Dad?" Linda asks.

"Let's all go meet Dr. Stone," Mom says. "It's a special occasion."

Dr. Stone is a thin man in a polo shirt with a bandage on the side of his forehead. This gives me the creeps, as if he's been operating on himself. The office is clean and bare, with just a dinged metal desk, a few chairs, and filing cabinets. There's no decoration except for two Harvard Medical School diplomas and a photo of him running the Boston Marathon, stringy and determined in a pair of very small shorts.

"It's gone very well," he says. "You should be pleased." We are.

"And you're seeing improvements at home?" We think so.

"He's put five pounds back on," Mom says. "And he got out his camera and started playing around with it."

"Very good," Stone says. He opens the schedule book he shares with his assistant. "I think another two to four treatments are all that will be needed to really lock it in."

Mom and Linda both fold their arms tightly over their

chests and recross their legs. Each has a leg swinging. Marty blinks as if he didn't hear right.

"I may be mistaken," Mom begins, "but I seem to recall hearing from you that this course of treatment would require eight visits total." She strokes the earpiece of her reading glasses slowly through her hair.

"Eight was a very good estimate," Stone says. "We've often had very good results with eight. The remaining two or three are just a bit of insurance, to make sure the improvements really jell."

"You're telling me," Marty says, "that my brother's brain has to jell?"

"Well, not his brain really, but the changes in his brain. If we want them to become permanent. We want them to coalesce, to firm up, to be cohesive. To really take hold, to lock in."

He keeps going, looking for a word we will accept. I would hear more about his reasons, but I am gone.

CORRIDORS

Water sears my eyes. I run blindly through corridors, left and right, right again, taking enough turns that I hope never to find my way back. The hallway is a moving watercolor of white, pink, and chrome.

"Paging Dr. Billy!"

I turn around to find Linda cupping her hands over her mouth and pinching her nose. She drops her hands. "Big brother," she says in her normal voice.

"*Incompetent. Just—incompetent.* I promised him he wouldn't have to come back here again."

"Well. Was that even your promise to make?"

We walk together until we come to an open door.

"Those idiots have no idea what they're doing. How many times did I try to tell Mom that this was a bad idea?"

Linda leans against the doorway. "Be quiet, Billy. God is here."

Inside the hospital chapel, the organist is playing the hymn that goes to the tune "Finlandia." We know this song from Dad's music collection—"Be still, my soul: The Lord is on thy side"—but the organist keeps stopping at a bad time to practice this phrase or that. We sit down and Linda bows her head, but I keep my head up and look around, at the dark paneling, and at the one narrow stained-glass window that a crowded city will allow.

While I may have called to God in moments of desperation, I still don't believe in Him. See, I have this deal with God: I don't believe in Him, and He doesn't believe in me. In fact, we view each other the way you might view fictional characters. We hear good things about each other, but we would never expect to see proof of each other's existence, either in a random meeting on the street or as a name on a tombstone.

Mom believes that there's a happy afterlife for everyone, even those who may not seem to deserve it, like murderers, terrorists, and pedophiles. Linda believes that anything you do will be forgiven, if you ask the people around you or ask God. Now that we bought the cake and the decorations and the gifts, I wonder who will be the one to tell Dad that his treatments aren't finished.

We return slowly through the zigzag of corridors. The halls are clear and distinct now, alive with workday sounds. We get to the waiting room, where Mom sits with Marty and the other patients. Marty goes to the swinging door that separates this room from the treatment room. He stands there until Dad comes in smiling, about to raise his arms in triumph.

"You sit, Adele," Uncle Marty says. "I'll tell him."

"Tell me what?" Dad asks.

Marty turns Dad's wheelchair toward the hall.

"Let's go for a walk, bro," he says.

DECELEBRATION

Linda keeps the decorations in her room that night. But we cut up the raspberry cake. And in spite of the lack of reasons to celebrate, the cake tastes good. *Really* good.

A READER'S QUESTION

Q: Does Dr. Mieux, the psychiatrist with a taste for fine
   furniture, ever reappear in this story?

A: No, he does not.

MARTY

Marty says he had a rough time telling Dad, as he puts it, "about the more treatments." When he talks to me in the driveway after the cake, Marty looks like he's falling through the ice again, into the cold place where no one but Dad wants him. "He was disappointed, but he kept telling me not to feel bad," Marty says. "He was worried more about *me*."

Throughout Dad's sickness Marty has seemed convinced that Dad was always thinking about him. His money problems, his business schemes, his trauma over the divorce from Aunt Stephanie . . . I got the idea that Marty was kidding himself, feeling all this sympathy from Dad that couldn't possibly have been there. That he was filling Dad with intelligence and other good qualities, like a little kid confiding in his teddy bear.

But along with the quiet and calmness that seeps into the house, something else seems to be happening for real.

It's like Dad was a snow globe that had no top on it, and all the stuff that was inside had somehow disappeared. Now it's as if the top has been put on and something is falling to the bottom, settling and collecting, flake by flake. Some recognizable stuff that can only be called the Spirit of Dad.

AN EXISTENTIAL MOMENT

Pudge starts calling the house nearly every day, outside of Mom's work hours. One day he hints that the museum is about to go under, and that her job will be at risk unless she takes responsibility for raising a big heap of money from the members. Mom talks to him from the kitchen for half an hour, pleading and arguing, but never in the taking-charge voice she uses on most people.

"If it's phone work, I'll do it," she says. "If it's e-mail, I'll do it. Tell me what I can do right now, Pudge. Tell me what I can do from home, without going in. I can get a laptop. Working from home, I can spend unlimited hours on the phone, and I will get you that money."

"It's extortion," she says when she hangs up. "He's actually threatening to fire me."

"Why don't you go in, Adele?" Dad says. "Go in in the mornings once in a while. I can take care of myself."

"What would you do by yourself in the morning?" Mom asks him.

"Read the newspaper, watch TV, listen to the news . . ."

"The news is so depressing, though," Mom says.

"I could always call Marty if I need someone to talk to."

"That's an idea. In fact, why don't we see if Marty is willing to come over a few mornings a week while I go in to work?"

And so our daily pattern begins to shift. Mom will go into the office from ten to noon a few days a week, as well as working three hours a day in the afternoon. Because Marty's bar/restaurant mostly needs him in the evenings, he can come by mornings most of the time. Dad will also stay home alone for an hour here or there, with the understanding that he will call Mom or Marty if he becomes agitated or needs company.

The first morning that Dad is to spend some time by himself, I see him rubbing his hands a little. Not in the old automatic, repetitive way, but more of a light buffing for good luck. It seems that he could use a booster, a dose of the old empowering phrases we used when he was really sick. But as of this moment we've dropped all the old techniques and are relying entirely on shock treatments to make Dad better. So, technically, I shouldn't do this anymore. Since Mom is just a few feet away gathering

the museum's financial records, I decide to come at it indirectly.

"You know, Dad," I begin, "everything is for the good."

"Everything is for the good? What in the world do you mean?"

"That everything is for the best. Ultimately. In the universe. It all works out, you know. Like a kind of perfection. Even your having been sick, I guess. Maybe some good will eventually come of it. It all happens for a reason, as part of some massively perfect scheme."

"You know, you can't believe everything you hear, son. The fact that someone said something and it sounded catchy doesn't mean it's true."

"What are you two talking about?" Mom says, putting a ledger book in her briefcase.

With one finger, Dad pushes Mom's glasses farther up her nose. "Whether the universe is moving toward perfection. Which in your case it clearly is."

"Well!" Mom says. "That's so sweet." Mom actually blushes, and I sort of want to leave the room. From what I can tell, this is the first time in a long time that Dad has said something in a husband-type way rather than as someone who needs her help, and I wish I hadn't been here. He used

to say poetic things to Linda, too. Like "Anon there drops a tear . . . for the cold strange eyes of a little Mermaiden and the gleam of her golden hair" (Matthew Arnold).

"I would say no, Billy," Mom says. "The universe doesn't seem to be moving toward perfection. At least, I don't see evidence that that's happening. It's just something people say when they're desperate. Something they grab at when they're drowning. I'm not sure those little sayings really work."

"But Fritz thinks they do, right? And we're back to Fritz again. I mean, he's back up on the pedestal. He's God now because Dad is getting better."

"Fritz isn't God. Can't you get through a single conversation without wallowing in sarcasm? He's just a regular person, but he seems to know what he's doing. Don't think of him as God. Think of him as a tool we can use, which is what that idiot Mieux is, and what they all are."

I leave for school thinking of a line from "Desiderata": "No doubt the universe is unfolding as it should." At first it seemed like more of the same, but it really isn't. It doesn't say the world is headed for perfection or destruction, just that it is going in the direction it's intended to go. Old Max Ehrmann was obviously hedging his bets there.

TREATMENT REPORT: DAY 128

Marty has been having such a good time talking to Dad (or *at* Dad would be more accurate) that he has decided to take complete responsibility for Dad's remaining two or three treatments. Although Marty usually closes the bar and cleans up at two a.m., he is changing his schedule and retraining himself to get up at five. This allows Mom to add more mornings to her workweek.

COMING UP NEXT

"Dad! Come on!" I shout.

I turn on the TV in the den and settle into my side of the couch with a bowl of cheese curls. I move the ottoman with my feet so it's in just the right spot. Dinky accordion music plays, and the camera pans across a wall of canvases. The paintings show windows, crystal glasses, and chandeliers, all painted with starry highlights.

"Dad! It's starting!"

Dad stands in the doorway with the newspaper while the Light-Teacher begins his introduction: "Even if you've never held a paintbrush. Even if you've never learned to draw. You can become a—"

"Billy! What are you watching this for?"

Dad blocks my view as he switches off the TV. Then he goes back to the living room to read.

ADOLESCENCE: IDYLLIC OR INSIPID?

Mom tells me to plan on another follow-up session with Dr. Fritz. After school on Wednesday afternoon, I am expecting Mom to pick up Linda, Dad, and me. Instead, Marty pulls up at the house, and after killing the drive time with a story about a bartender who may be stealing, he drops me off at Fritz's by myself. Although I've been to Fritz several times now with the family, in the waiting room the old nervousness comes back. Why am I being seen by myself, when Dad is the one who's sick? Why am I being placed under the microscope? Or is Fritz going to ask my advice in planning the rest of Dad's treatment? Mom mentioned some talk of trying another antidepressant once the shock treatments had started to take effect.

Here is Fritz in his lumberjack clothes. Here is the photo of Fritz's sailboat. I sit down opposite his desk.

"How are things going with you, Billy?" Staring. He likes me again!

"All right, I guess. Dad seems better."

"And how are you, apart from how your dad is doing?"

"Fine. Tired, maybe."

Fritz links his hands over his chest. "I asked you here, Billy, because your parents, in particular your mother, are concerned with how you are recovering from your father's illness. Do you have any idea what she might be talking about?"

"Not really."

"Well, from what she's told me—and correct me if I'm wrong—you seem to be having trouble letting go. You still spend a great deal of time at home. You don't seem to be, as I might put it, *reengaging* with life. Could there be any truth to that?"

I decide to withhold my own stare from Fritz. Instead, I look at the photo. Two guys out on the open seas. Well, that's one kind of adventure. But with all I've been through, how could anyone say I haven't been engaged with life?

"Look, Fritz, I mean Dr. Fritz. I just want to make sure everything goes okay—I mean, that things don't get worse again. My mother is all into her career again, and there has to be someone looking after things at home."

"And does that person have to be you?"

"Well, who else is there?"

"Who else is there? You tell me."

"Tell me, Dr. Fritz, how is your sailboat? Is she a good seaworthy vessel? Does she win you any big sailing races?"

Dr. Fritz tilts his head and smiles slightly. "That isn't my sailboat, unfortunately. Billy . . . You have to let go of caring so much for your father and get back to normal. That would be better for him, and for you. Do you have any reason not to let go?"

"I already told you that someone needs to stay home."

Fritz presses both sets of fingertips onto the closed file detailing the problems of my family. It's as if he's saying it's simple, it's self-explanatory, it's all there . . . but you're not allowed to read it.

"It's praiseworthy that you have such feelings of loyalty, Billy. I can understand your anxiety about all the difficulties you've been through recently. But I don't think you have to be so afraid anymore, now that your father is getting adequate care. Can you accept that?"

There is this folder, my life, with a big hole in it that everyone is talking about.

"Billy? Can you accept that?"

I'm studying the sailboat photo again. All at once I realize, after all these visits, that the colors and the clothes in

the photo date it by about forty years. The person I thought was Dr. Fritz is a lookalike, probably Fritz's father, and the small boy is Fritz himself. For some reason, this makes me tremendously sad.

"So I really do wonder what is prompting you to occupy so much of your time with your father and his illness."

I nod. I know something bad is happening to my face.

"I guess . . . I just don't think I'll ever do anything this important again."

"You think helping your father is important. Is anything else in your life important?"

Every thought seems to have left my head, as if I just woke up or was just born.

"Deep breath, Billy. *Mmmmmph-pheeww*. Now tell me. What else do you think is important?"

"I used to think writing songs was important, but now I don't know anymore."

"You don't know anymore."

"No."

"What are some of the things you've been missing out on since your father became ill?"

"Having music in the house, really loud, bouncing off of everything."

"Having music in the house."

"Having music in the house."

"What?"

"Dr. Fritz, you're repeating me."

Fritz just waits, doesn't rise to the bait.

"And maybe seeing my old friend Mitchell."

"This friend Mitchell, what is he like?"

"Oh, sort of fat. A big brain but doesn't care about anything. Sarcastic. Makes fun of everything, laughs at everything. Thinks everything's funny."

"Does he make you laugh too?"

"No. Not right now, anyway. I'm not in the mood for him now."

"Well, tell me, Billy. Is it any more true to say that everything is serious than to say that everything is funny?"

"Could you repeat that, please?"

"Is life so serious?"

"Well, that's easy to say now. It's easy to laugh and joke afterward, when everyone is safe. You yourself seemed to think everything was serious just a few weeks ago."

Fritz raises one hand, a variation on his old "Welcome" gesture. "Look, why don't you call this friend and make some plans?"

"Because he isn't serious enough. I could never tell him what happened to Dad. He would never understand how serious that was."

It's warm in the office, but I pull the zipper of my parka way up to my chin.

"If you do spend time with Mitchell or other friends, does it have to be serious?"

I picture something sparkling on the ground—a piece of treasure that turns out to be a gum wrapper. Those are my heroic moments, turned to ribald jokes for Andy's amusement. My Best Of's turned to America's Funniest.

"I guess I could just see him but not tell him what happened."

Fritz nods, a rolling nod, three times. "You can do that, or you can do something else, whatever you feel most comfortable with."

"I guess—the thing about Mitchell—I don't think he's really suffered in his life."

"Do you know that for sure?"

"No, but I think if he did I would have known about it."

"Maybe."

We sit for a while not saying anything.

"Why don't you reconnect with him and see how you

feel? Try reconnecting with all the things you used to like about your friend Mitchell."

"I don't like thinking about it that way."

"Then just call Mitchell."

BOULEVARD

In East Hawthorne, near where Gordy lives, is a wall about waist-high that stands between a broad sidewalk and the harbor. I'm showing it to him because everyone from the old regime knows it's the perfect wall to walk on. He pulls himself up easily and begins cantering along the top.

"Have you ever thought of riding your bike up here?" he asks.

"I've thought of it, but never actually done it. I don't think anyone has."

"Maybe you can be the first."

An elderly woman in a black nylon tracksuit stops a few yards away and glares at us.

"Sorry, ma'am," Gordy says, hopping to the ground. Then to me he says, "I guess it isn't very polite to walk on a wall that's inscribed with the names of dead fishermen."

"Everyone does it," I tell him. "She should be glad

someone's taking an interest. Let's jump back up as soon as she's gone."

"That's all right," Gordy says. "I've experienced it."

"Say, Gord."

"Say, Billy."

"I was wondering: Did she say anything particular? At the very end?"

"At what end?"

"You know, when she died."

"My mother?" Gordy looks out toward the water.

Now I wish I hadn't brought it up. Maybe I should have kept my mouth shut. Maybe the answer is something really horrible like "I can't breathe."

"Not really. She was in and out. She said a few things like that I should work hard and have goals and try to do something with my life. The typical things parents say."

"Except that this time you felt you had to pay attention?"

Gordy laughs and steps up onto a metal railing while still looking out to sea. The white sun of early April is reflected in one curve of the harbor, making it look like a bowlful of snow. "Yeah."

"Is that why you're good at stuff, because you work hard?"

"I don't know."

Tactical error. I shouldn't ever let on that I admire him. If I say something like that again I bet he won't want to be my friend anymore.

"I'm just trying to make some plans, you know? I'm just trying to decide what to do next," I explain.

But I already know—I can almost tell by the texture of the way my brain feels most days—that I am not cut out to do a lot of things well. One thing, maybe. One big thumper of a thing. The type of thing that will earn me a gravestone with just three words: I DID THIS.

Two a.m. Everyone's asleep. Everyone but me, that is. Linda's passed out under her mad photos and her Garfields. Someone in Mom and Dad's bedroom is snoring like a pack of wolves. But I'm wide awake.

Why can't I have the sleep that I deserve? Did I get so used to being up at night that I forgot how to sleep? Is something nagging at me? Have I forgotten to do something?

Then it comes back.

Why does a man feel tired
Why does a man feel dead
When misfortune comes to misery
Comes to (something) in his head

It's a world of trouble, baby
Oh Mister Trouble, let me go
Get your fingers off my (something)
And leave me to my—radio?

STRIVE TO BE HAPPY

"Hello?"

"Mitchell?"

"Yes?"

"It's Billy."

"I know this."

"Promise me one thing, okay?"

"What's that?"

"That you won't ask me any questions."

"I will not ask you any questions."

"Okay, then. Do you want to come by after school tomorrow?"

MISSING

For the first time in a long time, I've overslept. Sleep filled me up so completely that I actually felt myself getting taller. The clock reads 8:37 (it's Thursday, though—good, not a treatment day), and Linda's standing in the doorway to my bedroom.

"Billy," she says, "Dad's gone."

"He's gone? Where is he?"

"I don't know. He's just gone."

She leads me down the hall to our parents' room and opens the door. Mom is asleep with her mouth open and her arm flung over her eyes to block the bits of daylight that creep around the curtains. Dad's side of the bed is empty. Linda pushes the door open a bit more, making it creak, and Mom sits up and says, "Where is he?"

"Oh, Mom," Linda says. "He's gone."

"What do you mean?"

"He isn't anywhere in the house."

Mom gets out of bed and puts on her bathrobe. We move softly into the main rooms. No one, not even Linda, is getting hysterical, and that makes it scarier somehow. The calmness is something fearsome. That's how accustomed we are to Dad's actions/communications/requests/needs being part of our consciousness. With the house so quiet and nothing to advocate for or resist, we're like astronauts working around the capsule whose lifeline somehow becomes unattached. We're floating out toward the infinite.

"Bill!" Mom calls into the hallway. No answer from the living room or other rooms.

Mom's face is grim. We follow her, like baby ducks, to the big bathroom, where she looks up at the shower rod. Nothing. Next she goes into the kitchen and stares at the floor around the oven. Nothing.

"All right," Mom says. "I'm sure it's all right."

Nonsensically, I open the oven door. Linda, even more nonsensically, peers into the microwave. Of course, nothing. Mom opens the kitchen curtains and looks into the backyard. Nothing.

Mom stops at the kitchen phone. She chews the inside of her mouth while dialing Marty's number. "Bill's missing. Is he with you? Can you call back right away?"

"We should fan out," Linda says. But we don't. I open the door to the den. The couch is there, empty, with the remote and some newspapers. It's as quiet as when we went to sleep last night, and I get a sick feeling that this room is historical, they all are—they can be preserved just the way he left them, a Museum of Dad.

"All right," Mom says again.

We go to the utility room and push aside brooms, skis, and tennis rackets. Mom pulls on a ceiling cord that brings down the ladder for the attic crawlspace. She scrambles up the stairs. The metal strongbox is still in its spot at the edge of the crawlspace. I hear Mom pull it onto her lap, shake it, and test the padlock.

"It's all right. It's all here," she says—the knives, the poisons, and the sashes of our bathrobes. Mom's bare legs reappear on the ladder, and her bare feet touch down quickly on each step.

"All right," I say.

"It's going to be all right, you know, Mom," Linda says. Her voice is getting trembly. "Either way, it will be all right."

"Either way?" Mom asks her.

"We'll still have each other."

"Honey . . ."

"Wait," Linda says. "What's this?"

Passing through the kitchen a second time, we see something we missed before, a folded sheet of paper resting on the counter by the bins of flour and sugar. It has one word on the front: "Adele."

"It's a note," I tell Mom. I pick up the paper, wanting to open it, but it's really Mom's, and so I surrender it to her.

"I don't know if I want to open it," she says. "Maybe you should leave me alone for a few minutes. No, on the other hand, stay here."

"Do you want me to read it first?"

"No, I'll read it." She unfolds the paper. I can see through the back that it contains only one sentence.

"Okay," Mom says. She turns the paper around so we can both see it. "Gone for a walk," it says.

We rush to our rooms and pull on yesterday's clothes. Put on our boots by the living-room door—it's mud season. Run to the driveway, where both cars are empty, and look up and down our hill to find more nothing. The highway is noisy since it's rush hour. We follow Mom into the backyard. Here is the plastic bench where Mom and Dad sit in summer, between the rosebushes, drinking store-brand diet cola and listening to the highway noise. Here is the statue

of Athena, goddess of wisdom, lying on her side wrapped in a blue tarpaulin like a shroud.

We stop at the stockade fence that blocks our house from the highway.

"I'll run back there," I say.

I swing around the fence post and stagger into Mom's compost heap. A small ravine separates our yard from the highway itself. I cross it in a few wobbly steps. Then Linda is behind me, standing in the partly frozen compost. I scan the northbound and southbound lanes as cars whoosh by just feet from my rubber boots.

"I don't see him!" I call back to Mom.

Linda and I look at one another. A few yards away is the entrance to the tunnel. We stumble into the ravine toward the cement ring of the entrance.

"Where are you?" Mom calls from the other side of the fence.

"Just a minute!" Linda calls back.

We peer into the tunnel. It's four feet high, with eighteen inches of muddy water.

"He wouldn't do that," Linda says.

"Sometimes people do," I tell her. "They take pills or something and crawl in someplace small to die."

"Dad wouldn't do that to us. He wouldn't make us look for him here. He wouldn't do that to Mom."

"What are you two doing?" Mom yells. "Get back where I can see you."

I decide to concur with Linda. "We can come back. Later. If we have to."

The three of us run to the front of the house. Along our street neighbors are pulling out of their driveways to go to work, to take their toddlers to nursery school.

"We need a plan," I tell the other two. "Mom, you go uphill. I'll go downhill. Linda, you stay here and wait for the phone to ring." But I'm so agitated that when Mom starts to rush uphill I forget and go with her. Linda follows us too.

The woman next door, the shadow maker, is getting into her enormous van.

"Have you seen my husband?" Mom calls.

"I just got out here," the neighbor responds, chirpy and regular. "Have a good one!" At the front of her house a wind chime strums: *throm, blikblik.*

We clop down to the end of our street, lurching and lunging in our big galoshes. The only place to go is around a bend in the road. When we turn the bend, we see a

wooded lot, the only spot in the neighborhood that hasn't been built on yet.

"What's that?" Linda calls out, pointing.

"It's him!"

Dad's between the trees, awfully still, with his back to us and his head at an angle.

"Bill!" Mom calls. She breaks into a sprint. "Bill!"

Are his feet on the ground? I ask the no one in my mind. *Tell me his feet are on the ground.*

Dad's eyes are closed, and he stands with his head cocked, hands in his coat pockets. His white tennis sneakers are inch-deep in spring mud.

"Bill?" Mom puts her hand on Dad's shoulder.

"Hello!" he says to all three of us, opening his eyes.

"Oh, Bill," Mom says. "We were so scared."

"Dad." Linda winds her arms around Dad and squashes her head against him. Just what I wanted to do. Mom leans on both of them, trying to collect some air.

"Bill, why didn't you tell us you wanted to go for a walk?"

"You were asleep," Dad says, "so I just went. I felt like going, and I went."

"You could have woken us up, Dad," I tell him. "That would have been no problem. I would have gone with you."

"You wanted to go by yourself?" Mom asks, standing on a dry patch and scraping one boot against the other.

"I'm all right by myself," he says.

"But you should have asked us to come," I continue automatically. "You might . . ." But I don't know what he might. Forget how to walk in traffic, and step in front of a car? Turn his ankle on a wet piece of pavement? Obstruct the progress of a school bus? Bump into someone's trash can?

"Why are you hiding in these woods?" Mom asks, looking around at the nearly leafless trees and the coals and cans left over from someone's beer party.

"Something called me in here," Dad explains. "Up there." He points to a spot in the crown of the trees, where a single branch jitters against a freshly washed sky. "Shhh. Listen!"

At first there are only the usual morning sounds of highway noise and slamming car doors. And then we hear it.

Trlrlrlrlrlrlrlrlrlrl.

Then a funny thing happens to Mom's face. She begins to smile, and the smile grows, exceeding what you would consider normal limits and turning into a half circle. It grows until it seems like it's taking up two-thirds of her face. Her cheeks turn into Ping-Pong balls, while her eyes get smaller and smaller. Then her eyes completely disappear.

I DECIDE TO BECOME A
PSYCHOLOGIST

I never thought I would say this. But I have. Fritz showed me the way.

I've made many mistakes in my life so far. This experience with Dad is no exception. When I think of some of the things I've done, I pour a bucket of shame over my own head. Then I writhe in the shame.

But I learned that I have too much of something, and maybe I can take whatever it is that I have too much of, and instead of putting it all on Dad, I could spread it out usefully among many people.

Whatever that thing is, could I productively harness it? Could I distribute it to a different customer each time in a series of scheduled appointments? Could I channel it with a steady, Fritz-like gaze?

This might be a good time, then, to do some homework. Not the kind I usually do, but the regular kind.

Schoolwork. Whatever it is that's been weighing down my satchel.

THE ISLAND

Mom, you returned the library books and threw away the nutritional supplements. A muscle pulsed in your jaw, like a Morse code of regret. You were wishing for a do-over.

But we were like a family on an island, Mom. When we were on the island, we couldn't tell how big the island was, what its shape was, or how long we would be there. We couldn't know the island until we were in a boat speeding away from it. We can see everything, now that it's too late. *It was just a little island.*

Dad, you whistle a tune that sounds like music. You sound the way you did before, when you thought the world could be trusted.

Will we see the island again? If we do, will we all still be together, or will it be Linda or me alone? And who will spot it first? Who will be the one to say, "I've been here before. I remember that rocky beach and that shadow"?

But it's spring, and the sand is gone from the streets of our suburb.

Now fly, Triumph.